Mastering MongoDB 7.0

Achieve data excellence by unlocking the full potential of MongoDB

Marko Aleksendrić

Arek Borucki

Leandro Domingues

Malak Abu Hammad

Elie Hannouch

Rajesh Nair

Rachelle Palmer

Mastering MongoDB 7.0

Fourth edition

Copyright © 2024 Packt Publishing

Acquisition Editor: Sathya Mohan

Lead Development Editor: Siddhant Jain

Development Editors: Afzal Shaikh and Rhea Gangavkar

Content Development Editors: Asma Khan and Saba Umme Salma

Copy Editor: Safis Editing

Project Coordinator: Yash Basil

Proofreader: Safis Editing

Production Designer: Deepak Chavan

Production reference: 1300124

Published by Packt Publishing Ltd.

Grosvenor House, 11 St Paul's Square, Birmingham, B3 1RB, UK.

ISBN 978-1-83588-350-1

www.packtpub.com

Contributors

About the authors

Marko Aleksendrić is an analyst, an ex-scientist, and a freelance self-taught web developer with over 20 years of experience. Marko has authored the book *Modern Web Development with the FARM Stack*, published by Packt Publishing. With a keen interest in backend and frontend development, he has been an avid MongoDB user for the last 15 years for various web and data analytics-related projects, with Python and JavaScript as his main tools.

Arek Borucki, a recognized MongoDB Champion and certified database administrator, has been working with MongoDB technology since 2016. As a principal SRE database engineer, he works closely with technologies such as MongoDB, Elasticsearch, PostgreSQL, Kafka, Kubernetes, Terraform, AWS, and GCP. His extensive experience includes working with renowned companies such as Amadeus, Deutsche Bank, IBM, Nokia, and Beamery. Arek is also a Certified Kubernetes Administrator and developer, an active speaker at international conferences, and a co-author of questions for the MongoDB Associate DBA Exam.

Leandro Domingues is a MongoDB Community Champion and a Microsoft Data Platform MVP alumnus. Specializing in NoSQL databases, focusing on MongoDB, he has authored several articles and is also a speaker and organizer of events and conferences. In addition to teaching MongoDB, he was a professor at one of the largest universities in Brazil. Leandro is passionate about MongoDB and is a mentor and an inspiration to many developers and administrators. His efforts make MongoDB a more comprehensible tool for everyone.

Malak Abu Hammad is a seasoned software engineering manager at Chain Reaction, with a decade of expertise in MongoDB. She has carved a niche for herself not only in MongoDB but also in essential web app technologies. Along with conducting various online and offline workshops, Malak is a MongoDB Champion and a founding member of the MongoDB Arabic Community. Her vision for MongoDB is a future with an emphasis on Arabic localization, aimed at bridging the gap between technology and regional dialects.

Elie Hannouch is a senior software engineer and digital transformation expert. A driving force in the tech industry, he has a proven track record of delivering robust, scalable, and impactful solutions. As a start-up founder, Elie combines his extensive engineering background with strategic innovation to redefine how enterprises operate in today's digital age. Apart from being a MongoDB Champion, Elie leads the MongoDB, Google, and CNCF communities in Lebanon, and works toward empowering aspiring tech professionals by demystifying complex concepts and inspiring a new generation of tech enthusiasts.

Rajesh Nair is a software professional from Kerala, India, with over 12 years of experience working in various MNCs. He started his career as a database administrator for multiple RDBMS technologies, including Progress OpenEdge and MySQL. Rajesh also managed huge datasets for critical applications running on MongoDB as a MongoDB administrator for several years. He has worked on technologies such as MongoDB, AWS, Java, Kafka, MySQL, Progress OpenEdge, shell scripting, and Linux administration. Rajesh is currently based out of Amsterdam, Netherlands, working as a senior software engineer.

Rachelle Palmer is the Product Leader for Developer Database Experience and Developer Education at MongoDB, overseeing the driver client libraries, documentation, framework integrations, and MongoDB University. She has built sample applications for MongoDB in Java, PHP, Rust, Python, Node.js, and Ruby. Rachelle joined MongoDB in 2013 and was previously the director of the technical services engineering team, creating and managing the team that provided support and CloudOps to MongoDB Atlas.

About the reviewers

Jeff Allen is a technical writer at MongoDB. Based in the New York City area, he mainly focuses on server documentation. Before joining MongoDB, he worked in software development, specifically full-stack web development in C# and .NET. He is passionate about writing documentation that is easy to use and understand. He enjoys the challenge of documenting complex topics. Jeff regularly collaborates with Product and Engineering teams to craft examples that match real-world use cases and has been involved in large-scale improvements to the Indexes and Schema Design documentation.

Alex Bevilacqua is an advocate for open standards, as well as a passionate and enthusiastic open source developer with over 10 years of experience. He is skilled in Ruby, Python, C#, Flash, Flex, JavaScript, and others. He is the author of several Redmine extensions and plugins, two of the most popular being Redmine Knowledgebase and Redmine Dropbox Attachments. He currently works for a leading digital marketing company in Toronto where he handles process automation, data collection, and aggregation initiatives.

Nicholas Cottrell has used MongoDB as the data layer for dozens of software development projects since MongoDB 2.0, long before joining the company as a consulting engineer in 2017. He now helps technical services engineers learn about all aspects of MongoDB to support an ever-growing range of customer use cases. He holds dual Australian and Swedish citizenship and lives in Normandy, France.

Joseph Dougherty is a developer-turned-writer who has been working in tech for over 15 years. He has been a technical writer at MongoDB since 2020, contributing to the documentation of the core server product. Joseph has also worked with financial data models, built web apps, programmed guitar effects pedals, and documented it all along the way. In his spare time, he is an avid cyclist and enjoys working with open source audio production tools.

Kenneth P. J. Dyer is a Senior Technical Writer on the Server Documentation team at MongoDB. He joined MongoDB in 2021 and has 12 years of experience in documenting various content and database management systems and related products. With a background in creative writing and philology, he's passionate about language and literature and technologies that facilitate developments in these areas. He lives in Austin, Texas.

Corry Root is a Senior Technical Writer at MongoDB with 15+ years of experience. She holds an MS in Human Factors in Information Design and is passionate about innovative design and collaboration. Corry specializes in technical documentation for MongoDB's Cloud team. She covers products such as MongoDB Atlas CLI, embracing the *Docs as Code* approach. She believes in testing documentation for user-friendliness. Corry resides in Princeton, Massachusetts, with her family, and actively engages in the local community as the chair for the Princeton Cultural Council. She also enjoys jazz and ballet classes, her passion since childhood.

John Williams joined MongoDB in 2019 and co-leads the Cloud documentation team. His team documents MongoDB Atlas and other enterprise tools. He has more than a decade of experience in writing developer docs.

Kailie Yuan is a Technical Writer for the Cloud Enterprise team and holds a lot of knowledge regarding MongoDB drivers, Atlas Search, and MongoDB Atlas Charts. Throughout her time at the company, she worked on a handful of features and constantly strives to provide users with a great experience. Kailie loves to educate others and would like to see more people pursue roles in the technology field. She aspires to help more people understand the tech field better, which is why she took on a second job to teach at her alma mater.

Note from Author

When I joined MongoDB, our cloud engineering team was nascent, our server engineering team fit in a single room, and there were only four program managers in the entire company. At the time, I remember thinking whether joining a start-up, even a well-funded one with a big idea, was the right thing to do. Now, after working with MongoDB for almost 10 years, I have helped us grow from a big idea to a billion-dollar business.

It was a bitterly cold morning in December 2013 when I joined MongoDB; I didn't know what to expect. I certainly could not have predicted the features we would build, the IPO that would eventually happen, or that one day in the future, my job would be defining the experience of MongoDB for you—the developers around the world.

Making databases clearer and more user-friendly for developers is a necessity and something I'm constantly racking my brain over. And while there's so much that sets MongoDB apart from other databases, we've always focused on the foundation of our uniqueness—making it easier for you to work with data. Everything I find tedious about working with data, I strive to make simpler and more accessible in MongoDB.

That's the goal. That's the mission. That's the strategy.

In this book, you'll learn all about MongoDB: the major features, the use cases, the best practices, and the new functionalities we've added in MongoDB 7.0. You'll learn the tips and tricks from some of our community champions and most distinguished engineers. Since this is our first book as a company, we wanted to make it not just technically accurate, but also exciting!

I've realized that the best way to learn is by exploring, and transposing theory into practice. Look at the code, and go beyond it; access the GitHub examples, clone them, and build your own practice applications. You can create an account on MongoDB Atlas and host a production app on the free tier. By the end of this book, you will have the skills to build an application that runs at scale.

Thank you for reading, and for using MongoDB.

Rachelle Palmer

Director, Product Management

MongoDB, Inc.

Table of Contents

3

Developer Tools   33

4

Connecting to MongoDB   55

5

CRUD Operations and Basic Queries   71

6

7

8

Aggregation   155

9

Multi-Document ACID Transactions   173

10

Index Optimization   189

11

MongoDB Atlas: Powering the Future of Developer Data Platforms 211

12

Monitoring and Backup in MongoDB   243

13

14

Integrating Applications with MongoDB   281

15

Security   309

16

17

Preface

Mastering MongoDB 7.0 is a technical guide for developers and database professionals wanting to implement advanced functionalities and master complex database operations in MongoDB. Exploring the latest version of MongoDB, it helps with gaining the skills necessary to create efficient, secure, and high-performing applications using MongoDB.

This book is an excellent collection of real-world examples, practical insights, and invaluable tips. It is a comprehensive guide to equip developers with the skills needed to handle the challenges of modern data management, application integration, and security.

How will this book help you?

This book provides hands-on examples that will help you become proficient in creating efficient, secure, and high-performing applications using MongoDB. You'll gain the confidence to undertake complex queries, integrate robust applications, and ensure data security to overcome modern data challenges.

Who is this book for?

This book is for developers with an intermediate skill level, who aim to become MongoDB experts. This book is not for beginners. Working knowledge of MongoDB is recommended to get the most out of this guide. Ideal for database administrators, app developers, and software engineers, this book will assist you in developing advanced skills to conquer intricate data tasks.

What does this book cover?

Chapter 1, Introduction to MongoDB, provides a quick introduction to MongoDB, the world's most versatile developer data platform, through the lens of the creators. This chapter will build your curiosity around exploring MongoDB and all its new features.

Chapter 2, The MongoDB Architecture, shows how to increase reliability and availability for your applications by implementing various methods in MongoDB, using replication and sharding. It also covers the new sharded cluster features introduced in MongoDB 7.0.

Chapter 3, Developer Tools, explores different MongoDB developer tools and shows how to use them to increase your productivity.

Chapter 4, Connecting to MongoDB, showcases the multi-language facets of MongoDB, providing a walkthrough of the direct driver methods, ODM libraries, and MongoDB integration across Ruby, PHP, Python, and Node.js.

Chapter 5, CRUD Operations and Basic Queries, demonstrates CRUD operations and basic queries in action. It provides hands-on examples of using the MongoDB Shell for database administration operations.

Chapter 6, Schema Design and Data Modeling, covers MongoDB schema design principles and techniques for effective data representation—which are essential for optimizing performance and scalability.

Chapter 7, Advanced Querying in MongoDB, offers a more profound exploration of MongoDB's capabilities, including the aggregation framework, indexing techniques, and optimization.

Chapter 8, Aggregation, delves into the aggregation framework and explores numerous stages and expression operators suitable for the most diverse problems.

Chapter 9, Multi-Document ACID Transactions, shows how MongoDB handles multi-document ACID transactions and what significance this concept has in sectors with strict requirements, such as finance, fintech, and mission-critical applications.

Chapter 10, Index Optimization, discusses and shows how MongoDB supports a plethora of indexes—from single-field to compound indexes, from geospatial to hashed and partial, as well as some recently introduced indexing types.

Chapter 11, MongoDB Atlas: Powering the Future of Developer Data Platforms, provides an in-depth walk-through of MongoDB Atlas—the most advanced cloud database service on the market.

Chapter 12, Monitoring and Backup in MongoDB, focuses on the essential aspects of monitoring the health and performance of the system, along with strategies and tools for effective data backup and recovery.

Chapter 13, Introduction to Atlas Search, shares insights on the capabilities integrated into MongoDB Atlas. It shows how to use sophisticated search functionalities for your data.

Chapter 14, Integrating Applications with MongoDB, delves into the various methods of integrating applications with MongoDB—both the native and cloud versions of MongoDB Atlas.

Chapter 15, Security, discusses the critical role of security in MongoDB, delving into robust authentication and authorization methods such as SCRAM, x.509, LDAP, and Kerberos.

Chapter 16, Auditing, provides an in-depth look at the features, benefits, and challenges of auditing in MongoDB, with an understanding of and practical guidelines for its effective implementation.

Chapter 17, Encryption, summarizes the different types of encryption and shows the practical implementation of each type in your database.

To get the most out of this book

You will require the following software:

Software/hardware covered in the book	Operating system requirements	Resources for installation steps
MongoDB version 4.4 or newer	Windows, macOS, or Linux	`https://www.mongodb.com/docs/manual/installation/`
MongoDB Atlas Search	Windows, macOS, or Linux	`https://www.mongodb.com/docs/atlas/getting-started/`
MongoDB Shell	Windows, macOS, or Linux	`https://www.mongodb.com/docs/manual/administration/install-community/`
MongoDB Compass	Windows, macOS, or Linux	`https://www.mongodb.com/docs/compass/current/install/`

After reading this book, we encourage you to check out some of the other resources available at `https://www.mongodb.com/developer` or `https://learn.mongodb.com/`.

If you're using the digital version of this book, we advise you to type the code yourself or access the code from the book's GitHub repository (a link is available in the next section). Doing so will help you avoid any potential errors related to the copying and pasting of code.

Download the example code files

You can download the example code files for this book from GitHub at `https://github.com/PacktPublishing/Mastering-MongoDB-7.0`. If there's an update to the code, it will be updated in the GitHub repository.

We also have other code bundles from our rich catalog of books and videos available at `https://github.com/PacktPublishing/`. Check them out!

Conventions used

There are a number of text conventions used throughout this book.

`Code in text`: Indicates code words in text, database collection names, folder names, filenames, file extensions, pathnames, dummy URLs, user input, and Twitter handles. Here's an example: "The `mongoid` gem can be added to your application by modifying the `Gemfile`."

A block of code is set as follows:

```
class Shape
    include Mongoid::Document
    field: x, type: Integer
    field: y, type: Integer embedded_in: canvas
end
```

Bold: Indicates a new term, an important word, or words that you see onscreen. For instance, words in menus or dialog boxes appear in **bold**. Here's an example: "Click on the **Schema** tab to check the schema distribution of the collection."

> **Tips or important notes**
> Appear like this.

Get in touch

Feedback from our readers is always welcome.

General feedback: If you have questions about any aspect of this book, email us at `customercare@packtpub.com` and mention the book title in the subject of your message.

Errata: Although we have taken every care to ensure the accuracy of our content, mistakes do happen. If you have found a mistake in this book, we would be grateful if you would report this to us. Please visit `www.packtpub.com/support/errata` and fill in the form.

Piracy: If you come across any illegal copies of our works in any form on the internet, we would be grateful if you would provide us with the location address or website name. Please contact us at `copyright@packt.com` with a link to the material.

If you are interested in becoming an author: If there's a topic that you have expertise in and you're interested in either writing or contributing to a book, please visit `authors.packtpub.com`.

Download a free PDF copy of this book

Thanks for purchasing this book!

Do you like to read on the go but are unable to carry your print books everywhere?

Is your e-book purchase not compatible with the device of your choice?

Don't worry, now with every Packt book you get a DRM-free PDF version of that book at no cost.

Read anywhere, any place, on any device. Search, copy, and paste code from your favorite technical books directly into your application.

The perks don't stop there, you can get exclusive access to discounts, newsletters, and great free content in your inbox daily

Follow these simple steps to get the benefits:

1. Scan the QR code or visit the link below

https://packt.link/free-ebook/9781835883501

2. Submit your proof of purchase

3. That's it! We'll send your free PDF and other benefits to your email directly

1

Introduction to MongoDB

MongoDB, the most popular document database, is a NoSQL, non-relational key-value store, a JSON database, and more. It is a robust, feature-rich developer data platform with various built-in features that you need for modern applications, such as machine learning and AI capabilities, streaming, functions, triggers, serverless, device sync, and full-text search.

Though MongoDB is non-relational, it can easily handle relational data. It offers courses, tutorials, and documentation at `learn.mongodb.com` on how to best model and handle that data, even while using the document format.

Who uses MongoDB

10 years ago, the use of MongoDB was somewhat niche. It was a young database with compelling features for developers like you. Now, in 2023, MongoDB is used by a myriad of varied industries, and its use cases span across all kinds of situations and types of data stored. Some of the largest banks, automakers, government agencies, and gaming companies in the world use MongoDB for their production applications. The most famous users of MongoDB are *Coinbase*, *Epic Games*, *Morgan Stanley*, *Adobe*, *Tesla*, *Canva*, *Ulta Beauty*, *Cathay Pacific*, *Dongwha*, and *Vodafone*.

The MongoDB Atlas platform has millions of users, all of whom trust that their data will be managed safely and effectively in the cloud. This popularity has taken MongoDB to great heights, not just in terms of its growth and value as a company but also in terms of its raw developer mindshare. As of 2023, one in four developers uses MongoDB extensively in production. This ratio is much larger in other developer communities such as Go and JavaScript (approximately 40%).

Why developers love MongoDB

Along with its versatality, and robust features, MongoDB is the preferred choice for several reasons, such as:

- **Flexibility and schema-less**: Unlike traditional relational databases, MongoDB allows you to store and retrieve data without strict schemas or predefined structures. This flexibility is particularly useful when data evolves over time or when you are dealing with unstructured or semi-structured data.

- **Scalability and performance**: MongoDB is highly scalable and performs exceptionally well, making it suitable for both large-scale applications and personal projects. MongoDB Atlas provides a free-forever tier for side projects.

- **Rich query language**: MongoDB offers a powerful query language and indexing capabilities, simplifying common operations such as `findOne` and `updateOne`.

- **Developer-friendly data format**: Data in MongoDB closely resembles objects in popular programming languages, reducing data mapping complexities and expediting development.

- **Simplicity and quick start**: MongoDB's simplicity and hassle-free setup makes it easy to adapt. No complex sales processes or licensing hassles are involved.

What attracts most developers is the simplicity of working with MongoDB on a daily basis, in particular, the seamless experience of creating, updating, and interacting with data. For example, consider a Python developer attempting to insert a document, query that document, and receive a set of results, using the following code:

```python
from pymongo import MongoClient

# Connect to MongoDB
client = MongoClient('mongodb://localhost:27017/')
db = client['mydatabase']  # Specify the database name
collection = db['mycollection']  # Specify the collection name

# Create a document to be inserted
document = {
    'name': 'Jane Doe',
    'age': 30,
    'email': 'janedoe@example.com'
}

# Insert the document into the collection
result = collection.insert_one(document)
```

```
# Check if the insertion was successful
if result.acknowledged:
    print('Document inserted successfully.')
    print('Inserted document ID:', result.inserted_id)
else:
    print('Failed to insert document.')
```

Note that the developer creates a dictionary representing the document to be inserted. In this case, it contains the `name`, `age`, and `email` details. The developer doesn't need to create an ID for the document, because MongoDB automatically creates a unique identifier on each document.

To retrieve this document, you can filter the query by using any of the document's field individually, or in combination. Let's see that in action:

```
from pymongo import MongoClient

# Connect to MongoDB
client = MongoClient('mongodb://localhost:27017/')
db = client['mydatabase']  # Specify the database name
collection = db['mycollection']  # Specify the collection name

# Retrieve documents based on specific conditions
query = {
    'age': {'$gte': 29},  # Retrieve documents where age is greater than or
equal to 29
}
documents = collection.find(query)

# Iterate over the retrieved documents
for document in documents:
    print(document)
```

Pretty simple! The preceding example demonstrates how you can use a MongoDB query operator such as `$gte` (greater than or equal to) to filter your query. But the real magic happens when the document is returned. When MongoDB returns a document, it will be represented as a Python dictionary. Each field in the document is a key-value pair within the dictionary, similar to the following example:

```
{
    '_id': ObjectId('60f5c4c4543b5a2c7c4c73a2'),
    'name': 'Jane Doe',
    'age': 30,
    'email': 'janedoe@example.com'
}
```

MongoDB has a suite of language libraries and drivers that act as a translation layer between the client and server, intercepting each operation and translating it into MongoDB's query language. With this, you can interact with the data using your native programming language in a purely idiomatic way.

Alongside the other offerings of the MongoDB Atlas developer data platform, it truly abstracts away the difficulties of working with a database, and instead allows you to interact with data purely via your code and IDE. This is infinitely preferable while using a separate database shell, database UI, and other database-specific tools. Since MongoDB Atlas offers a completely managed MongoDB database, you can set up and register via a command-line interface.

At its heart, the mission of MongoDB is to be a powerful database for developers, and its features are tuned to the programming language communities and framework integrations, rather than to database administration tools. This will become more apparent in the subsequent chapters, where you'll learn more about *MongoDB Atlas*, *Atlas Vector Search*, *full-text search*, and features such as *aggregation*—all through the lens of a developer.

By the end of this book, you'll learn how effective these tools can be and make database management simpler!

Efficiency of the inherent complexity of MongoDB databases

The most interesting part of the modern database is understanding its architecture and why it's built that way. Fundamentally, MongoDB is a distributed system. The database server itself was originally built with the anticipation that most users would run it with a default configuration—*replica set*, sometimes also referred to as a *cluster*. When you explore this architecture in-depth, you'll notice the true complexities.

By default, replica set of MongoDB is a three-node configuration. All three nodes are data-bearing, which means that there is a complete copy of the database available on each node. Each database is hosted on a separate instance or host, which can be in the same availability zone, data center, or region. This default configuration is to ensure both *redundancy* and *high availability*. *Chapter 2, The MongoDB Architecture* will discuss replica sets in more detail.

If one of the instances becomes unresponsive or unavailable, a healthy node is promoted to become the primary node. This failover between members occurs automatically, and there's no impact on operations for the users of the database. This process considers many different factors, including node availability, data freshness, and responsiveness. This election process and protocol, while simple to understand at a high-level, is very nuanced. But since the operations continue without interruption, you hardly know or understand these details.

How is this possible?

Behind the scenes, write operations to MongoDB are propagated from the primary node to the secondary nodes via a process called *replication*. The best way to explain replication is with the example of a single write to the database. An inbound write from the client application (your *app*) will be first directed to the primary node. That primary node will apply the write to its copy of the database. Then, the write is recorded in the **operations log** (**oplog**), which is tailed by secondary nodes.

Replication in MongoDB is based on the RAFT consensus protocol. One particular example of how this implementation varies is *leader elections*. In the traditional RAFT protocol, leader and primary node election occurs through a combination of randomized election timeouts and message exchanges. In MongoDB, there are settings for node priority. This priority is considered along with data freshness and response time when electing a primary node.

It is often true that the write operation is not written simultaneously to all nodes—there is a lag heavily influenced by factors such as network latency, the distance between nodes, hardware configuration, and workload. If one of the mongod nodes falls behind, it will catch up or resync itself when it is able to do so using the oplog to determine the gaps in its operations. The MongoDB system monitors the replication lag between nodes to track this metric and assess whether the delay between primary and secondary nodes is acceptable, and if not, takes necessary action. This process is unique among databases as well.

This default configuration of MongoDB is a replica set with three members, where replication of data between nodes and failover between nodes are all handled automatically. This configuration is both durable and highly available, which makes it easy to use. For developers who require larger, global deployments, MongoDB has a sharded cluster model. The first thing to understand is that a sharded cluster consists of replica sets. It is a way of further dividing your data into effectively replicated partitions.

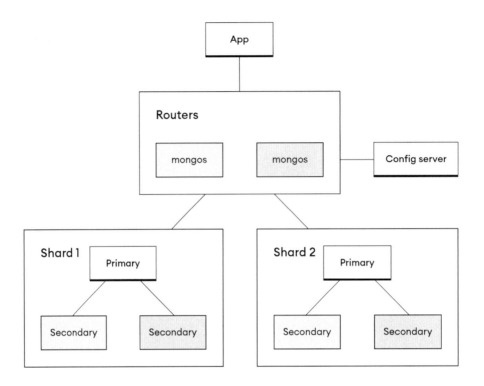

Figure 1.1: Replicated partitions set with primary and secondary nodes

If you require a global deployment with multiple terabytes of data, get started with *Chapter 2, The MongoDB Architecture*. It will cover how to split data, how to migrate data between regions or shards, how to marry data from multiple regions for analytics, and the performance of sharded cluster architectures.

Summary

MongoDB is a simple yet powerful database. It abstracts away many of the more complicated implementation details so that you can focus on building applications. It's easy to get started with and offers a powerful, idiomatic developer experience that allows you to interact with the database, exclusively in the programming language of your choice, via your IDE.

The rest of the book details how powerful and flexible MongoDB is, the new features in MongoDB 7.0, and how you can use it to your advantage. Besides being a great database for web applications, transactional data, flexible schemas, and high-performance workloads, it is also a great database for learning through hands-on experience and building proofs of concept.

In the next chapter, you'll see how replication and sharding can help increase reliability and availability for your applications.

2

The MongoDB Architecture

MongoDB enables you to meet the demands of modern apps with a developer data platform built on several core architectural foundations. It lets you access the best ways to innovate in building transactional, operational, and analytical applications. This chapter examines the MongoDB architecture with a special emphasis on two key elements: replication and sharding.

Replication is a crucial component in MongoDB's distributed architecture, ensuring data accessibility and resilience to faults. It enables you to spread identical datasets across various database servers, safeguarding against the failure of a single server.

Additionally, you will learn about sharding, a horizontal scaling strategy for spreading data across several machines. As applications grow in popularity, and the volume of data they produce increases, scaling across machines becomes essential to ensure sufficient read and write throughput.

This chapter will cover the following topics:

- How replication and sharding increase reliability and availability
- Various methods in MongoDB for replication and sharding
- New sharded cluster features in MongoDB 7.0

Replication vs sharding

People often confuse replication with sharding. While both are sets of systems utilized in database management, they serve distinct purposes and are employed for different reasons. Replication is a process where data is duplicated and stored in multiple locations to ensure redundancy and reliability, playing a vital role in data protection and accessibility.

On the other hand, sharding involves dividing a larger database into smaller, more manageable parts, called shards. Each shard stores a portion of the total dataset on a separate database server instance. However, it's important to note that each shard must also implement replication to maintain data integrity and availability.

The goal of combining sharding with replication is to ensure data durability and high availability. When a shard's server instance fails and there's only a single copy of data on that shard, it can result in unavailability of data until the server is restored or replaced. By employing replication within each shard, the sharded cluster can maintain data availability and prevent any disruptions caused by server failures. This approach enables rolling upgrades of the sharded cluster without downtime, allowing for smooth and uninterrupted system maintenance.

The next few sections will take an in-depth look at both replication and sharding, and their respective components.

Replication

A replica set in MongoDB refers to a collection of mongod processes that uphold the same dataset. They offer redundancy and high availability, serving as the foundation for all production implementations. By having numerous data copies across various database servers, replication ensures a degree of fault tolerance, protecting against the failure of a single database server.

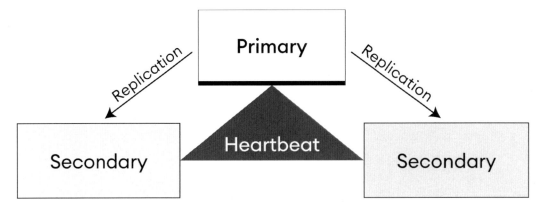

Figure 2.1: A replica set

The primary node handles all write operations, and logs all dataset changes in its **operations log** (**oplog**). A MongoDB replica set can only have one primary node.

The secondary nodes replicate the primary's oplog, and implement the operations on their own datasets, ensuring that they mirror the primary's dataset. In the event of the primary becoming inaccessible, a qualified secondary will initiate an election to become the new primary.

With data stored across multiple servers, replication increases the reliability of the system. Furthermore, support for rolling upgrades lets you upgrade the software or hardware of individual servers without interruption, ensuring continuous availability of the database. Replication significantly improves the performance of read-heavy applications, distributing the read load across multiple servers to ensure fast data retrieval.

Replica set elections

MongoDB employs a protocol built on top of the Raft consensus algorithm to orchestrate replica set elections, ensuring data consistency across distributed systems. This protocol includes a voting mechanism used by replica sets to select which member will assume the primary role.

Several events can initiate an election, including the following:

- Adding or removing a node from the replica set

- Initializing the replica set

- A heartbeat failure between any of the secondary nodes and the primary that exceeds the preset timeout duration (default is 10 seconds for self-managed hosts, or 5 seconds in MongoDB Atlas)

Your application's connection-handling logic should be designed to account for automatic failovers and the ensuing elections. MongoDB drivers have the capability to identify the loss of the primary and automatically retry specific read or write operations, offering an additional layer of built-in resilience to elections.

When a primary replica becomes unavailable, secondary replicas vote for a new primary. The replica with the most recent write timestamp is more likely to win the election. This strategy minimizes the chance of rollback when a previous primary rejoins the set. Post-election, nodes enter a *freeze* period during which they cannot initiate another election. This is designed to prevent continuous, rapid elections, which can destabilize the system. Currently, MongoDB replica sets only support the protocol known as protocol version 1 (pv1).

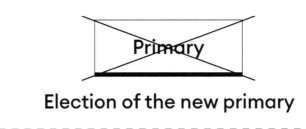

Election of the new primary

New primary elected

Figure 2.2: Electing a new primary

The replica set is unable to execute write operations until the election has been successfully concluded. However, the replica set can still handle read operations if they're configured to target secondary nodes.

Under normal circumstances, with default replica set configuration settings, the average time taken for a cluster to elect a new primary should not exceed 12 seconds. This duration encompasses the time needed to declare the primary as inaccessible, and to initiate and finalize an election. This time frame can be adjusted by altering the `settings.electionTimeoutMillis` replication configuration option.

Member priority

Once a stable primary is established, the election algorithm enables the highest-priority secondary to initiate an election. Member priority affects both the timing and the outcome of elections, where secondaries with higher-priority are likely to initiate an election sooner and win. Nevertheless, lower-priority members may briefly serve as a primary, despite higher-priority members being available. The process of elections persists until the highest-priority member ascends to the primary. Members with a priority value of 0 can't become a primary and don't seek election.

Since a replica set can accommodate a maximum of 50 members, with only seven of them being voting members, the inclusion of non-voting members enables the set to exceed the limit of seven. Non-voting members, characterized by having zero votes, must possess a priority of 0.

Replica set oplog

The oplog is a unique capped collection that maintains a continuous log of all operations that alter the data housed in MongoDB databases. It can expand beyond its set size limit to prevent the deletion of the majority commit point.

Write operations in MongoDB are executed on the primary and subsequently logged in the primary's oplog. The secondary members asynchronously replicate and apply these operations. Every member of the replica set holds a copy of the oplog, located in the `local.oplog.rs` collection, enabling them to keep up with the current state of the database.

To support replication, all members of the replica set exchange heartbeats (pings) with each other. Any secondary member can import oplog entries from any other member. Each operation within the oplog is idempotent, meaning that whether applied once or multiple times to the target dataset, oplog operations yield the same outcome.

The oplog window

Oplog entries carry timestamps. The oplog window refers to the time interval between the most recent and earliest timestamps in the oplog. If a secondary node loses connectivity with the primary, it can resynchronize using replication only if the connection is reestablished within the duration of the oplog window. MongoDB allows the definition of both a minimum duration (in hours), and a specific size for retaining an oplog entry. The system will discard an oplog entry only under the following conditions:

- The oplog has filled up to its maximum configured capacity, and the oplog entry has exceeded the specified retention period based on the host system's clock.

- Without a specified minimum oplog retention period, MongoDB defaults to its standard behavior. It begins truncation of the oplog from the oldest entries, ensuring the oplog doesn't exceed the configured maximum size.

Replica set deployment architectures

The typical deployment for a production system involves a three-member replica set. These sets offer redundancy and resilience to faults. While it's advisable to steer clear of unnecessary complexity, the architecture should ultimately be guided by the needs of your application. Generally, one should adhere to the following rules:

- Ensure the replica set has an odd number of voting members to prevent split decisions during network partitions, enabling the larger segment to accept writes.

- If your set of voting members is even, consider adding another voting member that carries data. If limitations prevent this, introduce an arbiter.

- Incorporate hidden or delayed members to support dedicated functions, such as backup or reporting.

- To safeguard your data in the event of a data center failure, ensure there is at least one member located in an alternate data center.

Replica set arbiter

Under conditions where you have a primary and a secondary, but budget limitations prevent you from adding another secondary, you may incorporate an arbiter into your replica set. While an arbiter takes part in primary elections, it doesn't hold a copy of the dataset and is incapable of becoming a primary. An arbiter carries a single vote in elections. By default, its priority is set to 0.

Hidden replica set members

Hidden members form an integral part of a replica set; however, they cannot assume the primary role, and remain unseen by client applications. Despite being invisible, hidden members retain the ability to participate and vote in elections. Hidden nodes can be utilized as dedicated replica set members to perform backup operations or to run some reporting queries. To set up a hidden node and prevent a member from being promoted to a primary, you can set its priority to 0, and also configure the hidden parameter to true, as shown in the following example:

```
cfg = rs.conf()
cfg.members[n].hidden = true
cfg.members[n].priority = 0
rs.reconfig(cfg)
```

Delayed replica set members

Delayed members, which are also hidden members, replicate and apply operations from the source oplog with a deliberate delay, representing a previous state of the set. For example, if the current time is 08:01, and a member has a delay set to one hour, then the most recent operation on the delayed member will be no later than 07:01:

```
cfg = rs.conf()
cfg.members[n].hidden = true
cfg.members[n].priority = 0
cfg.members[0].secondaryDelaySecs = 3600
rs.reconfig(cfg)
```

Delayed members act as a continuous backup or a live *historical* record of the dataset, providing a safety net against human errors. For instance, they can facilitate recovery from failed application updates and operator errors, such as accidental deletion of databases and collections.

Write concern

The write concern determines how MongoDB confirms write operations on replica sets. It provides a mechanism to ensure that the data is written to a specified number of nodes before acknowledging the write operation.

Components of a write concern

The following fields can be included in a write concern:

```
{ w: <value>, j: <boolean>, wtimeout: <number> }
```

w: specifies the required number of replica set members that must acknowledge the write. The following w: <value> write concerns are available:

- 0: No acknowledgement. This provides the least durability but the highest performance.

- 1: Acknowledgement from the primary node.

- majority: Acknowledgment from the majority of the replica set members. It is the default as of MongoDB 5.0; previously, the default was 1.

- <number>: Acknowledgment from a specific number of replica set members.

- j: Requests acknowledgment that the write operation has been written to the on-disk journal. If set to true, the write operation waits for a journal acknowledgment.

- wtimeout: Sets a time limit, in milliseconds, for the write concern. If the specified level of acknowledgment is not reached within this time, the write operation returns an error. This error does not mean the write won't complete or be rolled back; it prevents the write from blocking beyond the specified threshold.

Beginning with MongoDB 4.4, both replica sets and sharded clusters have the capability to establish a global default write concern. Any operations that don't define a specific write concern will automatically adopt the settings of this global default write concern. The administrative command setDefaultRWConcern is used to establish the global default configuration for either read or write concerns:

```
db.adminCommand({
    setDefaultRWConcern : 1,
    defaultReadConcern: { <read concern> },
    defaultWriteConcern: { <write concern> },
    writeConcern: { <write concern> },
    comment: <any>
})
```

From MongoDB 5.0 onward, the default write concern is set to { w: "majority" }. However, there are exceptions when the deployment includes arbiters:

- The voting majority is calculated as half the number of voting members plus 1, rounded down. If the count of data-bearing voting members doesn't exceed this voting majority, then the default write concern is adjusted to { w: 1 }.

- In any other situation, the default write concern remains { w: "majority" }.

Significance of the write concern

The choice of write concern can influence both the performance and the durability of the data:

- **Performance**: A lower write concern (e.g., `w: 0`) can enhance performance by reducing the latency of the write operation. However, it risks data durability.

- **Durability**: A higher write concern (e.g., `w: "majority"`) ensures that the data is durable by waiting for acknowledgments from the majority of the nodes. This might introduce a slight latency in the write operation.

Read preference

In MongoDB, the read preference determines how MongoDB clients route read operations to the members of a replica set. By default, MongoDB directs all read operations to the primary member. However, by adjusting the read preference, it's possible to distribute the read load to secondary members, improving the overall performance and availability of the system.

Components of the read preference

MongoDB supports five read preference modes:

- `primary`: All read operations are directed to the primary member (default).

- `primaryPreferred`: Reads are directed to the primary member if available; otherwise, they are routed to secondary members.

- `secondary`: All read operations are directed to secondary members.

- `secondaryPreferred`: Reads are directed to the available secondary members, if any; otherwise, they are routed to the primary member.

- `nearest`: Read operations are directed to the member with the lowest network latency, irrespective of the member's status.

In addition to the read preference modes, you can also specify the following options:

- **Tag sets**: Tag sets allow customizing read preferences by associating custom tags with replica set members. Clients can then target read operations to members with specific tags.

- **Max staleness**: Staleness refers to the lag in replication from the primary to the secondary. This option specifies how stale a secondary can be before the client stops using it for read operations.

Significance of read preference

The choice of read preference can influence both the performance and the availability of the data:

- **Performance**: Distributing read operations to secondary members can enhance performance by reducing the load on the primary.

- **Availability**: In case of primary unavailability, read operations can still be served by secondary members if the read preference mode allows it.

Read concern

The read concern determines the consistency and isolation properties of the data read from replica sets and sharded clusters. By adjusting the read concern, it's possible to control the visibility of data in read operations, thereby ensuring the desired level of consistency and isolation.

Components of read concern

The following read concern levels are supported by MongoDB:

- `"local"`: Returns the most recent data available to the MongoDB instance at the start of the query, irrespective of the state of replication (default).

- `"available"`: Returns the data that is currently available in the distributed system at the time of the query. This level provides the most minimal latency but does not guarantee consistency.

- `"majority"`: Returns data that has been acknowledged by a majority of the replica set members. This ensures a high level of consistency.

- `"linearizable"`: Provides the highest level of consistency by returning data that reflects all successful majority-acknowledged writes that completed prior to the start of the read operation.

- `"snapshot"`: Returns data from a specific point in time across all replica set members.

Significance of the read concern

The choice of read concern can influence both the consistency and the isolation of the data:

- **Consistency**: Higher levels of read concern (e.g., `"majority"` or `"linearizable"`) ensure that the data returned is consistent across the replica set members.

- **Isolation**: By using the `"snapshot"` read concern, it's possible to isolate a transaction from concurrent writes, ensuring a consistent view of the data throughout the transaction.

Replication methods

The MongoDB Shell (`mongosh`) provides a set of shell helper methods designed to facilitate interaction with a replica set. They serve as crucial tools for managing a replicated MongoDB deployment. Let's examine some of the important methods needed for managing replication in MongoDB:

- `rs.add()`: Adds a member to a replica set
- `rs.addArb()`: Adds an arbiter to a replica set
- `rs.conf()`: Shows the replica set configuration document
- `rs.initiate()`: Initializes a new replica set
- `rs.printReplicationInfo()`: Summary of the replica set's status as seen from the primary
- `rs.status()`: Provides a document detailing the current status of the replica set
- `rs.reconfig()`: Reconfigures an existing replica set, overwriting the existing replica set configuration
- `rs.stepDown()`: Triggers a transition where the current primary becomes a secondary, triggering an election

For a detailed list of replication methods, visit the following resource: `https://www.mongodb.com/docs/manual/reference/method/js-replication/`

In addition to the preceding replication methods, you can also use replication commands for specific operations. For instance, `replSetResizeOplog` changes the size of the variable oplog in a replica set. The command takes the following fields:

- `replSetResizeOplog`: Set to 1.
- `size`: Specifies the maximum size of the oplog in MBs. The minimum size that can be set is 990 MB, and the maximum is 1 PB. Explicitly cast the size as a double in mongosh using `Double()`.
- `minRetentionHours`: Represents the minimum number of hours to retain an oplog entry, where decimal values indicate fractions of an hour (e.g., `1.5` means 1 hour and 30 minutes). The value must be equal to or greater than `0`. A value of `0` means that mongod should truncate the oplog starting with the oldest entries to maintain the configured maximum oplog size.

```
'db.adminCommand({
  replSetResizeOplog: <int>,
  size: <double>,
  minRetentionHours: <double>
})'
```

To learn more about replication commands, visit the following resource: `https://www.mongodb.com/docs/manual/reference/command/nav-replication/`

Sharding

MongoDB supports horizontal scaling through sharding. Sharding involves the distribution of data across numerous processes and plays an essential role in managing and organizing large-scale data. This method divides a larger database into smaller, more manageable components known as shards. Each shard is stored on a separate database server instance, which distributes the load and offers an effective approach to data management. Moreover, this technique allows for the creation of distributed databases to support geographically distributed applications, enabling policies that enforce data residency within specific regions.

Why do you need sharding?

Consider a scenario where your data is expanding swiftly and your database is approaching its maximum capacity. This circumstance could manifest a multitude of challenges. Typically, the most pressing problem is performance deterioration. As your database grows, the time required to query and retrieve data can increase significantly. This deceleration negatively impacts the user experience, making your applications appear sluggish or unresponsive.

Another potential hurdle is storage constraints. Most systems have a set limit of data they can manage efficiently. If your data growth exceeds your system's storage capability, it can culminate in system failure. When it comes to managing the growth of a system, there are two principal strategies—vertical scaling and horizontal scaling:

- **Vertical scaling** enhances a single server's capacity, for example, by upgrading the CPU, increasing RAM, or expanding the storage space. However, technological limitations can prevent a single machine from handling certain workloads, as there are strict upper limits. Hence, vertical scaling has practical constraints.

- **Horizontal scaling** involves dividing a system's data and workload across multiple servers, adding to the number of servers needed. Each machine handles only a fraction of the total workload, which can be more efficient than one powerful server. While this approach might be more cost-effective than investing in expensive hardware, it increases the complexity of the infrastructure and system maintenance.

Key elements of a sharded cluster

A MongoDB sharded cluster consists of the following key elements:

- **Shard**: This is a replica set that stores a portion of the data in the cluster. The cluster can have anywhere from 1 to n shards, with each shard containing a distinct subset of the overall data. MongoDB Atlas offers different storage capacities based on the cluster tier: 4 TB for `M10-M40`, 8 TB for `M50-M60`, and 14 TB for `M80+`.

- mongos: Serves as a query router for client applications, efficiently managing both read and write operations. It directs client requests to the appropriate shards and consolidates the results from multiple shards into a coherent client response. Clients establish connections with mongos instances, rather than directly with individual shards. It is recommended to run multiple instances of mongos in production deployments to ensure high availability.

- **Config servers**: Function as a replica set and fulfill the role of a specialized database by serving as the primary repository for sharding metadata. This metadata encompasses the state and structure of the sharded data, including essential information such as the list of sharded collections and routing details. It plays a crucial role in enabling efficient data management and query routing within the cluster.

Figure 2.3 illustrates the interaction of components within a sharded cluster.

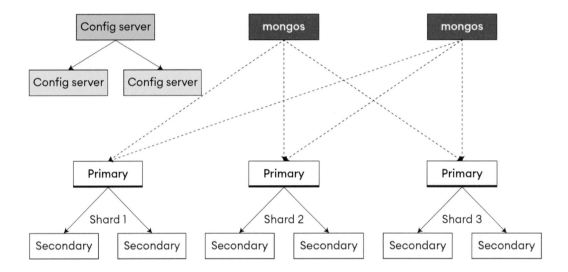

Figure 2.3: A sharded cluster

In MongoDB, data sharding occurs at the collection level, meaning that the data of a collection is distributed across multiple shards within the cluster. It's important to note that each database in a sharded cluster has its own primary shard, which is responsible for storing all the unsharded collections within that database. It's worth mentioning that the concept of a primary shard in a sharded cluster is different from the primary in a replica set; they serve different purposes and are not related to each other.

When creating a new database, the primary shard is selected by the mongos process. It chooses the shard in the cluster that contains the least amount of data. The totalSize field returned by the listDatabases command is used as one of the factors in the selection criteria.

It's possible to move the primary shard after its initial assignment using the movePrimary command. The movePrimary command initially alters the primary shard in the cluster's metadata, followed by migrating all unsharded collections to the designated shard.

Microsharding

In certain scenarios, MongoDB offers a more advanced sharding configuration known as microsharding. Unlike the traditional approach of allocating each shard to a dedicated machine, microsharding allows for more granular control and optimization of resources by collocating multiple shards on a single host.

Microsharding can be an effective strategy, particularly when dealing with smaller data sizes per shard. By consolidating multiple shards on a single host, resource utilization can be maximized, resulting in improved hardware efficiency.

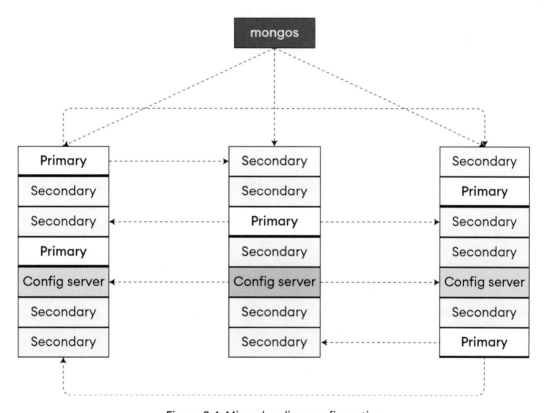

Figure 2.4: Microsharding configuration

However, it's important to note that this approach requires careful resource management to prevent conflicts between different MongoDB processes running on the same host. Each MongoDB process needs to be allocated sufficient resources to operate effectively. When implementing a microsharding strategy, it's crucial to properly configure the cache size for each MongoDB process. The cache size of the WiredTiger storage engine in MongoDB can be adjusted via the `storage.wiredTiger.engineConfig.cacheSizeGB` setting. This cache should be large enough to accommodate the working set of each MongoDB process. If the cache lacks the necessary space to load more data, WiredTiger will remove pages from the cache to create room.

By default, the `storage.wiredTiger.engineConfig.cacheSizeGB` is configured to be 50% of the total RAM, less than 1 GB. However, when running multiple MongoDB processes on the same machine, you should adjust this setting to ensure that the total memory usage of all MongoDB processes don't exceed the available RAM.

For instance, if you're running two MongoDB processes on a machine with 16 GB RAM, you can set `storage.wiredTiger.engineConfig.cacheSizeGB` to 25% (or 4 GB) for each process, rather than the default 50%. This prevents MongoDB processes from collectively consuming more than the total available RAM, leaving enough memory for the operating system and other applications.

Advantages of sharding

Sharding offers several benefits, such as:

- **Enhanced read/write speed**: Spreading your dataset across multiple shards allows for parallel processing. Each additional shard increases your total throughput, and a well-distributed dataset improves query performance. Multiple shards can process queries simultaneously, speeding up response times.

- **Expanded storage capacity**: Increasing the number of shards enhances your total storage. If one shard holds 4 TB of data, each additional shard adds another 4 TB. This allows for nearly limitless storage capacity, enabling scalability as your data needs increase.

- **Data locality**: Zone sharding allows for databases to be distributed across different geographical locations, making it ideal for distributed applications. Policies can confine data within specific regions, with each region holding one or more shards, improving efficiency and adaptability in data management. In zone sharding, different ranges of shard key values can be associated with each zone, enabling faster and more precise data access based on geographical relevance.

Data distribution

Correct data distribution in a sharded MongoDB cluster is vital for a balanced workload, improved performance, and enhanced scalability, preventing bottlenecks and ensuring efficient resource use.

Shard key

MongoDB performs sharding at the collection level, allowing you to choose which collections to shard. Selecting the shard key is critical in sharding clusters, as an improper choice can lead to inefficient data distribution, unbalanced load distribution across shards, and diminished query performance. Such issues may overload some shards while underutilizing others, reducing system efficiency. In extreme cases, a single shard, known as a *hot shard*, could become a bottleneck, significantly impacting cluster performance. Thus, choosing the right shard key is vital for optimal performance in a sharded environment.

By using a shard key, made up of one or more document fields, MongoDB distributes a collection's documents across shards. The data is divided into non-overlapping *chunks* by breaking down the range of shard key values. The goal is to evenly distribute these chunks among a cluster's shards, ensuring efficient distribution.

In recent versions of MongoDB, notable modifications have been made to the sharding functionality:

- Beginning in MongoDB 4.4, documents in sharded collections can omit shard key fields. In such cases, these missing shard key fields are considered to have null values during the distribution of documents across shards.

- Starting in MongoDB 4.4, you can enhance a shard key by appending a suffix field or fields to the existing shard key.

- In MongoDB 5.0, you can reshard a collection by modifying its shard key.

Sharding strategy

MongoDB supports two sharding strategies for distributing data across sharded clusters:

- **Ranged sharding** involves segmenting data into continuous sequences based on shard key values. Documents with similar shard key values are likely to be in the same shard or chunk, facilitating effective queries for continuous sequences. However, improper shard key selection can impact read/write performance. Range-based sharding is the default method unless options for hashed sharding or zones are configured. Ranged sharding is most efficient when the shard key exhibits the following traits:

  - **High cardinality**: The cardinality of a shard key sets the upper limit for the number of chunks that the balancer can produce. Whenever feasible, opt for a shard key that has high cardinality. Selecting a shard key with low cardinality diminishes the efficiency of horizontal scaling within the cluster.

  - **Low frequency**: The frequency of the shard key denotes the recurrence of a specific shard key value in the data. When a substantial proportion of documents hold just a fraction of potential shard key values, the chunks housing the documents with those values can turn into a cluster bottleneck. As these chunks expand, they may evolve into jumbo chunks, given their inability to undergo further splitting. This situation diminishes the efficiency of horizontal scaling within the cluster.

  - **Non-monotonically changing values**: A shard key based on a value that progressively increases or decreases is more prone to directing insert operations to a single chunk within the cluster. This happens because each cluster contains a chunk that includes a range with an upper bound of `MaxKey`. `MaxKey` is always regarded as greater than any other value. Similarly, there's a chunk that holds a range with a lower limit of `MinKey`, which is always considered lower than all other values.

- **Hashed sharding** operates by calculating a hash value of the shard key field's value and then assigns each chunk a range determined by the hashed shard key values. Although a range of shard keys may appear to be *close* in terms of their values, their hashed values are unlikely to fall within the same chunk. It is important to note that hashed sharding is not efficient for performing range-based operations. Hashed keys are ideal for shard keys with fields that change monotonically, such as `ObjectId` values or timestamps. A good example of this is the default `_id` field, assuming it only contains `ObjectId` values.

MongoDB 4.4 introduced the capability to construct compound indexes with a solitary hashed field. To create such a compound hashed index, designate `hashed` as the value of any single index key during index creation. A compound hashed index calculates the hash value for a single field in the compound index; this value, along with other fields in the index, is used as your shard key. Take the following example:

```
db.planets.createIndex({ "name":1, "_id": "hashed" })
sh.shardCollection("sample_guides.planets", { "name": 1, "_id": "hashed" })
```

The preceding commands create a compound hashed index on the `name` field in ascending order, `_id` as the hashed field, and shard the `planets` collection.

Features such as zone sharding are supported by compound hashed sharding, where the prefix (i.e., the first) non-hashed field or fields define zone ranges, while the hashed field ensures a more equitable distribution of the sharded data. Additionally, compound hashed sharding provides support for shard keys with a hashed prefix, which helps address data distribution issues tied to fields that increase monotonically.

Shard key index

To shard a populated collection, it is necessary for the collection to have an index that begins with the shard key. However, when sharding an empty collection, MongoDB automatically generates the required supporting index if the collection does not already have a suitable index for the specified shard key.

Chunks

MongoDB organizes sharded data into distinct sections, called a chunk or a range (starting in MongoDB 5.2, the default size is 128 MB; it was 64 MB prior to this version). Each chunk is characterized by an inclusive lower limit and an exclusive upper limit, which are defined by the shard key. These chunks contain an uninterrupted sequence of shard key values within a specific shard. Starting in MongoDB 6.1, chunks are not subject to auto-splitting. Instead, chunks are split only when moved across shards.

> **Note**
> Prior to MongoDB 6.1, chunks were split by the auto-splitter when the chunk size grew beyond the max chunk size.

Balancer and uniform chunk distribution

Starting in MongoDB 6.0.3, data in sharded clusters is distributed based on data size rather than the number of chunks. To ensure a balanced distribution of chunks, a background process called the *balancer* keeps track of the data volume on each shard for every sharded collection and also moves chunks between various shards. Once the amount of data for a sharded collection on a particular shard reaches specific migration limits, the balancer attempts to redistribute data across shards, aiming for an equal data distribution per shard while honoring the zones. By default, this balancing process is constantly active.

The balancer runs on the primary of the **config server replica set (CSRS)**. The balancing process for sharded clusters is completely invisible to the user and the application layer, although minor performance effects may be observed during its execution.

The balancer tries to mitigate this impact by attempting to:

- Restrain a shard to participate in only one migration at a time. In other words, a shard can't be involved in multiple data migrations simultaneously. The balancer performs range migrations one after the other.

  MongoDB can execute parallel data migrations; however, a shard is limited to being part of only one migration at any moment. With a sharded cluster consisting of n shards, MongoDB can perform up to $n/2$ (rounded down) concurrent migrations.

- Start a balance round when the data discrepancy between the most heavily loaded shard and the least loaded shard for a particular sharded collection hits the migration threshold. A collection is perceived as balanced when the data variation between shards (for that specific collection) is less than three times the established range size for the collection. If the range size is set at the default of 128 MB, a migration will be triggered if the data size difference between any two shards for a certain collection is at least 384 MB.

It is possible to set a specific timeframe for the balancer's operation to prevent it from interfering with production traffic. This is called the *balancing window* or *balancer window*.

Chunk administration

There are scenarios in which manual management of chunks is necessary.

Jumbo chunks

In MongoDB, a chunk that exceeds the specified range size and can't be automatically split by MongoDB is labeled as `jumbo`. While MongoDB manages chunk splitting and balancing automatically, there are situations where manual intervention is required to manage jumbo chunks. The preferred way to clear the jumbo flag from a chunk is to try to split the chunk. If the chunk can be divided, MongoDB removes the flag upon successful splitting of the chunk. You can use either the `sh.splitAt()` or `sh.splitFind()` method to split the jumbo chunk.

Indivisible chunks

In certain cases, MongoDB in unable to split a no-longer-jumbo chunk, for instance, a chunk with a range of single shard key value. As such, you cannot split the chunk to clear the flag. In such cases, you can modify the shard key (you can reshard a collection) to make the chunk divisible or you can manually remove the flag.

To manually clear the flag, in the `admin` database, initiate the `clearJumboFlag` command, providing the namespace of the sharded collection and either of the following:

- The boundaries of the jumbo chunk:

```
db.adminCommand({
    clearJumboFlag: "sample.customers",
    bounds: [{ "x": 5 }, { "x": 6 }]
})
```

- The `find` document with a shard key and value that falls within the jumbo chunk:

```
db.adminCommand({
    clearJumboFlag: "sample.customers",
    find: { "x": 5 }
})
```

In the case where the collection employs a hashed shard key, refrain from using the `find` field with `clearJumboFlag`. For collections with hashed shard keys, it's more appropriate to utilize the `bounds` field.

Pre-splitting the ranges

In most scenarios, a sharded cluster will automatically generate, divide, and allocate data ranges without the need for manual oversight. Nonetheless, there are cases where MongoDB can't produce sufficient ranges, or disseminate data at a pace that can keep up with the necessary throughput.

If you're about to load a large amount of data into a new sharded cluster, pre-splitting can help distribute the data evenly across shards from the beginning. This prevents a single shard from becoming a bottleneck.

> **Note**
> It is advised to only pre-split ranges for a collection that is currently empty. Attempting to manually split ranges for a collection that already contains data can result in irregular range boundaries and sizes and may also cause the balancing behavior to function inefficiently or not at all.

To manually split empty ranges, the `split` command can be used. This command divides a chunk in a sharded cluster into two separate chunks. The `split` command must be executed in the `admin` database.

Let's take a look at an example. Suppose you have a collection named `myapp.products`, and you want to pre-split the ranges into four distinct price categories. The shard key is set on the `price` field. This can be achieved using the following code in `mongosh`:

```
// Split the collection into chunks based on the specified split points
var splitPoints = [20, 50, 100];

// Note: The 'split' command can take either middle, find, or bounds
// as options.In this example, you're using the middle option to specify
// the split points.

for(var i = 0; i < splitPoints.length; i++) {
  db.adminCommand({
    split: "myapp.products",
    middle: {
      price: splitPoints[i]
    }
  });
}
```

This code will divide the data into four price categories:

- Products priced under $20

- Products priced between $20 to $50

- Products priced between $50 to $100

- Products priced over $100

Starting in MongoDB 6.0, the balancer distributes data across shards based on data size. Simply splitting the ranges might not ensure that data is evenly distributed across shards. Therefore, you have to manually move the chunks to ensure a balanced distribution:

```
// List of shards to which you want to move the chunks
var shards = ["shard0000", "shard0001", "shard0002", "shard0003"];
for (var i = 0; i < splitPoints.length; i++) {
  var lowerBound = { price: MinKey };
  if (i > 0) {
    lowerBound = { price: splitPoints[i-1] };
  }

  var upperBound = { price: MaxKey };
  if (i < splitPoints.length - 1) {
    upperBound = { price: splitPoints[i] };
  }
```

```
// Manually move the chunk to the desired shard
db.adminCommand({
  moveChunk: "myapp.products",
  find: lowerBound,
  to: shards[i],
  bounds: [lowerBound, upperBound]
});
}
```

This approach helps distribute the data evenly across shards from the start.

Querying sharded data

Querying data from a MongoDB sharded cluster differs from querying data in a single-server deployment or a replica set. Instead of connecting to the single server or the primary of the replica set, you connect to mongos, which acts as a query router and decides which shard to ask for data. In the next section, you will explore how the mongos router operates.

The mongos router

mongos instances provide the only interface and entry point to your MongoDB cluster. Applications connect to mongos instead of connecting to the underlying shards directly. mongos executes queries, gathers results, and passes them to the application. The mongos process doesn't hold any persistent state and typically doesn't use a lot of system resources. It acts as a proxy for requests. When a query comes in, mongos examines it, decides which shards need to execute the query, and establishes a cursor on all targeted shards.

find

If a query includes the shard key or a prefix of the shard key, mongos will perform a targeted operation, only querying the shards that hold the keys you are looking for.

Let's assume the compound shard key for the user collection is _id, email, country:

```
db.user.find({ _id: 1 })
db.user.find({ _id: 1, "email": "packt@packt.com" })
db.user.find({ _id: 1, "email": "packt@packt.com" , "country": "UK" })
```

These queries consist of either a prefix (as is the case with the first two) or the complete shard key. On the other hand, a query on { email, country } or { country } will not be able to target the right shards, resulting in a broadcast operation. A broadcast operation is any operation that doesn't include the shard key or a prefix of the shard key, and results in mongos querying every shard. They are also known as scatter-gather operations or fan-out queries.

sort(), limit(), and skip()

If you want to sort results, you have the following two options:

- If you're using a shard key in the sort criteria, then mongos can determine the order in which it has to query a shard or shards. This results in an efficient and targeted operation.

- If you're not using the shard key in the sort criteria, then—as is the case with a query without any sort criteria—it's going to be a fan-out query. To sort the results when you are not using the shard key, the primary shard executes a distributed merge sort locally before passing on the sorted result set to mongos.

A limit on the queries is enforced on each individual shard and then again at the mongos level, as there may be results from multiple shards. A skip operator, on the other hand, cannot be passed on to individual shards and will be applied by mongos after retrieving all the results locally.

If you combine the skip() and limit() cursor methods, mongos will optimize the query by passing both values to individual shards. This is particularly useful in cases such as pagination. If you query without sort() and the results are coming from more than one shard, mongos will round robin across shards for the results.

Update and delete

Starting in MongoDB 7.0, the process for document modifier operations such as *update* and *delete* have been streamlined. If the find() section of the modifier contains the shard key, mongos can continue to route the query to the appropriate shard. Yet, if the shard key is absent from the find section, it no longer triggers a fan-out operation as it did in earlier versions.

For updateOne(), deleteOne(), or findAndmodify() operations, there's no longer a strict requirement to have the shard key or the _id value. Any field can be used to match documents, similar to a non-sharded collection. However, using the shard key in these operations is still more efficient as it allows for targeted queries.

For example, in MongoDB 6.0, you must pass a shard key to updateOne():

```
db.cities.updateOne({ "city": "New York City" },
{ $set: { "population" : 8500000 }});
```

In the preceding example, city represents the shard key. However, in MongoDB 7.0, you can run the updateOne() operation without having to include the shard key in the filter:

```
db.cities.updateOne({ "population" : 293200 },{ $set: { "areaSize" : 211 }});
```

Table 2.3 sums up operations in MongoDB 7.0 that you can use for sharding:

Operation	Description
`insert()`	Must include the shard key
`update()`	Can include the shard key, but not mandatory
Query with shard key	Targeted operation
Query without shard key	A scatter-gather operation behind the scenes
Index sorted, query with shard key	Targeted operation
Index sorted, query without shard key	Distributed sort merge
`updateOne()`, `replaceOne()`, `deleteOne()`	Can use any field to match on, but more efficient with shard key

Table 2.1: Sharding operations

Hedged reads

Beginning in MongoDB 4.4, `mongos` instances can hedge reads that utilize non-primary read preferences. The `mongos` instances direct read operations to two members of the replica set for each queried shard, and then return the results from the first respondent per shard.

The operations that support hedged reads include `collStats`, `count`, `dataSize`, `dbStats`, `distinct`, `filemd5`, `find`, `listCollections`, `listIndexes`, and `planCacheListFilters`.

Sharding methods

To manage the distribution of data, MongoDB provides a set of helper methods. These methods are used to enable sharding, define how data should be distributed, and monitor the state of sharding. They are essential tools for managing a sharded MongoDB deployment, allowing for efficient scaling of data across multiple machines. Various `mongosh` shell helper methods are listed here:

- `sh.shardCollection()` is essential for setting up sharding in MongoDB. Once a collection has been sharded, MongoDB does not provide a method to unshard it. However, the shard key can be changed later if needed.

- `db.collection.getShardDistribution()` provides a detailed breakdown of data distribution across the shards for a specific sharded collection. Here's a summary of the output information this command displays:

Output	Type	Description
`<shard-x>`	String	Holds the shard name
`<host-x>`	String	Holds the host name(s)
`<size-x>`	Number	Includes the size of the data, including the unit of measure
`<count-x>`	Number	Reports the number of documents in the shard
`<number of chunks-x>`	Number	Reports the number of chunks in the shard
`<size-x>/<number of chunks-x>`	Calculated value	Reflects the estimated data size per chunk for the shard, including the unit of measure
`<count-x>/<number of chunks-x>`	Calculated value	Reflects the estimated number of documents per chunk for the shard
`<stats.size>`	Number	Reports the total size of the data in the sharded collection, including the unit of measure
`<stats.count>`	Number	Reports the total number of documents in the sharded collection
`<calc total chunks>`	Calculated value	Reports the number of chunks from all shards
`<estDataPercent-x>`	Calculated value	Signifies the estimated data size for each shard as a percentage of the collection's total data size
`<estDocPercent-x>`	Calculated value	Reflects the estimated number of documents for each shard as a percentage of the total number of documents for the collection

Table 2.2: Output information for db.collection.getShardDistribution()

- `sh.status()` provides information about the sharded cluster. The level of detail in the output can be adjusted with the verbose parameter, allowing for either a high-level overview or a detailed report. The information provided by this command includes the sharding version, details about each shard, the status of active `mongos` instances, the status of auto-splitting, the state of the balancer, and information about databases and sharded collections.

- Beginning in MongoDB 5.0, the `sh.reshardCollection()` method makes it possible to modify the shard key of a collection to alter how your data is distributed throughout a cluster. However, before starting a resharding operation, ensure that your application can tolerate a two second write block during resharding, which may increase latency. If this is unacceptable, consider adjusting your shard key. Your database server should also have the necessary resources:

  - **Storage**: Ensure the available storage on each shard is at least 2.2 times the size of the collection to be resharded. For instance, for a 1 TB collection, each shard should have at least 2.2 TB of free storage.

    To determine the storage required for each shard, use the following formula: Available storage required on each shard = (collection storage size * 2.2) / number of shards the collection will be distributed across

    Supposedly, a collection occupies 2 TB of storage and is distributed across four shards, each shard would require at least 1.1 TB of available storage.

    Example calculation: (2 TB * 2.2) / 4 shards = 1.1 TB/shard

  - **I/O**: Your I/O capacity should not exceed 50%.

  - **CPU usage**: Keep CPU usage below 80%.

- `sh.getBalancerState()` returns a boolean value indicating whether the balancer is presently active.

- `$shardedDataDistribution`, at this aggregation stage, returns information on the distribution of data in a sharded cluster.

New sharded cluster features in MongoDB 7.0

MongoDB 7.0 continues to simplify the management and understanding of sharded clusters for both operations and developer use cases. This version provides additional insights that assist in making the best decisions for both initial and future shard key selections. Furthermore, starting in MongoDB 7.0, developers can experience a consistent interface when using these commands on sharded or unsharded clusters, while still retaining the option to optimize for performance when necessary. Let's have a look at the new sharding features introduced in MongoDB 7.0.

Shard key advisor commands

Choosing a shard key is complex due to intricate data patterns and trade-offs. Yet, the new features in MongoDB 7.0 aim to ease this task:

- `analyzeShardKey` provides the ability to evaluate a candidate shard key against existing data. Shard key analysis in MongoDB 7.0 offers metrics to evaluate a shard key's suitability, including its uniqueness (cardinality), frequency, and whether it increases or decreases steadily (monotonicity). This command can be run on a replica set as well as a sharded cluster.

- `configureQueryAnalyzer` offers metrics about query routing patterns across the cluster, helping spot unbalanced loads and hot shards. It returns a document containing fields that describe the old configuration, if one exists, and fields describing the new configuration. With these two commands, the initial shard key can be confidently set, or live resharding prepared for, backed by the necessary data to ensure confidence in the chosen shard key.

- The `mergeAllChunksOnShard` command is designed to consolidate or merge all the mergeable chunks of data that a specific shard owns for a given collection. It helps address decreased performance during sharding maintenance operations by finding all chunks on a specific shard that can be merged, and then merging them. This can help to reduce fragmentation and improve performance by reducing the number of chunks that need to be queried during sharding maintenance operations.

AutoMerger

`AutoMerger` is a feature that automatically merges chunks that meet certain *mergeability* requirements. This process runs in the background as part of balancing operations. Unless disabled, `AutoMerger` starts when the balancer is first enabled and pauses for a set interval (`autoMergerIntervalSecs`) after each run. It performs automerging at every interval when enabled. For each collection, it ensures a minimum delay (`autoMergerThrottlingMS`) between subsequent merges. If a balancing window is defined, `AutoMerger` operates only within that window. Two or more contiguous chunks in the same collection are mergeable when they meet all of the following conditions:

- Belong to the same shard.

- Are not jumbo chunks (which can't participate in migrations).

- Have a migration history that can be safely purged without disrupting transactions or snapshot reads. This means the last migration of the chunk occurred at least as far back as the `minSnapshotHistoryWindowInSeconds` and `transactionLifetimeLimitSeconds` values.

You can use the following methods to control the `AutoMerger` behavior:

```
sh.startAutoMerger()
sh.stopAutoMerger()
sh.enableAutoMerger()
sh.disableAutoMerger()
```

Command support without shard keys

The usage of commands such as `updateOne`, `deleteOne`, and `findAndmodify` will be consistent across both sharded and unsharded clusters, while providing the option to optimize for performance when required.

Summary

Replication in MongoDB is a process that synchronizes data across multiple servers, providing redundancy and increased data availability. This is achieved through replica sets, a group of MongoDB servers that maintain the same dataset. Within a replica set, one node acts as the primary node, receiving all write operations, while the secondary nodes replicate the primary's operations to their datasets. This structure provides a robust system for failover and recovery. If a primary node fails, an election among the secondaries determines a new primary, allowing for continuous client operations.

Sharding in MongoDB is a method for splitting and distributing data across multiple servers or shards. Each shard is an independent replica set, and collectively, the shards make up a single logical database—the *sharded cluster*. This approach is used to support deployments with very large datasets and high-throughput operations, effectively addressing scalability issues.

In the next chapter, you'll explore different categories of MongoDB developer tools, and how you can use MongoDB Shell, MongoDB CLI, MongoDB Compass, and MongoDB for VS code to increase your productivity.

3

Developer Tools

Mastering the art of MongoDB development can be challenging and requires more than just an understanding of the core concepts and syntax. To truly harness the full potential of MongoDB and its ecosystem, you should familiarize yourself with the array of developer tools that MongoDB offers.

MongoDB has a long history of ensuring that developers have access to the best tools to work with their MongoDB clusters and data. In 2011—only two years after MongoDB 1.0 was released—10gen (now known as MongoDB Inc.) released **MongoDB Management Service** (**MMS**), later rebranded as Ops Manager. Ops Manager has played a vital role for developers using MongoDB products as a portal to manage and monitor their systems. The management tool, being part of the MongoDB ecosystem from early releases, reflects the importance of MongoDB, aiming to provide developer tools, along with growing its database system architecture.

This chapter will cover the following topics:

- Categories of developer tools
- Using MongoDB Shell (`mongosh`)
- Using MongoDB CLI (`mongocli`)
- Using MongoDB Compass
- Using the MongoDB for VS Code

Technical requirements

For all the developer tools discussed in this chapter, you will need a running MongoDB cluster that you can connect to. This can be done either locally, or by spinning up a free cluster via the managed service—MongoDB Atlas.

- Download MongoDB Community Edition from the official website: `https://www.mongodb.com/try/download/community`
- Create a free account on MongoDB Atlas (`https://www.mongodb.com/try`) to use the MongoDB tools

Introduction to developer tools

To facilitate efficient database management and query optimization, MongoDB tools are designed for enhanced productivity, performance monitoring, and seamless integration with developers' preferred development environments. In this section, you will learn about various MongoDB tools and explore their functionalities, use cases, and best practices, all aimed at empowering you to wield the capabilities of MongoDB to their fullest.

Categories of developer tools

Developer tools, officially designed by MongoDB, serve users across different scenarios. Some tools are meant to manage the data you store inside your MongoDB instance, some are plugin tools for third-party software, whereas some tools are used for the management and performance monitoring of the cluster itself. Based on the use case scenario, these tools can be classified as follows:

Administrative tools

These tools are used for the administration and management of database systems. Some examples of administrative tools are as follows:

- **MongoDB Shell** (`mongosh`): A fully functional JavaScript and Node.js REPL environment for interacting with MongoDB deployments. You can use `mongosh` to test queries and operations directly with your database.
- **MongoDB Compass**: A powerful GUI for querying, aggregating, and analyzing your MongoDB data in a visual environment.

Backup and restore tools

These tools are designed for creating a backup of your MongoDB database to external storage, or to restore database backups to existing MongoDB clusters. Some examples of backup and restore tools are as follows:

- `mongodump`: A command-line utility for creating a binary export of a database's contents
- `mongorestore`: A command-line tool for loading data from a binary database dump created by `mongodump`

Performance monitoring tools

These tools provide insight into the performance of your database clusters and monitor the health diagnostics of your database systems. Some examples of performance monitoring tools are as follows:

- `mongostat`: A command-line tool for monitoring real-time performance statistics of a MongoDB instance
- `mongotop`: A command-line tool for tracking the amount of time a MongoDB instance spends reading and writing data

Development and integration tools

These tools enable seamless integration with various third-party software and tools, widening the spectrum of development capabilities:

- **MongoDB Connector for BI**: Traditional business intelligence tools are designed to work with tabular, row-and-column data. The MongoDB Connector for BI allows you to query MongoDB data with SQL using tools such as Tableau, Power BI, and Excel.
- **MongoDB for Visual Studio Code**: Work with your MongoDB data seamlessly within VS Code, using features such as syntax highlighting, code snippets, IntelliSense (code suggestions), connection management, and query execution.

Deployment and orchestration integration tools

These tools assist in the deployment and orchestration of an application by integrating with major integration and deployment solutions:

- **Kubernetes Operator**: MongoDB offers an official Kubernetes Operator that simplifies deployment, scaling, and management of MongoDB clusters in Kubernetes environments
- **Terraform template support**: Integration with Terraform allows for automated infrastructure provisioning, making it easier to set up and maintain MongoDB clusters on various cloud platforms

These categories are not exhaustive, since some tools may fall into multiple categories depending on their functionalities. Each project's requirements and application goals are different, so a suitable tool can be chosen as per your development workflow.

MongoDB Shell

The MongoDB Shell (mongosh) is a fully functional JavaScript and Node.js-based REPL environment used to interact with MongoDB deployments. mongosh is a powerful and versatile command-line interface that serves as an interpreter. You can use mongosh to talk to the database directly and perform **create**, **read**, **update**, **delete** (**CRUD**) operations, administrative operations, aggregations, indexing, and much more on the database.

Installation

You can install mongosh using any of the following methods:

- mongosh is available as a standalone package from the MongoDB Download Center: https://www.mongodb.com/download-center/community/releases.

- Download and install mongosh by following the steps provided in the MongoDB documentation: https://www.mongodb.com/docs/mongodb-shell/install/#std-label-mdb-shell-install.

- You can use **Node Package Manager** (**npm**), as it's built on Node.js:

  I.   Open the terminal

  II.   Run the following command to install mongosh globally on your system:

```
npm install -g mongosh
```

Connecting to a MongoDB deployment using mongosh

Once mongosh is installed, start it by simply typing mongosh in the Terminal or Command Prompt. By default, this will attempt to connect to a MongoDB deployment running on localhost with the default port 27017. To establish connection with a remote MongoDB deployment, you can run mongosh without any options, or as seen in the following command, use a connection string with the chosen host and port:

```
mongosh "mongodb://username:password@hostname:port/test"
```

Once you're connected to the MongoDB deployment, you should see the MongoDB test> shell prompt, indicating that the shell is connected to the test database and is ready to execute commands.

A successful connection to a local MongoDB deployment using mongosh should resemble the following output in your terminal:

```
Packt Server $ mongosh
Current Mongosh Log ID:     64c3fd54ca5106d524ea1c5c
Connecting to:
mongodb://127.0.0.1:27017/?directConnection=true&serverSelectionTimeoutMS
=2000&appName=mongosh+2.0.0
```

```
Using MongoDB:              7.0.0
Using Mongosh:              2.0.0

For mongosh info see: https://docs.mongodb.com/mongodb-shell/
------
test>
```

Once you're connected to the MongoDB deployment on localhost, you will get a prompt with the database name, as seen in the preceding code block. Now, you can execute commands on the MongoDB cluster, such as displaying all databases using show dbs, switching to a particular database, or running CRUD operations on collections in your database from the mongosh interface, as seen in the following code block:

```
test> show dbs
admin 132.00KiB
config 36.00KiB
core 890.00KiB
local 92.00KiB
org 80.00KiB
test> use org
org> show collections
clients
employees
infra
accounts
org> db.employees.find()
[
  {
    "_id": ObjectId("5f5b047b7e59b56c5878df4c"),
    "first_name": "John",
    "last_name": "Doe",
    "email": "johndoe@example.com",
    "department": "HR",
    "salary": 60000
  },
  {
    "_id": ObjectId("5f5b04ac7e59b56c5878df4d"),
    "first_name": "Jane",
    "last_name": "Smith",
    "email": "janesmith@example.com",
    "department": "Engineering",
    "salary": 75000
  },
```

```
 {
   "_id": ObjectId("5f5b04c67e59b56c5878df4e"),
   "first_name": "Alice",
   "last_name": "Johnson",
   "email": "alicejohnson@example.com",
   "department": "Sales",
   "salary": 55000
 }
]
```

mongosh provides intelligent autocomplete and suggestions, which can help you write commands faster and with fewer errors. If you want to explore additional options, you can run the help command:

```
test> help
Shell Help:


use                Set current database
show               'show databases'/'show dbs': Print a list of all databases
                   'show collections'/'show tables': Print a list of all
                   collections for current database.
                   'show profile': Prints system.profile information
                   'show users': Print a list of all users for current database.
                   'show roles': Print a list of all roles for current database.
                   'show log <type>': log for current connection,
                   if type is not set uses 'global'
                   'show logs': Print all logs.
exit               Quit the MongoDB shell with exit/exit()/.exit
quit               Quit the MongoDB shellwith quit/quit()
Mongo              Create a new connection and return the Mongo object.
connect            Create a new connection and return the Database object.
it                 result of the last line evaluated; use to further iterate
version            Shell version
load               Loads and runs a JavaScript file into the current shell env
enableTelemetry    Enables collection of anonymous usage data
disableTelemetry   Disables collection of anonymous usage data
passwordPrompt     Prompts the user for a password
sleep              Sleep for the specified number of milliseconds
print              Prints the contents of an object to the output
printjson          Alias for print()
                   convertShardKeyToHashed Returns the hashed value for the input
cls                Clears the screen like console.clear()
isInteractive      Returns whether the shell will enter
```

Refer to following MongoDB documentation for an overview of the help features available in mongosh: https://www.mongodb.com/docs/mongodb-shell/reference/access-mdb-shell-help/.

For detailed instructions on installing `mongosh` on your local machine, check the documentation at `https://www.mongodb.com/docs/mongodb-shell/install/`.

mongosh vs legacy shell

`mongosh` offers numerous advantages over the legacy shell (`mongo`), such as:

- **Intelligent auto-complete**: You can get help on command syntax by using the *Tab* button while typing in the command.

- **Syntax highlighting**: When you write commands and view results, you'll see colors that match your command line setup, as well as pretty-print formatting, making the code readable and easy to process.

- **Logging**: MongoDB Shell uses `ndjson` to store session logs. You can view or tail the logs for a MongoDB Shell session based on its log ID.

- **Legacy method compatibility**: To ensure backward compatibility, `mongosh` supports legacy methods using the same syntax as the corresponding methods in the legacy `mongo` shell.

Key features of mongosh

`mongosh` is an invaluable tool for both database administrators and developers like yourself, offering real-time feedback and a wide range of functionalities that enhance your MongoDB experience. As you become more familiar with `mongosh`, you will discover various features to empower you to interact with databases and collections more efficiently. Some of the most prominent features in `mongosh` include:

- **Administrative methods**: You can use `mongosh` to execute administrative methods to manage the database and troubleshoot data or cluster configuration issues.

  You can create a new user with specific roles assigned to it by using the following command:

```
org> db.runCommand({
        createUser: "mark",
        pwd: "test123",
        roles: [
                { role: "dbOwner", db: "admin" }
                ]
})
{ ok: 1 }
org>
```

- **Write scripts**: `mongosh` can be used to write scripts for modifying data in MongoDB or for performing administrative tasks on a cluster. The scripts can be used as snippets for easier distribution, management, and reuse of the code.

  You can execute a `.js` file from within `mongosh`. Since `mongosh` is a Node.js REPL environment, it can execute Node.js code by using a script to perform the desired operation.

To load and execute a `.js` file within `mongosh`, use the `load()` method:

```
mongosh> load("connect-and-insert.js")
```

You can also execute the script file directly from the command line before logging in to `mongosh` by using the `file` parameter:

```
mongosh --file loadMovies.js
```

You can use script execution to initialize the database with predefined collections, documents, and indexes. You can also load a script to perform scheduled tasks or perform data migration operations. Writing a script for complex queries helps with documentation and improves code reusability for multiple executions.

- **Retrieve shell logs**: `mongosh` uses ndjson to store session logs. Starting in `mongosh` version 1.0.5, the MongoDB Shell log format has been updated to match the MongoDB server log format. You can view or tail the logs for a `mongosh` session based on its log ID.

  The log ID can be retrieved from the startup message loaded when `mongosh` starts on terminal or command prompt. MongoDB Shell logs are stored in a subdirectory of the home directory of a user with a filename that corresponds to the log ID. You can interact with the logs using standard text processing tools like CAT.

- **Use as an editor for commands**: `mongosh` provides an interface to execute one command at a time. Thus, to perform a series of operations on the database, you need to write and execute operations one by one or execute operations as a script, as explained earlier. Another way to perform multiline functions is to use an editor within `mongosh` to type in all the executable commands in one go. You can set an editor within `mongosh` by using the `config.set()` command:

```
config.set( "editor", "vi" )
```

  Now, you can enter the editor set by using the `edit` command. To use the built-in editor, you can use the `.editor` command. Press *Ctrl + D* to exit and run your function.

Use cases for mongosh

`mongosh` is a modern, user-friendly, and feature-rich interactive tool, ideal for the following use case scenarios:

- **Interactive database exploration and querying**: `mongosh` is great for exploring your MongoDB database interactively. You can run queries, examine documents, and experiment with different commands directly in the shell.

- **Administration and management**: You can perform administrative tasks such as creating databases, collections, and indexes using `mongosh`. It's particularly useful for setting up your database structure.

- **Data manipulation**: `mongosh` allows you to insert, update, and delete documents, making it useful for manipulating data within your collections.

- **Scripting and automation**: You can write scripts using `mongosh` to automate repetitive tasks, such as data migrations, backups, and maintenance operations.

- **Aggregation framework**: `mongosh` supports the MongoDB aggregation framework, a powerful tool for performing complex data transformations and analysis tasks.

- **Working with replica sets and sharded clusters**: You can use `mongosh` to manage and monitor replica sets and sharded clusters, including viewing their status and managing failover scenarios.

- **Performance analysis and monitoring**: `mongosh` provides commands for monitoring the performance of your MongoDB deployment, such as `db.serverStatus()` and `db.stats()`.

Best practices for using mongosh

Here are some best practices for using the `mongosh` tool:

- **Install and update regularly**: Keep your `mongosh` version up to date to benefit from the latest features, improvements, and bug fixes.

- **Use the connection string**: Instead of specifying individual connection parameters, use the MongoDB connection string to connect to your database. This makes your connection settings more portable and easier to manage.

- **Write code with ease**: `mongosh` provides intelligent autocomplete and syntax highlighting features, making it easy for you to navigate and execute commands.

- **Understand the output**: Become familiar with the output format of commands such as `find()` and `aggregate()`, as they can display large amounts of data. You might want to use cursor methods, such as `forEach()`, for better control.

- **Use the help command**: Utilize the `help` command to get information about available commands, syntax, and usage examples.

- **Practice in a safe environment**: When experimenting with administrative tasks or scripts, it's good practice to work in a test or development environment before applying changes to production data.

- **Security best practices**: Ensure that you connect to your MongoDB deployment securely using appropriate authentication mechanisms and authorization roles.

- **Back up data**: Before performing any potentially destructive operations, back up your data to prevent accidental data loss.

MongoDB CLI

The MongoDB CLI is a modern command-line interface tool that enables you to manage your MongoDB services from the terminal. It is used to deploy and manage MongoDB clusters in Atlas, Cloud Manager, and Ops Manager.

Installation

You can install MongoDB CLI from the official website: `https://www.mongodb.com/try/download/mongocli`.

Once installed, you can use it to interact with your cloud deployments and manage clusters remotely for Atlas, Cloud Manager, and Ops Manager deployments through its user-friendly command-line interface.

Configuration

Follow these steps to configure and authenticate MongoDB CLI to your cluster:

1. **Create API keys**: In the Atlas UI, create an API key to programmatically access your organization or project.

2. **Create a project**: If you don't have an existing project, create one to group clusters that share users, settings, or environments.

3. **Establish a connection**: Add your IP or CIDR block to the API access list for your MongoDB service.

Once the prerequisites are completed, create the profile by running the `mongocli configure` command in the terminal:

```
~ mongocli config
```

This will set up a profile for MongoDB CLI. You will be prompted to optionally provide public or private API keys, an org, and a project of the Atlas cluster you want to configure.

> **Note**
> By default, the MongoDB CLI will store the configuration settings in `~/.config/mongocli.toml`.

Working with MongoDB CLI

After creating your profile, you can access the Atlas cluster from the shell and script any interaction with it by running commands to simulate responses as you would see in the Atlas GUI. For example, you can list the users in the database of your configured cluster along with their roles, using the following command:

```
Packt Server $ mongocli atlas dbusers list
[
{
  "databaseName": "admin",
  "ldapAuthType": "NONE",
  "x509Type":  "NONE",
```

```
  "awsIAMType": "NONE",
  "groupId": "620173c921b1ab3de3e83610",
  "roles": [
    {
      "roleName": "readWriteAnyDatabase",
          "databaseName": "admin"
  }
  ],
  "scopes": [],
  "username": "admin"
  ]
```

You should then enable access to your database from your IP address. By default, MongoDB Atlas databases are not open to external connections, including the admin IP. To change that, you can execute the following command to enable your current IP to connect:

```
mongocli atlas accessLists create --currentIp
```

The output should resemble the following:

```
{
  "links": [
    {
      "rel": "self",
      "href": "https://cloud.mongodb.com/api/atlas/v1.0/groups"
    }
  ],
  "results": [
    {
      "cidrBlock": "A.B.C.D/32",
      "comment": "My IP Address",
      "groupId": "620173c921b1ab3de3e8e610",
      "ipAddress": "A.B.C.D"
    }
  ],
  "totalCount": 1
}
```

You can create, update, and delete IP blocks that are allowed to connect to MongoDB Atlas and add whole subnets to it. For example, an entry formatted as 192.168.1.0 would allow clients coming from any IP starting with 1.2.3... to connect. Other than using the MongoDB CLI as an interface to connect to the Atlas cluster, you can also use it to authenticate your cloud deployments using the mongocli auth command.

mongocli auth

The `mongocli auth` command lets you manage the authentication state of the command-line interface. You can use `auth to` command to authenticate Atlas (`mongocli auth login`) or Cloud Manager (`mongocli auth login --cm`). You can use `mongocli logout` to log out of the command-line interface.

> **Note**
> The MongoDB CLI will accept singular and plural naming for the same command. For example, both `accessList` and `accessLists` will result in invoking the same command.

Key features of MongoDB CLI

MongoDB CLI provides a convenient way to manage and administer MongoDB deployments without needing a GUI or writing extensive scripts. Key features of MongoDB CLI include:

- **Cluster management**: MongoDB CLI enables you to manage MongoDB clusters, including creating, updating, and deleting clusters.

- **Database operations**: You can perform various database-related operations, such as creating databases, collections, and documents, as well as querying and updating data, directly from the command line.

- **Data import and export**: It allows you to import and export data to and from MongoDB databases using various formats, such as `.json` and `.csv`. This is helpful when you need to migrate data between environments, or back up and restore databases.

- **User and role management**: The MongoDB CLI enables you to manage users and roles for authentication and authorization purposes. You can create users, assign roles, and update user credentials.

- **Integration with other tools**: The MongoDB CLI can be used in conjunction with other tools and scripts for automation and orchestration purposes. For instance, you can incorporate commands into your deployment scripts.

Use cases for MongoDB CLI

As an interactive tool for managing cloud-based MongoDB solutions, the MongoDB CLI can help you:

- Create, update, and manage MongoDB Atlas clusters
- Move data between your local environment and MongoDB Atlas
- Manage database users, roles, and access control settings
- Monitor cluster health, performance, and perform maintenance
- Integrate MongoDB Atlas management into existing automation workflows

Best practices for MongoDB CLI

The following are a few best practices for using the MongoDB CLI tool:

- Ensure that you have proper authentication and authorization settings in place when you're using the MongoDB CLI tool with MongoDB Atlas.

- Use MongoDB CLI to create and manage clusters programmatically, and perform cluster maintenance tasks, such as resizing and upgrading.

- Utilize MongoDB CLI for backup operations to create regular backups of your data.

- Use MongoDB Atlas CLI to automate user and role management, while adhering to the principle of least privilege for user roles while doing so.

- Use Atlas CLI as part of your CI/CD pipeline for database-related tasks to integrate with other tools using scripts, and streamline your development and deployment processes.

MongoDB Compass

MongoDB Compass is a powerful and intuitive GUI tool designed to simplify database management, query building, and data visualization for MongoDB. It offers a user-friendly alternative to the command-line interface by providing a visual representation of MongoDB data and collections.

Compass is a free interactive tool. With Compass, you can explore databases and collections, view and analyze the data, and perform CRUD operations without writing complex queries manually. Compass provides visualizations for most queries and index performance, allowing database administrators to monitor and troubleshoot clusters seamlessly through a TLS-encrypted connection. It exposes an API that can be used to import or develop plugins. Compass also has the ability to download a read-only edition so that you can limit access to non-destructive operations. There is also an isolated edition of this tool that can be used to restrict connections to a single chosen server.

Installation

1. Compass is freely available for Windows, macOS, Red Hat, and Ubuntu as an executable download: `https://www.mongodb.com/docs/compass/current/`.

2. Once the download is complete, install the Compass tool.

Configuration

To configure connection parameters to a local or remote MongoDB cluster, or a deployment hosted on MongoDB Atlas, you should provide the connection string scheme either as a URI or by specifying the hostname, port, and authentication details in the dialog box for connection parameters. Since you're connecting to a local MongoDB deployment, select **mongodb** as the **Connection String Scheme**. To connect to an Atlas deployment, use the **mongodb+srv** schema.

As shown in *Figure 3.1*, when you open MongoDB Compass, it will prompt a window for a new connection. You can provide the connection parameters with the connection URI and also other additional details required for the connection by selecting each tab. Click *Connect* to connect to the MongoDB instance or click on *Save & Connect* to save the configuration and connect.

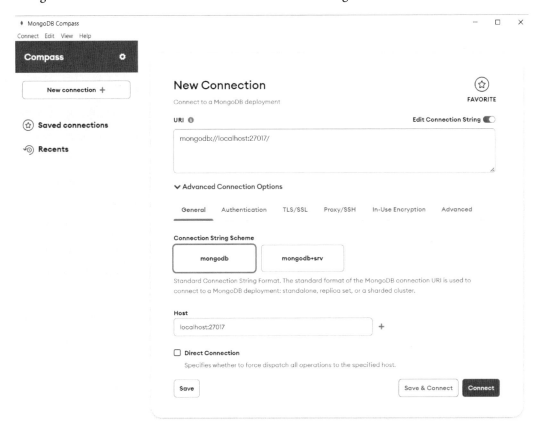

Figure 3.1: New connection configuration

Visually explore data using Compass

Once connected to the database, MongoDB Compass can be used to accomplish tasks such as importing your data from CSV or JSON into your connected MongoDB cluster or managing data from an easy-to-navigate interface. You can write ad hoc queries to filter your data and explore trends and commonalities in collections. You can also write aggregation pipelines that allow documents in a collection, or you can view them to pass through multiple stages where they are processed into a set of aggregated results. You can also use the embedded MongoDB Shell in Compass to operate over your data in an interactive JavaScript environment.

Figure 3.2 shows the MongoDB Compass environment once you're connected to a cluster. In the navigation bar, you can see all your databases listed on the left side of the Compass window. You can select a database from the list to see the collections in that database.

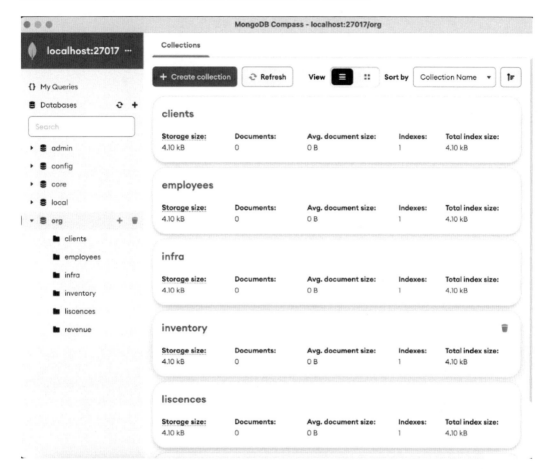

Figure 3.2: The MongoDB Compass environment

When you select a particular collection, you can see the sample set of data and query the collection using the query textbox. In the latest version, you can get insights for any query you run. For example, in *Figure 3.3*, Compass is used to run a query on the *employees* collection in the *org* database to find all documents with `lastname` not equal to `nair`. As you type the query, you will notice a suggestion pop up on the right side of the window, prompting to add an index for optimizing the executed query.

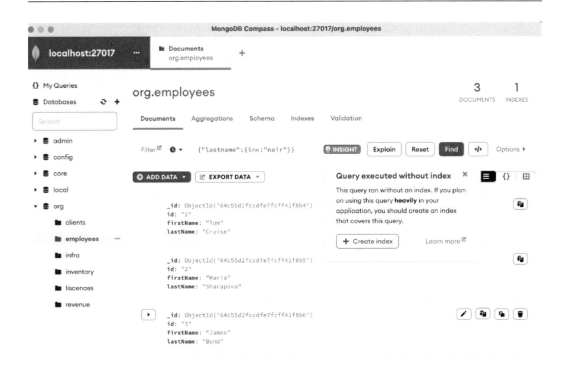

Figure 3.3: The optimization popup

As shown in *Figure 3.3*, you can click on the **Schema** tab to view the schema distribution of the collection as it lists out the fields in your collection and its distribution ratio across all documents in the collection. You can add and list indexes in the collection using the **Indexes** tab, and add rules to enforce the data structure of documents on updates and inserts using the **Validation** tab.

Key features of MongoDB Compass

MongoDB Compass offers several features for querying, aggregating, and analyzing your MongoDB data in a visual environment, such as:

- **Visual data exploration**: Compass presents your data in an easy-to-navigate, tree-like structure, making it simple to browse through documents and nested fields.

- **Query building**: The intuitive query builder allows you to construct complex queries using a point-and-click interface. This feature is especially beneficial when working with large datasets and complex filtering conditions.

- **Real-time performance monitoring**: Compass allows you to analyze the real-time performance of your MongoDB server. You can monitor query execution times, index usage, and more to optimize the performance of your database.

- **Schema analysis**: Compass automatically generates a visual representation of the schema of your data, offering valuable insights into how your data is structured.

- **Data visualization**: Compass provides built-in data visualization tools, enabling you to create charts and graphs from your MongoDB data for easy analysis and reporting.

- **Index management**: You can create, modify, and analyze indexes directly from Compass to optimize query performance.

- **Aggregation pipeline builder**: The pipeline builder helps construct complex aggregation pipelines effortlessly, simplifying the process of data transformation and analysis.

Use cases for MongoDB Compass

With its interactive GUI and tools, MongoDB Compass enables you to:

- Quickly explore your database by visually querying and filtering data using the intuitive query builder

- Design and visualize the structure of your collections and documents using the Compass schema view

- Build and visualize complex aggregation pipelines for data transformations and analysis

- Analyze and optimize query performance by viewing query execution plans

- Manage user accounts, roles, and privileges for authentication and authorization

Best practices for MongoDB Compass

The following are some best practices for using MongoDB Compass:

- Always connect to your MongoDB instance securely using appropriate connection settings and authentication.

- Regularly update MongoDB Compass to ensure you're using the latest features, improvements, and bug fixes.

- Before making significant changes to your data or schema, create backups to prevent data loss. When performing administrative tasks or testing new queries, use a development or staging environment to prevent any impact on production data.

- Use the *Indexes* tab in Compass to view existing indexes and identify areas for optimization.

- Learn how to use the query builder effectively, and utilize features such as *filtering*, *sorting*, and *projection* to retrieve the data you need.

- When experimenting with Compass features, consider using sample documents or creating a test dataset to avoid affecting production data.

MongoDB for VS Code

MongoDB provides an extension for VS Code that lets you work with your data directly within the coding environment. By using the MongoDB for VS Code extension, you can take advantage of the powerful features and extensibility of VS Code while seamlessly working with MongoDB databases.

Installation

Setting up the MongoDB for VS Code extension follows the generic installation method used for any other extension installed on VS Code or similar IDE tools. To install the extension, follow the steps given below:

1. Download and install the Visual Studio Code installer from `https://code.visualstudio.com/`.

2. Open the *Extensions* view by clicking on the *Extensions* icon in the *Activity* bar.

3. Alternatively, you can open the *Extensions* view by pressing *Ctrl + Shift + X* or *Cmd + Shift + X*. Search for *MongoDB* for *VS Code* in the extension marketplace.

4. Click *Install* on the MongoDB for VS Code extension.

5. Once the installation is complete, the *Install* button changes to the *Manage gear* button.

Explore data using Playground

Once you've installed MongoDB for VS Code, you can view data in your deployment and create Playgrounds to interact with your data. MongoDB Playgrounds are JavaScript environments where you can prototype queries, aggregations, and MongoDB commands with helpful syntax highlighting. You can create a new playground from the *Playgrounds* panel, the MongoDB for VS Code *Overview* page, or the Microsoft VS Code Command Palette.

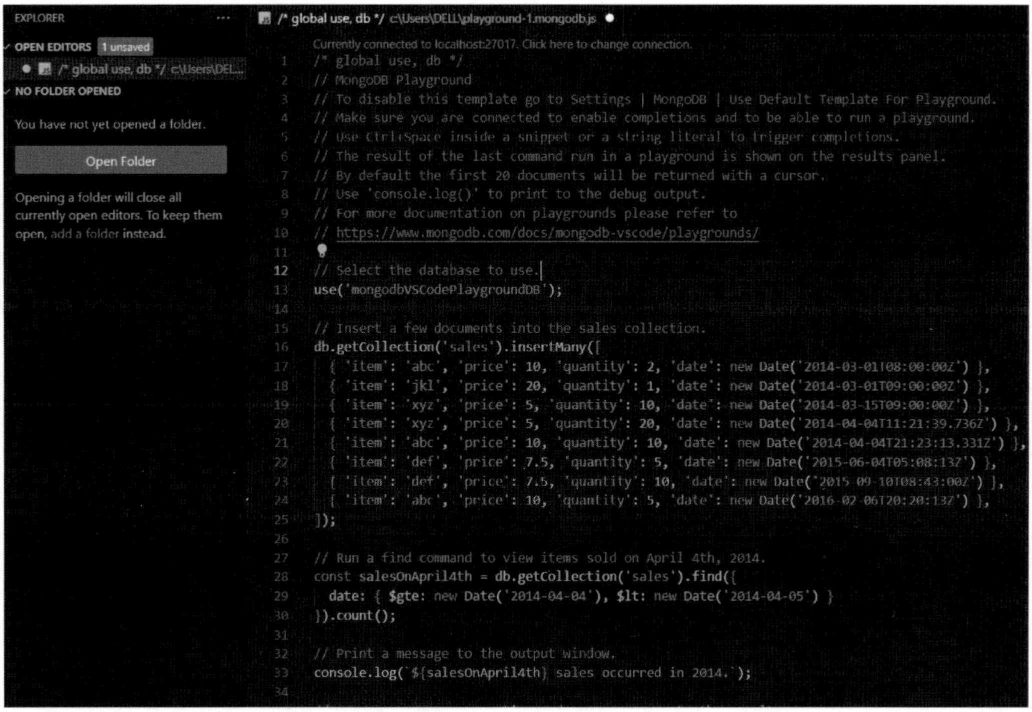

Figure 3.4: The Microsoft VS Code Command Palette

Use Terraform to create an Atlas cluster

If you have an Atlas account with an API key in an organization and Terraform installed, you can use the Atlas template for Terraform files included with the MongoDB for VS Code extension to create *Shared Tier* Atlas clusters. After loading the template, configure the cluster and provide details about the Atlas account. You can now use Terraform commands to plan, apply, or destroy your Atlas cluster.

Key features

The MongoDB for VS Code extension transforms application development within VS Code, offering substantial features such as:

- MongoDB Shell and VS Code integration for enhanced development capabilities, and using VS Code as an extension interface for MongoDB

- Autocomplete and syntax highlighting for MongoDB queries and commands

- Simplified connection management to the MongoDB database, and support for JSON editing and CRUD operations

- A graphical interface with tree views and sidebar panel options to visualize database structures and collections for constructing complex MongoDB queries
- Support for using Atlas templates for Terraform to create Shared Tier Atlas clusters

Use cases for the MongoDB for VS Code extension

The MongoDB for VS Code extension is a powerful tool that facilitates database interactions, schema design, query execution, and much more. With the MongoDB for VS Code extension, you can:

- Quickly prototype and test MongoDB queries without switching between different tools or interfaces
- Visualize the structure of your collections and documents to aid in database design and understanding
- Configure and manage connection settings, including authentication
- Quickly run queries and explore your MongoDB collections to retrieve and analyze data
- Perform administrative tasks such as creating, deleting, and modifying databases and collections
- Experiment with data transformations, formatting, and calculations

Best practices for the MongoDB for VS Code extension

Here are a few best practices for using the MongoDB for VS Code extension:

- Store your code snippets and experiments in version control to track changes and collaborate with others
- Familiarize yourself with the syntax and features of MongoDB Playground to maximize its utility
- Regularly update MongoDB Playground to use the latest features and improvements
- Take advantage of MongoDB IntelliSense features for autocompletion, syntax highlighting, and suggestions to write queries efficiently

Summary

In this chapter, you explored different MongoDB developer tools and learned how to use them to increase your productivity. The chapter introduced MongoDB Shell—mongosh, the command-line interface serving as a direct gateway to MongoDB databases. After that, you learned about MongoDB CLI, which is a command-line interface to connect to cloud-based MongoDB Atlas clusters.

Then, you explored the powerful GUI tool MongoDB Compass, which provides an intuitive and visual representation of data. Finally, you had a look at the MongoDB for VS Code extension. This extension offers you a seamless experience, combining powers of a code editor with the capabilities of MongoDB development. Throughout the chapter, the significance of each tool was highlighted along with their functionalities, use cases, and best practices.

In *Chapter 4, Connecting to MongoDB*, you will explore the multi-language facets of MongoDB. The chapter will guide you through direct driver methods, ODM libraries, and MongoDB integration across Ruby, PHP, Python, and Node.js.

4

Connecting to MongoDB

In the world of database management, MongoDB stands out as a powerful, flexible, and scalable NoSQL solution. As businesses and developers adapt to an increasingly data-centric paradigm, the demand for seamless integration of databases with a myriad of programming languages takes center stage.

Whether you're an experienced developer aiming to expand your toolkit or a beginner who's eager to integrate MongoDB into different development environments, this chapter is structured to provide clear step-by-step instructions.

This chapter will cover the following topics:

- Direct driver methods
- **Object-Document Mapping (ODM)** libraries
- MongoDB integration across the spectrum of PHP, Python, Ruby, and Node.js and TypeScript

Connecting methods

MongoDB provides an array of methods to connect with its databases. This ranges from direct driver interactions to the convenience of **Object-Document Mapping (ODM)** layers, which elegantly handles the mapping of your model objects. While MongoDB boasts extensive language support, including but not limited to Java, C++, C#, Kotlin, and Rust, this chapter focuses on four distinct and widely used languages—PHP, Ruby, Node.js, and Python. Each language offers a unique set of features and strengths, demanding tailored connection techniques to harness the full potential of MongoDB.

Connecting using Ruby

Ruby is at the forefront of languages supported by MongoDB, boasting an official driver that provides excellent compatibility. To successfully establish the connection to a local MongoDB host, follow these simple steps:

1. To install, you must add the driver to the Gemfile, as shown in the following example:

    ```
    gem 'mongo'
    ```

2. Then, you can connect to a database, as shown in the following example:

    ```
    require 'mongo'
    client = Mongo::Client.new(['127.0.0.1:27017'], database: 'test')
    ```

    Or, you can also use a URI connection string:

    ```
    require 'mongo'
    client = Mongo::Client.new('mongodb://127.0.0.1:27017/test')
    ```

3. This is the simplest example: connecting to a single database instance called test in your *localhost*. In most use cases, you would at least have a replica set to connect to, as shown in the following snippet:

    ```
    client_host = ['server1_host:server1_port_number, server2_host:server2_
    port_number']
    client_options = {
        database: 'YOUR_DATABASE_NAME',
        replica_set: 'REPLICA_SET_NAME',
        user: 'YOUR_USERNAME',
        password: 'YOUR_PASSWORD'
    }
    client = Mongo::Client.new(client_host, client_options)
    ```

    Or you can connect using URI syntax as shown in the following code snippet:

    ```
    client = Mongo::Client.new("mongodb://127.0.0.1:27017,127.0.0.1:27018/
    mydb")
    ```

4. The client_host servers act as seed servers for the client driver, providing a list of servers that can be used for connection. Once connected, the driver determines the appropriate server to connect, based on the primary/secondary read or write configuration. To establish a successful connection, the replica_set attribute must match the REPLICA_SET_NAME specified.

5. Username and password are optional but highly recommended in any MongoDB instance. It is a good practice to enable authentication by default in the `mongod.conf` file. Connecting to a sharded cluster follows a process similar to a replica set, with one key distinction. Instead of providing the server host/port, connect to the MongoDB process serving as the MongoDB router.

```
require 'mongo'
#Assuming mongos is running on localhost
#and default port 27017
client = Mongo::Client.new(['localhost:27017'], :database =>'my_sharded_
database')
```

You can connect to a shared cluster, as shown in the following example:

```
require 'mongo'
#Assuming mongos is running on localhost
#and default port 27017
client = Mongo::Client.new(['localhost:27017'], :database =>'my_sharded_
database')
```

If you have multiple `mongos` instances for high availability, you'd simply extend the list of hosts in the array:

```
require 'mongo'
#Connecting to multiple mongos instances
client = Mongo::Client.new(['mongos1_host:27017', 'mongos2_host:27017',
'mongos3_host:27017'], :database => 'my_sharded_database')
```

Now that you've learned how to connect using the Ruby library, you'll cover how to use an ODM library in the next section.

Mongoid

The Mongoid ODM stands out as a streamlined choice for connecting to MongoDB from your Ruby or Rails application. It not only maintains the flexibility inherent to the Ruby driver but also optimizes the process by necessitating less development time and code. Drawing parallels to **Object-relational mapping (ORM)** solution tools, ODMs seamlessly bridge the gap between your models and the database.

The benefits of the Mongoid ODM include:

- **Data abstraction**: Mongoid provides a higher-level programming interface, allowing you to interact with databases using objects instead of dealing directly with the document representation.

- **Consistency**: By using a standardized interface provided by Mongoid, you can ensure that data access patterns remain consistent throughout the application.

- **Reduce boilerplate code**: Mongoid automates many repetitive database operations, which can reduce the volume of code that you need to write and maintain.

- **Schema management and validation**: Even though MongoDB is schema-less, Mongoid allows for the definition of schemas, providing a structured way to validate data before it's stored.

- **Optimized performance**: Mongoid offers performance benefits by implementing caching mechanisms.

- **Middleware and plugins**: ODMs may support middleware or plugins that execute during different stages of database operations, providing hooks for custom logic, data transformation, logging, and more.

- **Easy transition**: If you are familiar with ORMs from the relational database world, Mongoid might feel more intuitive when transitioning to MongoDB.

- **Seamless integration**: Mongoid bridges the gap between application models and the underlying MongoDB database, ensuring smooth data translation and handling.

- **Support for transactions**: Mongoid offers support for transactions, ensuring that any series of operations is executed atomically.

For those using Ruby's most prevalent MVC framework—*Ruby on Rails*—Mongoid emerges as an exemplary tool, modeling data with elegance and simplicity reminiscent of Active Record.

The `mongoid` gem can be added to your application by modifying the `Gemfile` as follows:

```
gem 'mongoid'
```

You may need to configure the ORM for your Rails application to use Mongoid by adding the following to `application.rb`:

```
config.generators do |g|
    g.orm: mongoid
end
```

Connection to the database is established through a `mongoid.yml` configuration file. Configuration options are passed as key-value pairs with semantic indentation. The `mongoid.yml` configuration file is similar to `database.yml`, used for relational databases.

Some of the options that you can pass through the `mongoid.yml` file include:

Option	Description
`database`	The database name
`hosts`	The database hosts
`write/w`	The write concern (default = { w: 1 })
`auth_mech`	The authentication mechanism. Valid options are `:aws`, `:gssapi`, `:mongodb_cr`, `:mongodb_x509`, `:plain`, `:scram`, and `:scram256`
`min_pool_size/max_pool_size`	The maximum and minimum number of connections in the connection pool. Default values: `min_pool_size: 1` `max_pool_size: 5`
`ssl`, `ssl_cert`, `ssl_key`, `ssl_key_pass_phrase`, `ssl_verify`	SSL configurations and options
`include_root_in_json`	Include the root model name in JSON serialization (default: `false`)
`include_type_for_ serialization`	Include the `_type` field in serialization (default: `false`)

Table 4.1: Mongoid configuration options

Now, you must adapt your models to be stored in MongoDB. All it takes is a single line of code included in the model declaration, as illustrated in the following example:

```
class Person
    include Mongoid::Document
    include Mongoid::Timestamps
end
```

Adding `Mongoid::Timestamps` as shown above will ensure `created_at` and `updated_at` fields will be generated in a similar way to Active Record.

Data fields do not need to be declared by type in your models, but it is good practice to do so. The supported data types include:

Data type	Alias	Description
ObjectId		ObjectId is small, likely unique, fast to generate, and ordered. ObjectId values are 12 bytes in length, consisting of the following: • A 4-byte timestamp, representing the ObjectId creation, measured in seconds since the Unix epoch • A 5-byte random value generated once per process. This random value is unique to the machine and process • A 3-byte incrementing counter, initialized to a random value
Double	double	A floating-point number
String	String	A string of characters; must be valid UTF-8
Object	Object	Embedded documents, which can contain one or more fields
Array	Array	A list of values
Binary data	binData	Any binary data
Boolean	Bool	A Boolean value (true or false)
Date	Date	BSON date type, storing dates in milliseconds since the Unix epoch (1 January 1970)
Null	Null	A null value
Regular expression	Regex	Stores a JavaScript regular expression
JavaScript	Javascript	Same as JavaScript type but with a scope (a set of variables with values)
32-bit integer	Int	A 32-bit integer value
Timestamp	timestamp	A BSON timestamp type

Data type	Alias	Description
64-bit integer	`Long`	A 64-bit integer value
Decimal128	`decimal`	A 128-bit decimal-based floating-point number. Useful for representing exact monetary values
Min key	`minKey`	A value that is less than all other possible BSON values
Max key	`maxKey`	A value that is greater than all other possible BSON values

Table 4.2: Data types and their descriptions

Explicitly defining field types can improve performance and support for all the data types. If you do not explicitly define field types, MongoDB will cast the fields to the object and store them in the database.

However, this approach does not support all data types, such as `BigDecimal`, `Date`, `DateTime`, or `Range`. If you try to use these data types, you will get an error.

Inheritance with Mongoid models

The following code is an example of inheritance using Mongoid models:

```
class Canvas
    include Mongoid::Document
    field: name, type: String embeds_many: shapes
end
class Shape
    include Mongoid::Document
    field: x, type: Integer
    field: y, type: Integer embedded_in: canvas
end
class Circle < Shape
    field: radius, type: Float
end
class Rectangle < Shape
    field: width, type: Float
    field: height, type: Float
end
```

In the preceding example, you have a `Canvas` class with many `Shape` objects embedded in it. `Mongoid` will automatically create a field, which is `_type`, to distinguish between parent and child node fields. When a document is inherited from its fields, the relationships, validations, and scopes will propagate down into the child document.

The opposite doesn't happen; using `embeds_many` and `embedded_in` pair creates embedded subdocuments to store the relationships. If you want to store these by referencing to `ObjectId`, you can do so by substituting these with `has_many` and `belongs_to`.

Connecting using Python

Another option is to connect using Python. Like the `Mongoid` ODM for Ruby, the `MongoEngine` ODM exists for Python as well as the official MongoDB Python driver called *PyMongo*.

Installing PyMongo can be done using `pip` or `easy_install`, as shown in the following code:

> **Note**
>
> The minimum required PyMongo version is 4.4, and the minimum required Python version is 3.7.

```
python - m pip install pymongo python - m easy_install pymongo
```

Then, in your class, you can connect to a database, as shown in the following example:

```
from pymongo import MongoClient
client = MongoClient()
```

Connecting to a replica set requires one or more members of the set for the client to find out what the primary, secondary, or arbiter nodes in the set are, as indicated in the following example:

```
client = pymongo.MongoClient('mongodb://user:passwd@
node1:port1,node2:port2,node3:port3/?replicaSet=rsname')
```

Using the connection string, you can pass a `username` and `password` and the `replicaSet` name all in a single string. Some of the most interesting options for the connection string URL are presented in the next section.

Connecting to a shard requires the server host and IP for the `mongos` server.

MongoEngine ODM

MongoEngine offers a powerful way to interact with MongoDB from Python, blending the flexibility of MongoDB with a familiar, Pythonic API. It is more suitable for developers transitioning from relational databases and ORMs. However, like any tool, it's crucial to understand its strengths and limitations for effective usage.

Installing `mongoengine` can be done via `pip`, as shown in the following code:

```
pip install mongoengine
```

Always ensure that the version of MongoEngine you are using is compatible with the version of MongoDB installed.

The options must be pairs of `name=value` with an & between each pair. Some interesting options are shown in *Table 4.3*.

Option	Description
`max_pool_size/` `min_pool_size`	The maximum and minimum number of connections in the connection pool
`W`	The write concern
`w_timeout`	The timeout of the write concern operations
`Journal`	The journal options
`read_preference`	Used for replica sets, with the following valid options: `Primary`, `primaryPreferred`, `secondary`, `secondaryPreferred`, `nearest`
`maxStalenessSeconds`	Specifies in seconds how stale (data lagging behind the primary) a secondary can be before the client stops using it for read operations
`Ssl`	SSL configurations and options
`authentication_source`	Used in conjunction with the username and specifies the database associated with the user's credentials When external authentication mechanisms are being used, this option should be `$external` for LDAP or Kerberos
`authentication_mechanism`	The authentication mechanism, with the following valid options: `SCRAM-SHA-1`, `SCRAM-SHA-256`, `MONGODB-X509`, `MONGODB-AWS` MongoDB Enterprise offers two more options: `GSSAPI` (Kerberos), `PLAIN` (LDAP SASL)

Table 4.3: MongoEngine configuration options

The following code shows a sample class to define a document:

```
from mongoengine import Document, StringField
class User(Document):
    email = StringField(required=True, unique=True, primary_key=True)
    name = StringField(max_length=50)
```

This has a `User` class with `name` and `email` fields, where `email` is the primary field.

Like any object-document mapper or object-relational mapper, MongoEngine introduces some overhead. While this overhead is often negligible and is compensated by the increased developer productivity, for performance-critical applications, it might be worth considering PyMongo (the native Python driver of MongoDB) directly as an option.

Connecting using PHP

The architecture of MongoDB's PHP driver is made up of many layers, as shown in *Figure 4.1*:

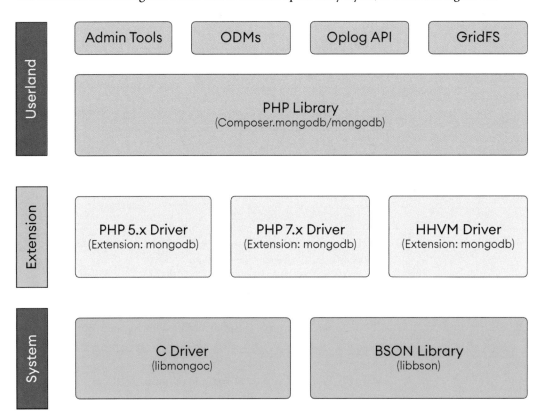

Figure 4.1: PHP driver architecture

At the top of this stack sits a PHP library, which is distributed as a Composer package. This library provides an API consistent with other MongoDB drivers. Sitting below that library is a PHP extension, which is distributed through PECL. The extension forms the glue between PHP and MongoDB's system libraries (libmongoc, libbson, and libmongocrypt). While the extension can be used directly, the library has minimal overhead and should be a common dependency for most applications built with MongoDB.

Installation is a two-step process:

1. The first step is to install the MongoDB extension. This extension is dependent on the version of PHP that you have installed and can be done using PECL.

   ```
   pecl install mongodb
   ```

   The minimum requirements to work with MongoDB 7.0 are PHP 7.2 and PHP Driver ext + lib 1.16.

   Then, copy the following line and place it at the end of your php.ini file:

   ```
   extension=mongodb.so
   ```

   The php --ri mongodb output should then reference libmongoc and libmongocrypt.

2. The second step is to use composer (a widely used dependency manager for PHP), as shown in the following example:

   ```
   composer require mongodb/mongodb
   ```

   To connect to the database, create a client instance using the connection string along with an array of options:

   ```
   $client = new MongoDB\Client('mongodb://
   myUsername:myPassword@rs1.example.com,rs2.example.
   com/?ssl=true&replicaSet=myReplicaSet&authSource=admin');
   ```

   Alternatively, you can use the $uriOptions set for passing parameters without using the connection string:

   ```
   $client = new MongoDB\Client(
       'mongodb://rs1.example.com,rs2.example.com/'
       [
           'username' => 'myUsername',
           'password' => 'myPassword',
           'ssl' => true,
           'replicaSet' => 'myReplicaSet',
           'authSource' => 'admin',
       ],
   );
   ```

   The $uriOptions set and the connection string options available are analogous to the ones used for Ruby and Python.

Eloquent ORM

Laravel is renowned for its elegant syntax and expressive coding style, particularly evident in its Eloquent ORM. Eloquent provides a rich, fluent interface for interacting with databases and is particularly known for its Active Record implementation, in contrast to Doctrine's Data Mapper pattern.

To begin using Eloquent with MongoDB, you need to install the package that bridges Laravel's Eloquent ORM with MongoDB. To install, run the following Composer command:

```
composer require mongodb/laravel-mongodb
```

Defining Eloquent models

Eloquent models for MongoDB are defined like all other Eloquent models, except that they extend from a different Model base class. Here is an example model designed to work with MongoDB:

```
namespace App\Models;
use MongoDB\Laravel\Eloquent\Model;

class Students extends Model{
    protected $connection = 'mongodb';
    protected $collection = 'students';
    protected $fillable = ['firstname', 'lastname'];
    // Define a relationship to 'Class' model
    public function classes() {
        return $this->hasMany(Class::class);
    }
    public function address() {
        return $this->embedsOne(Address::class);
    }
    public function Grades() {
        return $this->embedMany(Grade::class);
    }
}
```

This Laravel model example demonstrates the use of MongoDB with Eloquent ORM, highlighting three key relationship types: hasMany for a one-to-many relationship, embedsOne to define a relationship where a single embedded document is nested within another document, and embedMany to define a relationship where multiple embedded documents are nested within a single parent document. These relationships exemplify how Laravel elegantly handles both relational and embedded document structures in MongoDB.

Connecting using Node.js

Node.js is an open source, cross-platform runtime environment that became one of the most popular web technologies due to its exceptional performance. MongoDB and Node.js, along with Express.js (a Node.js web framework) and React.js (a client-side JavaScript framework), have become known as the *MERN stack*. This gang of four gets its power from being all built on top of JavaScript, allowing the creation of full stack web solutions. This frees engineers up from learning many languages and spending valuable time trying to make them work together. Nowadays, there are several **content management systems** (**CMSs**) built using MERN, such as Strapi.

So, it's crucial to cover connecting with MongoDB using Node.js. Installing the Node.js driver can be done using **node package manager** (**NPM**), as shown in the following code:

```
npm install mongodb
```

Then, in your code, you can connect to a database, as shown in the following example:

```
const { MongoClient } = require("mongodb");
// Replace the uri string with your connection string.
const uri = "mongodb://user:pass@host:27017/?w=majority";
const client = new MongoClient(uri);
async function run() {
  try {
    const database = client.db('productions');
    const movies = database.collection('movies');
    // Query for a movie that has the title '200 meters'
    const query = { title: '200 meters' };
    const movie = await movies.findOne(query);
    console.log(movie);
  } finally {
    // Ensures that the client will close when you
    // finish/error
    await client.close();
  }
}
run().catch(console.dir);
```

Connecting to a replica set requires a set of seed servers for the client to find out what the primary, secondary, or arbiter nodes in the set are, as indicated in the following example:

```
const uri = "mongodb://user:pass@
host1:27017,host2:27017,host3:27017/?replicaSet=mySet";
const client = new MongoClient(uri);
```

Using the connection string, you can pass a username, password, and replicaSet name all in a single string. Some of the most interesting options for the connection string are presented in the next section.

Here, you must use a connection string that has the following structure:

```
mongodb://[username:password@]host1[:port1][,host2[:port2],...
[,hostN[:portN]]][/[database][?options]]
```

Options have to be pairs of `name=value` with an & between each pair. Some interesting options are shown in the following table:

Option	Description
maxPoolSize	Specifies the maximum number of clients or connections the driver can create in its connection pool. This count includes connections in use.
minPoolSize	Specifies the number of connections the driver should create and maintain in the connection pool even when no operations are occurring. This count includes connections in use.
authMechanism	Specifies the authentication mechanism method to use for connection to the server. If you do not specify a value, the driver uses the default mechanism, either SCRAM-SHA-1 or SCRAM-SHA-256 depending on the server version. See the documentation on authentication mechanisms for more information https://www.mongodb.com/docs/drivers/go/current/fundamentals/auth/
authSource	Specifies the database that connections should authenticate against.
directConnection	Specifies whether to force dispatch all operations to the host specified in the connection URI.
journal	Specifies the default write concern j field for the client.
ssl	ssl is an alias for the tls option.
tls	Specifies whether TLS is required for connections to the server. Using a srvServiceName value of mongodb+srv, or specifying other tls prefixed options, will default tls to true.
w	Specifies the default write concern w field for the client.
wTimeoutMS	Specifies the default write concern wtimeout field for the client.

Table 4.4: Node.js configuration options

Connection compression

Like all drivers, the Node.js driver provides the option to compress messages, which reduces the amount of data passed over the network between MongoDB and the application.

The Node.js driver supports three compression algorithms:

- **Snappy**: This algorithm aims for very high speeds and reasonable compression.
- **zlib**: zlib is a lossless data-compression library.
- **Zstandard**: Zstandard, or zstd, is a fast lossless compression algorithm, targeting real-time compression scenarios at zlib-level and better compression ratios.

If you specify multiple compression algorithms, the driver selects the first one in the list supported by your MongoDB instance.

To enable compression using the connection string, add the `compressors` parameter in the connection string. If you want to specify one or more compression algorithms, separate them with commas:

```
const uri = "mongodb+srv://<user>:<password>@<cluster-
url>/?compressors=snappy,zlib";
const client = new MongoClient(uri);
```

Connecting using TypeScript

TypeScript is a typed superset of JavaScript, offering better tooling and static typing for large-scale applications. Combining TypeScript with Node.js can provide a robust backend solution, ensuring type safety and enhanced developer productivity. Given that MongoDB and TypeScript are both widely used in modern application development, understanding their connection mechanics is critical.

To work with MongoDB in a TypeScript project, use the same Node.js driver. However, TypeScript can benefit from the type definitions provided by MongoDB, which provide autocompletion, type checking, and other benefits.

In a TypeScript file, you can now set up and connect to MongoDB:

```
import { MongoClient, Db, Collection } from "mongodb";
const uri = "mongodb://user:pass@host:27017/?w=majority";
const client: MongoClient = new MongoClient(uri);
async function run(): Promise<void> {
  try {
    const database: Db = client.db('productions');
    const movies: Collection = database.collection('movies');
    // Sample query with type
    interface Movie {
      title: string;
      [key: string]: any;
    }
    const query: Partial<Movie> = { title: '200 meters' };
    const movie: Movie | null = await movies.findOne(query);
    console.log(movie);
  } finally {
    await client.close();
  }
}
run().catch(console.dir);
```

In the preceding code, you used TypeScript interfaces to define the shape of your data, providing a clearer understanding of the data structure and ensuring type safety when querying the database.

Connecting to a replica set with TypeScript is similar to the Node.js version, but with added type annotations:

```
const uri = "mongodb://user:pass@
node1:port1,node2:port2,node3:port3/?replicaSet=mySet";
const client: MongoClient = new MongoClient(uri);
```

The connection string's structure remains the same as in the Node.js example. However, with TypeScript, when you define configuration objects or handle results from MongoDB, you benefit from interfaces and types to ensure type safety and clarity.

Connecting with compression in TypeScript remains similar to the Node.js example. However, if you're defining compressors programmatically, you will benefit from enumerations:

```
enum Compressors {
    SNAPPY = 'snappy',
    ZLIB = 'zlib',
    ZSTANDARD = 'zstd'
}
const uri = 'mongodb+srv://<user>:<password>@<cluster-
url>/?compressors=${Compressors.SNAPPY},${Compressors.ZLIB}';
const client: MongoClient = new MongoClient(uri);
```

In conclusion, while connecting MongoDB using TypeScript is similar to Node.js, the addition of type definitions and interfaces enhances the developer experience, ensuring type safety and clarity in your application code.

Summary

This chapter was a meticulous guide on connecting to MongoDB using PHP, Ruby, Node.js, and Python. It explored each language's connection process in-depth, ensuring that you are equipped with hands-on knowledge, encompassing code snippets and vital configurations related to performance and security.

This chapter also highlighted the strategic advantage of using an ODM in the connection process. Along with the benefits of ODMs, it explored its efficiency, reduced development time, and the seamless bridge it offers between models and the MongoDB database.

In the next chapter, you will see CRUD operation and basic queries in action.

5

CRUD Operations and Basic Queries

In this chapter, you will learn how to use the MongoDB Shell for database administration. Starting with simple **create**, **read**, **update**, and **delete** (**CRUD**) operations using Ruby and Python drivers, you will master scripting and get a broader perspective on how to interact with MongoDB across different programming environments. You will learn what the MongoDB Stable API (previously labeled the *Versioned API*) means for developers, and the features it provides. Finally, you will explore authentication and authorization using the MongoDB Community Edition and its paid counterpart, the Enterprise Edition.

This chapter will cover the following topics:

- Understanding MongoDB CRUD operations

- Performing CRUD operations using Ruby and Python drivers

- Executing batch operations using `mongosh`

- Administering and implementing authentication with MongoDB

Technical requirements

To follow along with the code in this chapter, you will need to install MongoDB locally or connect to a MongoDB Atlas database. You can download the MongoDB Community Edition from `mongodb.com` or use the fully managed **database-as-a-service** (**DBaaS**) MongoDB Atlas offering, which provides a free tier as well as seamless upgrades to the latest version.

Most examples are compatible with the new `mongosh` shell, but you may want to use the legacy shell, `mongo`, or enable `mongosh` backwards compatibility using `mongosh` snippets.

You will also need to download the official drivers for the language of your choice—Ruby or Python: `https://www.mongodb.com/docs/drivers/`.

To follow along with the code in this chapter, you will need the following:

- `mongosh` shell
- Connection with the MongoDB Atlas database
- Official drivers for the language of your choice—Ruby or Python

MongoDB CRUD operations

Regardless of why you are using a MongoDB server, you'll need to perform CRUD operations on it. These fundamental methods, collectively known as CRUD operations, form the basis of interacting with a MongoDB server. To modify MongoDB documents, the process involves connecting to the server, querying the relevant documents, adjusting the specified properties, and subsequently transmitting the data back to the database for updates. Each CRUD operation serves a distinct purpose:

- The *create* operation is used to insert new documents in the MongoDB database
- The *read* operation is used to query a document in the database
- The *update* operation is used to modify existing documents in the database
- The *delete* operation is used to remove documents in the database

CRUD using mongosh

`mongosh` is equivalent to the administration console used by relational databases.

1. To connect to `mongosh`, enter the following command:

```
mongosh "mongodb+srv://mycluster.packt.mongodb.net/myDatabase"
--apiVersion 1 --username <username> --password <password>
```

2. The preceding connection string connects to an Atlas deployment. Within the shell, you can view available databases by typing the following command:

```
show dbs
```

3. Next, connect to a database by specifying the database name:

```
use <db name>
```

4. mongosh can be used to query and update data in your databases. For instance, you can insert a document into the books collection as follows:

```
db.books.insertOne({ title: 'Mastering MongoDB 7.0', isbn: '101' });

{
  acknowledged: true,
  insertedId: ObjectId("652024e7ab44f3bf77788a3d")
}
```

5. To find your document from a collection named books using a selection filter { isbn: '101' }, type the following code:

```
db.books.find({ isbn: '101' });

[
  {
    _id: ObjectId("652024e7ab44f3bf77788a3d"),
    title: 'Mastering MongoDB 7.0',
    isbn: '101'
  }
]
```

6. The result you get back from MongoDB informs that the write has succeeded and inserted one new document in the database.

7. To update this document, use the mongosh method updateOne():

```
db.books.updateOne({ isbn: '101' }, { $set: { price: 30 } });

{
  acknowledged: true,
  insertedId: null,
  matchedCount: 1,
  modifiedCount: 1,
  upsertedCount: 0
}
```

8. Now, use the `find()` method once again to display the updated document:

```
db.books.find({ isbn: '101' });

[
  {
    _id: ObjectId("652024e7ab44f3bf77788a3d"),
    title: 'Mastering MongoDB 7.0',
    isbn: '101',
    price: 30
  }
]
```

Deleting this document has a similar syntax and results in the following code:

```
db.books.deleteOne({ isbn: '101' });

{
  acknowledged: true,
  deletedCount: 1
}
```

Here, you will notice a couple of things:

*   The JSON document `{ isbn: '101' }` in the `updateOne()` method serves as the query filter to identify the specific document you want to update
*   The `matchedCount` object notifies that the query matched one document
*   The `modifiedCount` object notifies that the query modified one document
*   The `$set` operator allows you to set the value of a field with a specified value:

```
db.books.updateOne({ isbn: '101' }, { $set: { price: 30 } });

{
  acknowledged: true,
  insertedId: null,
  matchedCount: 1,
  modifiedCount: 1,
  upsertedCount: 0
}
```

When several documents meet the filter's criteria, only the first matching document is modified by the updateOne() method. Now, using the find() method, you will see that your document matches what you expected:

```
db.books.find({ isbn: '101' });

[
  {
    _id: ObjectId("652024e7ab44f3bf77788a3d"),
    title: 'Mastering MongoDB 7.0',
    isbn: '101',
    price: 30
  }
]
```

To delete a document, there are multiple approaches. The simplest method involves filtering based on the document's unique _id field value. As an example, let's delete the document isbn: 101:

```
db.books.deleteOne({ isbn: '101' });

{
  acknowledged: true,
  deletedCount: 1
}

> db.books.find({ isbn: '101' });
```

Here, you can see that when there are no results, mongosh will not return anything other than the shell prompt itself: >.

MongoDB 7.0 removes most of the time series limitations from these operations that are based on the delete command. However, there is only one time series-related limitation on these delete commands:

- delete
- deleteOne()
- deleteMany()
- Bulk.find.delete()
- Bulk.find.deleteOne()

> **Note**
> You cannot use these commands for multi-document transactions.

Scripting for mongosh

Administering the database using built-in commands is helpful, but it's not the main reason for using the shell. The true power of mongosh comes from the fact that it provides a JavaScript REPL environment. This means that you can perform complex administrative tasks that require a set of commands to execute as one.

You can declare and assign variables in the shell, as follows:

```
let title = 'MongoDB in a nutshell';
print(title);

db.books.insertOne({ title: title, isbn: 102 });

{
  acknowledged: true,
  insertedId: ObjectId("65205285f7f90f88bce3909d")
}

db.books.find({ title: title, isbn: 102 });

[
  {
    _id: ObjectId("65205285f7f90f88bce3909d"),
    title: 'MongoDB in a nutshell',
    isbn: 102
  }
]
```

The preceding example declares a new title variable as MongoDB in a nutshell, and uses the variable to insert a new document into your books collection.

Since it is a JavaScript REPL environment, you can use it for functions and scripts that generate complex results from your database:

```
queryBooksByIsbn = function (isbn) { return db.books.find({ isbn: isbn }); }
[Function: queryBooksByIsbn]
```

This one-line command creates a new function named queryBooksByIsbn that takes a single argument, which is the isbn value.

With the data that you have in your collection, you can use the new function and fetch books by isbn, as shown in the following code snippet:

```
queryBooksByIsbn(102)
[
  {
    _id: ObjectId("65205285f7f90f88bce3909d"),
    title: 'MongoDB in a nutshell',
    isbn: 102
  }
]
```

You can use mongosh to write and test these scripts. Once you're satisfied, you can store them in the .js file and invoke them directly from the command line, as follows:

```
'mongosh <script_name.js>'
```

Here are some useful notes regarding the default behavior of these scripts:

- Write operations use a default write concern of w: "majority". The majority of the write concern is calculated as the minimum value between the calculated majority of all nodes and the number of data-bearing nodes. This means that when you have arbiters that are not data-bearing nodes, they will not be included in the calculation of a majority. For example, in a replica set comprising three servers, including one being an arbiter, the calculation of the majority involves determining the minimum value between the calculated majority of all nodes (2, the closest number to bring the figure over 50%) and the number of data-bearing nodes, which, in this case, is also 2.

- To retrieve operation results from a script back to **standard output** (**stdout**), you must use JavaScript's built-in print() function.

The next section will examine the difference between scripting for mongosh and using it directly.

Scripting for mongosh vs direct use

When writing scripts for mongosh, you cannot use shell helpers. MongoDB's commands such as use <database_name>, show collections, and other helpers, are built into the shell and remain inaccessible from the JavaScript context where your scripts execute. Fortunately, there are equivalents available from the JavaScript execution context, as shown in *Table 5.1*:

Shell helpers	JavaScript equivalents
show dbs, show databases	db.adminCommand('listDatabases')
use <database_name>	db = db.getSiblingDB('<database_name>')
show collections	db.getCollectionNames()
show users	db.getUsers()
show roles	db.getRoles({ showBuiltinRoles: true })
show log <logname>	db.adminCommand({ 'getLog' : '<logname>' })
show logs	db.adminCommand({ 'getLog' : '*' })

it	cursor = db.collection.find()
	
	if (cursor.hasNext()){
	
	   cursor.next();
	
	}

Table 5.1: Shell helpers and JavaScript equivalents

In *Table 5.1*, it is the iteration cursor that the mongosh shell returns when you query and get back too many results to show in one batch.

Using mongosh, you can script almost anything from the client. It is a powerful tool for prototyping and getting quick insights into your data.

Batch inserts using mongosh

If you want to insert many documents programmatically using the shell, the simplest implementation, since you're using the JavaScript shell, involves iterating through a loop, generating each document sequentially, and executing a write operation in each iteration, as outline below:

```
authorMongoDBFactory = function() {
    for (let loop = 0; loop < 1000; loop++) {
        db.books.insertOne({ name: "MongoDB factory book" + loop });
    }
}
```

The preceding example creates an authorMongoDBFactory() method for an author, generating 1000 books on MongoDB, each with a slightly different name:

```
> authorMongoDBFactory()
```

This will result in `1000` writes being issued to the database. While it is simple from a development point of view, this method can put a strain on the database.

As an alternative, you can use a `bulk` write to issue a single database `insert` command with the `1000` documents that you've prepared beforehand:

```
fastAuthorMongoDBFactory = function() {
    let bulk = db.books.initializeUnorderedBulkOp();
    for (let loop = 0; loop < 1000; loop++) {
        bulk.insert({ name: "MongoDB factory book" + loop });
    }
    bulk.execute();
}

> fastAuthorMongoDBFactory();
```

The end result will be the same as before, with the insertion of `1000` documents into your `books` collection, each adhering to the following structure:

```
db.books.find({ name: /MongoDB factory/ });

[
  {
    _id: ObjectId("652059aff7f90f88bce39486"),
    name: 'MongoDB factory book0'
  },
  {
    _id: ObjectId("652059aff7f90f88bce39487"),
    name: 'MongoDB factory book1'
  },
  {
    _id: ObjectId("652059aff7f90f88bce39488"),
    name: 'MongoDB factory book2'
  },
  {
    _id: ObjectId("652059aff7f90f88bce39489"),
    name: 'MongoDB factory book3'
  },
  ...
  {
    _id: ObjectId("652059aff7f90f88bce3948a"),
    name: 'MongoDB factory book999'
  }
]
```

The difference from the user's perspective lies in the speed of execution and reduced strain on the database.

In the preceding example, `initializeUnorderedBulkOp()` was used for the `bulk` operation builder setup. This is because you didn't have to worry about the order of insertions being in the same order as they were added in to your `bulk` variable with the `bulk.insert()` command. This makes sense when you can make sure that all operations are unrelated to each other or idempotent.

If you want to preserve the order of insertions, you will have to use `initializeOrderedBulkOp()` by changing the second line of the function, as illustrated below:

```
let bulk = db.books.initializeOrderedBulkOp();
```

In the next section, you will see how batch operations can be used with `mongosh` to improve operational performance.

Batch operations using mongosh

In the case of inserts, the order of operations is negligible. However, the `bulk` command can be used with many more operations than just insert. In the following example, you have a single book with `isbn : 101`, and a `name` value of `Mastering MongoDB` in the `bookOrders` collection. The `available` field denotes the number of copies available for purchase, set at 99 books:

```
db.bookOrders.find()
[
  {
    _id: ObjectId("652065fcf7f90f88bce39c57"),
    isbn: 101,
    name: 'Mastering MongoDB 1',
    available: 99
  }
]
```

In a single `bulk` operation, executing the following series of actions will involve adding one book to the inventory and then proceeding to purchase 100 books, resulting in a final count of 0 available copies:

```
let bulk = db.bookOrders.initializeOrderedBulkOp();
bulk.find({ isbn: 101 }).updateOne({ $inc: { available: 1 } });
bulk.find({ isbn: 101 }).updateOne({ $inc: { available: -100 } });
bulk.execute();
```

With the preceding code, you will get the output shown in *Figure 5.1*:

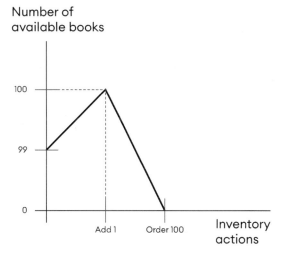

Figure 5.1: Book count over a period of time

Using `initializeOrderedBulkOp()`, you can make sure that you add one book before ordering 100 books, so that you are never out of stock. On the contrary, if you were using `initializeUnorderedBulkOp()`, you wouldn't have such a guarantee, and you might end up with the 100-book order coming in before the addition of the new book, resulting in a logical error, as you don't have that many books to fulfill the order.

When executing through an ordered list of operations, MongoDB splits the operations into batches of 100,000, and groups these by operation. For example, if you have `100,004` inserts, `99,998` updates, `100,004` deletes, and 5 inserts, you will end up with the following:

```
[100,000 inserts]
[4 inserts]
[99,998 updates]
[100,000 deletes]
[4 deletes]
[5 inserts]
```

Figure 5.2 explains the preceding code:

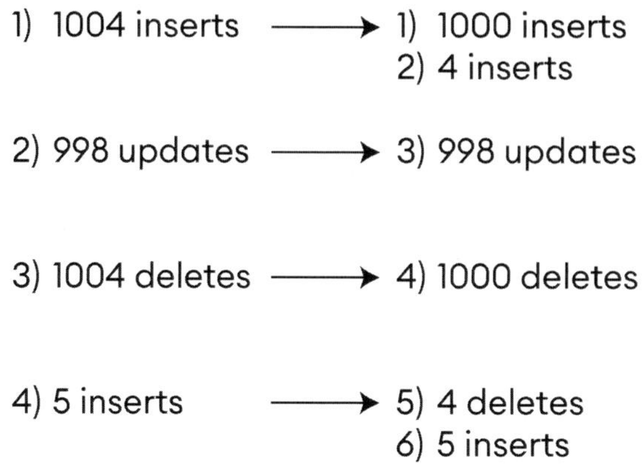

1) 1004 inserts ⟶ 1) 1000 inserts
                   2) 4 inserts

2) 998 updates ⟶ 3) 998 updates

3) 1004 deletes ⟶ 4) 1000 deletes

4) 5 inserts ⟶ 5) 4 deletes
               6) 5 inserts

Figure 5.2: Bulk operations ordering

This doesn't affect the series of operations, but it implicitly means that your operations will leave the database in batches of 100,000. This behavior is not guaranteed to stay in future versions.

> **Note**
>
> Starting in MongoDB 3.2, there's an alternative command for bulk writes: `bulkWrite()`.

In the following code snippet, the arguments for `bulkWrite` include the sequence of operations you wish to execute, the `writeConcern` (with the default being 1), and whether the write operations should be applied in the order they appear in the array (they will be ordered by default):

```
db.collection.bulkWrite(
    [ <operation 1>, <operation 2>, ... ],
    {
        writeConcern : <document>,
        ordered : <boolean>
    }
)
```

The following operations are the same ones supported by `bulk`:

- `insertOne()`
- `updateOne()`
- `updateMany()`

- deleteOne()
- deleteMany()
- replaceOne()

updateOne(), deleteOne(), and replaceOne() have matching filters. If they match more than one document, they will only operate on the first one. It's important to design these queries so that they don't match more than one document; otherwise, the behavior will be undefined.

In this section, you learned how to write scripts for the mongosh. In the next section, you'll go through administration tasks using mongosh.

CRUD using the Ruby driver

The Ruby driver was originally maintained by an external community member who was later hired by MongoDB. Subsequently, Ruby became one of the first languages to receive official support from MongoDB with an official driver.

MongoDB Ruby driver includes an integrated query cache. Once activated, this cache retains outcomes from previous *find* and *aggregation* operations. When those queries are executed again, the driver serves the cached results, eliminating redundant database interactions. An example of using the query cache can be found later in this chapter, in the *Mongoid ODM* section.

The recommended method for connecting to a MongoDB instance with Ruby is through the official MongoDB Ruby driver on GitHub.

Connecting to a database

Add mongo to your Gemfile, as follows:

```
gem "mongo"
```

To install the driver manually, execute the following command:

```
gem install mongo
```

Then, in your class, you can connect to a database, as shown in the following example:

```
connection_string = "mongodb://HOST:PORT/DATABASE_NAME"
client = Mongo::Client.new(connection_string)
db = client.database
db.collection_names # returns a list of collection names
db.list_collections # returns a list of collection metadata hashes
```

Creating documents

Consider, you have a @collection instance variable pointing to your books collection in a mongodb_book database. To insert a single document with your definition, execute the following code:

```
@collection = client[:books]
document = {
isbn: '101',
      name: 'Mastering MongoDB 7.0',
price: 30}

result = @collection.insert_one(document)
      puts result.n
```

Similarly, to insert two documents with isbn values of 102 and 103, use insert_many instead of insert_one:

```
documents = [ { isbn: '102', name: 'MongoDB in 7 years', price: 50 },
{ isbn: '103', name: 'MongoDB for experts', price: 40 } ]

result = @collection.insert_many(documents)
```

The resulting object is now a Mongo::BulkWrite::Result class, meaning that the BulkWrite interface was used for improved performance. The main difference is that you now have an attribute, inserted_ids, which can return the ObjectId of inserted objects from the BSON::ObjectId class:

```
#<Mongo::BulkWrite::Result:0x000055e707ea5d28 @results={"n_inserted"=>2,
"n"=>2, "inserted_ids"=>[BSON::ObjectId('6521706eb2e05257537b2fea'),
BSON::ObjectId('6521706eb2e05257537b2feb')]}, @acknowledged=true>
```

Reading data

Finding documents works in the same way as creating them, at the collection level:

```
@collection.find({ isbn: '101' })
```

Multiple search criteria can be chained and are equivalent to the AND operator in SQL:

```
@collection.find({ isbn: '101', name: 'Mastering MongoDB 7.0' })
```

The CRUD functionality of the MongoDB Ruby driver provides several query options to optimize queries. *Table 5.2* outlines some of the most commonly used query options.

Option	Description
`allow_partial_results`	This is used with sharded clusters. If a shard is down, it allows the query to return results from the shards that are up, potentially getting only a portion of the results.
`batch_size (Integer)`	This can change the batch size that the cursor will fetch from MongoDB. This is done on each `GETMORE` operation.
`comment (String)`	With this command, you can add a comment in your query for documentation reasons.
`hint (Hash)`	You can force the usage of an index using `hint()`.
`limit (Integer)`	You can limit the result set to the number of documents specified by Integer.
`no_cursor_timeout`	If you don't specify this parameter, MongoDB will close any inactive cursor after 600 seconds. With this parameter, your cursor will never be closed.
`projection (Hash)`	You can use this parameter to fetch or exclude specific attributes from your results. This will reduce data transfer over the wire. Example: `client[:books].find.projection(:price => 1)`.
`read (Hash)`	You can specify a read preference to be applied only for this query. Example: `client[:books].find.read(:mode => :secondary_preferred)`.
`skip (Integer)`	This can be used to skip the specified number of documents. It's useful for paginating results.
`sort (Hash)`	You can use this to sort your results; for example, `client[:books].find.sort(:name => -1)`.

Table 5.2: Query options for the MongoDB Ruby driver

On top of the query options, the MongoDB Ruby driver provides some helper functions that can be chained at the method call level:

- `count_documents`: Gets the total count of documents that align with a specified filter or retrieve the overall count of documents within a collection.

- `estimated_document_count`: Gets a rough estimate of the number of documents present in the collection. Note that this method does not allow for filtering.

- `distinct(:field_name)`: Distinguishes between the results of the preceding query.

- `find()`: Returns a cursor containing the result set that you can iterate using `.each` in Ruby, such as every other object:

```
result = @collection.find({ isbn: '101' })
result.each do |doc|
      puts doc.inspect
end
```

The output for the `book` collection will appear as follows:

```
{"_id"=>BSON::ObjectId('65216d4bb2e05254b3022d2f'), "isbn"=>"101",
"name"=>"Mastering MongoDB 7.0", "price"=>30}
```

Chaining operations in find()

By default, `find()` uses an `AND` operator to match multiple fields. If you want to use an `OR` operator, your query needs to resemble the following:

```
result = @collection.find('$or' => [{ isbn: '101' }, { isbn:'102' }]).to_a
puts result
```

The output of the preceding code is as follows:

```
{"_id"=>BSON::ObjectId('65216d4bb2e05254b3022d2f'), "isbn"=>"101",
"name"=>"Mastering MongoDB 7.0", "price"=>30}
{"_id"=>BSON::ObjectId('6521706eb2e05257537b2fea'), "isbn"=>"102",
"name"=>"MongoDB in 7 days", "price"=>50}
```

You can also use `$and` instead of `$or` in the previous example:

```
result = @collection.find('$and' => [{ isbn: '101' }, { isbn: '102' }]).
to_a puts result
```

This, of course, will return no results since no document can posses `isbn` values of `101` and `102`.

Nested operations

The MongoDB Ruby driver simplifies the process of inserting documents with nested structures. As shown in the following example, you can create a document with both top-level fields (`isbn`, `name`, and `price`), and a nested field (`meta`) containing its own subfields. The document can then be inserted into the MongoDB collection using the `insert_one` method:

```
document = {
  'isbn': '104',
  'name': 'Python and MongoDB',
  'meta': {
    'version': 'MongoDB 7.0'
  },
  'price': 60
}
@collection.insert_one(document)
```

When retrieving data, the driver provides a succinct method. You can use dot notation together with find to access the desired embedded data:

```
result = @collection.find({ 'meta.version': 'MongoDB 7.0' }).to_a
puts result
```

> **Note**
>
> You need to enclose the key name in quotes (") to access the embedded object, just as you need it for operations starting with $, such as $set.

Updating data

To update documents using the MongoDB Ruby driver, they must first be located or identified. Using your example book collection, issue the following command:

```
@collection.update_one({ 'isbn': '101'}, { '$set' => { name:'Mastering MongoDB
7.0' } })
```

This finds the document with an isbn value of 101 and changes its name to Mastering MongoDB 7.0.

Similar to update_one, you can use update_many to update multiple documents retrieved via the first parameter of the method.

Deleting data

Deleting documents works in a similar way as finding documents. You need to find documents and then apply the delete operation. For example, using your book collection, issue the following code:

```
@collection.find({ isbn: '101' }).delete_one
```

This will delete a single document. In your case, since isbn is unique for every document, this is expected. If your find() clause had matched multiple documents, then delete_one would've deleted just the first document that find() returned, which may or may not have been what you wanted.

If you want to delete all documents matching your find() query, use delete_many, as follows:

```
@collection.find({ price: { $gte: 30 } }).delete_many
```

In the preceding example, you are deleting all books that have a price greater than or equal to 30.

Batch operations

You can use the bulkWrite method for batch operations. As seen in the *insert many documents* example in the *Creating documents* section, this would resemble the following:

```
@collection.bulk_write([{ insertMany: documents }], { ordered: true });
```

The `bulkWrite` method supports the following parameters:

- `insertOne`

- `updateOne`

- `updateMany`

- `replaceOne`

- `deleteOne`

- `deleteMany`

Methods ending in `*One` affect only a single document, even if multiple documents match the provided filter. Therefore, when using these methods, ensure your filters accurately target a single document to prevent unintended actions. In contrast, methods ending in `*Many` are designed to act on multiple documents that match the filter criteria.

Mongoid ODM

Mongoid, a popular **Object-Document Mapper (ODM)** for MongoDB, offers developers a seamless and intuitive way to work with MongoDB databases within the Ruby on Rails framework. While low-level drivers provide a vast range of flexibility, Mongoid further enhances the developer experience by offering a higher-level abstraction that aligns closely with Rails naming conventions. This harmonious integration simplifies tasks such as schema definition, querying, and data modeling, allowing you to focus more on application logic and less on database intricacies. Just like ORMs, ODMs bridge the gap between your models and the database. In Rails, the most widely used MVC framework for Ruby—Mongoid—can be used to model your data in a similar way to Active Record.

Installing gem is similar to the MongoDB Ruby driver. Add a single file in `Gemfile`, as shown in the following command:

```
gem 'mongoid'
```

Depending on the version of Rails, you may need to add the following to `application.rb` as well:

```
config.generators do |g|
    g.orm :mongoid
end
```

Connecting to the database is done through a `mongoid.yml` configuration file. Configuration options are passed as *key-value* pairs with semantic indentation.

Reading data

Finding documents is done using a query DSL similar to Active Record. As with Active Record, where a relational database is used, Mongoid assigns a class to a MongoDB collection and any object instance to a document:

```
Book.find('592149c4aabac953a3a1e31e')
```

This will find the document by _id field and return the document with ISBN 101, as will the query by the name attribute:

```
Book.where(name: 'Mastering MongoDB')
```

In a similar fashion to the dynamically generated queries by an attribute, you can use the helper method:

```
Book.find_by(name: 'Mastering MongoDB')
```

This query is similar to the previous one, where you used the name attribute. You can enable QueryCache to avoid hitting the database for the same query multiple times:

```
Mongoid::QueryCache.enabled = true
```

This can be added to any code block that you want to enable, or to the initializer for Mongoid.

Scoping queries

You can scope queries in Mongoid using class methods, as follows:

```
class Book
  include Mongoid::Document
  field :price, type: Float
  scope :premium, -> { where(price: { '$gt' => 20 }) }
end
```

Then, you can use the following query:

```
Book.premium
```

This query will find books with a price greater than 20.

Create, update, and delete

Mongoid's interface for creating documents is similar to what you'd expect if you're already familiar with Active Record's APIs:

```
Book.where(isbn: 202, name: 'Mastering MongoDB, 4th Edition').create
```

To update documents, you can use update or update_all. Using the update method will update only the first document retrieved by the query part, whereas update_all will update all of them:

```
Book.where(isbn: 202).update(name: 'Mastering MongoDB, 4th Edition')
Book.where(price: { '$gt': 20 }).update_all(price_range:'premium')
```

Deleting a document is like creating it; you provide delete to skip callbacks and destroy to execute any available callbacks in the affected document.

delete_all and destroy_all are convenient methods for multiple documents.

CRUD using the Python driver

Python is a powerful programming language that provides robust web development capabilities, when paired with frameworks such as FastAPI. For MongoDB integration with Python, you can use MongoEngine as well as the official MongoDB low-level driver, PyMongo. PyMongo can be easily installed using `pip`:

```
$ python -m pip install pymongo
```

You can use the following connection snippet to test the connection to your MongoDB deployment:

```python
from pymongo import MongoClient

# Replace the placeholder with your connection string
uri = "<connection string>"

# Create a new client and connect to the server
client = MongoClient(uri)

# Send a ping to confirm a successful connection
try:
    client.admin.command('ping')
    print("Pinged your deployment. You successfully connected to MongoDB!")
except Exception as e:
    print(e)
```

PyMongo is MongoDB's officially supported driver for Python, providing a seamless bridge between the dynamic world of Python programming and the efficient, document-oriented NoSQL database of MongoDB.

Alongside PyMongo, the MongoDB community has another significant tool: Motor. Motor is the official asynchronous driver for Python. In the age of real-time web applications and the need for non-blocking operations, Motor allows you to use MongoDB in Python's asynchronous frameworks. This ensures efficient database operations, especially in I/O bound scenarios, such as web applications handling many simultaneous users. Motor can be easily installed using `pip`:

```
$ python -m pip install motor
```

You can use the following connection snippet to test the connection to your MongoDB deployment on Atlas using the `asyncio` asynchronous framework:

```python
import asyncio
from motor.motor_asyncio import AsyncIOMotorClient
from pymongo.server_api import ServerApi

async def ping_server():
```

```
    # Replace the placeholder with your Atlas connection string
    uri = "<connection string>"

    # Set the Stable API version when creating a new client
    client = AsyncIOMotorClient(uri, server_api=ServerApi('1'))

    # Send a ping to confirm a successful connection
    try:
        await client.admin.command('ping')
        print("Pinged your deployment. You successfully connected to MongoDB!")
    except Exception as e:
        print(e)

asyncio.run(ping_server())
```

This code snippet leverages the MongoDB Stable API feature. To utilize this, ensure you're using Motor driver version 2.5 or newer when connecting to MongoDB Server version 5.0 and beyond.

In the next section, you'll see how to use PyMongo for creating, reading, updating, and deleting documents in MongoDB.

Inserting documents

MongoDB's Python driver offers a comprehensive suite of CRUD APIs, akin to what's available in Ruby. This makes it simple to interact with your MongoDB collections using Python.

Here's a simple example demonstrating how to insert a document into the books collection within the mongodb_books database:

```
# Use the 'mongodb_books' database and the 'books' collection
books = client.mongodb_books.books

# Insert a new book document
book = {
    'isbn': '301',
    'name': 'Python and MongoDB',
    'meta': {'version': 'MongoDB 7.0'},
    'price': 60
}
insert_result = books.insert_one(book)
pprint(insert_result)
```

Upon executing the script, the insertion result will be displayed, followed by the newly inserted document:

```
[{'_id': ObjectId('6521ae0a0e542d46b87947a4')]
```

In the above example, the `insert_one()` method is employed to insert a singular document. This document is crafted using Python's dictionary notation. Subsequently, you can query the collection to retrieve and display all its documents.

Finding documents

When you want to retrieve documents based on specific attributes, the process is intuitive. For top-level attributes, a dictionary with the desired key-value pairs will do the trick.

Here's an example that demonstrates how to find documents in the `books` collection of the `mongodb_books` database based on the book name:

```python
# Use the 'mongodb_books' database and the 'books' collection
books = client.mongodb_books.books

# Fetch documents with the name "Python and MongoDB"
result = books.find({"name": "Python and MongoDB"})

# Print the fetched documents
for document in result:
    pprint(document)
```

The preceding script prints all the documents in the `books` collection that have the name `Python and MongoDB`. If the document you inserted earlier exists in the collection, you'll see its details printed in the console:

```
{'_id': ObjectId('6521ae0a0e542d46b87947a4'),
 'isbn': '301',
 'name': 'Python and MongoDB',
 'meta': { 'version': 'MongoDB 7.0' },
 'price': 60 }
```

To retrieve documents containing specific fields within embedded documents, you can employ the dot notation. In the subsequent example, utilize `metadata.version` to pinpoint the version field nested within the `meta` document:

```python
query = {
    'meta.version': {
        "$regex": ".*?g.*?7\.0$",
        "$options": "i"
    }
}

# Fetch the document(s) matching the query
result = books.find(query)

# Print the fetched documents
for document in result:
    pprint(document)
```

In the demonstrated example, a regular expression was used to search for any occurrence of the string pattern ending with 7.0 and possibly containing the letter g within the metadata.version field of the documents. This search is case-insensitive, thanks to the $options parameter set to i. This approach leverages the $regex notation in PyMongo, which corresponds to MongoDB's method for handling regular expressions. By executing this script, you can retrieve and display documents from the books collection in the mongodb_books database that match this specific pattern in their metadata.version field.

Comparison operators are also supported in a similar way. Common comparison operators include $eq (equals), $gt (greater than), $gte (greater than or equal to), $lt (less than), $lte (less than or equal to), and $ne (not equal). Below is an example:

```
# Define the query using the $gt comparison operator
query = {
    'price': {
        "$gt": 50
    }
}

# Fetch the document(s) matching the query
result = books.find(query)

# Print the fetched documents
for document in result:
    pprint(document)
```

The script returned two documents where the price is greater than 50. Both are titled Python and MongoDB and are priced at $60, but they have distinct ISBNs and metadata:

```
{'_id': ObjectId('6521ae0a0e542d46b87947a4'),
 'isbn': '301',
 'name': 'Python and MongoDB',
 'meta': { 'version': 'MongoDB 7.0' },
 'price': 60}
{'_id': ObjectId('6521c1a0379c18f8df180e57'),
 'isbn': '302',
 'meta': {'version': 'MongoDB 7.0'},
 'name': 'Python and MongoDB',
 'price': 60}
{'_id': ObjectId('6521d7e309731cfd8fa0ca04'),
 'isbn': '303',
 'name': 'Advanced MongoDB Techniques',
 'price': 70}
```

Let's add multiple dictionaries to your query results in a logical AND query:

```
# Define the query with logical AND conditions
query = {
    'name': 'Advanced MongoDB Techniques',
    'price': 70
}

# Fetch the document(s) matching the query
result = books.find(query)

# Print the fetched documents
for document in result:
    pprint(document)
```

You can check the result:

```
{'_id': ObjectId('6521d7e309731cfd8fa0ca04'),
 'isbn': '303',
 'name': 'Advanced MongoDB Techniques',
 'price': 70}
```

Now, query the books collection to retrieve documents that either have the name Advanced MongoDB Techniques or an ISBN number of 301, using the $or operator:

```
# Define the query with $or conditions
query = {
    "$or": [
        {'name': 'Advanced MongoDB Techniques'},
        {'isbn': '301'}
    ]
}

# Fetch the document(s) matching the query
result = books.find(query)

# Print the fetched documents
for document in result:
    pprint(document)
```

The result will appear as follows:

```
{'_id': ObjectId('6521ae0a0e542d46b87947a4'),
 'isbn': '301',
 'name': 'Python and MongoDB',
 'meta': {'version': 'MongoDB 7.0'},
 'price': 60}
{'_id': ObjectId('6521d7e309731cfd8fa0ca04'),
 'isbn': '303',
 'name': 'Advanced MongoDB Techniques',
 'price': 70}
```

Updating documents

In the following code block, you will see an example of updating a single document using the update_one helper method. This operation matches one document in the search phase and modifies one document based on the operation to be applied to the matched documents:

```
# Update the price of the book with the name "Advanced MongoDB Techniques"
update_result = books.update_one(
    {"name": "Advanced MongoDB Techniques"},
    {"$set": {"price": 75}}  # Setting the new price to 75
)

# Print the result of the update operation
pprint(update_result.raw_result)

# Fetch the updated document to verify the change
updated_document = books.find_one({"name": "Advanced MongoDB Techniques"})
pprint(updated_document)
```

This script will update the price of the book titled Advanced MongoDB Techniques to 75. After the update operation, it fetches and prints the updated document to verify the changes:

```
{'n': 1, 'nModified': 1, 'ok': 1.0, 'updatedExisting': True}
{'_id': ObjectId('6521d7e309731cfd8fa0ca04'),
 'isbn': '303',
 'name': 'Advanced MongoDB Techniques',
 'price': 75}
```

Deleting documents

The `delete_one` method in PyMongo allows you to remove a single document from a collection based on a specified filter. For situations where you might want to remove multiple records that match certain criteria, PyMongo offers the `delete_many` method. This is particularly useful when you want to remove specific records or a group of records from your dataset. Let's see an example of `delete_one`:

```python
# ISBN number of the book to be deleted
isbn_to_delete = '303'

# Delete the book with the specified ISBN number
delete_result = books.delete_one({"isbn": isbn_to_delete})

# Print the result of the delete operation
pprint(delete_result.raw_result)
```

The result indicates a successful deletion operation. Specifically, `'n': 1` signifies that one document was deleted, and `'ok': 1.0` confirms that the operation was executed without any errors:

```python
{'n': 1, 'ok': 1.0}
```

Regular expressions

There are several considerations that you have to take into account when querying in MongoDB. Let's look at some best practices for using regular expressions, query results, cursors, and deleting documents:

```
db.books.find({"name": /mongo/})
```

This is done to search for books in your `books` collection that contain the `mongo` name. It is the equivalent of an SQL `LIKE` query.

> **Note**
> MongoDB uses **Perl Compatible Regular Expression** (**PCRE**) version 8.42 with UTF-8 support.

While querying, you can use the following options:

Option	Description
i	This option queries case insensitivity.
m	This option only applies to multiline strings with anchors (* for the start and $ for the end). In this case, defining the m option will match the pattern at the beginning or end of each line. Without the m option, the anchors will match at the beginning or end of the string.

Table 5.3: Query options for regular expressions

In the previous example, if you wanted to search for mongo, Mongo, MONGO, or any other case-insensitive variation, you would need to use the i option, as follows:

```
db.books.find({"name": /mongo/i})
```

Alternatively, you can use the $regex operator, which provides more flexibility. The same queries using $regex are written as follows:

```
db.books.find({'name': { '$regex': /mongo/ }})
db.books.find({'name': { '$regex': /mongo/i }})
```

By using the $regex operator, you can also use the options shown in the following table:

Option	Description
x	This option ignores all whitespace characters in the $regex pattern. It also ignores any content between and including an unescaped hash or pound character, and the next newline. This can be used to include comments. It will not have any effect if the characters are included in a character class or escaped otherwise. It will not have any effect on handling the VT character.
s	This option allows the dot character (that is, .) to match all characters, including newline characters.

Table 5.4: Query options for the $regex operator

Expanding matching documents using $regex makes your queries slower to execute. Indexes that use regular expressions can only be used if your regular expression does queries for the beginning of a string that is indexed; that is, regular expressions starting with ^ or \A. If you only want to query using a string with a regular expression, you should avoid writing lengthier regular expressions, even if they match the same strings.

Take the following code block as an example:

```
db.books.find({ 'name': { '$regex': /mongo/ } });
db.books.find({ 'name': { '$regex': /^mongo.*/ } });
```

Both queries will match name values starting with mongo (case-sensitive), but the first one will be faster as it will stop matching as soon as it hits the sixth character in every name value.

Administration

Integration with MongoDB offers a seamless experience due to its non-relational, schema-free design. Without the constraints of schema migrations, you can streamline your database operations, thus minimizing database administrative overhead.

However, for optimal speed and performance in MongoDB, there are various tasks that experienced MongoDB developers or architects can perform. Management typically spans four distinct levels, each with increasing granularity: *process*, *database*, *collection*, and *index*.

At the process level, there is the shutDown command to shut down the MongoDB server.

At the database level, you have the following commands:

- dropDatabase: To drop the entire database
- listCollections: To retrieve the collection names in the current database

In comparison, at the collection level, the following commands are used:

- drop: To drop a collection
- create: To create a collection
- renameCollection: To rename a collection
- cloneCollectionAsCapped: To clone a collection into a new capped collection
- convertToCapped: To convert a collection to a capped one. However, MongoDB does not support the convertToCapped command in a sharded cluster
- compact: To release unneeded disk space to the operating system on WiredTiger databases

At the index level, you can use the following commands:

- createIndexes: To create new indexes in the current collection
- listIndexes: To list existing indexes in the current collection
- dropIndexes: To drop all indexes from the current collection
- reIndex: To drop and recreate an index in the current collection
- createSearchIndexes: To create one or more Atlas Search indexes on a specified collection
- dropSearchIndex: To delete an existing Atlas Search index
- updateSearchIndex: To update an existing Atlas Search index

The following sections will focus on a few other commands that are more important from an administration standpoint.

currentOp() and killOp()

db.currentOp() returns a document that contains information on in-progress operations for the mongod instance together with the operation ID.

killOp() terminates an operation as specified by the operation ID. Always terminate running operations with extreme caution. Only use killOp() to terminate operations initiated by clients and do not terminate internal database operations.

The `killOp()` command is used in the following way:

```
db.adminCommand(
    {
        killOp: 1,
        op: <opid>,
        comment: <any>
    }
)
```

collMod

`collMod` makes it possible to add options to a collection or to modify view definitions. For example, you can add an index option that can change the properties of an existing index, or you can add a validator that allows users to specify validation rules or expressions for a collection. You can also resize capped collections or modify time series collections.

For instance, take a look at the document validation option. Document validation can specify a set of rules to be applied to new updates and insertions into a collection. This means that current documents will be checked if they get modified.

You can only apply validations to documents that are already valid if you set `validationLevel` to `moderate`. By specifying `validationAction`, you can log documents that are invalid by setting it to `warn` or prevent updates from happening altogether by setting it to `error`.

For example, with the previous example of `bookOrders`, you can set `validator` on the `isbn` and name fields present for every insertion or update, as demonstrated in the following code snippet:

```
db.runCommand({
collMod: "bookOrders",
    validator: {
        $and: [
            {
                "isbn": {
                    $exists: true
                }
            },
            {
                "name": {
                    $exists: true
                }
            }
        ]
    }
});
```

Now, when you try to insert a new document with only the isbn field present, you'll get an error, as shown here:

```
db.bookOrders.insertOne({ isbn: 102 })
Uncaught:
MongoServerError: Document failed validation
Additional information: {
  failingDocumentId: ObjectId("6521162942094e44892aa6f6"),
  details: {
    operatorName: '$and',
    clausesNotSatisfied: [
      {
        index: 1,
        details: {
          operatorName: '$exists',
          specifiedAs: { name: { '$exists': true } },
          reason: 'path does not exist'
        }
      }
    ]
  }
}
```

This is because your validation has failed. Managing validation from the shell is useful as you can write scripts to manage it, and also make sure that everything is in place.

After learning how to administer your MongoDB server, you'll learn how to secure access to MongoDB with authentication and authorization in the next section.

Secure access to MongoDB

As the volume and sensitivity of data stored in databases grows, the importance of robust security measures becomes paramount. MongoDB recognizes this and has designed a suite of security tools and protocols to ensure that your data remains protected against unauthorized access and potential breaches. It provides various features, such as authentication, access control, and encryption, to secure your MongoDB deployments. It's crucial to understand the overarching principles that guide MongoDB's approach to database security.

Authentication and authorization

Authentication and authorization are closely connected. Authentication is the process of verifying the identity of a client. When access control (authorization) is enabled, MongoDB requires all clients to authenticate themselves in order to determine their access.

Authorization is about determining which actions a user can take on a resource. In the next sections, you'll explore authentication and authorization with these definitions in mind. You'll also examine some security tips for MongoDB as per the most current version.

Authorization with MongoDB

MongoDB's most basic authorization relies on the username/password method. To enable it, you need to start your server with the `-auth` parameter, as follows:

```
mongod --auth
```

Localhost exception

The localhost exception grants you the capability to turn on access control and subsequently establish the initial user or role within the system. Once access control is activated, you can link to the localhost interface to set up the first user within the `admin` database. For a `mongod` instance, this `localhost` exception is only relevant when no users or roles have been defined in the MongoDB environment.

Setting up the first `admin` user is simple, as shown in the following code snippet:

```
use admin
db.createUser(
   {
     user: <adminUser>,
     pwd: passwordPrompt(),  // Or  "<cleartext password>"
     roles: [ { role: <adminRole>, db: "admin" } ]
   }
)
```

Here, `<adminUser>` is the name of the user you want to create, `<cleartext password>` is the password, and `<adminRole>` can be any of the following values ordered from the most powerful to the least powerful for self-hosted deployments, as shown in the following list:

- `root`
- `dbAdminAnyDatabase`
- `userAdminAnyDatabase`
- `readWriteAnyDatabase`
- `readAnyatabase`
- `dbOwner`
- `dbAdmin`
- `clusterAdmin`

- `clusterManager`
- `clusterMonitor`
- `hostManager`
- `backup`
- `restore`
- `userAdmin`
- `readWrite`
- `read`

MongoDB Atlas also has some built-in roles dedicated only to Atlas, such as `atlasAdmin`.

Of these roles, `root` is the superuser that allows access to everything. However, this isn't recommended to be used, except in special circumstances.

All the `AnyDatabase` roles provide access to all databases, of which `dbAdminAnyDatabase` combines the `userAdminAnyDatabase` and `readWriteAnyDatabase` scopes, being an administrator again in all databases.

The rest of the roles are defined in the database that you want them to apply to. By changing the roles subdocument of the preceding `db.createUser()`; for example, if you want to create a `dbAdmin` role for your `mongodb_book` database, you can use the following code:

```
use admin
db.createUser(
    {
      user: "adminUser",
      pwd: "passwordPrompt()",  // Or  "<cleartext password>"
      roles: [ { role: "adminRole", db: "admin" } ]
    }
)
```

Authentication and authorization are essential prerequisites for any production-level MongoDB system. For more in-depth information on security practices, please refer to *Chapter 15, Security*. This chapter will help you understand how to ensure robust protection for your MongoDB deployments.

MongoDB Stable API

Introduced in MongoDB 5.0, the Stable API provides a guarantee that the API will not break for client-server communication. The Stable API is declared when using any driver or `mongosh`, in a similar fashion to the following `mongosh` example:

```
mongosh --apiVersion 1
```

> **Note**
>
> 1 is the only API version available as of MongoDB 7.0.

StableAPI guarantees backward compatibility between MongoDB server upgrades. This means that you can continue upgrading your MongoDB server without any significant risk, i.e., your application connected to the MongoDB server will behave differently.

This guarantee holds correct under the following three constraints:

- You need to declare apiVersion in the client
- You need to use a supported version of the official MongoDB client
- You can only use commands and features that are supported in this API version

Following the third constraint, as of apiVersion='1', you can use any of the following commands:

Command	Stable API version	Added to Stable API
count	V1	MongoDB 6.0, 5.0.9
abortTransaction	V1	MongoDB 5.0
aggregate (with limitations)	V1	MongoDB 5.0
authenticate	V1	MongoDB 5.0
collMod	V1	MongoDB 5.0
commitTransaction	V1	MongoDB 5.0
create (with limitations)	V1	MongoDB 5.0
createIndex (with limitations)	V1	MongoDB 5.0
delete	V1	MongoDB 5.0
drop	V1	MongoDB 5.0
dropDatabase	V1	MongoDB 5.0
dropIndex	V1	MongoDB 5.0
endSession	V1	MongoDB 5.0
explain	V1	MongoDB 5.0

Command	Stable API version	Added to Stable API
find (with limitations)	V1	MongoDB 5.0
findAndModify	V1	MongoDB 5.0
getMore	V1	MongoDB 5.0
insert	V1	MongoDB 5.0
hello	V1	MongoDB 5.0
killCursors	V1	MongoDB 5.0
listCollections	V1	MongoDB 5.0
listDatabases	V1	MongoDB 5.0
listIndexes	V1	MongoDB 5.0
ping	V1	MongoDB 5.0
refreshSessions	V1	MongoDB 5.0
update	V1	MongoDB 5.0

Table 5.5: Stable API commands and corresponding MongoDB version

The preceding methods in *Table 5.5* that have the note (*with limitations*) are only partially supported by the Stable API guarantee. You can also set the apiStrict boolean flag to True to prohibit clients from using commands that are not whitelisted. MongoDB will return an apiStrictError in such cases.

> **Note**
> apiStrict defaults to False.

Summary

This chapter explored the basics of CRUD operations. Starting from mongosh, you learned how to insert, delete, read, and modify documents, and learned the difference between one-off inserts and inserting data in batches for performance. Additionally, the chapter discussed administration tasks and how to perform them in mongosh. Finally, the chapter briefly covered security and authentication with MongoDB, the new versioning scheme, and the new shell, mongosh.

The next chapter will explore MongoDB schema design principles and techniques for effective data representation—essential for optimizing performance and scalability.

6

Schema Design and Data Modeling

In the dynamic world of database management, the decisions you make about structuring and representing data, significantly impact efficiency, adaptability, and overall system performance. With the advent of modern databases such as MongoDB, there's a heightened emphasis on employing distinct strategies that cater to flexible and scalable data environments. This chapter delves into the core principles of schema design and data modeling, offering clear guidance on selecting and implementing strategies that best suit your application's needs.

This chapter will cover the following topics:

- The foundation of schema design
- Technical aspects of MongoDB
- Data modeling and schema design patterns in MongoDB

Schema design for relational databases

In terms of structured relational databases, the paramount considerations are making sure your data is reliable, and everything runs efficiently. Two foundational principles drive this focus:

- Avoiding data anomalies
- Reducing data redundancy

In the context of a **relational database management system (RDBMS)**, a data anomaly is an inconsistency in the dataset resulting from a write operation, such as insert, delete, or update. For example, a university stores student information such as email, phone numbers, and addresses in multiple tables or columns. Over time, a student's phone number changes, and the university administration updates the phone number field in one of the tables or columns but forgets to update the others. As a result, the system now has conflicting information for the same student's phone number. Such a situation creates a data anomaly known as an *update anomaly*.

Data redundancy refers to the unnecessary duplication of data across different tables in the database. Such a situation can lead to data inconsistency and make data integrity difficult to maintain. For example:

Student

StudentID	Name	Email	DOB	Phone number
001	John	john@example.com	12/01/2000	00-123456

Table 6.1: Student table

Enrollment

EnrollID	StudentID	CourseID	StudentEmail
B43	001	C32	john@example.com

Table 6.2: Enrollment table

In this scenario, the StudentEmail field is redundant between different fields across the tables. In such a case, if John's email is updated in the Student table without updating the Enrollment table, the data will become inconsistent between the two tables.

Normal forms

In relational databases, normal forms serve as a benchmark to guide the design process. Normal forms minimize data duplication and prevent anomalies related to adding, removing, or modifying data. These forms are structured hierarchically, meaning each level builds upon the one before it, and advancing to a higher level requires fulfilling the criteria of the preceding levels. There are different levels of normal forms:

- **First normal form (1NF)**: Eliminates duplicates and simplifies queries
- **Second normal form (2NF)**: Eliminates redundant data, where all the non-key attributes are fully dependent on the primary key
- **Third normal form (3NF)**: All attributes are functionally dependent only on the primary key
- **Boyce-Codd normal form (BCNF)**: A stricter version of 3NF, where every non-trivial dependency is a super key
- **Fourth normal form (4NF)**: Ensures that a table does not contain any multi-valued dependency

- **Fifth normal form (5NF)**: The highest level in the normalization process. It involves splitting the table into smaller tables to remove any redundancy and improve integrity

In relational databases, tables and columns are structured using functional dependencies between different data units. Following such a formal method ensures that your data is normalized, with the downside that you can, in some scenarios, end up with many more tables than the domain model objects that you originally started with from your systems model.

When you're working with data, its nature often guides your approach to database modeling. Consider that you're developing applications using the **model-view-controller** (**MVC**) pattern. More often than not, you'll lean on representations from the **unified modeling language** (**UML**) to help shape your data models. These UML diagrams act as a foundational guide, assisting in structuring your MVC models. As a result, your design decisions are centered around the specific queries or data needs you foresee for your application.

Schema design for MongoDB

Transitioning from relational databases and SQL to MongoDB requires a shift in modeling strategy tailored to specific application data patterns. A pivotal step in this design process is to clearly define the data retrieval needs of users, effectively determining the structure of system entities. In traditional RDBMSs, normalization is paramount, with data duplication and denormalization often viewed negatively. Conversely, MongoDB frequently employs both data duplication and denormalization for valid performance and flexibility reasons.

The MongoDB document model offers a unique advantage: each document within a collection can vary, possessing different fields or even data types for the same field. Given the capability of MongoDB to execute detailed queries, even at the embedded document level, there's significant flexibility in document design. By understanding data access patterns, you can determine which fields to embed directly and which to distribute and refer to across separate collections.

Consider the following example showcasing two user documents from the user collection. While there are similarities between the documents, they are not identical:

```
{                                               {
  "_id": ObjectId("5ef2d4b45b7f11b6d7a"),         "_id": ObjectId("6ef8d4b32c9f12b6d4a"),
  "user_id": "Sherlock Holmes",                   "user_id": "John Watson",
  "age": 40,                                      "age": 45,
  "address":                                      "address":
{                                               {
  "Country": "England",                           "Country": "England",
  "City": "London",                               "Street": "221B Baker St."
  "Street": "221B Baker St."                    },
},                                                "Medical license": "Active",
  "Hobbies":[ "violin", "crime-solving" ]         "Job": "Software Engineer"
}                                               }
```

Table 6.3: Examples of user documents from the user collection

Data modeling in MongoDB

Data modeling in MongoDB is a nuanced process, distinct from traditional relational databases. On one hand, you have the demands of your application and the way users interact with it. On the other hand, there's the need for efficient performance and the specific patterns employed to access the data. Striking this balance influences the structure of the data itself, which in MongoDB is represented as documents.

Document structure

A standout feature of MongoDB is its versatile document structure. It can handle nested BSON documents and arrays up to an impressive depth of 100 levels. This depth not only showcases the flexibility of the database but also ensures data can be represented in ways that truly resonate with your application needs. Such a structure reduces the need for joins, streamlines data retrieval, and simplifies queries, making MongoDB a powerful choice for complex data architectures.

Here's a sample document, illustrating the MongoDB document structure:

```
{
    "_id": ObjectId("407f1f77bcf86cd799429012"),
    "name": "Alice Smith",
    "addresses": [
        {
            "street": "123 Main Street",
            "city": "New York"
        },
        {
            "street": "456 Pine Street",
            "city": "San Francisco"
        }
    ],
    "certificates":[
        {
            "_id": ObjectId("407f1f77bcf86cd799429013"),
            "name": "Software Development",
            "date": "2023-01-01",
            "details": {
                "issuer": "Tech University",
                "duration": "1 Year",
                "modules": [
                    {
                        "name": "Introduction to Python",
                        "score": 90,
                        "topics": [
                            {
                                "title": "Basic Syntax",
```

```
                                "description": "Understanding the basics."
                        }
                    ]
                }
            ]
        }
    }
  ]
}
```

Embedded data

MongoDB can encapsulate related data within a single document structure, making it easy to show relationships between different pieces of data. This model enables the inclusion of nested document structures within a field or an array inside a document. By employing these denormalized data models, applications can access and modify correlated data through just one database operation.

The following example showcases a book document in MongoDB with embedded author details, demonstrating the database's ability to nest information seamlessly:

```json
{
    "_id": "f4a38c6edf1a2e86d7f726b",
    "title": "Journey to the Center of the Earth",
    "published_year": 1864,
    "genres": ["Adventure", "Science Fiction"],
    "author": {
        "first_name": "Jules",
        "last_name": "Verne",
        "birth_year": 1828,
        "nationality": "French",
        "biography": "A pioneering author of science fiction..."
    },
    "ratings": 4.5,
    "copies_sold": 1500000
}
```

References

In MongoDB, references establish connections between data by using links or pointers from one document to another, referring to different collections. Applications can then resolve these references to fetch related data, making it easier to access associated information. Broadly, these are normalized data models.

The following example depicts a university where courses reference professor details using their document's "_id" value as a reference. This approach allows for efficient cross-referencing between collections, ensuring data normalization:

```
// Course Collection
{
    "_id": ObjectId("60e428f2c9a7e24d8c90a01a"),
    "course_name": "Introduction to Artificial Intelligence",
    "professor_id": ObjectId("60e428f2c9a7e24d8c90a02b"),
    "duration": "6 months",
    "credits": 3
}


// Professor Collection
{
    "_id": ObjectId("60e428f2c9a7e24d8c90a02b"),
    "first_name": "Alan",
    "last_name": "Turing",
    "department": "Computer Science",
    "publications": 45
}
```

Denormalization

Denormalization in MongoDB is a design choice that balances redundancy and performance by introducing intentionally redundant data with an aim to improve read performance.

By embedding fields such as authorName directly in the book document, you can fetch details faster, as only a single operation is required. Here's an example:

```
// Book Document
{
    "_id": ObjectId("5f1d2a3b8b0c9a0b4c3d2a3b"),
    "title": "Mastering Linux",
    "author_id": ObjectId("507f191e810c19729de860ea"),
    "authorName":"John Smith"
}
```

In contrast to the referencing approach, this example directly incorporates the author's name. By doing so, you can reduce additional queries when fetching book details that require the author's name.

Now that you have an understanding of the MongoDB data modeling structure, let's explore how this data is stored. In the next section, you will learn about BSON, the format MongoDB uses to save designed models in binary form.

BSON and its data types

Binary JSON (BSON) forms the bedrock for storing data in MongoDB. While it shares similarities with JSON, BSON comes equipped with additional data types and optimization for storage and scanning speed.

BSON was designed to have the following three characteristics:

- **Lightweight**: Keeping the spatial overhead to a minimum is important for any data representation format, especially when used over the network.

- **Traversable**: BSON is designed to be traversed easily. This is a vital property in its role as the primary data representation for MongoDB.

- **Efficient**: Encoding data to BSON and decoding from BSON can be performed very quickly in most languages due to the use of C data types.

> **Note**
>
> For a comprehensive list and a detailed explanation of all BSON data types, please refer to the official MongoDB documentation: `https://www.mongodb.com/docs/manual/reference/bson-types/`.

BSON offers a versatile storage format in MongoDB, supporting a broader range of data types than standard JSON:

```
{
    "_id": ObjectId("407f1f77bcf86cd799439012"),
    "doubleField": 55.4,
    "stringField": "Hello, everyone!",
    "objectField": {
        "name": "John",
        "age": 35
    },
    "arrayField": [1,2,3,4,5],
    "binaryField": BinData(0,"binary-content"),
    "booleanField": true,
    "dateField": ISODate("2023-08-01T10:00:00Z"),
    "nullField": null,
    "regexField": /^abc/,
    "javascriptField": Code("function () { print('success!'); }"),
    "javascriptWithScopeField": Code("return this.x + this.y;",{x: 3, y: 5}),
    "int32Field": 42,
    "timestampField": Timestamp(1601410400,1),
    "int64Field": NumberLong(9876543210),
    "decimal128Field": NumberDecimal("0.123456789123456789"),
    "minKeyField": MinKey(),
    "maxKeyField": MaxKey()
}
```

Each field in the preceding document exemplifies a unique BSON data type, showcasing the diversity and depth MongoDB offers in terms of data representation. As you design and model your databases, being familiar with these BSON types will empower you to make informed decisions on data storage and retrieval.

Design considerations and best practices for MongoDB modeling

When you're crafting data models in MongoDB, it's not just about representing the data—it's about doing so *efficiently* and *effectively*. The design decisions you make can greatly influence your application's performance, scalability, and maintainability. While MongoDB offers great flexibility, consider the following best practices while structuring your data to help achieve peak efficiency.

Read-write ratio

Understanding your application's read-write ratio can guide how data is stored and retrieved to optimize performance:

- **Read considerations**: When reading data in sharded clusters, you want to avoid the scatter-gather approach, where multiple shards are queried. Data modeling, especially the decision to embed related data within a single document, can help reduce the number of queries required to fetch related data. This provides performance benefits in terms of reduced I/O operations. However, it's crucial to strike a balance since excessive embedding can lead to large documents and potential update inefficiencies.

- **Write considerations**: To optimize write performance, especially in a sharded environment, it's essential to distribute write operations across multiple servers or shards. This can be achieved using appropriate sharding strategies and ensuring your shard key provides a good distribution of write operations.

- **Query-update ratio**: Analyzing the ratio of read queries to update queries can help in determining how often data is modified versus how often it is accessed. This insight can guide indexing strategies, as frequently accessed or modified fields might benefit from indexing.

Design patterns and schema design

Schema design in MongoDB is crucial for optimizing performance and scalability. Through the understanding and application of distinct patterns, you can tailor your data model effectively. The following is an overview of various MongoDB design patterns:

- **Bucket pattern**: This is a great solution for managing streaming data, such as time-series, real-time analytics, or **Internet of Things** (**IoT**) applications. It reduces the overall number of documents in a collection, simplifies data access, and improves index performance.

  Consider an IoT application where a sensor sends temperature readings every minute. Instead of creating a new document for every reading, the data can be bucketed together in hourly intervals:

```
{
    "_id": ObjectId("50bf1fbbbcf86cd799439051"),
    "sensor_id": "S123",
    "start_date": ISODate("2023-10-03T08:00:00Z"),
    "end_date": ISODate("2023-10-03T08:59:59Z"),
    "readings": [
        {"value": 22, "timestamp": ISODate("2023-10-03T08:00:01Z")},
        {"value": 23, "timestamp": ISODate("2023-10-03T08:01:10Z")},
        // ... readings for the entire hour
    ]
}
```

- **Attribute pattern**: This is ideal for large documents with many similar fields. The attribute pattern targets a subset of fields that share common characteristics for sorting or querying. This pattern is especially effective when these fields appear in a limited number of documents.

  Consider an e-commerce platform with a catalog of products. Each product has a set of attributes that can vary based on the type of product:

```
{
    "_id": ObjectId("50cf1fcbcf86cd799439061"),
    "product_name": "Smartphone XYZ",
    "category": "Electronics",
    "attributes": [
        {"name": "color", "value": "black"},
        {"name": "storage", "value": "128GB"},
        {"name": "camera", "value": "12MP"},
        {"name": "battery", "value": "4000mAh"}
    ]
}
```

- **Polymorphic pattern**: This solution is useful when there are a variety of documents that have more similarities than differences and the documents need to be kept in a single collection.

  Consider a medical database storing different types of medical records—general check-ups, surgical procedures, and dental check-ups:

```
// Document 1
{
    "_id": ObjectId("50df1fdbcf86cd799439071"),
    "patient_id": "P45678",
    "type": "surgical",
    "surgery_name": "Appendectomy",
    "surgeon": "Dr. Smith",
    "date": ISODate("2023-10-04T10:00:00Z")
},
```

```
// Document 2
{
    "_id": ObjectId("50ef1febbcf86cd799439081"),
    "patient_id": "P45678",
    "type": "dental",
    "dentist": "Dr. White",
    "procedure": "Tooth extraction",
    "date": ISODate("2023-09-04T11:00:00Z")
}
```

- **Schema versioning pattern**: This pattern involves adding a version field to documents, allowing for evolution of data structures over time. By tracking schema versions, applications can handle multiple schema variations, facilitating smoother data migrations and updates.

  Consider a user profile collection on a social media platform. Over time, as the platform evolves, the structure of the user profile might change:

```
{
    "_id": ObjectId("50gf1ffbbcf86cd799439091"),
    "username": "alice123",
    "email": "alice@email.com",
    "birthdate": ISODate("1990-01-01"),
    "schema_version": 1
},
{
    "_id": ObjectId("50hf1fgbbcf86cd799439101"),
    "username": "bob456",
    "email": "bob@email.com",
    "birthdate": ISODate("1992-05-05"),
    "contact": {
        "phone": "+1234567890",
        "address": "123 Main St"
    },
    "schema_version": 2
}
```

- **Extended reference pattern**: This pattern is most useful when your application is experiencing many repetitive JOIN operations to bring together frequently accessed data. By identifying fields on the lookup and bringing frequently accessed fields into the main document, the extended reference pattern helps improve performance. This is achieved through faster reads and a reduction in the overall number of JOINs.

Consider an e-commerce platform with products and orders. When displaying an order, it's common to show the product name and price without fetching all the product details:

```
// products collection:
{
    "_id": ObjectId("50if1ghbbcf86cd799439111"),
    "product_name": "Laptop ABC",
    "price": 1200,
    "specs": {...},
    "reviews": [...],
    // ... other product details
}
// orders collection:
{
    "_id": ObjectId("50jf1hibbcf86cd799439121"),
    "customer_id": "C7890",
    "products": [
        {
            "product_id": ObjectId("50if1ghbbcf86cd799439111"),
            "product_name": "Laptop ABC",
            "price": 1200
        },
    ],
    "order_date": ISODate("2023-10-05T13:00:00Z")
}
```

- **Approximation pattern**: This is useful when exact values are not critical, but performance is. Instead of performing resource-intensive calculations or aggregations in real time, this pattern uses precalculated, estimated, or cached values to provide quick responses. It's beneficial in scenarios such as real-time analytics or counters, where close-enough values are acceptable for faster query performance.

Consider a website that tracks the number of views on its articles. Due to high traffic, updating the exact view count in real time for each view can be taxing. Instead, the approximation pattern can be used:

```
{
    "_id": ObjectId("50kf1ijbbcf86cd799439131"),
    "title": "Understanding MongoDB Patterns",
    "content": "...",
    "approximate_views": 5000,
    "exact_views": 5123,
    "last_update": ISODate("2023-10-06T14:30:00Z")
}
```

- **Computed pattern**: This pattern involves precomputing the results of certain calculations and storing them within the document, rather than computing them on the fly during read operations. This pattern is particularly useful for frequently accessed data that involves complex aggregations or calculations. By precomputing and storing the result, you can optimize read operations and achieve faster query performance.

  Consider an e-commerce application where products have ratings from users. Instead of calculating the average rating every time a product is accessed, the application can store a computed average and update it periodically, or whenever a new rating is added:

  ```
  {
      "_id": ObjectId("5f50a123d1a7d7f78f9b7e6b"),
      "product_name": "Laptop XYZ",
      "reviews": [
          { "user": "Alice", "rating": 5 },
          { "user": "Bob", "rating": 4 },
      ],
      "computed_avg_rating": 4.5,
      "total_reviews": 200
  }
  ```

- **Outlier pattern**: This works around the idea of handling outliers in your data. In many datasets, the majority of data often belongs to a standard structure, but there might be a small percentage that deviates from this norm. Instead of designing the entire schema around these exceptions, which could lead to inefficiencies, the outlier pattern suggests storing the standard data in one way and the exceptions in another.

  Consider a school system where most students take a standard set of courses, but a few students have special courses due to specific needs or advanced programs:

  ```
  {
      "_id": ObjectId("5f50b123d1a7d7f78f9c8e6b"),
      "student_name": "John",
      "standard_courses": ["Math", "Science", "History"],
      "new_courses": ["Advanced Astrophysics", "Special Language Studies"]
  }
  ```

- **Pre-allocation pattern**: When you know your document structure and your application simply needs to fill it with data, the pre-allocation pattern is the right choice. By pre-establishing the necessary space or documents in MongoDB, you can streamline data insertion and updates, minimizing overhead and ensuring efficient write operations.

Imagine a weather application that tracks daily weather data for various cities. At the start of each month, the application pre-allocates a document for each city with placeholders for every day of the month:

```
{
    "_id": ObjectId("508f1f99bcf86cd799439021"),
    "city": "New York",
    "month": "October",
    "daily_data": [
        {"day": 1, "temperature": null, "condition": null},
        {"day": 2, "temperature": null, "condition": null},
    ]
}
```

- **Subset pattern**: Improves data access efficiency for applications with a predetermined page size for reviews (or a similar use case), particularly when dealing with large documents that have much of the data in the document not being used by the application.

Consider a library system where each book has hundreds of reviews. However, when displaying a list of books, the application only shows the latest five reviews for quick browsing:

```
{
    "_id": ObjectId("509f1faabcf86cd799439031"),
    "title": "Moby Dick",
    "author": "Herman Melville",
    "subset_reviews": [
        {"user": "Alice", "rating": 5, "comment": "Loved it!", "date":
ISODate("2023-10-01T10:00:00Z")},
        {"user": "Bob", "rating": 4, "comment": "Good read.", "date":
ISODate("2023-09-29T08:30:00Z")},
        // ... 3 more recent reviews
    ]
}
```

- **Tree pattern**: This is used to represent hierarchical data structures. It's ideal for scenarios where data has parent-child relationships or needs to be represented in a tree-like format. By using references or embeddings, this pattern can efficiently depict structures such as organizational charts, filesystems, or comment threads.

Consider a forum application where users can post comments and reply to other comments, forming a comment thread:

```
{
    "_id": ObjectId("50af1fabbcf86cd799439041"),
    "text": "This is the original comment.",
    "user": "Alice",
    "timestamp": ISODate("2023-10-02T12:00:00Z"),
    "replies": [
        {
            "text": "This is a reply to the original comment.",
            "user": "Bob",
            "timestamp": ISODate("2023-10-02T12:10:00Z"),
            "replies": [
                {
                    "text": "This is a nested reply.",
                    "user": "Charlie",
                    "timestamp": ISODate("2023-10-02T12:15:00Z"),
                    "replies": [...]
                }
            ]
        },
        // ... more replies to the original comment
    ]
}
```

In MongoDB, various design patterns enable tailored schema designs for optimal performance and scalability. By using these patterns, you can skillfully structure data to fit diverse application needs.

Summary

This chapter explored the intricacies of database design, focusing specifically on schema design for MongoDB. It touched on different MongoDB data modeling techniques, BSON data types, and essential design considerations for MongoDB modeling. Through a series of design patterns, practical insights were provided for various application scenarios. The examples and information shared, set the stage for a solid understanding of data modeling and schema design in MongoDB.

In the next chapter, you will learn about the aggregation framework, advanced querying techniques, and master the art of indexing, helping you elevate your MongoDB querying expertise from beginner to advanced.

7

Advanced Querying in MongoDB

MongoDB offers a rich set of advanced query features that extend beyond basic data retrieval and manipulation. These features allow you to optimize query performance, create aggregation pipelines, and perform complex aggregations.

This chapter offers a more profound exploration of MongoDB's capabilities. You will refine your expertise with advanced querying techniques, understand transactions and concurrency, and get a clearer picture of MongoDB's backend processes.

This chapter will cover the following topics:

- Overview and benefits of the MongoDB aggregation framework
- Key stages in the MongoDB aggregation framework
- Advanced querying techniques for database management
- Query optimization using indexes

Introduction to the aggregation framework

The aggregation framework in MongoDB is a data processing tool that helps you perform complex data transformations and computations. You can use the framework to filter, transform, and get insights from data instead of writing scripts outside the database to process it.

The framework was designed around the concept of a data processing pipeline in which the data enters, and the transformation occurs as it passes from one stage to the next.

The flexibility and expressive syntax of the aggregation framework helps you shape data in various ways, from simple filtering and grouping to reshaping entire documents. Here's an example to better understand the true value of aggregation.

Imagine that you're managing the academic records of a university using MongoDB. Among various collections, such as courses, students, and faculty, you have a student_grades collection. Each document in this collection represents a course grade for a student. The document structure might look something like this:

```
{
    "_id": ObjectId("5f4b7de8e8189a46aaf6e3ad"),
    "student_id": ObjectId("5f4b7de8e7139a46aaf5e4a5"),
    "course_id": ObjectId("5f4b7de8e7179a56aaf6e1b2"),
    "grade": 76,
    "semester": "Fall 2023"
}
```

Suppose the university wants a report at the end of each academic year, and they're interested in computing the average grade for each student. With the vast number of courses and students, calculating this manually or even with a traditional script would be tedious and time consuming. However, with the MongoDB aggregation framework, you can construct an efficient and powerful pipeline to:

1. **Filter the grades**: By using the $match stage, you can filter only the grades needed from the target semester.

2. **Group the grades by student**: Using the $group stage, you can group grades by student_id. At the same time, you can calculate both the total grade and the count of subjects for each student.

3. **Compute the average grade**: After grouping, you can use the $project stage to compute the average grade for each student by dividing the total grade by the count of subjects.

Here's an example of filtering, grouping, and computing the average:

```
db.student_grades.aggregate([
  {
    $match: { semester: "Fall 2023" }
  },
  {
    $group: {
      _id: "$student_id"
    }
  },
```

```
  {
    $project: {
      // Calculate average
      averageGrade: { $divide: ["$totalGrade", "$totalCourses"] }
    }
  }
])
```

Benefits of aggregation in MongoDB

Aggregation is a powerful tool in MongoDB that allows you to process data records and return computed results. By using the aggregation framework, you can transform and combine data in various ways, making it easy to analyze and derive meaningful insights.

Aggregating in MongoDB provides a range of benefits, such as:

- **Performance**: Native database operations are often faster than extracting data and processing it externally.

- **Flexibility**: The aggregation framework provides a vast array of tools and operators to transform data in complex ways, often reducing the need for external data processing logic.

- **Data integrity**: Operating at the database level ensures consistency and integrity, unlike external processes, which might be prone to synchronization or transactional issues.

- **Resource efficiency**: Reducing the need to move large datasets out of the database for processing can lead to less network bandwidth usage and reduced memory or CPU overhead in application servers.

The MongoDB aggregation framework provides you with a robust, efficient, and reliable method for data processing, underscoring its pivotal role in achieving optimal system performance and comprehensive data analysis.

In the following sections, you will explore aggregation stages to better understand their capabilities and the role they play in modern data-driven applications.

Aggregation stages

An aggregation stage represents a specific step in the pipeline where the data transformation process takes place. Each stage processes data and outputs documents that can be further processed by the subsequent stages.

Let's explore some key stages that act as the building blocks of a pipeline:

- `$match`: Use `$match` to filter the documents so that only those that meet the specified condition(s) are passed to the next pipeline stage. This stage should be used early in the pipeline, because filtering out unnecessary documents leads to processing only the relevant documents in the following stages, leading to significant performance improvements.

Example: Find all users older than 22.

Input

```
[
    { "_id": 1, "name": "Alice", "age": 21 },
    { "_id": 2, "name": "Bob", "age": 25 },
    { "_id": 3, "name": "Charlie", "age": 23 },
    { "_id": 4, "name": "David", "age": 20 }
]
```

Pipeline

```
db.users.aggregate([{ $match: { age: { $gt: 22 } } }]);
```

Output

```
[
    {
        "_id": 2,
        "name": "Bob",
        "age": 25
    },
    {
        "_id": 3,
        "name": "Charlie",
        "age": 23
    }
]
```

- `$limit`: If you know you only need a subset of the results, use `$limit` early in the process to reduce the number of documents passed to subsequent stages.

Example: Get only three users.

Input

```
[
    { "_id": 1, "name": "Alice", "age": 21 },
    { "_id": 2, "name": "Bob", "age": 25 },
    { "_id": 3, "name": "Charlie", "age": 23 },
    { "_id": 4, "name": "David", "age": 20 },
    { "_id": 5, "name": "Eve", "age": 29 },
    { "_id": 6, "name": "Frank", "age": 26 },
    { "_id": 7, "name": "Grace", "age": 24 }
]
```

Pipeline

```
db.users.aggregate([{ $limit: 3 }]);
```

Output

```
[
    { "_id": 1, "name": "Alice", "age": 21 },
    { "_id": 2, "name": "Bob", "age": 25 },
    { "_id": 3, "name": "Charlie", "age": 23 }
]
```

- $sort: If sorting is necessary, use this stage to optimize performance, especially if there's an index that supports your sort order.

Example: Sort users by age in descending order.

Input

```
[
    { "_id": 1, "name": "Alice", "age": 21 },
    { "_id": 2, "name": "Bob", "age": 25 },
    { "_id": 3, "name": "Charlie", "age": 23 },
    { "_id": 4, "name": "David", "age": 20 },
    { "_id": 5, "name": "Eve", "age": 29 },
    { "_id": 6, "name": "Frank", "age": 26 },
    { "_id": 7, "name": "Grace", "age": 24 }
]
```

Pipeline

```
db.users.aggregate([{ $sort: { age: -1 } }]);
```

Output

```
[
    { "_id": 5, "name": "Eve", "age": 29 },
    { "_id": 6, "name": "Frank", "age": 26 },
    { "_id": 2, "name": "Bob", "age": 25 },
    { "_id": 7, "name": "Grace", "age": 24 },
    { "_id": 3, "name": "Charlie", "age": 23 },
    { "_id": 1, "name": "Alice", "age": 21 },
    { "_id": 4, "name": "David", "age": 20 }
]
```

- $skip: Use this stage to skip the first N documents, where N is a positive integer, and pass the remaining documents unmodified to the next pipeline stage.

Example: Skip the first 10 users.

Input

```
[
    { "_id": 1, "name": "Alice", "age": 21 },
    { "_id": 2, "name": "Bob", "age": 25 },
    { "_id": 3, "name": "Charlie", "age": 23 },
    { "_id": 4, "name": "David", "age": 20 },
    { "_id": 5, "name": "Eve", "age": 29 },
    { "_id": 6, "name": "Frank", "age": 26 },
    { "_id": 7, "name": "Grace", "age": 24 },
    { "_id": 8, "name": "Hannah", "age": 27 },
    { "_id": 9, "name": "Ian", "age": 22 },
    { "_id": 10, "name": "Jack", "age": 28 },
    { "_id": 11, "name": "Katie", "age": 30 },
    { "_id": 12, "name": "Liam", "age": 24 }
]
```

Pipeline

```
db.users.aggregate([{ $skip: 10 }]);
```

Output

```
[
    { "_id": 11, "name": "Katie", "age": 30 },
    { "_id": 12, "name": "Liam", "age": 24 }
]
```

- `$project` / `$set` / `$addFields`: Use these stages to reshape documents. A `$project` stage should normally be the last stage in your pipeline to specify which fields to return to the client.

  Example: Return only the username and phone number of each user.

> **Note**
>
> Each record includes an `_id` field. This is because the `_id` field is included in query results by default in MongoDB. It serves as a unique identifier for each document. Unless explicitly excluded in the query, the `_id` field will appear in the output.

Input

```
[
    {
        "_id": 1,
        "username": "Alice01",
        "age": 21,
        "phoneNumber": "123- 456-7890",
        "email": "alice@example.com"
    },
```

```
  {
    "_id": 2,
    "username": "Bob02",
    "age": 25,
    "phoneNumber": "234-567- 8901",
    "email": "bob@example.com"
  },
  {
    "_id": 3,
    "username": "Charlie03",
    "age": 23,
    "phoneNumber": "345- 678-9012",
    "email": "charlie@example.com"
  },
  {
    "_id": 4,
    "username": "David04",
    "age": 20,
    "phoneNumber": "456- 789-0123",
    "email": "david@example.com"
  }
]
```

Pipeline

```
db.users.aggregate([{ $project: { username: 1, phoneNumber: 1 } }]);
```

Output

```
[
  { "_id": 1, "username": "Alice01", "phoneNumber": "123-456-7890" },
  { "_id": 2, "username": "Bob02", "phoneNumber": "234-567-8901" },
  { "_id": 3, "username": "Charlie03", "phoneNumber": "345-678-9012" },
  { "_id": 4, "username": "David04", "phoneNumber": "456-789-0123" }
]
```

- $group: After filtering and reducing the dataset, group your data as needed with this stage.

  Example: Get the average age of users, and group them by their country.

  Input

```
[
  { "_id": 1, "username": "Alice", "age": 21, "country": "USA" },
  { "_id": 2, "username": "Bob", "age": 25, "country": "USA" },
  { "_id": 3, "username": "Charlie", "age": 30, "country": "UK" },
  { "_id": 4, "username": "David", "age": 28, "country": "UK" },
  { "_id": 5, "username": "Eve", "age": 29, "country": "Canada" }
]
```

Pipeline

```
db.users.aggregate([
  { $group: { _id: "$country", averageAge: { $avg: "$age" } } }
])
```

Output

```
[
  { "_id": "Canada", "averageAge": 29.0 },
  { "_id": "UK", "averageAge": 29.0 },
  { "_id": "USA", "averageAge": 23.0 }
]
```

- $unwind: Use this stage when you need to flatten array fields and produce a new document for each element.

  Example: For each user, unwind the hobbies array and produce a document for each hobby they have.

  Input

```
[
  {
    "_id": 1,
    "username": "Alice",
    "hobbies": ["reading", "hiking", "swimming"]
  },
  {
    "_id": 2,
    "username": "Bob",
    "hobbies": ["cycling", "painting"]
  },
  {
    "_id": 3,
    "username": "Charlie",
    "hobbies": ["dancing", "cooking"]
  },
  {
    "_id": 4,
    "username": "David",
    "hobbies": ["fishing"]
  },
  {
    "_id": 5,
    "username": "Eve",
    "hobbies": []
  }
]
```

Pipeline

```
db.users.aggregate([{ $unwind: "$hobbies" }]);
```

Output

```
[
    { "_id": 1, "username": "Alice", "hobbies": "reading" },
    { "_id": 1, "username": "Alice", "hobbies": "hiking" },
    { "_id": 1, "username": "Alice", "hobbies": "swimming" },
    { "_id": 2, "username": "Bob", "hobbies": "cycling" },
    { "_id": 2, "username": "Bob", "hobbies": "painting" },
    { "_id": 3, "username": "Charlie", "hobbies": "dancing" },
    { "_id": 3, "username": "Charlie", "hobbies": "cooking" },
    { "_id": 4, "username": "David", "hobbies": "fishing" }
]
```

- $lookup: Use this stage to perform a left outer join with another collection. It allows documents from the input collection (the one you're aggregating on) to be combined with documents from a different collection. To effectively utilize the $lookup stage, you must understand its key components. Each of these components play a distinct role in deciding how documents from one collection are combined with those from another collection. These components include the following:

  - The from field, which identifies the collection with which you want to join.

  - localField and foreignField specify the fields from the input documents and the documents in the from collection, respectively.

  - The as field, which determines the name of the new array field added to the input documents. This array contains the matching documents from the from collection.

Example 1:

Orders collection

```
[
    { "_id": 1, "product_id": 100, "quantity": 2 },
    { "_id": 2, "product_id": 101, "quantity": 5 }
]
```

Products collection

```
[
    { "_id": 100, "name": "Laptop", "price": 1000, "stock": 10 },
    { "_id": 101, "name": "Mouse", "price": 50, "stock": 0 }
]
```

Pipeline

```
db.orders.aggregate([
  {
    $lookup: {
      from: "products",
      localField: "product_id",
      foreignField: "_id",
      as: "productDetails"
    }
  }
])
```

Output

```
[
  {
    "_id": 1,
    "product_id": 100,
    "quantity": 2,
    "productDetails": [
      {
        "_id": 100,
        "name": "Laptop",
        "price": 1000
      }
    ]
  },
  {
    "_id": 2,
    "product_id": 101,
    "quantity": 5,
    "productDetails": [
      {
        "_id": 101,
        "name": "Mouse",
        "price": 50
      }
    ]
  }
]
```

Example 2:

In this example, you will utilize MongoDB's $lookup stage to join orders with in-stock products, adding a productDetails field to each order that includes the product's name and price. This approach dynamically links orders to relevant product information based on stock availability.

Pipeline

```
db.orders.aggregate([
  {
    $lookup: {
      from: "products",
      let: { order_product_id: "$product_id" },
      pipeline: [
        {
          $match: {
            $expr: {
              $and: [
                { $eq: ["$_id", "$$order_product_id"] },
                // Matches only in-stock products
                { $gt: ["$stock", 0] }
              ]
            }
          }
        },
        { $project: { name: 1, price: 1 } },
      ],
      as: "productDetails",
    }
  }
])
```

Output

The result is an array of orders documents, where each document includes the original orders fields (_id, product_id, quantity) plus the productDetails array containing relevant products information (only the name and price of the in-stock products).

```
[
  {
    "_id": 1,
    "product_id": 100,
    "quantity": 2,
    "productDetails": [
      {
        "name": "Laptop",
        "price": 1000
      }
    ]
  },
  {
    "_id": 2,
    "product_id": 101,
    "quantity": 5,
```

```
      "productDetails": []
    }
  ]
```

- $geoNear: Use this stage to order documents based on their proximity to a specified point, ranging from the nearest to the farthest. To effectively utilize $geoNear, the collection must include a field with a geospatial index. It's important to note that $geoNear can only be used as the first stage in an aggregation pipeline.

Example: Find the closest restaurants to a specific location.

Input

```
[
  {
    "_id": 1,
    "name": "Deli Delight",
    "location": {
      "type": "Point",
      "coordinates": [-73.993, 40.7185]
    }
  },
  {
    "_id": 2,
    "name": "Pizza Palace",
    "location": {
      "type": "Point",
      "coordinates": [-73.995, 40.717]
    }
  },
  {
    "_id": 3,
    "name": "Burger Bliss",
    "location": {
      "type": "Point",
      "coordinates": [-73.99, 40.721]
    }
  },
  {
    "_id": 4,
    "name": "Taco Tower",
    "location": {
      "type": "Point",
      "coordinates": [-73.997, 40.714]
    }
  }
]
```

Pipeline

```
db.restaurants.aggregate([
  {
    $geoNear: {
      near: {
        type: "Point",
        coordinates: [-73.99279, 40.719296],
      },
      distanceField: "distance",
      maxDistance: 2000,
      spherical: true
    }
  }
])
```

Output

```
[
  {
    "_id": 1,
    "name": "Deli Delight",
    "location": {
      "type": "Point",
      "coordinates": [-73.993, 40.7185]
    },
    "distance": 88.12345678
  },
  {
    "_id": 2,
    "name": "Pizza Palace",
    "location": {
      "type": "Point",
      "coordinates": [-73.995, 40.717]
    },
    "distance": 255.12345678
  },
  {
    "_id": 3,
    "name": "Burger Bliss",
    "location": {
      "type": "Point",
      "coordinates": [-73.99, 40.721]
    },
    "distance": 200.12345678
  }
]
```

- $redact: Use this field to restrict the contents of your documents based on information stored in the documents themselves. This is often used for data access control.

Example: Display only the documents that the users have read access to.

Input

```
[
  {
    "_id": 1,
    "title": "Document A",
    "content": "This is document A.",
    "access": "read"
  },
  {
    "_id": 2,
    "title": "Document B",
    "content": "This is document B.",
    "access": "write"
  },
  {
    "_id": 3,
    "title": "Document C",
    "content": "This is document C.",
    "access": "read"
  },
  {
    "_id": 4,
    "title": "Document D",
    "content": "This is document D.",
    "access": "none"
  }
]
```

Pipeline

```
db.docs.aggregate([
  {
    $redact: {
      $cond: {
        if: { $eq: ["$access", "read"] },
        then: "$$DESCEND",
        else: "$$PRUNE"
      }
    }
  }
])
```

Output

```
[
  {
    "_id": 1,
    "title": "Document A",
    "content": "This is document A.",
    "access": "read"
  },
  {
    "_id": 3,
    "title": "Document C",
    "content": "This is document C.",
    "access": "read"
  }
]
```

- $replaceWith: Use this field to replace the input document with the specified document.

Example: Replace the document with its profile field.

Input

```
[
  {
    "_id": 1,
    "name": "Alice",
    "age": 25,
    "profile": {
      "hobbies": ["reading", "hiking"],
      "city": "New York"
    }
  },
  {
    "_id": 2,
    "name": "Bob",
    "age": 30,
    "profile": {
      "hobbies": ["cycling", "painting"],
      "city": "Los Angeles"
    }
  },
  {
    "_id": 3,
    "name": "Charlie",
    "age": 28,
    "profile": {
      "hobbies": ["dancing", "cooking"],
      "city": "Chicago"
```

```
        }
      }
    ]
```

Pipeline

```
db.users.aggregate([
  {
    $replaceWith: "$profile"
  }
])
```

Output

```
[
  { "hobbies": ["reading", "hiking"], "city": "New York" },
  { "hobbies": ["cycling", "painting"], "city": "Los Angeles" },
  { "hobbies": ["dancing", "cooking"], "city": "Chicago" }
]
```

In conclusion, the MongoDB aggregation framework is a powerful tool for data manipulation and analysis. The aggregation stages offer a flexible and efficient approach to *transforming, filtering,* and *deriving* insights from your data, going well beyond simple CRUD operations. With the knowledge of these aggregation stages, you are now equipped to tackle a wide array of tasks—from complex data transformations to generating intricate analytics reports. Furthermore, the ability to chain multiple stages together offers endless possibilities, which enables you to craft sophisticated queries tailored to your specific needs. Embracing these capabilities not only optimizes database operations but also empowers you to derive greater value from your data.

This section outlines a number of MongoDB aggregation stages, but for a deeper dive into this topic, see the book, *Practical MongoDB Aggregations* by Paul Done, published by Packt Publishing Ltd.

Query Techniques

In this section, you will explore advanced querying techniques for database management. Proper querying is essential for efficient data retrieval and analysis. This section will provide detailed methods and best practices to ensure precision and efficiency in queries.

Logical and comparison operators

In *MongoDB Query Language*, logical and comparison operators are fundamental constructs that allow users to filter and select data based on specific conditions. They provide a means to perform tests on data and determine which documents match the given criteria:

- $or: Use this operator to perform a logical OR operation and return documents that match any of the conditions specified in its array.

  Example: Find documents where the age is either 18 or 25.

Input

```
[
    { "_id": 1, "name": "Alice", "age": 18 },
    { "_id": 2, "name": "Bob", "age": 25 },
    { "_id": 3, "name": "Charlie", "age": 20 },
    { "_id": 4, "name": "David", "age": 25 },
    { "_id": 5, "name": "Eve", "age": 19 }
]
```

Query

```
// Finds documents where the age is either 18 or 25.
db.users.find({ $or: [{ age: 18 }, { age: 25 }] })
```

Output

```
[
    { "_id": 1, "name": "Alice", "age": 18 },
    { "_id": 2, "name": "Bob", "age": 25 },
    { "_id": 4, "name": "David", "age": 25 }
]
```

- $and: Use this operator to perform a logical AND operation. It's often used explicitly for clarity because if conditions are specified without an operator, MongoDB assumes an AND operation.

Example: Find documents where the age is 22 and the name is Elie.

Input

```
[
    { "_id": 1, "name": "Alice", "age": 22 },
    { "_id": 2, "name": "Elie", "age": 22 },
    { "_id": 3, "name": "Charlie", "age": 22 },
    { "_id": 4, "name": "David", "age": 25 },
    { "_id": 5, "name": "Elie", "age": 23 }
]
```

Implicit $and operation

```
// Finds documents where the age is 22 and the name is Elie.
db.users.find({ age: 22, name: "Elie" })
```

Output

```
[{ "_id": 2, "name": "Elie", "age": 22 }]
```

Explicit $and operation

```
db.users.find({ $and: [ { age: 22 }, { name: "Alice" } ] })
```

Output

```
[{ "_id": 2, "name": "Alice", "age": 22 }]
```

- $not: Use this operator to negate the effect of the condition, which returns documents that don't match the specified condition.

  Example: Return documents where the age is not 18.

  Input

  ```
  [
      { "_id": 1, "name": "Alice", "age": 18 },
      { "_id": 2, "name": "Bob", "age": 25 },
      { "_id": 3, "name": "Charlie", "age": 22 },
      { "_id": 4, "name": "David", "age": 18 },
      { "_id": 5, "name": "Eve", "age": 23 }
  ]
  ```

  Query

  ```
  // Returns documents where the age is not 18.
  db.users.find({ age: { $not: { $eq: 18 } } })
  ```

  Output

  ```
  [
      { "_id": 2, "name": "Bob", "age": 25 },
      { "_id": 3, "name": "Charlie", "age": 22 },
      { "_id": 5, "name": "Eve", "age": 23 }
  ]
  ```

- $nor: Use this operator to match documents that fail to meet all the provided conditions.

  Example: Return documents where the age isn't 22 and the name isn't Elie.

  Input

  ```
  [
      { "_id": 1, "name": "Alice", "age": 22 },
      { "_id": 2, "name": "Elie", "age": 23 },
      { "_id": 3, "name": "Charlie", "age": 22 },
      { "_id": 4, "name": "David", "age": 24 },
      { "_id": 5, "name": "Eve", "age": 25 }
  ]
  ```

  Query

  ```
  // Returns documents where the age isn't 22 and the name isn't Elie.
  db.users.find({ $nor: [ { age: 22 }, { name: "Elie" } ] })
  ```

  Output

  ```
  [
      { "_id": 4, "name": "David", "age": 24 },
      { "_id": 5, "name": "Eve", "age": 25 }
  ]
  ```

- $in and $nin: Use these operators to match any or none of the values specified in an array.

Example: Using $in to match only those people with a specific age, and $nin to match only those without.

Input

```
[
    { "_id": 1, "name": "Alice", "age": 18 },
    { "_id": 2, "name": "Bob", "age": 20 },
    { "_id": 3, "name": "Charlie", "age": 22 },
    { "_id": 4, "name": "David", "age": 23 },
    { "_id": 5, "name": "Eve", "age": 25 }
]
```

$in operator

```
db.users.find({ age: { $in: [18, 20, 22] } }) // age is 18, 20, or 22
```

Output

```
[
    {
        "_id": 1,
        "name": "Alice",
        "age": 18
    },
    {
        "_id": 2,
        "name": "Bob",
        "age": 20
    },
    {
        "_id": 3,
        "name": "Charlie",
        "age": 22
    }
]
```

$nin operator

```
db.users.find({ age: { $nin: [18, 20, 22] } })
```

Output

```
[
    {
        "_id": 4,
        "name": "David",
        "age": 23
    },
    {
        "_id": 5,
        "name": "Eve",
```

```
        "age": 25
    }
]
```

- $eq: Use this operator to match documents where the value of a field is equal to the specified value.

  Example: Using $eq to find airplanes with exactly 200 seats.

  Input

  ```
  [
      { "_id": 1, "model": "Boeing 737", "seats": 200 },
      { "_id": 2, "model": "Airbus A320", "seats": 180 },
      { "_id": 3, "model": "Boeing 747", "seats": 400 },
      { "_id": 4, "model": "Airbus A330", "seats": 200 },
      { "_id": 5, "model": "Boeing 777", "seats": 250 }
  ]
  ```

  Implicit $eq

  ```
  db.airplanes.find({ seats: 200 });
  ```

  Explicit $eq

  ```
  db.airplanes.find({ seats: { $eq: 200 } });
  ```

  Output

  ```
  [{ "_id": 1, "model": "Boeing 737", "seats": 200 }]
  ```

- $ne: Use this operator to match documents where the value of a field is not equal to the specified value.

  Example: Using $ne to retrieve all airplanes except those with the model Boeing 777.

  Input

  ```
  //retrieve all airplanes except the ones
  //that have a model named "Boeing 777".
  db.airplanes.find({ model: { $ne: "Boeing 777" } })
  ```

  Output

  ```
  [
      { "_id": 1, "model": "Boeing 737", "seats": 200 },
      { "_id": 2, "model": "Airbus A320", "seats": 180 },
      { "_id": 3, "model": "Boeing 747", "seats": 400 },
      { "_id": 4, "model": "Airbus A330", "seats": 200 },
      { "_id": 5, "model": "Boeing 777", "seats": 250 }
  ]
  ```

- $gt (**greater than**) and $lt (**less than**): Use the $gt operator to match documents where the value of a field is greater than the specified value. In contrast, the $lt operator is used to match documents where the value of a field is less than the given value.

- $gte (**greater than or equal to**) and $lte (**less than or equal to**): Use the $gte operator to match documents where the value of a field is greater than or equal to the specified value. On the other hand, the $lte operator matches documents where the value of a field is less than or equal to the given value.

Example: Using $gte and $lte together to retrieve airplanes with maxSpeed greater than 500 and lower than 700.

Input

```
[
   { "_id": 1, "model": "Boeing 737", "maxSpeed": 485 },
   { "_id": 2, "model": "Airbus A320", "maxSpeed": 530 },
   { "_id": 3, "model": "Boeing 747", "maxSpeed": 570 },
   { "_id": 4, "model": "Airbus A330", "maxSpeed": 520 },
   { "_id": 5, "model": "Boeing 777", "maxSpeed": 710 },
   { "_id": 6, "model": "Concorde", "maxSpeed": 1350 },
   { "_id": 7, "model": "Lockheed SR-71 Blackbird", "maxSpeed": 2200 }
]
```

Query

```
db.airplanes.find({
   maxSpeed: {
      $gt: 500,
      $lte: 700
   }
})
```

Output

```
[
   {
      "_id": 2,
      "model": "Airbus A320",
      "maxSpeed": 530
   },
   {
      "_id": 3,
      "model": "Boeing 747",
      "maxSpeed": 570
   },
   {
      "_id": 4,
      "model": "Airbus A330",
      "maxSpeed": 520
   }
]
```

Logical and comparison operators in MongoDB provide a robust framework for filtering and retrieving documents based on specific conditions. These operators allow you to craft precise queries, ensuring that the retrieved data is both relevant and meaningful. By mastering the use of these operators, you can optimize database interactions, reduce unnecessary data retrieval, and ensure that applications access only the data they need. As with any toolset, the key is to understand each operator's nuances and apply them judiciously, balancing precision with performance.

Array querying and manipulation

In MongoDB Query Language, array querying and manipulation allow the precise selection and modification of documents based on array content. Using operators such as $elemMatch and $all, and array update operators such as $push and $pull, you can efficiently interact with and modify array-based data structures within your documents. Let's look at these operators in more detail:

- $all: Use this operator to match arrays that contain all elements specified in the query.

  Example: Find documents where tags contain both nosql and mongodb.

  Input

  ```
  [
    {
      "_id": 1,
      "title": "Intro to NoSQL",
      "tags": ["database", "nosql"]
    },
    {
      "_id": 2,
      "title": "Mastering MongoDB",
      "tags": ["mongodb", "database", "nosql"]
    },
    {
      "_id": 3,
      "title": "SQL for Beginners",
      "tags": ["database", "sql"]
    },
    {
      "_id": 4,
      "title": "MongoDB & NoSQL Exploration",
      "tags": ["mongodb", "nosql", "advanced"]
    }
  ]
  ```

  Query

  ```
  db.books.find({ tags: { $all: ["nosql", "mongodb"] } })
  ```

Output

```
[
  {
    "_id": 2,
    "title": "Mastering MongoDB",
    "tags": ["mongodb", "database", "nosql"]
  },
  {
    "_id": 4,
    "title": "MongoDB & NoSQL Exploration",
    "tags": ["mongodb", "nosql", "advanced"]
  }
]
```

- $elemMatch: Use this operator to match documents where an array field meets several conditions.

  Example: Imagine a *league* collection where each document has an array of results, and each result is a subdocument with fields for each player and their score.

  Input

```
[
  {
    "_id": 1,
    "results": [
      { "player": "Alice", "score": 82 },
      { "player": "Bob", "score": 90 }
    ]
  },
  {
    "_id": 2,
    "results": [
      { "player": "Charlie", "score": 78 },
      { "player": "David", "score": 83 }
    ]
  },
  {
    "_id": 3,
    "results": [
      { "player": "Eve", "score": 85 },
      { "player": "Frank", "score": 88 }
    ]
  }
]
```

Query

```
db.league.find({
  results: {
    $elemMatch: {
      score: {
        $gte: 80,
        $lt: 85
      }
    }
  }
})
```

Output

```
[
  {
    "_id": 1,
    "results": [
      { "player": "Alice", "score": 82 },
      { "player": "Bob", "score": 90 }
    ]
  },
  {
    "_id": 2,
    "results": [
      { "player": "Charlie", "score": 78 },
      { "player": "David", "score": 83 }
    ]
  }
]
```

- $size: Use this operator to match arrays that have a specified number of elements.

  Example: Find documents where the tags array has exactly three elements.

  Input

```
[
  {
    "_id": 1,
    "title": "Intro to NoSQL",
    "tags": ["database", "nosql", "beginner"]
  },
  {
    "_id": 2,
    "title": "Mastering MongoDB",
    "tags": ["mongodb", "database", "nosql", "advanced"]
  },
```

```
{
  "_id": 3,
  "title": "SQL for Beginners",
  "tags": ["database", "sql"]
},
{
  "_id": 4,
  "title": "MongoDB & NoSQL Exploration",
  "tags": ["mongodb", "nosql", "intermediate"]
}
]
```

Query

```
db.books.find({ tags: { $size: 3 } })
```

Output

```
[
  {
    "_id": 1,
    "title": "Intro to NoSQL",
    "tags": ["database", "nosql", "beginner"]
  },
  {
    "_id": 4,
    "title": "MongoDB & NoSQL Exploration",
    "tags": ["mongodb", "nosql", "intermediate"]
  }
]
```

- $push: Use this operator to add an item to an array.

  Example: Using $push to add a new AirFly route to Tokyo to a list of routes:

  Input

```
[
  {
    "_id": 1,
    "name": "AirFly",
    "destinations": ["New York", "London", "Paris"]
  },
  {
    "_id": 2,
    "name": "SkyHigh",
    "destinations": ["Sydney", "Delhi", "CapeTown"]
  }
]
```

Query $push

```
db.airlines.updateOne(
  { name: "AirFly" },
  { $push: { destinations: "Tokyo" } }
)
```

Query find: Performing a find query to retrieve the latest updated data

```
db.airlines.find({})
```

Output

```
[
  {
    "_id": 1,
    "name": "AirFly",
    "destinations": ["New York", "London", "Paris"]
  },
  {
    "_id": 2,
    "name": "SkyHigh",
    "destinations": ["Sydney", "Delhi", "Cape Town"]
  }
]
```

- $pull: Use this operator to remove a specified value from an array.

   Example: Using $pull to remove Paris from the list of AirFly destinations:

```
db.airlines.updateOne(
  { name: "AirFly" },
  { $pull: { destinations: "Paris" } }
)
```

   Query find: Performing a find query to retrieve the latest updated data after the pull

```
db.airlines.find({})
```

   Output

```
[
  {
    "_id": 1,
    "name": "AirFly",
    "destinations": ["New York", "London", "Tokyo"]
  },
  {
    "_id": 2,
    "name": "SkyHigh",
    "destinations": ["Sydney", "Delhi", "Cape Town"]
  }
]
```

- $addToSet: Use this operator to add a value to an array but only if it does not already exist.

  Example: Check that Berlin does not exist in the destinations array, then add it:

  Input

  ```
  [
    {
      "_id": 1,
      "name": "AirFly",
      "destinations": ["New York", "London", "Paris"]
    },
    {
      "_id": 2,
      "name": "SkyHigh",
      "destinations": ["Sydney", "Delhi", "Cape Town"]
    }
  ]
  ```

  Query

  ```
  db.airlines.updateOne(
    { name: "AirFly" },
    { $addToSet: { destinations: "Berlin" } }
  );
  ```

  Query find: Performing a find query to retrieve the latest updated data after addToSet

  ```
  db.airlines.find({})
  ```

  Output

  ```
  [
    {
      "_id": 1,
      "name": "AirFly",
      "destinations": ["New York", "London", "Paris", "Berlin"]
    }, // "Berlin" added as it wasn't in the array before.

    {
      "_id": 2,
      "name": "SkyHigh",
      "destinations": ["Sydney", "Delhi", "Berlin"]
    } // Remains unchanged as "Berlin" was already in the array.
  ]
  ```

- $pop: Use this operator to remove the first or last item from an array. A value of -1 removes the first item, and a value of 1 removes the last item.

  Query

  ```
  db.airlines.updateOne({ name: "AirFly" }, { $pop: { destinations: 1 } })
  ```

Query find: Performing a `find` query to retrieve the latest updated data after the `$pop` operation

```
db.airlines.find({})
```

Output

```
[
    {
        "_id": 1,
        "name": "AirFly",
        "destinations": ["New York", "London"]
    }, // "Paris" removed from the end of the array.

    {
        "_id": 2,
        "name": "SkyHigh",
        "destinations": ["Sydney", "Delhi", "Berlin"]
    } // Remains unchanged.
]
```

Array querying and manipulation capabilities in MongoDB offer a robust solution for managing intricate data structures. The direct interaction with and modification of array elements enhances both data retrieval and update processes. As data increasingly becomes complex, mastering these array operations becomes crucial for you to maintain flexibility and performance in evolving application environments.

Array field projection techniques

In MongoDB Query Language, projection techniques dictate which elements are returned from an array field in the result set. Using operators such as `$`, `$elemMatch`, and `$slice`, you can tailor the queries to retrieve specific data, optimizing bandwidth, and processing time for more efficient database interactions. Let's look at them in more detail:

- `$`: In projections, the `$` operator is used to project only the first element from an array that matches the query conditions.

    Example: Using `$` to find the first review by `Bob`.

    Input

    ```
    {
        "_id": 1,
        "title": "Mastering MongoDB",
        "reviews": [
            {
                "reviewer": "Alice",
                "comment": "Great book!"
            },
            {
                "reviewer": "Bob",
                "comment": "Informative."
            },
    ```

```
      {
        "reviewer": "Charlie",
        "comment": "A must-read for database enthusiasts."
      }
    ]
  }
```

Query

```
db.books.find({ "reviews.reviewer": "Bob" }, { "reviews.$": 1 });
```

Output

```
{
  "_id": 1,
  "reviews": [{ "reviewer": "Bob", "comment": "Informative." }]
}
```

- $elemMatch: Use this operator to specify multiple criteria on the elements of an array such that at least one array element satisfies all specified conditions. It is particularly useful when dealing with arrays of subdocuments.

  Example: Consider a collection of students where each student has an array of test scores.

  Input

```
[
  { "_id": 1, "name": "John", "scores": [85, 88, 92] },
  { "_id": 2, "name": "Jane", "scores": [78, 88, 89] },
  { "_id": 3, "name": "Doe", "scores": [92, 90, 85, 88] }
]
```

  Query

```
db.students.find({ scores: { $elemMatch: { $gte: 85, $lte: 90 } } });
```

  Output

```
[
  { "_id": 1, "name": "John", "scores": [85] },
  { "_id": 2, "name": "Jane", "scores": [88] },
  { "_id": 3, "name": "Doe", "scores": [90] }
]
```

- $slice: Use this operator to limit the number of elements projected from an array.

  Example: Return only the last three scores.

  Input

```
[
  { "_id": 1, "team": "Tigers", "scores": [85, 88, 90, 92, 95] },
  { "_id": 2, "team": "Lions", "scores": [78, 80, 82, 84, 86] }
]
```

Query

```
// Returns only the last 3 scores.
db.league.find({}, { scores: { $slice: -3 } });
```

Output

```
[
    { "_id": 1, "team": "Tigers", "scores": [90, 92, 95] },
    { "_id": 2, "team": "Lions", "scores": [82, 84, 86] }
]
```

Projection techniques in MongoDB empower you to retrieve only the necessary data, which optimizes efficiency and performance. By selectively shaping the output, you can streamline data processing and enhance response times. Mastering these techniques ensures precise, tailored, and effective database interactions.

Indexes and query optimization

Indexes in MongoDB are specialized data structures that play a crucial role in enhancing query efficiency. Without these indexes, MongoDB would have to sift through every document in a collection for query results. An available index can drastically reduce the number of documents MongoDB examines.

Benefits of using indexes

The benefits of indexes include the following:

- **Performance boost**: Indexes significantly speed up data retrieval operations, reducing the need to scan every document in a collection.

- **Reduced load**: By accelerating search queries, indexes decrease the system's workload, leading to better resource utilization.

- **Sort efficiency**: Indexes support efficient sorting operations, allowing results to be ordered without extra computational effort.

- **Support for complex queries**: Advanced query operations, such as geospatial searches or text-based searches, are made possible and efficient through specialized indexes.

- **Selective load**: Indexes can limit the data loaded into memory, allowing MongoDB to handle large datasets more efficiently.

Effectively leveraging indexes in MongoDB requires strategic considerations. While they optimize query performance, they also consume additional storage. A thoughtful selection of which fields to index can balance performance gains with space constraints.

Although indexes quicken reads, they introduce some latency to write operations due to necessary index updates. By being aware of these aspects of indexing and aligning them with your system's requirements, you can harness indexes' full potential while mitigating potential challenges.

Types of index

MongoDB provides a diverse range of index types, each tailored to optimize specific query patterns. By selecting the right index, you can significantly boost query performance. Here, you can explore the key index types, their primary use cases, and examples of their implementation:

Single field index

- **Description**: Creates an index on a single field of a document
- **Use case**: Useful for queries that search based on a single field
- **Example**: Optimize searches by username:

```
db.users.createIndex({ "username": 1 })
```

Compound index

- **Description**: Indexes on multiple fields within a document
- **Use case**: Ideal for queries that sort or search on multiple fields. This index orders firstname in ascending order and lastname in descending order.
- **Example**:

```
db.users.createIndex({ "firstname": 1, "lastname": -1 })
```

Multikey index

- **Description**: Creates indexes on array fields, indexing each element of the array
- **Use case**: Useful when querying array content, such as tags or categories
- **Example**:

```
db.collection.createIndex({ "tags": 1 })
```

Compound multikey index

- **Description**: Indexes several fields in documents, with at least one being an array. MongoDB indexes each array element, but with the limitation that only one array field can be indexed in a compound multikey index.
- **Use case**: Ideal for queries sorting or filtering on multiple fields, where at least one field might be an array. They're especially valuable for data with intricate relationships or multi-dimensional attributes.
- **Example**: Assume a collection of documents where tags is an array and rating is a numeric value, and you want to create a compound multikey index:

```
db.collection.createIndex({ "tags": 1, "rating": -1 })
```

Text index

- **Description**: Allows for full-text search across string content and arrays of string content. Text indexes can include any field whose value is a string or an array of string elements.

- **Use case**: Suited for searching textual content across multiple fields and assigning weights to fields for relevance.

- **Example**: Creating a `text` index on the `description` field:

```
db.post.createIndex({ "description": "text" })
```

Wildcard index

- **Description**: Indexes fields regardless of their location in a document. It's particularly useful when dealing with schema-less or evolving data models.

- **Use case**: Ideal for indexing fields in embedded documents without knowing the keys or for indexing every field in a document.

- **Example**: Index all fields from a document:

```
db.users.createIndex({ "$**": 1 })
```

Time-to-live (TTL) index

- **Description**: Enables automatic deletion of documents after a specified duration

- **Use Case**: Perfect for data such as logs or sessions that need expiration

- **Example**: Auto-remove each log entry 1 hour after it was made:

```
db.logs.createIndex({ "createdAt": 1 }, { expireAfterSeconds: 3600 })
```

Unique index

- **Description**: Enforces the uniqueness of the indexed field's value

- **Use case**: When you need to ensure fields such as `username` or `email` are unique

- **Example**: Ensure that the username is unique whenever someone new signs up:

```
db.users.createIndex({ "username": 1 }, { unique: true })
```

Partial index

- **Description**: Only indexes documents that satisfy a specified filter condition

- **Use Case**: For situations where only a subset of documents need to be indexed, such as active user accounts

- **Example**: Index only those 18 or older in the collection:

```
db.users.createIndex(
  { age: 1 },
  {
    partialFilterExpression: {
      age: {
        $gte: 18
      }
    }
  }
)
```

In conclusion, indexes are essential for improving performance in MongoDB. Choosing and managing the right types of indexes helps speed up database queries and improves the efficiency of your application. It's important to always consider the best indexing strategy for your data and query needs.

Geospatial features in MongoDB

Geospatial features in MongoDB are designed to support the creation of location-aware applications and facilitate location-based queries, catering to a diverse range of users. Through its specialized indexes and operators, MongoDB can efficiently manage geographical data, which makes it suitable for a wide range of applications, such as maps and location searching.

Legacy coordinate pairs are the traditional way of representing locations using two-element arrays with the longitude first and then the latitude. For example, [-73.97, 40.77] represents a point in New York City. When indexing such data, you can use the 2d index type. Following is an example of creating index for legacy coordinate pairs:

```
db.collection.createIndex({ loc: "2d" })
```

GeoJSON objects

GeoJSON objects are of three types:

- `Point`: Represents a single point in space with longitude and latitude coordinates
- `LineString`: A series of two or more points that form a line
- `Polygon`: A linear ring of points that forms a closed loop, defining an area

Geospatial indexes

Geospatial indexes are specialized data structures that optimize spatial queries in databases, enabling faster retrieval of location-based information.

- **2d index**: These indexes are designed to support queries on data represented as points on a two-dimensional plane. They are primarily used for legacy coordinate pairs. When creating a 2d index, you specify 2d as the index type. Here's an example:

```
db.collection.createIndex({ loc: "2d" })
```

- **2dsphere index**: These are specialized indexes in MongoDB designed for geospatial queries on a spherical surface, such as Earth. They allow operations such as identifying points within a certain area, calculating proximity to a designated point, and fetching exact coordinate matches. The indexed fields can be GeoJSON objects or legacy coordinate pairs. In case of legacy pairs, the 2dsphere index automatically converts them into GeoJSON points. Here's an example:

```
db.collection.createIndex({ loc: "2dsphere" })
```

Geospatial operators

Geospatial operators are specialized query tools that enhance spatial analysis in geospatial databases, enabling location-based data retrieval.

- $near: Returns objects sorted by proximity to a specific point, from the nearest to farthest

- $nearSphere: Returns geospatial objects in proximity to a point on a sphere

- $geoWithin: Finds documents with geometries that lie entirely within a specified shape

- $geoIntersects: Returns documents with geometries that intersect the shape defined in the query

- $maxDistance: Limits the results of a geospatial query that uses $near or $nearSphere. This operator specifies the maximum distance from a point, beyond which documents will not be included in the query results. It's important to note that the value specified for $maxDistance must be a non-negative number.

Here's an example for querying nearby places using $maxDistance:

```
//Creating a 2dsphere index:
db.places.createIndex({ location: "2dsphere" });
//Querying for nearby places (within 500 meters of a point):
db.places.find({
  location: {
    $near: {
      $geometry: { type: "Point", coordinates: [-73.9667, 40.78] },
      $maxDistance: 500
    }
  }
})
```

Here's another example for querying documents within a polygon shape:

```
//Querying for documents within a specified polygon:
db.places.find({
  location: {
    $geoWithin: {
      $geometry: {
        type: "Polygon",
        coordinates: [
          [
            [0, 0],
            [3, 6],
            [6, 1],
            [0, 0]
          ]
        ]
      }
    }
  }
})
```

Geospatial capabilities in MongoDB are pivotal for modern applications dealing with location data. From querying proximity to defining areas of interest on a spherical surface, these specialized indexes and features ensure efficient and precise spatial operations. As applications become more location-aware and data-driven, harnessing these geospatial tools becomes increasingly essential for delivering valuable insights and user experience.

Summary

In this chapter, you've taken a deep dive into many advanced features of MongoDB. You've explored the aggregation framework, honed your skills in querying, and learned the importance of indexing. With these tools in hand, you're better prepared to tackle complex database tasks and make the most of MongoDB. As you continue, apply what you've learned and keep building on this foundation.

In the next chapter, you will take an in-depth look at the aggregation framework, and explore the numerous aggregation stages and expression operators suitable for the most diverse problems.

8

Aggregation

Aggregations in MongoDB are operations consisting of several steps that process multiple documents and return computed results. Aggregations are built around the concept of pipelines, through which data flows are gradually processed. In a pipeline, the output from the current processing unit is fed as input to the next unit (similar to chaining commands in Linux or a data-wrangling script in Python). In a pipeline, at each stage, a set of documents is fed to the processing unit's input and the output is fed to the following unit. This process ultimately provides solutions to potentially complex problems by breaking them down into smaller and simpler stages.

In this chapter, you will dive deeper into some of the more interesting and useful features of the MongoDB aggregation framework.

This chapter will cover the following topics:

- The purpose of the MongoDB aggregation framework
- Principles of aggregation and aggregation stages
- Basic aggregation operators and expressions
- Role of bitwise operators in aggregation
- Advanced aggregation capabilities and best practices

Technical requirements

To perform the exercises covered in this chapter, you will need the following:

- A computer running macOS, Windows, or Linux
- MongoDB Compass – the GUI MongoDB client
- A MongoDB Atlas account

Connect to your Atlas account and enable the sample datasets that ship with Atlas. For instructions on connecting to your MongoDB database, please refer to *Chapter 4, Connecting to MongoDB*.

If you prefer the GUI tool, make sure to also download MongoDB Compass from the MongoDB website: `https://www.mongodb.com/try/download/compass`.

Now that you have your system set up, you are ready to begin exploring the MongoDB aggregation framework.

MongoDB aggregation framework

The MongoDB aggregation framework allows you to fine tune and process complex data on the server, drastically reducing the amount of data that is transferred to the application for further processing. The aggregation framework is an incredibly powerful data processing workhorse that enables you to:

- Handle custom data presentations through views
- Join data from different collections
- Perform data science tasks, such as data wrangling and analysis
- Handle big data
- Run real-time analytics, monitor data, and create dashboards

MongoDB is centered around the concept that data should be easily retrievable and accessible to fit your application. As shown in *Chapter 7, Advanced Querying in MongoDB*, the querying framework—with its tunable parameters—is powerful. However, it may not always provide the precise data in the required shape or format. It may also lack the accompanying descriptive statistics that are frequently necessary. Moreover, data often needs to be processed and transformed according to some business logic, before being delivered to the application. This is where the aggregation framework truly excels.

Recent MongoDB presentations[1] emphasize that the dividing line between the use cases for *find* and *aggregate* is becoming a blur. With over 150 operators and expressions, the ecosystem offers a vast range of possibilities, enabling incredibly complex and useful data operations through relatively simple steps.

---

1   Kamsky, Asya. "Recent Additions to Query and Aggregation You May Have Missed." YouTube, uploaded by MongoDB, December 20, 2022, `https://www.youtube.com/watch?v=FprmF6nmkWY`

To be clear about the terminology, *aggregation* refers to an analysis or summary of the data, a representation of existing data, while a *pipeline* is used to define a complete (simple or complex) aggregation consisting of *aggregation stages*.

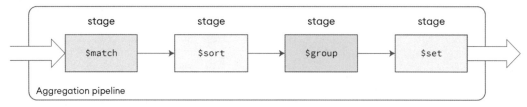

Figure 8.1: The aggregation pipeline structure, including stages

Modularity and composability

Aggregation pipelines are composed of stages or steps that can be viewed as individual data processing units, and can be parameterized and tuned according to your needs. The parameters for different stages, such as choosing a specific car brand from a collection or a user's ID, are sent through a REST or GraphQL API. This API returns a dataset that's already in the desired format or closely resembles the required data. This helps reduce the need for extensive server-side data processing.

The simplest possible stages in a pipeline are easily relatable to the relational database world. $match is used for selecting data according to a specific criteria, $project is used for selecting a subset of a collection's document properties or fabricating new ones, and $sort, $skip, and $limit are pretty self-explanatory.

If you're transitioning from the relational database world, *Table 8.1* illustrates the correlation between key SQL operations and their MongoDB counterparts. For a comprehensive list, visit https://www. mongodb.com/docs/v7.0/reference/sql-comparison/.

SQL terms, functions, and concepts	MongoDB aggregation operators
WHERE	$match
GROUP BY	$group
HAVING	$match
SELECT	$project
LIMIT	$limit
OFFSET	$skip
ORDER BY	$sort
SUM()	$sum
COUNT()	$sum and $sortByCount

SQL terms, functions, and concepts	MongoDB aggregation operators
`JOIN`	`$lookup`
`SELECT INTO NEW_TABLE`	`$out`
`MERGE INTO TABLE`	`$merge` (Available starting in MongoDB 4.2)
`UNION ALL`	`$unionWith` (Available starting in MongoDB 4.4)

Table 8.1: Corresponding SQL and MongoDB terminology and concepts

It is important to adopt an *aggregation mindset* as early as possible. MongoDB is built for unstructured data, and trying to build queries centered around relational database concepts can prove less effective. The data can be queried, filtered, joined, and transformed. However, before using the framework, it is essential, useful, and often mandatory to familiarize yourself with the most important tools at your disposal.

With over 150 operators and expressions, the MongoDB ecosystem offers a vast range of possibilities, enabling you to perform incredibly complex and useful data operations through relatively simple steps. All MongoDB language-specific drivers (JavaScript, Python, etc.) fully support the aggregation framework, making it convenient for you to write aggregations in any language. In this section, JavaScript is used because the MongoDB Shell employs a JavaScript interpreter. The examples are concise and illustrative, and the aggregation always consists of an array of objects, making **JSON** (**JavaScript Object Notation**) the natural choice.

From a strictly formal standpoint, the aggregation framework is a *Turing-complete*, proper **domain-specific language** (DSL), implying its capability to tackle any business problem. This term is used to distinguish between *powerful* and *complete* data manipulation systems (such as full-fledged programming languages) and less powerful sets of instructions. DSLs are computer languages specialized to a particular application domain. In case of the MongoDB aggregation framework, it offers the ability to use a real aggregation language and send specifications for a series of tasks—data processing instructions—to the database engine for execution. The framework itself consists of two parts:

- The *aggregation framework API*, which enables you to define a task through a pipeline and send it to the database through an appropriate MongoDB driver.

- The *aggregation runtime*, which acts as the receiver of the pipeline and executes it, providing the desired results.

If you're experienced in data processing, you may have used Python's pandas and NumPy libraries in a Jupyter Notebook. And if you come from a more traditional statistical background with a language such as R, the MongoDB aggregation framework and its functional nature will look familiar, and you will feel right at home. In the following section, you will examine the basic unit of a pipeline—*stages*—and how they can be used as building blocks for complex data manipulation.

Stages

The main unit of an aggregation pipeline is the *aggregation stage*—a stage that performs an operation on the input, without side effects, and sends it to the next stage. These processed groups of documents flow through the pipeline in a way that is very similar to a Linux pipeline of commands. Each stage is formatted to expect certain types of documents and perform some operations, before passing the result to the next stage, or ultimately, to a collection. These stages are parameterized and this process of defining the parameters and the aggregation objects is what defines a stage, and ultimately, a pipeline.

A complete, up-to-date list of all MongoDB aggregation stages is available on the MongoDB documentation website: `https://www.mongodb.com/docs/manual/reference/operator/aggregation-pipeline/`.

Before exploring the syntax and the form of an aggregation stage, let's look at some of the aggregation expressions. Stages define *what* you want to do with your dataset, while the expressions define *how* to do it.

Aggregation expressions

Expressions can be grouped based on their scope, covering practically every use case you might encounter. According to Asya Kamsky, Principal Engineer at MongoDB, MongoDB went from having 7 stages and 3 dozen expressions to over 30 stages and over 150 expressions.[2] That's a lot of tools, even for the best toolboxes.

Finally, before diving into the expression categories, it is useful to know that certain aggregation stages, such as `$limit`, `$skip`, `$sort`, `$count`, `$lookup`, and `$out` cannot use expressions. However, `$match` is a different case, since it is essentially a part of the MongoDB Query Language, and there is the possibility of embedding the `$expr` expression. But let's not delve into that as the regular MongoDB Query Language syntax is sufficient for 99% of the use cases that you might run into.

This chapter hasn't mentioned several other significant groups of expression operators—trigonometric expressions, data size expressions, and many others—as it's best to start with groups, and later, when the need arises, check the latest documentation and dive into more specialized expressions.

Basic aggregation operators

At this point, you should be familiar with the basic MongoDB stages used for querying (`$match`, `$limit`, `$search`, `$sample`, `$skip`, `$sort`, etc.), mutating (`$fill`, `$project`, `$set`, `$unset`, and others), summarizing (`$group`, `$count`, etc.), joining, and performing input/output operations on documents.

For a quick refresher, the MongoDB documentation provides an excellent starting point: `https://www.mongodb.com/docs/v7.0/reference/operator/aggregation/`.

---

2   Kamsky, Asya. Foreword to *Practical MongoDB Aggregations*, by Paul Done, vii. Birmingham, UK: Packt Publishing Ltd., 2023. `https://www.packtpub.com/product/practical-mongodb-aggregations/9781835080641`

Bitwise operators in aggregation

One of the new features in MongoDB 7.0 is the introduction of *bitwise operators* in aggregations. Bitwise operators are especially useful in cases where documents have a lot of bit-mask values (such as status, permission settings, or general settings).

There are four operators that allow developers to create aggregations based on bit-mask values:

- $bitAnd: Returns the result of a bitwise and operation on an array of integers or long values
- $bitOr: Returns the result of a bitwise or operation on an array of integers and long values
- $bitXor: Returns the result of a bitwise xor (exclusive or) operation on an array of integers and long values
- $bitNot: Returns the result of a bitwise not operation on a single integer or long value

If operands include both integers and long values in an aggregation, MongoDB will sign-extend the calculated integer result and output a long value. On the other hand, if an argument in the aggregation array has a different data type, such as a string, double, or decimal, MongoDB will return an error.

You can find an excellent use case given by *Cris Staufer*, Director of Product Management at MongoDB, in this video: https://www.youtube.com/watch?v=kFLjFRHA9Pg.

Suppose you have some UNIX-type user permissions that are encoded with each user as a permissions field. If you are familiar with the chmod Linux command, the permissions are denoted by the **read (r)**, **write (w)**, and **execute (k)** sequence, corresponding to the numbers 4 (100 binary), 2 (10 binary), and 1 (1 binary). If you wish to check whether a user has write permissions with a MongoDB aggregation, and set a new binary variable to hasWritePermissions, you can accomplish this functionality very quickly by using the bitwise operator $bitAnd:

```
db.user.aggregate([{
    $set: {
        hasWritePermissionsL {
            $eq: [{
                $bitAnd: ["$permissions", 2]
            }, 2]
        }
    }
}])
```

The preceding code checks the $bitAnd operation on the value of the *permissions* field and the value 2 (010 in binary) and sets hasWritePermissions accordingly.

Array expression operators

Mastering array expressions demands dedication, as these expressions constitute the core of the aggregation framework. They empower you to manipulate data containing embedded arrays of objects or documents in various ways, facilitating the desired data structure and format. In this section, you'll work with a couple of examples, since it is easier to demonstrate some key concepts with just a handful of appropriately formatted data.

The "power" array operators: $map and $reduce

Sometimes, when transforming data from an array field, a single high-level operator like $avg or $filter isn't enough to provide the desired functionality. In such cases, the MongoDB aggregation framework provides two tools known from majority of programming languages—the $map and $reduce array operators. These operators are not to be confused with the—now obsolete—Map-Reduce API.

$map allows you to perform logic against each element in an array and returns a processed array. Similarly, $reduce processes each element of an array field, and returns a single value, making it an excellent choice for summary results.

If you're familiar with JavaScript ES6, the map method used on JavaScript arrays resembles the following:

```
const array1 = [1, 2, 3, 5]
const map1 = array1.map(x => x ** 3)
// output
[1, 8, 27, 125]
```

Keeping this concept in mind is particularly useful when working with arrays in the aggregation framework, as well as understanding the concept of the conditional ternary operator:

```
function getPrice(isMember) {
    return isMember ? '$15.00' : '$30.00';
}
```

In the preceding function, the resulting price is computed by analyzing the boolean variable, isMember. If it evaluates to true, the first value after the question mark is returned ($15); if not, the value after the colon (:) is returned ($30).

The reduce() method in ES6 is illustrated in the following example. The reduce() method of array instances allows you to execute a reducer callback function on each element of the array, in order, passing in the return value from the calculation on the preceding element. You can use the reducer to multiply the items in an array while providing an initial value:

```
const someArray = [2, 3, 5]; const initialValue = 1;
const product = someArray.reduce(
(accumulator, currentValue) => accumulator * currentValue, initialValue
  );
console.log(product);
// expected output: 30
```

Among the useful sample datasets that ship with an Atlas account, you will find the sample_mflix database. This database contains thousands of documents on movies and related data, such as the cast, director, year of production, ratings, and more. You can connect to it once you've enabled the sample datasets in Atlas.

Now, create a new field—a simple, single string that will be used for populating a cast field without the need to iterate through the members in a hypothetical frontend application.

You will perform some introductory stages, filter by genre and rating, sort in descending order, and then use the powerful $reduce expression operator, as shown:

```
db.getCollection('movies').aggregate(
    [
        {
            $match: {
                'imdb.rating': { $gt: 8.5 },
                genres: 'Comedy'
            }
        },
        {
            $sort: {
                'imdb.rating': -1
            }
        },
        {
            $set: {
                castString: {
                    $reduce: {
                        input: '$cast', initialValue: 'Cast:', in:
                            {
                                $concat: ['$$value', '$$this', ';']
                            }
                    }
                }
            }
        },
        { $limit: 5 }
    ],
);
```

The preceding example will give you a new field called castString. This string will be composed of the initial value (the Cast: part), and every element of the corresponding cast array in the movie document:

```
[
    {
        _id: ObjectId("573a13f0f29313caabdd9d6e"),
        title: 'Over the Garden Wall',
        year: 2014,
        imdb: {
            rating: 9.2
        },
        castString: 'Cast:Elijah Wood;Collin Dean;Melanie Lynskey;'
    },
]
```

The $map expression allows you to define and apply some operations on each element in an array and return the resulting array. It is important to remember that the current item that is being iterated over can be accessed with the $$this keyword, similar to the $reduce example.

One of the most frequent uses for array processing is adding more data to each existing object in an array. For this, you will use a dataset provided by Atlas: the sample_supplies database and its sales collection.

Either select the database and the collection in Compass, or type the following command into your MongoDB Shell:

```
use sample_supplies
```

After executing the preceding command, take a moment and examine the data in the database. You might be especially interested in the sales collection, which contains the sales data.

The documents in the sales collection are fairly typical for an inventory sales-tracking application: there is a saleDate datetime field (when the purchase occurred), the store location, data about the customer in an object, the purchase method, and whether a coupon was used. What you would be really interested in is the array called items. This array contains objects that are included in the order: the name of the product, some tags, a price, and a quantity.

An example document from the collection looks like this:

```
{
  "_id": {
    "$oid": "5bd761dcae323e45a93ccfe8"
  },
  "saleDate": {
    "$date": "2015-03-23T21:06:49.506Z"
  },
  "items": [
    {
      "name": "printer paper",
      "tags": [
        "office",
        "stationary"
      ],
      "price": {
        "$numberDecimal": "40.01"
      },
      "quantity": 2
    },
    {
      "name": "notepad",
      "tags": [
        "office",
        "writing",
```

```
          "school"
        ],
        "price": {
          "$numberDecimal": "35.29"
        },
        "quantity": 2
      },
  …
    ],
    "storeLocation": "Denver",
    "customer": {
      "gender": "M",
      "age": 42,
      "email": "cauho@witwuta.sv",
      "satisfaction": 4
    },
    "couponUsed": true,
    "purchaseMethod": "Online"
}
```

You can enhance these objects, which represent individual sales, by calculating the total cost for each item. This involves multiplying the price and quantity for each item, and adding this value to every object within the array. Later, you must sum all these amounts in order to get a total for the money.

```
db.getCollection('sales').aggregate(
    [
        {
        $set: {
            items: {
                $map: {
                    input: '$items',
                    as: 'item',
                    in: {
                        $mergeObjects: [
                            '$$item',
                            {
                                cost: {
                                    $multiply: [
                                        '$$item.price',
                                        '$$item.quantity'
                                    ]
                                }
                            }
                        ]
                    }
                }
            }
        }
```

```
            }
        }
    },
    {
        $set: {
            totalAmount: {
                $sum: '$items.cost'
            }
        }
    }
    ]
)
```

There is a lot going on here, but if you recall the mapping method and try to break down part of the code, things become much clearer. Firstly, this is a set stage—you're setting the items field to something new—although, you're just adding a bit to each object in the items array.

Map, like $reduce, has its own syntax: it takes an input—in your case, it is the $items document field—and an alias for the current item being iterated. Instead of performing some operations on a primitive, such as a string or a number, $mergeObjects is used, which can be thought as a counterpart of the ES6 spread operator (the three dots). $mergeObjects takes an item (represented by $$item, i.e., the entire object) and adds a new field (named cost) by applying the multiplication expression operator (arithmetic) to the quantity and unit price fields.

In the final stage of this pipeline, it adds a new field to each document with the sum of all the costs to get the total value.

On the other hand, pipeline stages involving arrays are simpler, where you may need to find the maximum, minimum, and average value of a stock, along with the opening and closing prices ($max, $min, $avg, $first, and $last, respectively).

Other types of aggregations

There are many aggregation operator tools that can be used for specific tasks, and listing them all would be impractical. In this section, you will go through a couple of examples that illustrate the possibilities, simplicity, and elegance of aggregation operator tools.

> **Note**
>
> You can read more about aggregation operator tools in this documentation: https://www.mongodb.com/docs/manual/reference/operator/aggregation/

One interesting aggregation type that you might encounter on various e-commerce websites or even movie applications is faceting, or *faceted classification*. The $facet stage allows the creation of multi-faceted aggregations that characterize data across multiple dimensions—facets—within the same aggregation stage.

For example, working with your movie database, you need to quickly group films into categories such as above average, average, and below average based on metrics such as IMDb rating and Rotten Tomatoes critics rating.

The aggregation framework allows you to leverage the *facet aggregation stage operator* and automatically create a spread of values across the desired metric.

In order to simplify things, you will limit your analysis to the year 1995, and to movies that are categorized as Drama. The actual facet stage is highlighted (just the IMDb part, the other one is analogous):

```
db.getCollection('movies').aggregate(
    [{
            $match: {
                year: 1995,
                genres: 'Drama'
            }
        },
        {
            $facet: {
                by_imdb: [{
                        $bucketAuto: {
                            groupBy: '$imdb.rating',
                            buckets: 3,
                            output: {
                                count: {
                                    $sum: 1
                                },
                                movies: {
                                    $push: '$title'
                                }
                            }
                        }
                    },
                    {
                        $set: {
                            imdb_range: '$_id'
                        }
                    },
                    {
                        $unset: ['_id']
                    }
                ],
                by_tomato: [{
                        $bucketAuto: {
                            groupBy: '$tomatoes.critic.rating',
                            buckets: 3,
                            output: {
```

```
                                count: {
                                    $sum: 1
                                },
                                movies: {
                                    $push: '$title'
                                }
                            }
                        }
                    },
                    {
                        $set: {
                            rating_range: '$_id'
                        }
                    },
                    {
                        $unset: ['_id']
                    }
                ]
            }
        }
    ],
);
```

The facet stage returns only one document, with the keys indicating the metric used for faceting. In this case, you can call it by _imdb and use the $bucketAuto expression to automatically create the buckets. The $bucketAuto operator categorizes the incoming document into a specified number of groups or buckets. The bucket boundaries are determined automatically in a way that ensures an even distribution of documents into the specified number of buckets.

The grouping is performed by $imdb.rating as the metric, and you can choose to have three buckets. Finally, the output is set to be the number of movies in each bucket, together with the movie titles in an array. In a realistic web application, you can output the _id of the movie to build some clickable URLs.

The exact same procedure is repeated for the Rotten Tomatoes critic ratings and can potentially be applied to other metrics. Let's see (part of) the output:

```
[{
    by_imdb: [{
            count: 76,
            movies: [
                'Gordy',
                'I Shot a Man in Vegas',// …more movies here
            imdb_range: {
                    min: 3.9,
                    max: 6.6
                }
            },
```

Here, you see the lowest IMDb bucket, with movies rated from 3.9 to 6.6. There are 76 of them and an array of titles. This is repeated for every bucket (three in both cases) for two metrics, so you end up with six groups. Crafting this query without the powerful facet expression operator would be very difficult.

Here are some more specific aggregation tools that can save you time and help you design simpler and more powerful aggregations:

- `$lookup`: Used to perform a left outer join to a collection that must reside in the same database. Starting from MongoDB 5.1, these collections can be sharded.

- `$graphLookup`: Allows you to perform a recursive search on a collection, while specifying the desired depth and optional query filters.

- `$geoNear`: This is a real gem among the aggregation operators when it comes to finding the nearest gas station or a fancy restaurant. It returns documents in order of nearest to farthest from a point specified in the query.

Among the numerous time-series expressions that allow for analyzing time-varying data, the `$fill` and `$densify` expression operators are very interesting and powerful. Often, a need may arise to transform time-series data into a format that is better suited for analysis, be it a *Fourier* analysis or some fancy machine learning algorithm. The data being read is often inherently irregular, with missing values or irregular intervals. Enter the `$densify` operator, which allows you to essentially create new, initially missing documents between existing data points in a regularly spaced manner.

For example, consider a sensor measuring an engine's temperature at 60 second intervals. There might be missing or displaced data points at irregular intervals, like 65, 49, and 100 seconds. In such a scenario, the `$densify` expression can be used to fill these gaps by generating placeholder documents. These documents include the desired timestamps and typically contain empty or default values for the other fields.

The `$fill` expression operator is used to fill in the missing data by using a method you find most suitable for the specific problem. The `$fill` stage makes use of a sortable field, as it needs to interpolate the missing values. In most cases, a linear interpolation will do (if you have a value of 10 and the next value is 20, the middle point will probably be around 15). However, sometimes it is enough to simply carry over the last reading, for example, in some data acquisition or digital control systems.

Finally, it is important to underline two expression operators—`$out` and `$merge`—that appear towards the end, as the last stage of an aggregation pipeline, and instead of transferring their content to the next stage, they write the resulting document set to a collection.

There are some differences between the two that are worth noting:

	$out	$merge
Outputs to a different database	Prior to MongoDB 4.4: No After MongoDB 4.4: Yes	Yes, if available
Creates a new collection if the specified collection doesn't exist	Yes	Yes
Outputs to a sharded collection	No	Yes

Table 8.2: Difference between $out and $merge

All of your previously written pipelines could be easily written to a new collection just by adding $merge (ourPipeline) as the last stage.

Best practices

Writing and specifying good aggregations takes practice, and throughout this chapter, you have focused on some useful principles. The aggregation pipeline is a sequential set of stages, and it encourages high composability and modularity. Here are some best practices that you can keep in mind when using MongoDB aggregations:

Code modularity

No matter how complex an aggregation gets, it can and should always be broken down into simple, understandable stages that can be tested in isolation, reducing the cognitive load on the developer. If you're using Compass for prototyping your aggregations, there is an option for turning down certain stages without removing them. If you're coding in an editor, it's easier if the stages are separated, with an option to toggle the comments. The Visual Studio Code extension, introduced earlier in this book, is an excellent tool for debugging, analyzing, and synthesizing aggregation pipelines.

Finally, with JavaScript running in the MongoDB Shell, it is often easier to write the stages as separate variables that are then just added to the pipeline array:

```
var projectStage = {
    "$project": ["imdb.rating", "title"]
};
var sortStage = {
    "$sort": {
        "imdb.rating"
    }
};
var pipeline = [projectStage, sortStage];
db.getCollection('movies').aggregate(pipeline)
```

Query optimization

As discussed in *Chapter 7, Advanced Querying in MongoDB*, you can return information on query plans and execution with the `explain()` command. This feature is especially useful in complex pipelines, and it can help you detect potential issues. Note that MongoDB will attempt to apply its aggregation pipeline optimizations at runtime, but sometimes the changes must be made beforehand. You, as the developer, can see the *bigger picture* of the business problem and the potential bottlenecks. The explain plan is, however, very useful as it can provide accurate information about queries and pinpoint problems.

Streaming and blocking stages of a pipeline

There are two types of stages: *streaming stages*, in which the database engine streams each batch of documents through a stage, and *blocking stages*, when the stage must wait for all the batches to arrive and accumulate for further processing. Typical blocking stages are `$sort` and `$group`, while most other stages are streaming stages. Other blocking stages related to grouping include `$bucket`, `$count`, `$sortByCount`, and `$facet`.

Blocking stages are often essential and unavoidable, but if placed improperly, they can drastically reduce concurrency and increase latency. There are several ways to work around these problems, including the following:

- Using indexed fields for sorting near the beginning of a pipeline to make aggregations significantly faster.

- Using `$limit` with `$sort`, when only a subset of documents is needed. The aggregation engine collapses the sort and limit phases into a special internal command, performing both actions together. This allows the memory to handle only the predefined limited number of documents.

- Moving the sorting stage to a phase where the record set has already been limited by a `$match` filter. Matching early is always encouraged as it can reduce the amount of data flowing through the pipeline by orders of magnitude.

- Avoiding the `$unwind` and `$group_by` antipattern for modifying or reducing an array field. As discussed in this chapter, the use of array expression operators ensures superior performance in most cases.

- Using existing indexed fields for sorting and grouping before mutating them in accordance with the aggregation's specifications.

Sharded cluster considerations

Depending on the structure of your sharded database, and on the number and structure of the documents in a sharded collection, it might be possible to achieve significant reductions when it comes to the aggregation response time. Sharded clusters attempt to run as many aggregation stages in parallel as possible, but problems arise when a stage requires all the data to be present at the same stage.

The tips for aggregating over sharded collections remain largely the same as for unsharded ones, with the addition of trying to aggregate on a single shard (where possible) and trying to split a pipeline in a way that avoids `allowDiskUse`.

It is important to note that starting in MongoDB 6.0, pipeline stages that require more than 100 MB of memory to execute, write temporary files to disk by default. In earlier versions of MongoDB, it was necessary to pass `{ allowDiskUse: true }` to individual find and aggregate commands to enable this behavior.

For individual find and aggregate commands, you can override the `allowDiskUseByDefault` parameter. When `allowDiskUseByDefault` is set to `false`, you can use `{ allowDiskUse: true }` to permit writing temporary files to disk, and when `allowDiskUseByDefault` is set to `true`, you can use `{ allowDiskUse: false }` to prohibit writing temporary files to disk.

Summary

In this chapter, you delved deeply into the aggregation framework, exploring the possibilities and understanding how various stages and expression operators can be employed to tackle a wide range of problems.

You learned about aggregation stages and operators, examining real-life databases from Atlas that effectively demonstrate essential functionalities. The chapter included valuable tips and suggestions designed to make you proficient as quickly as possible, with a focus on practical and advanced functionalities.

In the next chapter, you will see how MongoDB handles multi-document ACID transactions, and the significance this concept has in sectors with strict requirements, such as finance, fintech, and mission-critical applications.

9

Multi-Document ACID Transactions

MongoDB has supported multi-document **atomicity**, **consistency**, **isolation**, and **durability** (**ACID**) transactions since the release of MongoDB 4.0 in 2018. Transactions are logical groups of processes, with each group containing several reads or writes across different documents. Although single-document operations in MongoDB already offer basic transactional features that meet the data integrity needs of most applications, the addition of multi-document ACID transactions provides you with increased flexibility.

This chapter will cover the following topics:

- Significance and properties of transactions
- Fundamentals and implementation steps for multi-document ACID transactions
- Best practices and limitations for multi-document ACID transactions

Why are transactions useful?

Before examining how MongoDB treats transactions and its technical requirements, let's examine what transactions are, when they're needed, and the benefits and constraints they bring to your applications.

Formally, transactions are logical units of work. Every transaction is self-contained and defined; performed within a database management system against a database, and generally composed of multiple databases read and/or write operations.

From a practical standpoint, a transaction can be viewed as a sequence of database operations, considered complete only when every operation within the transaction has been executed successfully.

There are numerous situations in which your databases may need to perform read and write operations *to* and *from* multiple documents. These documents may reside in the same collection, or they may belong to different collections. These operations often have the constraint that they should all either succeed, or they should be discarded altogether, without any change to the database state before the said transaction.

A classical transaction example is a bank transfer. Let's consider money is taken from account A, only if the balance permits, and is transferred to account B. Should an error arise during the transaction, after the money has been taken from account A, the transaction will abort, and the money will be immediately returned to account A, without modifying the balance prior to initiating the transaction.

Transactions have been a feature of relational databases for quite some time, but even then, some of the most popular relational database servers (such as MySQL) took years to reach full ACID compliance.

MongoDB is not a relational database, which is why the classical relational database approach to transactions is not applicable. First, it's important to acknowledge that MongoDB's existing operations on a single document already provide the semantics that meet the data integrity needs of most applications. The addition of multi-document ACID transactions to MongoDB provides developers with a plethora of use cases in which MongoDB really shines.

Before diving into the specifics of how MongoDB solves these problems, this chapter will define what ACID means.

ACID properties

ACID is widely accepted as a framework that a transaction must meet to be defined as a *proper* or *true* transaction. These properties ensure database transactions are reliable and consistent, serving as the criteria for a unit of work to be considered a transaction:

- **Atomicity** implies that all the operations in a transaction are either performed successfully or not at all, meaning that if one operation in a transaction fails, the entire transaction is rolled back.

- **Consistency** ensures that all the data in a database is consistent with the results of the transaction.

- **Isolation** prevents transactions from interfering with each other. The implication of this property is that two transactions will not see each other's changes until both transactions have been committed.

- **Durability** ensures that once a transaction is committed, the changes are permanent. In this way, changes are not lost even if the database crashes.

Let's look at these concepts in detail, and understand how ACID transactions can impact your MongoDB database design and the overall architecture.

Atomicity

Atomicity means that a transaction can have only one of two outcomes. If a transaction is successful, and all the operations defined within have been executed correctly, the result should be visible and readable to every subsequent user or operation. If a transaction fails, all the changes created by the transaction are rolled back to the point where the database was before the said transaction started.

Atomicity can also be observed as a property that ensures transactions (comprising one or more operations), occur all at once, and no other client can observe them as separate operations.

As discussed earlier, the classic example for atomicity is a bank transfer. When transferring a sum of money from account A to account B, money must first be debited from account A and then credited to account B. If some of these operations fail, both accounts A and B must revert their state and balance before the transaction.

In MongoDB, operations involving a single document are always atomic, even in cases where the operation (update, for instance) encompasses several subdocuments or arrays within the document.

Consistency

As already mentioned, consistency is a concept related to the database state. Every operation, regardless of its outcome (success or failure), must return the database to a consistent state. Additionally, future transactions must be able to see the result generated by the previous transaction.

There are several database consistency models, such as:

- **Eventual consistency** is the model that's most used when it comes to distributed data systems. This model guarantees that once you update your data, all future reads will eventually get the latest committed read value. With distributed systems, all data is replicated through a network of servers, and this is the only acceptable model in terms of performance.

- **Strong consistency** guarantees that every future read will always get to read the last committed written value. This model implies that every update has to be propagated and committed to every server before the next read operation arrives. This model can cause performance problems with distributed systems.

In MongoDB, the concept of consistency falls between these models, capitalizing on MongoDB's nearly decade-long work in ensuring fine-grained consistency and durability. MongoDB has achieved a balance between the number of possible concurrent operations on one hand, and the consistency of the data being read by the application on the other.

Isolation

The concept of isolation states that transactions should be secluded, and no phase of any transaction should *spill over* into another transaction running in parallel.

It is easy to think of a banking system in which a user receives a payment, but the transaction fails to recognize it and update the current balance. Due to this, a subsequent purchase could fall through, as the purchase transaction reads the bank account's old state, failing to acknowledge the income, thus invalidating the second transaction.

There are several problems that can cause violations of the isolation principle and they have different degrees of severity. The worst-case scenario is when an operational update's data is *lost*, rendering the database practically unusable.

Other limitations of the isolation principle include:

- **Phantom reads**: They occur when, during a transaction, another transaction modifies the results by adding or deleting rows that belong to the result set of the first transaction. If a strict isolation level is implemented (serializable isolation, as shown later in this section), it can induce serious performance degradation, since every update would need to wait for reads to commit their own transactions.

- **Non-repeatable reads**: These errors occur when, during a transaction, another transaction successfully modifies its result set (add or remove documents). The problem with non-repeatable reads is that a value might change during the transaction.

- **Dirty reads**: These errors occur when a transaction reads data that has been modified by another transaction but has not yet been committed. This can lead to inconsistent data, as the transaction may be reading data that is no longer valid. For example, when a value that doesn't correspond to reality is read from the database. For example, paying an amount of $100 from an account that has a balance of only $50.

Each of these errors is addressed by a different isolation level in different database systems. From the strictest to the laxest, these levels are: *serializable, repeatable read, read committed, and read uncommitted*. In MongoDB, the same granularity is achieved using write concern, read concern, and sessions.

Durability

Durability is arguably the most significant aspect of the ACID paradigm; every successful transaction needs to persist regardless of failure. This is usually accomplished by writing the transaction results in some sort of persistent storage. Relational database systems follow the principle of writing all committed transactions to a committed transactions log or to a **write-ahead log** (**WAL**).

MongoDB uses the powerful WiredTiger storage engine, and commits writes using WAL to an on-disk journal every 100 milliseconds. Durability is usually the last feature of the ACID paradigm to get relaxed.

MongoDB implementation of ACID

MongoDB ensures atomicity for single-document operations, and this is enough for most real-world cases. However, sectors such as *finance* and *fintech*, with stringent requirements, demand different treatment in MongoDB. In the case of financial and banking sectors, applications often handle huge numbers of accounts and financial transactions, all of which need verification. These transactions often span multiple documents—thousands or more.

Generally, multi-document ACID transactions are used when an unbounded number of entities that cannot fit into an array of subdocuments as the main document, outgrow the maximum BSON document size (16MB, currently supported by MongoDB). If you're experienced in **relational database management systems (RDBMS)**, you will find MongoDB's multi-document semantics very familiar and straightforward.

According to a MongoDB seminal white paper on ACID transactions (`https://www.mongodb.com/collateral/mongodb-multi-document-acid-transactions`), 80–90% of applications don't require multi-document transactions at all. This is something to keep in mind during the modeling and development stages. However, there are cases such as the financial sector, where ACID-compliant transaction support is mandatory. Other factors that might push you toward ACID transactions are future-proofing your application or relying on the support available for ACID transactions, should you ever need it.

MongoDB's data model is different from the relational one; instead of breaking the related data apart into several tables, MongoDB documents store related data in a rich, hierarchical structure with subdocuments and arrays.

Before the introduction of multi-document transactions, MongoDB developers had to programmatically implement transaction controls in their applications, ensuring all stages of an operation finished successfully, before committing. MongoDB reported that customers in the financial industry were able to significantly reduce the amount of code by implementing multi-document ACID transactions. However, this is not limited to the financial sector. Any application will benefit from the shift to server-side functionality and the reduced need to maintain application-level transaction controls.

The following example, taken from the PyMongo documentation, showcases the new method of interacting with transactions (`https://pymongo.readthedocs.io/en/stable/api/pymongo/client_session.html`):

```python
orders = client.db.orders
inventory = client.db.inventory

with client.start_session() as session:
    with session.start_transaction():
        orders.insert_one({"sku": "abc123", "qty": 100}, session=session)
        inventory. update_one(
            {"sku": "abc123", "qty": {"$gte": 100}},
            {"$inc": {"qty": -100}},
            session=session,
        )
```

This example shows that you don't have to deviate from MongoDB's regular query language syntax to implement distributed transactions across documents and collections. Through snapshot isolation, MongoDB's transactions are able to provide a consistent view of the data, along with enforcing all-or-nothing execution to secure data integrity.

It is also worth noting that changes inserted by multi-document transactions don't modify or impact the performance of workloads that don't actually need them. You've already seen that during its execution, a single transaction is able to read its own uncommitted writes. However, none of these writes are visible outside the transaction as they're not being replicated to secondary nodes. The transaction gets replicated only once it's committed, and then it's applied to all secondary replicas.

Read and write concerns in transactions

When working with transactions in replica sets and sharded clusters, you have to configure the read and write concerns at the start of every transaction. One way to set transaction-level read preferences at the start of a transaction is by using MongoDB drivers. If the transaction-level read preference is unset, the transaction uses the session-level read preference. Multi-document transactions that contain read operations must use a read preference of *primary*. All operations in each transaction must route to the same member.

Starting in MongoDB 4.4, read and write concerns can be configured cluster-wide, allowing applications to set the most sensible default values. This frees you from having to explicitly configure settings for each transaction.

Transactions in MongoDB support the following read concern levels:

- `"local"`: Returns the most recent data available from the node, but it can be rolled back. Note that for transactions on a sharded cluster, this read concern can't guarantee that data is from the same snapshot view across all shards. This is why the `"snapshot"` read concern is used if isolation is required.

- `"majority"`: Guarantees that the data read has been acknowledged by a majority of the replica set members. A `"majority"` read concern provides its guarantees only if the transaction commits with write concern `"majority"`, otherwise the `"majority"` read concern does not guarantee that read operations will get `"majority"`-committed data.

- `"snapshot"`: This read concern returns data from a snapshot of `"majority"`-committed data if the transaction commits with the `"majority"` write concern. Considering the previously defined levels, if the transaction does not use the `"majority"` write concern for the commit, this read concern provides no guarantee that the read operation used a snapshot of `"majority"`-committed data.

Transactions in MongoDB support the following write concern levels:

- `"majority"`: Requests majority of the servers in a replica set to acknowledge the data. This is the default write concern from MongoDB 5.0.

- The option requests acknowledgment that the write operation has been propagated to a specified number of mongod instances.

If the transaction-level write concern is unset, the transaction-level write concern defaults to the session-level write concern for the commit. Furthermore, if the transactional-level write concern and the session-level write concern are unset, the transaction-level write concern defaults to the client-level write concern of `"majority"` in MongoDB 5.0 or later.

Transaction limitations

Transactions are an extremely powerful feature. However, it's important to be aware of their limitations:

- Transactions cannot write to capped or system collections, and cannot read or write to the `admin`, `config`, and `local` databases.

- The supported operation's query plan (i.e. `explain`) cannot be returned.

- Starting in MongoDB 4.2, `killCursors` cannot be specified as the first operation in a transaction.

- Operation on a cursor must be created and accessed either inside or outside the transaction.

- Although transactions can perform certain **data definition language** (DDL) operations—such as creating collections—there are some limitations. Writes/updates cannot be performed across different shards in the same transaction, such as updating a document in a collection on shard 1 and in the same transaction, creating a collection on shard 2.

- For transactions on sharded clusters, `"local"` read concern cannot guarantee that the data is from the same snapshot view across the shards. If snapshot isolation is required, use `"snapshot"` read concern.

- The `listCollections` and `listIndexes` commands, and their helper methods cannot be used.

- Read concern `"snapshot"` returns data from a snapshot of majority committed data if the transaction commits with write concern `"majority"`.

- If the transaction doesn't use write concern `"majority"` for the commit, the `"snapshot"` read concern provides no guarantee that read operations used a snapshot of `"majority"`-committed data.

- For transactions on sharded clusters, the `"snapshot"` view of the data is synchronized across shards.

- Other non-CRUD and non-informational operations, such as `createUser`, `getParameter`, and `count`, and their helpers cannot be used.

An example of transaction

In this section, you will see a simplified example that demonstrates the mechanism and syntax. The example is inspired by the tutorial from Lauren Schaefer: `https://www.mongodb.com/blog/post/quick-start-nodejs--mongodb--how-to-implement-transactions`

To implement these transactions, you'll need a sharded cluster or a replica set. For the following example, use the MongoDB Atlas instance that was set up in the previous chapters.

The example will cover a fairly common scenario. You can use the Atlas `sample_airbnb` dataset—feel free to imagine any kind of booking application that you might have in mind—and add another collection for users. Users should be able to reserve properties and you will see how MongoDB transactions can help you ensure no property can be booked twice. Following the MongoDB rule of thumb (the data that is accessed together should be stored together), the reservations will be stored inside the `users` collection. This way, you will immediately see the reservations made by a user by inspecting their profile. For instance, if a user named `Leslie` makes two reservations, her document in the `users` collection would look like the following (other document properties like `specialRequests` and `breakfastIncluded` have been omitted for brevity):

```
{
  "_id": {"$oid":"5dd589544f549efc1b0320a5"},
  "email": "leslie@example.com",
  "name": "Leslie Yepp",
  "reservations": [
    {
      "name":"Nice room in Barcelona Center", "dates": [
        {"$date": {"$numberLong":"1577750400000"}},
        {"$date": {"$numberLong":"1577836800000"}}
      ],
      "pricePerNight": {"$numberInt":"180"},
    {
      "name": "Lovely Loft",
      "dates": [
        {"$date": {"$numberLong": "1585958400000"}}
      ],
    }
  ]
}
```

However, the main business problem is tied to the `listingsAndReviews` collection where users need to see immediately if a property is already reserved for the desired dates. So, you need to store the dates listings in the `listingsAndReviews` collection as well. The *Nice room in Barcelona Center* property that the user `Leslie` has reserved previously, should be updated to match, and list her reservation dates.

An example could be the following (additional fields are omitted for brevity):

```
{
  "_id": {"$oid":"5dbc20f942073d6d4dabd730"},
  "name":"Nice room in Barcelona Center",
  "summary":" Hi!  Cozy double bed room in amazing flat next to Passeig de Sant
Joan… ",
  "property_type": "House",
  "bedrooms": 1,
  "bathrooms":1.0,
  "beds":2,
```

```
  "datesReserved": [
    {"$date": {"$numberLong": "1577750400000"}},
    {"$date": {"$numberLong": "1577836800000"}}
  ]
}
```

The main purpose of transactions in this environment is to ensure that these two collections are in sync and that the booking process is only possible if the property is indeed available for the desired dates. In this example, you will see how to achieve the desired behavior through multi-document transactions.

> **Note**
>
> To utilize transactions, you must configure MongoDB as a replica set or a sharded cluster. Transactions are not supported on standalone deployments. Since you're using a database hosted on Atlas, you don't need to worry about this as every Atlas cluster is either a replica set or a sharded cluster.

Since the listingsAndReviews is the only collection inside the sample_airbnb dataset, you need to create a new users collection and insert the three users that should be unique. The following Node.js file, called users.js, accomplishes that. You only need to update the uri constant to reflect your own Atlas connection info in the following users.js file:

```
const { MongoClient } = require("mongodb");
async function createMultipleUsers(client, newUsers) {
  // function that inserts three users
  const result = await client
    .db("sample_airbnb")
    .collection("users")
    .insertMany(newUsers);

  console.log(
    '${result.insertedCount} new user(s) created with the following id(s):'
  );

  console.log(result.insertedIds);
}

async function main() {
  const uri = "mongodb+srv://your-connection-string/";

  const client = new MongoClient(uri);

  try {
    // Connect to the MongoDB cluster
    await client.connect();
```

```javascript
    // Create 3 new users in the users collection
    await createMultipleUsers(client, [
      {
        email: "leslie@example.com",
        name: "Leslie Yepp",
      },
      {
        email: "april@example.com",
        name: "April Ludfence",
      },
      {
        email: "tom@example.com",
        name: "Tom Haverdodge",
      },
    ]);

    const createIndexResults = await client
      .db("sample_airbnb")
      .collection("users")
      .createIndex({ email: 1 }, { unique: true });
    console.log('Index successfully created: ${createIndexResults}');
  } finally {
    await client.close();
  }
}

main().catch(console.error);
```

The script will create three new users in the users collection: Leslie Yepp, April Ludfence, and Tom Haverdodge. If the users collection doesn't already exist, MongoDB will automatically create it for you when you insert the new users. The script also creates an index on the email field in the users collection. The index requires that every document in the collection has a unique email, so running the script repeatedly will not create additional users.

After the users collection is set up and populated with users, you can build transaction.js to handle the property reservation process. The file transaction.js will be quite long, but you can build it gradually, inspecting each part of the code. First, you can create a helper function that will create the reservation object, and facilitate the reservation transaction process. So, let's begin:

```javascript
const { MongoClient } = require("mongodb");

function createReservationDocument(
  // Helper function for creating the reservation
  nameOfListing,
  reservationDates,
  reservationDetails
```

```
) {
  // Create the reservation
  let reservation = {
    name: nameOfListing,
    dates: reservationDates,
  };

  // Add additional properties from reservationDetails to the reservation
  for (let detail in reservationDetails) {
    reservation[detail] = reservationDetails[detail];
  }

  return reservation;
}
```

After importing the `MongoClient` from the MongoDB package (your sole dependency), you can create a simple function that is used to only format your reservation data in a more concise and approachable way throughout the following code.

In the same `transaction.js` file, you can now start working on the main functionality—creating a transaction:

```
async function createReservation(
  client,
  userEmail,
  nameOfListing,
  reservationDates,
  reservationDetails
) {
  const usersCollection = client.db("sample_airbnb").collection("users");
  const listingsAndReviewsCollection = client
    .db("sample_airbnb")
    .collection("listingsAndReviews");

  const reservation = createReservationDocument(
    nameOfListing,
    reservationDates,
    reservationDetails
  );
// … more code will follow
}
```

The previous code defines an async function—createReservation—that takes all the data necessary for booking a property: the MongoDB client, the unique user email, the name of the listing, the reservation dates, and the details of the property. After selecting the users collection that you created inside the sample_airbnb database, you can select the listingsAndReviews collection as well, and use your helper function to simplify the reservation data, and make it suitable for further processing inside the transaction. Continue going through the same createReservation function:

```
const session = client.startSession();
  const transactionOptions = {
    readPreference: "primary",
    readConcern: { level: "local" },
    writeConcern: { w: "majority" },
  };
```

The previous code creates a client session and defines the transaction options, as you've already seen in this chapter. Finally, you get to write the transaction code! After the previous snippet, which is still there inside the body of the createReservation function, insert the following:

```
try {
    const transactionResults = await session.withTransaction(async () => {
      const usersUpdateResults = await usersCollection.updateOne(
        { email: userEmail },
        { $addToSet: { reservations: reservation } },
        { session }
      );
      console.log(
        '${usersUpdateResults.matchedCount} document(s) found in the users
collection with the email address ${userEmail}.'
      );
      console.log(
        '${usersUpdateResults.modifiedCount} document(s) was/were updated to
include   the reservation.'
      );
```

The try/catch block begins a transaction session, updates the user data in the user collection, and prints a friendly informative message to the console. Now comes the part where you have to check if the property is actually available. You just need to find one user-selected date that is not available (using findOne), and if this date exists, the transaction must be aborted, otherwise the code will simply return the following:

```
      const isListingReservedResults =
        await listingsAndReviewsCollection.findOne(
          { name: nameOfListing, datesReserved: { $in: reservationDates } },
          { session }
        );
      if (isListingReservedResults) {
        await session.abortTransaction();
        console.error(
```

```
            "This listing is already reserved for at least one of the given
       dates. The reservation could not be created."
          );
          console.error(
             "Any operations that already occurred as part of this transaction
       will be rolled back."
          );
          return;
       }
```

Finally, you must update the property document in the listingsAndReviews collection by adding the selected dates and printing a couple of informative messages to the console. The try/catch block is closed by outputting any potential unexpected errors, and the finally clause is used to end the session:

```
       const listingsAndReviewsUpdateResults =
          await listingsAndReviewsCollection.updateOne(
             { name: nameOfListing },
             { $addToSet: { datesReserved: { $each: reservationDates } } },
             { session }
          );
       console.log(
          '${listingsAndReviewsUpdateResults.matchedCount} document(s) found in
       the listingsAndReviews collection with the name ${nameOfListing}.'
          );
       console.log(
          '${listingsAndReviewsUpdateResults.modifiedCount} document(s) was/were
       updated to include the reservation dates.'
          );
       }, transactionOptions);
    } catch (e) {
       console.log("The transaction was aborted due to an unexpected error: " +
    e);
    } finally {
       await session.endSession();
    }
```

To be able to test this code, create an asynchronous main function that will connect to your Atlas instance, and try to perform the previously defined transaction:

```
async function main() {
   const uri =
   // your Atlas connection string
    "mongodb+srv://your-atlas-URI/";

   const client = new MongoClient(uri);
   try {
      // Connect to the MongoDB cluster
      await client.connect();
      await createReservation(
```

```
        client,
        "leslie@example.com",
        "Nice room in Barcelona Center",
        [new Date("2023-12-31"), new Date("2024-01-01")],
        {
          pricePerNight: 180,
          specialRequests: "Late checkout",
          breakfastIncluded: true,
        }
      );
    } finally {
      // Close the connection to the MongoDB cluster
      await client.close();
    }
}
```

End the `transaction.js` file with a call to the main function that you just defined above:

```
main().catch(console.error);
```

After running the `transaction.js` code in the console with node `transaction.js`, you will get the following output:

```
1 document(s) found in the users collection with the email address leslie@
example.com.
1 document(s) was/were updated to include the reservation.
1 document(s) found in the listingsAndReviews collection with the name Nice
room in Barcelona Center.
1 document(s) was/were updated to include the reservation dates.
```

If you try to run the same code again, the shell will inform you that the transaction is not possible:

```
1 document(s) found in the users collection with the email address leslie@
example.com.
0 document(s) was/were updated to include the reservation.
```

This listing is already reserved for at least one of the given dates. Hence, the reservation is not created. Any operations that already occurred as part of this transaction will be rolled back.

You just implemented a multi-document transaction using MongoDB. If you run this code once, it will perform as advertised. However, the second time, it will throw an error because the collection already contains the reservation for the property named *Nice room in Barcelona Center*, and the transaction will abort.

In this section, you have seen a simple yet illustrative example of the power of transactions, as well as the simplicity of the syntax. You have used the MongoDB Node.js driver to demonstrate the example, as the language-specific drivers give you more control and flexibility to handle exceptions, and add custom logic. In the next section, you will explore some best practices that are encouraged when working with transactions in MongoDB.

Best practices

There are several best practices to help make your work with transactions simpler. This section will give a brief overview of these practices.

Generally, you can avoid multi-document ACID transactions by using rich document models through a careful process of data modeling. The modeling phase can help you avoid using transactions altogether, and in many cases, this is always something to keep in mind. However, if your application requires the use of transactions, they integrate seamlessly into your non-transactional workflow, but should be subject to some particular considerations.

As stated previously, transactions have a default maximum time limit set to 60 seconds. This value can be increased by modifying the `transactionLifetimeLimitSeconds` server parameter at the `mongod` level. If you're working with a sharded cluster, this parameter must be set on all shard replica members. After this period has expired, as you've seen in the example, the transaction will be considered expired, and will be eventually aborted by the cleanup process that runs periodically. To address this timeout constraint, special attention should be given to tuning the transaction operations.

As a rule of thumb, transactions shouldn't have to modify more than 1,000 documents at a time, although there is no limit on the number of documents read. For operations that need to modify a number of documents greater than 1,000, the transaction should be separated into multiple parts, and executed in batches.

Another thing to keep in mind is that the oplog records a single entry for any transaction and this entry is also subject to the 16 MB BSON document size limit. For transactions that perform updates, this will not be a problem as only the difference (delta) will be recorded, but if a transaction performs inserts, they will be fully recorded in the oplog as well.

MongoDB drivers support two APIs for working with transactions: the *Core API*, and the new *Callback API*. While the Core API requires explicit calls to start and commit the transactions, it also doesn't incorporate error-handling logic for `TransientTransactionError` and `UnknownTransactionCommitResult`. The Callback API, on the other hand, starts a transaction, executes the specified operation, and commits or aborts on errors. It incorporates logic for retrying the entire transaction if a `TransientTransactionError` error is encountered, and for retrying the commit operation in case of a `UnknownTransactionCommitResult` error.

Developers are required to handle the application logic that caters to failed transactions. Usually, this is done within the Callback API—tied to a specific language, and a MongoDB driver. The Callback API can wrap more functionality of a transaction, including the start of a transaction, executing a function supplied as the callback, and taking care of all edge cases. The complexity involved and the additional coding required for applications are the reason why the Callback API—introduced in MongoDB 4.2—is preferred over the Core API.

Other best practices mentioned in *Chapter 7, Advanced Querying in MongoDB*, become even more important in a transaction environment.

Summary

This chapter explored ACID-compliant multi-document transactions in MongoDB. You learnt the principles of the ACID transaction paradigm. Further, you saw how MongoDB handles these requirements, including the strictest requirements, which are sometimes unavoidable. You also learned when to use transactions, when it's best to avoid them, how to use them, their best practices, their limitations, and how to mitigate them.

You followed a simple yet illustrative transaction example, and tested a transaction from the MongoDB Shell. You explored the transaction behavior from within, and observed how it looks like from outside the transaction. You also saw how a transaction is committed, and how to handle failure conditions that require the transaction to be aborted.

The next chapter will address key facets of the MongoDB document model, encompassing indexing, index optimization, and its impact on your overall system.

10

Index Optimization

Every database system, whether relational or non-relational, relies on indexing to speed up data querying. This is why index optimization is crucial for using the database to its full speed and potential. MongoDB features a powerful granular indexing system that can improve the overall performance of the database.

This chapter discusses how MongoDB supports a variety of indexes, ranging from single-field to compound indexes, including geospatial, hashed, and partial indexes. Additionally, it covers recently introduced indexing types, such as compound wildcard indexes.

This chapter will cover the following topics:

- Introduction to indexing and its collections
- Defining indexes in MongoDB
- Types of indexes and strategies for optimal use
- Best practices and considerations

Introduction to indexes

An index is a special data structure that enables faster access to data in a collection, much like an old-school paper encyclopedia index. It is an ordered list of references to the actual contents—the documents—which allows MongoDB to query much faster, often by orders of magnitude. Indexes store values of a specific field or a set of fields, ordered by value. As you will see later in *The equality, sort, range (ESR) rule* section, MongoDB can return sorted results using the ordering of the index itself.

MongoDB indexes use a data structure known as *B-tree*, a self-balancing tree data structure that maintains sorted data, and allows sequential access, searches, insertions, and deletions in logarithmic time. The index can be thought of as a list of key-value pairs, where each key is a value of index, and the value of the key-value pair is the document itself. Like an index of a book, the keys are stored in order, and associated with one or more fields.

The B-tree structure is used to store index values and reduce the number of comparisons needed when performing a search. While with a collection scan, each new document insertion creates an extra comparison; with the B-tree structure, each new insertion doesn't necessarily imply a new comparison. For instance, in the following example, the insertion of a document with a value of 5 (left child leaf) wouldn't impact the search for a value of 9, as it ends up in the other part of the root node value (7).

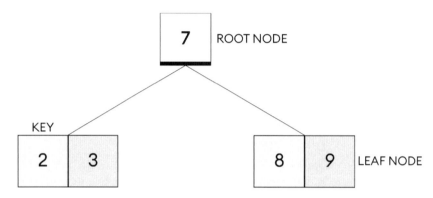

Figure 10.1: The B-tree data structure

Creating an index

To illustrate the basics of index creation and how it can affect queries, you can use the MongoDB Shell and create some data.

First, open the MongoDB Shell and select or create a database called *testing* (the following command will create a new database with the specified name if said database does not exist):

```
use testing
```

Before you begin creating indexes, populate the collection named books inside the currently selected database by executing the following script in the MongoDB Shell:

```
for (i = 0; i < 100000; i++){
  db.books.insertOne(
    {
      "i": i,
      "author": "Author_" + i, "title": "Book title " + i,
      "ISBN": Math.floor(Math.random() * 100000),
      "created": new Date(),
      "meta":
      {
```

```
        "price": Math.floor(Math.random() * 100),
        "rating": Math.random() * 5
      }
    }
  )
}
```

This simple script inserts 100,000 dummy books with some fake data—title, author, ISBN code, date, and some embedded meta fields for price and rating.

Now that you have a database with 100,000 entries, you can create your first query and use the `explain` command to see what MongoDB will do. In the same MongoDB Shell, type the following command:

```
db.books
  .find({'title': 'Book title 45678'})
  .explain('executionStats')
```

The shell will respond with a very long output:

```
executionStats: {
    executionSuccess: true,
    nReturned: 1,
    executionTimeMillis: 77,
    totalKeysExamined: 0,
    totalDocsExamined: 100002,
    executionStages: {
      stage: 'filter',
      planNodeId: 1,
      nReturned: 1,
      executionTimeMillisEstimate: 78,
      opens: 1,
      closes: 1,
      saveState: 100,
      restoreState: 100,
      isEOF: 1,
      numTested: 100002,
      filter: 'traverseF(s5, lambda(l1.0) { ((l1.0 == s8) ?: false) }, false)',
      inputStage: {
        stage: 'scan',
        planNodeId: 1,
        nReturned: 100000,
        executionTimeMillisEstimate: 77,
        opens: 1,
        closes: 1,
        saveState: 100,
        restoreState: 100,
        isEOF: 1,
```

```
        numReads: 100002,
        recordSlot: 6,
        recordIdSlot: 7,
        fields: [ 'title' ],
        outputSlots: [ Long("5") ]
    }
```

The same command using MongoDB Compass will yield a slightly less verbose output as shown in *Figure 10.2*:

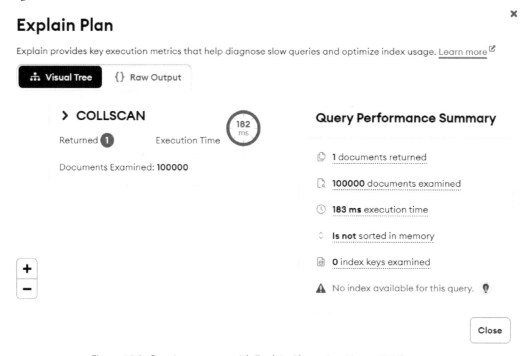

Figure 10.2: Creating a query with Explain Plan using MongoDB Compass

For now, you can focus on one key bit—the executionStats object, which looks something like the following:

```
executionStats: {
    executionSuccess: true,
    nReturned: 1,
    executionTimeMillis: 42,
    totalKeysExamined: 0,
    totalDocsExamined: 100000,
}
```

The rule of thumb for creating MongoDB indexes is to ensure they align with your expected query shape. More precisely, an index supports a query when it contains all the fields scanned by the query. In this scenario, the query scans the index rather than the collection. The creation of indexes that align with queries enhances query performance. In MongoDB Compass, the aforementioned query will run after the **Explain** button is pressed from the query bar.

Here, the query executes successfully and returns one result (nReturned) since the titles and authors are unique. After the execution time (42 milliseconds), you will be informed that the query didn't examine any keys (indexes), and that it examined 100,000 documents to complete the query.

In this case, you can create your first index on the book title field. The syntax is simple:

```
db.books.createIndex({ "title":1 })
```

This command is used to create a *single-field index* on the title field, while number 1 denotes the index order. Here, it's in the ascending order. The number can be 1 or -1, similar to the direction specified when sorting query results using sort. If you want your application to access data in descending order, you can set it to -1.

If you inspect the collection in MongoDB Compass now, under the **Indexes** tab as shown in *Figure 10.3*, you will see another index (along with the default _id_ index) with the automatically generated name, title_1.

Figure 10.3: The collection in MongoDB Compass

Now, let's repeat the previous explain query:

```
db.books
  .find({'title': 'Book title 45678'})
  .explain('executionStats')
```

The output from MongoDB will be similar to the following (results on your system might vary):

```
executionStats:
  {
    executionSuccess: true,
    nReturned: 1,
    executionTimeMillis: 6,
    totalKeysExamined: 1,
    totalDocsExamined: 1,
  }
```

The difference is notable even on a small database with a simplified document structure and relatively few documents. You still get your document, but the execution time is much shorter (42 milliseconds instead of 6), and only one document is examined from the database.

In a database with many complex documents, indexes are necessary. The proper choice of indexes is an important part of mastering MongoDB. You'll get guidelines on how and where to place indexes later in the chapter. If you are tempted to index each and every possible field, embedded document, or array in your database, remember that indexes come with a price. Each and every write operation (insert, update, and delete) can take slightly longer since the indexes have to be updated.

Dropping indexes is also simple. Use the following command to do it:

```
db.books.dropIndex({ "title": 1 })
```

If you want to drop an index by name, run the following command:

```
db.books.dropIndex("title_1")
```

After reviewing the basics of index creation, it is time to get acquainted with various index types that MongoDB provides.

Index types

In the following section, you will explore different index types, understanding how and when to utilize them for optimal outcomes.

Single-field indexes and indexing embedded documents

The simplest and the most common type of index is the single-field index. By default, MongoDB automatically generates single-field indexes for every collection—a unique index on the _id field. This index prevents the insertion of a second document with the same value for the _id field into the collection.

In the previous section, you saw an example of the simplest possible single-field index. You can further enhance your books collection by adding a couple more indexes—one for the titles and one for the price, which is an embedded field, to make it unique.

Execute the following command:

```
db.books.createIndex({ "title": 1 }, { "unique": true })
```

> **Note**
> Two indexes cannot have the same shape even in cases when the options are different. For instance, the following would *not* be possible:
> ```
> { title: 1 }
> { title: 1 }, { unique: true }
> ```

The preceding command resembles the one for creating a generic index on a field; however, it enforces uniqueness on the `title` field. With a unique `title` field, you can't insert a book with an existing title (which is not desirable in a real system). The following command will create an index on an embedded field:

```
db.books.createIndex({ "meta.price": 1 })
```

You can always check your indexes in MongoDB Compass, under the *Indexes* tab, after refreshing the data. Your new index in the `meta.price` field now enables you to perform quick queries on the price range, making full use of the efficient B-tree structure.

The preceding command shows that indexing an embedded field is simple with the dot notation. If you expect queries against the entire subdocument (in this case, it is called `meta`), you can index the whole subdocument, similar to the embedded field, retaining the quotes around it:

```
db.books.createIndex({ "meta": 1 })
```

One key difference here is that with indexing embedded fields, you can perform range queries on them using the index. On the other hand, if you index the whole subdocument, you can only perform comparison queries using the index.

Compound indexes

Compound indexes get and sort data from two or more fields in each document in a collection. Data is grouped by the first field in the index and then by each subsequent field.

In scenarios where you where you expect several fields to be used in your queries, the compound index is often the best solution. For example, you can create an index composed of two fields—the author and the ISBN code of the book in your database, as follows:

```
db.books.createIndex({ "author": 1, "ISBN": 1 })
```

This command creates a compound index that uses the `author` and `ISBN` fields. You can also keep it unique, so no combination of the two fields could be repeated.

With compound indexes, the order determines which types of sorting you can perform index-wise. For the above example, the index will support sorting on the following field combinations:

```
db.books.find().sort({ "author": 1,"ISBN": 1 })
db.books.find().sort({ "author": -1,"ISBN": -1 })
```

But the index will not be used for the following:

```
db.books.find().sort({ "author": 1,"ISBN": -1 })
db.books.find().sort({ "author": -1,"ISBN": 1 })
```

Notice the placement of the *minus* sign. The sign indicates the sorting direction: ascending or descending.

Another important attribute of compound indexes is the fact that they can be used for multiple queries on prefixes of the indexed fields. For example, the compound index from the previous example can be used for a query against the author and ISBN code, or on the author field alone as it is the first field declared in the index. Querying just by the ISBN code will not make use of the index at all, and will instead perform a collection scan.

The order of the fields in the query is insignificant; MongoDB will rearrange the fields as needed to match the query. However, the order of the fields in the index is crucial. The values of the fields are stored in the index as secondary, tertiary, etc., each one embedded into the previous one.

Compound indexes contain references to documents according to the order of the fields in the index. For example, *Figure 10.4* shows a compound index where documents are first grouped by userid in ascending order (alphabetically). Then, the scores for each userid are sorted in descending order:

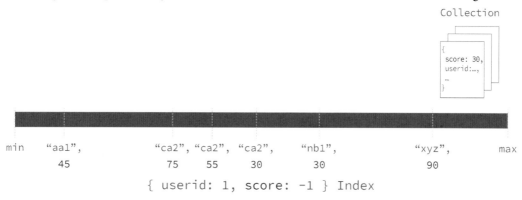

Figure 10.4: An example of a compound index

As a simple example, consider that you have a variety of clothes that you wish to organize in a series of closets following this logic: each closet will be sorted by the type of clothes—shirts, underwear, socks, trousers, jackets, and so on. Within each closet, you further sort the garments by color, ranging from red, orange, and yellow to violet.

It is intuitively clear that this system will work very well if you are searching for a piece of clothing to wear starting by the type of garment, and that you will be able to find your favorite orange shirt quickly by traversing your index. However, trying to find a generic garment by color only would be problematic—you will have to perform a manual search, analogous to a collection scan.

Compound indexes are created in a manner similar to the other indexes shown in the previous example, by specifying a field and a sort order.

Let's look at an example from MongoDB's extensive documentation:

```
db.students.insertMany(
  [
    {
      "name": "Alice",
      "gpa": 3.6,
```

```
      "location": { city: "Sacramento", state: "California" }
    },
    {
      "name": "Bob",
      "gpa": 3.2,
      "location": { city: "Albany", state: "New York" }
    }
  ]
)
```

The preceding code inserts a couple of students, along with their locations and GPAs. To create a compound index containing the name and gpa fields, the following will suffice:

```
db.students.createIndex(
  {
    name: 1,
    gpa: -1
  }
)
```

In this example, the index on the name field is in ascending order (1), while the index on the gpa field is in descending order (-1).

This created index supports queries that select on either both the name and gpa fields or only the name field since the name is a prefix of the compound index.

The following queries will thus be supported by this index:

```
db.students.find({ name: "Alice", gpa: 3.6 })
db.students.find({ name: "Bob" })
```

This index, however, will not support queries on only the gpa field, since gpa isn't part of the index prefix.

If a compound index is created on attributes A, B, and C, respectively, this index will be used to optimize queries against A, A and B, or A and B and C, but not for B or C or B and C.

Compound indexes should be used for queries that will use the attributes together in a find() or $match. Preferably, the first field should be the one on which equality is tested, followed by range matches (i.e., last name, then age).

To create efficient compound indexes, the ESR rule should be followed, which is a simple rule that perfectly formalizes the indexing process.

The equality, sort, range (ESR) rule

As you saw earlier, an index that references more than one field is called a compound index, and it improves the query response times dramatically. In most cases, the ESR rule for arranging index keys will help create an efficient compound index.

Equality

Equality refers to an exact match on a single value. The following example scans a car collection for documents whose `model` field matches `Cordoba`:

```
db.cars.find({ model: "Cordoba" })
```

Index searches use exact matching efficiently and limit the number of documents that need to be examined for a query to be satisfied. Therefore, the fields requiring exact matches should be placed first in the index.

Indexes can have multiple keys for queries with exact matches, and they can appear in any given order. However, they must come before any other index keys. MongoDB's search algorithm eliminates any need to arrange the exact matching fields in any particular order.

For example, if you wanted to execute the following query:

```
db.cars.find({ model: "Cordoba", color: "Black" })
```

Here, the index could be either `{ model: 1, color: 1 }` or `{ color: 1, model: 1 }`, and still be appropriate. The exact matches should be highly selective. MongoDB's documentation recommends ensuring that equality texts eliminate at least 90% of possible document matches.

Sort

The *sort* part of the rule determines the order of the results. It follows equality matches as these matches reduce the number of documents requiring sorting. This ensures that the index can satisfy the sort requirements without the need for a blocking sort. It is important to emphasize that sorting after equality matching allows MongoDB to do a *non-blocking sort*. An index can support sorting when the query fields are a subset of the index keys.

Returning to the cars example, sorting on a car model and matching on the manufacturer would look as follows:

```
db.cars.find({ manufacturer: "GM" }).sort({ model: 1 })
```

In order to improve query performance, the index should be as follows:

```
db.cars.createIndex({ manufacturer: 1, model: 1 })
```

In the previous example, `manufacturer` is the first key as it supports an equality match, while `model` satisfies the sort requirements of the query.

Range

The *range* stage scans a subset of index keys. To improve query efficiency, the range bounds should be as tight as possible. To enable MongoDB to perform a non-blocking sort, it is advisable to place range bounds after sorting since MongoDB cannot perform index sorting on the result of a range filter. It should be noted that `$ne`, `$nin`, and `$regex` are all range operators.

In the following query, the cars collection is searched for vehicles produced by Ford, with a cost higher than $15,000, and sorted by model:

```
db.cars.find(
   {
      manufacturer: "Ford",
      cost: { $gt: 15000 }
   }
).sort({ model: 1 })
```

This query contains all the elements of the ESR rule—an equality match, a sorting phase, and a range-based match on the price. Following the rule, the optimal index for this query would be as follows:

```
{ manufacturer: 1, model: 1, cost: 1 }
```

Multikey indexes

The ability of MongoDB to store arrays of values is extended to indexing as well. Indexing arrays of documents or fields is achieved by using a *multikey index*—an index that can store arrays of scalar values (text or numbers) or nested documents.

The example database doesn't have any arrays, but you can insert a document that looks like this:

```
db.books.insert(
   {
      "title": "Book with tags",
      "author": "Jane Doe",
      "ISBN": 1111,
      "tags": [ "MongoDB", "Mastering", "Packt Publishing" ]
   }
)
```

You can add a multikey index as well, and it is quite similar to creating a standard index:

```
db.books.createIndex({ "tags": 1 })
```

If you try to query for a book containing one of the tags, and use the `explain` command, you will see that the index was used and that the number of documents read is equal to one:

```
db.books.find({ tags: "MongoDB" }).explain("executionStats")
```

Multikey indexes also enable the creation of compound indexes, but with the limitation of using only one array in each index at most. It is worth knowing that multikey indexes can't cover a query completely. A query will be covered completely when an index contains all the values requested by a query, so that the result can be retrieved entirely from the index.

Querying for multiple values in multikey indexes involves a two-step process. In the first step, the index is used to retrieve the first value of the array. Subsequently, a sequential scan is performed to iterate through the rest of the elements in the array. An example is as follows:

```
db.books.find({ tags: [ "mongodb", "index", "Packt" ] })
```

This query will first search for all entries in multikey index tags that have a mongodb value, and subsequently scan through them to find the ones that also have index and Packt.

Covered queries

A covered query, as mentioned in the previous section, is a query that can be satisfied entirely using the index and does not need to examine any documents.

An index is said to cover a query when all the following conditions are met:

- All the fields in the query are part of an index
- All the fields returned in the results are in the same index
- No fields in the query are equal to null

For instance, a collection inventory has the following index on the type and item fields:

```
db.inventory.createIndex({ type: 1, item: 1 })
```

This index will cover the operation that queries on the type and item fields, but returns only the item field, without the _id value, since the index does not include the _id field:

```
db.inventory.find(
   {
      type: "food",
      item: "bread"
   },
   { item: 1, _id: 0 }
)
```

An index can also cover a query on fields within embedded documents. Say you have a collection, userdata, containing some login data as follows:

```
{ id: 1, user: { login: "tester" }}
```

You will have the following index:

```
{ "user.login": 1 }
```

For this index, the following query will be required:

```
db.userdata.find(
    { "user.login": "tester" },
    { "user.login": 1, _id: 0 }
)
```

Now, let's explore another very interesting and useful type of index: hashed indexes.

Hashed index

A hashed index contains the hashed values of the indexed fields, and they are ideal for equality matching. However, they cannot be used for range queries. To create a hashed index on the book titles in your `books` collection, you can use the following command:

```
db.books.createIndex({ "title": "hashed" })
```

Hashed indexes create more evenly distributed values. The field you choose for your hashed shard key should have higher cardinality (a large number of different values). Therefore, hashed indexing is the ideal solution for shard keys with fields that are monotonically growing functions, such as `ObjectId` values or timestamps.

In scenarios where your data does not contain a single field with high cardinality, consider creating a compound hashed index. A compound hashed index provides more unique indexed values and can increase cardinality. A compound hashed key is created by hashing one value and providing the sorting orders for the others. Take the following example:

```
db.books.createIndex(
    {
        "created": "hashed",
        "title": 1,
        "author": -1
    }
)
```

The decision to hash some of the indexes can usually be postponed after the main optimizations have been applied.

However, you should take into account the following limitations of hashed indexes:

- The hashing function does not support multi-key indexes, so you cannot create a hashed index on a field that contains an array.

- You cannot insert an array into a hashed index field.

- Unique constraints cannot be specified on a hashed index. The solution is usually to create an additional, non-hashed index with the unique constraint, and then let MongoDB use that non-hashed index to enforce uniqueness on the desired field.

Text indexes

MongoDB supports full-text searching through text indexes—special indexes on string value fields. Creating the text index is similar to other types of indexes, replacing the order 1 or -1 with text.

If you don't have a real text field apart from the title in your dummy books collection, you could use the title for the text field as follows:

```
db.books.createIndex({ "author": "text" })
```

Text indexing provides performance improvements when searching for a substring within a string, and these indexes are bound to some rules.

Since a collection can have at most one text index, and this index will support multiple fields (textual or not), it is important to carefully choose the fields for text indexing. Reconstructing the text index can take some time compared to other types of indexes.

Text indexes will apply word stemming (removing common suffixes and removing stop words, such as *a*, *an*, *the*, etc.).

With the possibility of creating a text index based on several fields, MongoDB also provides you with the opportunity to specify how much importance each text field should have. For instance, you can value match the title or subtitle of a document compared to the same matches in a simple paragraph of an article.

In case of a hypothetical newspaper application, with a collection of articles that have a title, a teaser, and the body, you could create a text index resembling the following:

```
db.articles.createIndex(
  {
    "title": "text",
    "teaser": "text",
    "body": "text"
  },
  {
    weights: { title: 10, teaser: 8, body: 1 }
    name: "TextIndex"
  }
)
```

The preceding code would create a text index on three fields, but search matches on the title would be scored 10 times more than matches on the body, and slightly more (1, 25) than on the teaser.

While other indexes can use a full collection scan and resolve the query without an index, text searches cannot. So, if text searching is needed, the use of a text index is mandatory.

Since MongoDB performs a full index search for every single search term, text index performance is directly proportional to the number of search terms. To improve the performance of a text query, limit the number of documents by using a compound index including maybe the author of the document or a date range, thus partitioning the documents and speeding up the text-index search by reducing the search space.

MongoDB Atlas has a *full-text search index* based on *Apache Lucene*, which has additional capabilities compared to *MongoDB text indexing*, so if text searching is of paramount importance, Atlas Search indexes may be a better fit.

MongoDB suggests always having enough memory on your system to keep the text index in memory. Additional factors to consider when building text indexes include the following:

- Text indexes can consume lots of RAM as they must contain one index entry for each unique post-stemmed word in each indexed field for each document inserted. This index can grow very quickly!

- Although building a text index is similar to building a large, multikey index, it takes longer than building a simple ordered (scalar) index on the same data.

- Text indexes can impact write performance because MongoDB must add an index entry for each unique post-stemmed word in each indexed field of each new source document.

- Text indexes store individual words of a text string and not phrases or any data about the proximity of the words in the documents. As a consequence, queries that specify multiple words run faster when the entire collection fits in RAM.

Atlas Search Indexes

The Atlas Search Index is a MongoDB data structure that is used for categorizing data in an efficiently and easily searchable format. This index creates mapping between terms and documents containing said terms, enabling fast retrieval of documents using identifiers.

Atlas Search indexes must be configured to be able to query data in your Atlas Cluster using Atlas Search. Atlas Search Indexes can be created on a single field or on multiple fields and the process is quite straightforward, as you will see in *Chapter 13, Introduction to Atlas Search*. Similar to other index types, it is recommended to index fields that you will regularly use for searching and sorting.

TTL indexes

Time-to-live (**TTL**) indexes are special indexes used to automatically delete documents after an expiry period, specified in seconds. They are configured through a field that must contain a date or an array of dates (in which case the earliest one will be used as a reference) and an expiration time.

Returning to the `books` collection, you could create an index on the created field, and specify 60 * 60 * 24 = 86,400 seconds, which is equivalent to one day:

```
db.books.createIndex(
    { "created": 1 },
    { expireAfterSeconds: 86400 }
)
```

After exactly one day, the MongoDB background job, which runs every 60 seconds, will select the index and delete all the books with a `created` datetime value that is older than the `expireAfterSeconds` period of `86400` seconds or one day. It is worth considering that if the number of documents to be deleted is large, it would be wise to schedule the deletion in batches.

TTL indexes are useful for deleting documents that represent data such as user sessions or logs, for instance, after a prescribed period of time. They come with some limitations: they cannot be compound indexes. Starting in MongoDB 7.0, you can, however, create partial TTL indexes on time series collections.

Partial indexes

Partial indexes are often used to optimize queries. They are simple indexes applied on documents that satisfy an expression, specified in the `partialFilterExpression` query.

For instance, you can create an index on the title and on the price of your books, but only for books that cost more than $50:

```
db.books.createIndex(
    { "meta.price": 1, "title": 1 },
    { partialFilterExpression:
        {
            "meta.price": { $gt: 50 }
        }
    }
)
```

Partial indexes use less storage than full indexes and they are much quicker to create. The supported expressions provide a comfortable environment for specifying criteria:

- Equality expressions (that is, `field: value`, or using the `$eq` operator)
- `$exists: true` expression
- `$type` expressions
- Comparison expressions ($gt, $gte, $lt, and $lte)
- The $and operator on the top level only

For queries that might use only a subset of the data—the most recent social network status, the latest news, or something similar, a partial index can be very helpful as it concentrates only on the data that matters the most.

Geospatial indexes

Geospatial indexes enable you to create powerful geo-aware applications. There are two types of geospatial indexes:

- 2d geospatial indexes store geospatial data on a two-dimensional plane, and are mostly kept for legacy reasons. The 2d index is intended for queries on legacy coordinate pairs. Newer applications should always use 2dsphere indexes unless the data points are already stored in a legacy 2d plane format.

- 2dsphere coordinates calculate their geometries on an earth-like sphere surface, taking into account the curvature of the Earth, thus providing more accuracy compared to the 2d coordinates. For example, 2dsphere indexes can determine points within a specified area, calculate proximity to a specified point, and return exact matches on coordinate queries.

Geospatial querying is a rich topic as it enables you to use an array of querying operators, such as the following:

- $near: For finding nearby points or shapes starting from a given GeoPoint (a specific location on the Earth's surface)

- $geoWithin: For finding all data points that are within an area (for instance, in GeoJSON format)

- $geoIntersects: For determining which area intersects with which objects

An excellent example of a geospatial index can be found in the MongoDB Atlas sample dataset—the sample_geospatial database. The shipwrecks collection is a dataset of shipwrecks with coordinates for longitudes and latitudes, and the documents can be queried by using the geoNear operator.

In order to see geospatial indexing, you can open the sample sample_geospatial database from Atlas in MongoDB Compass, and select the sole collection within, named shipwrecks. The sample_geospatial database contains data specifically designed to help familiarize you with GeoJSON data.

After inspecting the fields in the collection document, let's paste the following query into the *Filter* of the *Documents* tab in MongoDB Compass in order to search for all the documents within a certain distance from a point in space:

```
{
  coordinates:{
    $near:{
      $geometry:{
        type: "Point",
        coordinates: [-80, 9.3]
      },
      $maxDistance: 10000
    }
  }
}
```

This query takes a single coordinates field, denoted by the longitude and latitude, and searches for the nearest points within a maximum distance of 10,000 meters.

Figure 10.5: Searching for nearest points

Note that due to the nature of MongoDB's geospatial operators, 2d and 2dsphere indexes cannot create covered queries.

Wildcard indexes

Wildcard indexes allow you to use the wildcard operator (*) to define a pattern that will be used for including or excluding a field. Use wildcard indexes to support queries against arbitrary or unknown fields. This is useful when you don't know the exact fields that'll be present in the document beforehand.

Theoretically, you can use this type of index to index all the attributes:

```
db.books.createIndex({ "$**": 1 })
```

However, this will recursively index every attribute for every subdocument and array type. Hence, it is not preferred in many cases.

Examining your artificially created books collection, a sample document might look like the following:

```
{
    "_id": {
     "$oid": "651726fe01c6f61ad8ee6460"
    },
    "i": 0,
    "author": "Author_0",
    "title": "Book title 0",
    "ISBN": 74498,
    "created": {
      "$date": "2023-09-29T19:35:26.394Z"
    },
    "meta": {
      "price": 56,
      "rating": 0.16225525931335527
    }
}
```

In your case, it'll make sense to just target the meta field, since you may decide to add other subfields to the meta field later:

```
db.books.createIndex({ "meta.$**": 1 })
```

This will cover all the possible values inside a potentially varying meta field.

Wildcard indexes can use the wildcardProjection option. However, this option is only valid when you create a wildcard index on all document fields. You can't specify the wildcardProjection option when you create a wildcard index on a specific field path and its subfields.

Consider using a wildcard index in the following scenarios:

- If your application queries a collection in which field names vary between documents, a wildcard index can support queries on all possible document field names.

- If your application repeatedly queries an embedded document field where the subfields are not consistent, a wildcard index will support queries on all of the subfields.

- If your application queries documents that share common characteristics. A compound wildcard index can efficiently cover many queries for documents that have common fields.

It's important to bear in mind that, while initially appealing, wildcard indexes are not a universal solution. Having large, unbounded number of fields indexed can result in poor performance under certain circumstances. The documentation on wildcard indexing is available on the MongoDB website: https://www.mongodb.com/docs/manual/core/indexes/index-types/index-wildcard/.

Hidden indexes

Hidden indexes are indexes that are not visible to the MongoDB query planner but are nevertheless present. These indexes are not used to speed up queries but operate as intended: a TTL hidden index will delete documents after an expiration period, unique hidden indexes will enforce uniqueness on a field, and so on.

Creating a hidden index on your books collection will have the following syntax:

```
db.books.createIndex(
  { "title": 1 },
  {
    hidden: true,
    name: "hidden_name_index"
  }
)
```

To unhide the index, keep it, and at the same time remove the hidden property, you can issue the following command:

```
db.books.unhideIndex("hidden_name_index")
```

Similarly, you can use the hideIndex command to hide an existing index.

Compound wildcard indexes

One of the most exciting features introduced in the MongoDB 7.0 release is the introduction of *compound wildcard indexes*. These indexes support performant and fast queries against a combination of fields and an always-present field. They help solve numerous practical problems.

Similar to a regular compound index, which has multiple index terms, a compound wildcard index has one wildcard term and one or more additional index terms.

> **Tip**
> The example provided by Cris Stauffer, Director of Product Management at MongoDB, is highly illustrative for this purpose. You can find the link to his presentation on YouTube: https://youtu.be/kFLjFRHA9Pg.

Consider a scenario, where you own a store, and you have different sets of attributes for groups of products that you have in stock. These attributes will not be the same for jewelry, clothing, or electronics. A sample document could look like the following:

```
{
  "seller_id": "123",
  "name": "Ring",
  "attributes":
    {
      "color": "blue",
      "size": "S",
      "material": "silver",
    },
  "stock":2
}
```

This type of document can be indexed with a compound wildcard index as shown:

```
db.products.createIndex(
  {
    seller_id: 1,
    "attributes.$**": 1,
    name: 1,
    stock: 1
  }
)
```

This type of indexing enables sophisticated aggregations and queries. For instance, you could query for a product that is short on stock, and has a particular `seller_id`, but also match on attributes, which could be different across multiple sellers. These queries are highly optimized, leveraging the strengths of both regular indexing and wildcard indexing for certain fields.

Best practices for index optimization

Now that you have covered a lot of ground and explored various MongoDB indexes, let's look at the best practices and guidelines for optimizing indexes.

Creating indexes for your MongoDB database is an important task that can—and will—determine the speed and performance of the queries and the overall database performance. As you've seen throughout this chapter, creating indexes is easy and intuitive, and there are many types of indexes that cover almost every possible use case. However, having too many or inadequate indexes can hamper the database performance, and special care should be taken when deciding on what to index and how to index.

One of the most important features of an index is its *selectivity*—the measure of the number of documents associated with a single index value. An index is said to be selective if it has many unique values and few duplicates. Cardinality, on the other hand, refers to several unique values in a document attribute or index. Selectivity can then be defined as the ratio between cardinality and the total number of documents in a collection.

Highly selective indexes are more efficient than less selective ones since they can quickly point to the desired dataset. MongoDB always tries to optimize the queries to use the most selective index. Although unique indexes are usually created to enforce uniqueness in a specific field, they are highly selective.

Summary

In this chapter, you discovered MongoDB indexes, their types, and their uses. You explored how carefully crafted indexes can speed up your queries, and gained insights into best practices for database optimization. You learned about single-field indexes, compound indexes, wildcard indexes, and multikey indexes, illustrating how each can contribute to optimizing queries and aggregations.

Additionally, the chapter delved into specialized indexes, including geospatial, hidden, and the newly introduced compound wildcard index, addressing the challenge of indexing fields not known in advance. Finally, it delved into tips and strategies for constructing optimized indexes to maximize the efficiency of your queries.

In the next chapter, you will learn about MongoDB Atlas—the most advanced cloud database service on the market.

11

MongoDB Atlas: Powering the Future of Developer Data Platforms

MongoDB Atlas is more than just a database service. It's a comprehensive solution, carefully crafted for developers to simplify and enhance data management. This platform is tailored according to the needs of modern applications, which are often characterized by large data volumes, automation requirements, rapid scalability, and the need for adaptability amidst change.

MongoDB Atlas enables a user-friendly GUI for database maintenance, automated backups, and point-in-time data snapshots. It offers various features such as automated upscaling, monitoring, alerting, Vector Search, Full-text Search, Triggers and Functions, Device Sync, and performance optimization tools for diagnosing poorly constructed queries.

These features aim to consolidate various workloads into a single-developer data platform across the enterprise. Whether a start-up or a well-established enterprise, MongoDB Atlas caters to all cloud-based database needs. As you delve further into this chapter, you'll explore the capabilities of MongoDB Atlas in depth and breadth.

This chapter will cover the following topics:

- Extensive features offered by MongoDB Atlas as a database-as-a-service

- Integration of MongoDB Atlas resources with Kubernetes clusters

- Features such as Atlas Vector Search, Atlas Stream Processing, Atlas Data Federation, and Atlas SQL Interface

Understanding MongoDB Atlas as a database-as-a-service

MongoDB Atlas can manage a wide spectrum of data types across an organization—from real-time updates to unstructured data residing in data lakes. Its multi-cloud compatibility further extends its utility, offering a unified environment for a variety of data and application services. This integration empowers development teams to rapidly build with the performance, scalability, and capabilities demanded by contemporary applications.

The MongoDB Atlas developer data platform is built on the infrastructure of **Amazon Web Services (AWS)**, **Google Cloud Platform (GCP)**, and Azure to enable database scaling to over 95+ cloud regions. This provides a high degree of flexibility and control in data management. Users have the choice to either utilize MongoDB Atlas on a single cloud provider or take advantage of its multi-cloud capabilities for enhanced flexibility and resilience.

Its comprehensive platform for managing MongoDB clusters automates several aspects of database management, including deployment and upscaling, thus streamlining the process for developers and DevOps engineers. This enables a quick setup of a MongoDB cluster accessible via a web interface, or through Atlas CLI, Terraform MongoDB Atlas Provider, or MongoDB Kubernetes Operator.

As a **database-as-a-service (DaaS)** offering, MongoDB Atlas also handles maintenance tasks such as software patching, hardware provisioning, setup configuration, and failure recovery. MongoDB Atlas has an updated upgrade process where it schedules and performs minor upgrades during regular maintenance windows. These upgrades are done by MongoDB, requiring no user intervention, and necessitating no downtime. Thus, using MongoDB Atlas ensures that your database is always running the latest and most secure version of MongoDB.

Some of the other features of MongoDB Atlas include:

- Automated security measures, including network isolation using **virtual private clouds (VPCs)**, encryption at rest, and in-transit, and **role-based access control (RBAC)**

- Automated backup solutions, taking regular snapshots of the data and allowing for point-in-time recovery

- Cross-region availability, automatically replicating data across regions based on configuration

Figure 11.1 shows some of the key features of MongoDB Atlas:

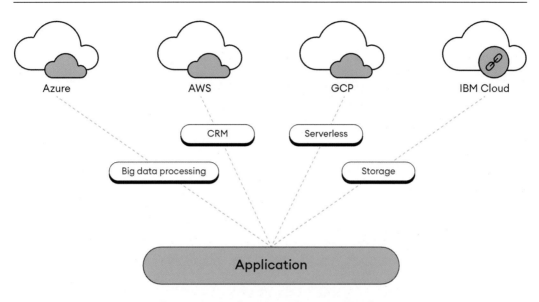

Figure 11.1: Key features of MongoDB Atlas

MongoDB Atlas offers big data processing, serverless computing, and storage. The following section will delve into MongoDB Atlas as a hosted database that offers different options for deployment of applications.

Hosted database

Fundamentally, MongoDB Atlas is a hosted DaaS solution where you receive a ready-made database that is fully administrated by MongoDB Inc. Every hosted database is catered to your specific needs, but in most cases, you'll simply look for a secure deployment with a connection string.

The default deployment is a three-node replica set in a region, a zone, and on a cloud provider of your choice. There is a free-forever tier, a shared infrastructure tier, and dedicated hardware options for the user to select from.

If you do have more specific requirements, MongoDB Atlas provides many different variants of deployment, which are detailed below.

Global Clusters

Atlas Global Clusters allow for geographically local read and write operations by defining single- or multi-region zones. Each Global Cluster can have up to nine distinct zones, each with a *Highest Priority* region and one or more *Electable*, *Read-only*, or *Analytics* nodes:

- **Highest Priority region**: Hosts the primary replica set member for associated shards, directing write operations

- **Electable region**: Hosts electable secondary replica set members, providing fault tolerance during regional outages

- **Read-only region**: Hosts non-electable secondary replica set members, supporting secondary read operations
- **Analytics region**: Hosts analytics nodes, isolating reporting queries and reducing latency for local reads

MongoDB Atlas distributes shard nodes across the configured regions for each shard associated with a zone. It supports upto 50 shards per sharded cluster, irrespective of the number of zones.

Cross-region and cross-cloud replication

Cross-region and cross-cloud replication provide data redundancy and low-latency read access. During setup, the MongoDB Atlas service automatically distributes the nodes in your replica sets across the availability zones in your selected region, enabling failover during incidents that affect a single cloud data center. Cross-region replication supports failover to a different region during incidents affecting an entire region. It also allows data copies to be spread across regions for low latency read access for distributed users of the data.

Multi-cloud clusters

MongoDB Atlas facilitates the deployment of a single database cluster across multiple cloud platforms, including AWS, GCP, and Azure. Multi-cloud clusters enable applications to simultaneously use the services from different cloud providers seamlessly, as well as facilitating migrations between cloud providers. This mitigates the operational complexity of managing data replication and migration across clouds.

In case of an issue with one cloud provider, automated failover to another cloud provider serving the same geographical location is possible. Further, it supports a single database spanning any combination of the 95+ supported regions, catering to specific regional or cloud preferences.

Serverless instances

Atlas serverless instances provide a flexible, scalable, and cost-effective solution for deploying databases. They are designed to automatically adjust to the changing demands of your application, eliminating the need for manual capacity planning.

The key feature of Atlas serverless instances is their ability to dynamically scale based on your workload. Unlike traditional databases that require pre-allocation of resources, Atlas serverless instances automatically adjust their capacity based on the incoming traffic. This means that during periods of high demand, the serverless instance will automatically scale up to ensure consistent performance. Conversely, during periods of low demand, it scales down to save costs. This dynamic scaling happens in real-time and can support up to 1 TB of storage.

Atlas serverless instances follow a pay-as-you-go pricing model. Instead of paying for pre-allocated resources, you pay only for the actual reads, writes, and storage that your application uses. This model ensures you're not paying for idle resources, making it a cost-effective solution for applications with unpredictable traffic patterns.

All these variants of deployment also offer built-in security features and adhere to compliance regulations.

Secure by default

MongoDB Atlas has undergone rigorous auditing processes to achieve certifications such as *HIPAA* and *GDPR compliance, ISO, PCI*, and *FedRAMP Moderate*. These certifications demonstrate the commitment of MongoDB Atlas to maintaining high levels of data protection, privacy, and compliance:

- HIPAA compliance ensures that MongoDB Atlas is suitable for handling sensitive health information.

- GDPR compliance guarantees that the platform adheres to data protection and privacy standards for handling the data of European Union citizens.

- ISO certification indicates that MongoDB Atlas meets international standards for data security.

- PCI compliance ensures that the platform can securely handle cardholder data, making it suitable for e-commerce applications.

- FedRAMP Moderate certification signifies that MongoDB Atlas meets the security requirements needed to handle federal government data.

MongoDB Atlas offers robust security defaults. It provides built-in security controls for all data, whether managed in a customer environment or through MongoDB Atlas. It enables enterprise-grade security features and simplifies the deployment and management of databases. *Figure 11.2* shows some of the security features:

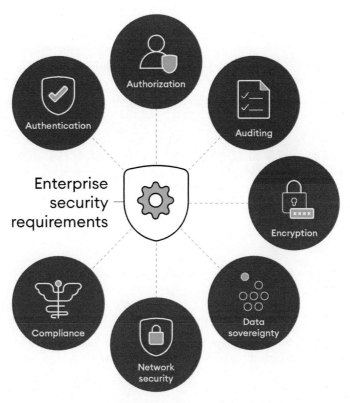

Figure 11.2: Security features of MongoDB Atlas

- **Authentication**: Users can authenticate Atlas UI with their Atlas credentials or use single sign-on via their GitHub or Google accounts. MongoDB Atlas also supports **multi-factor authentication (MFA)** with various options including OTP authenticators, push notifications, FIDO2 (hardware security keys or biometrics), SMS, and email. Users can also authenticate the MongoDB database using mechanisms including SCRAM, x.509 certificates, LDAP, password-less authentication with AWS **Identity and Access Management (IAM)**, and OpenID Connect support.

- **Authorization**: RBAC is available to manage all cloud resources, including MongoDB deployments. Users can be granted one or more roles that determine their access privileges for their organizations and projects. Fine-grained database roles for database operations can also be granted. With identity federation, access to MongoDB Atlas can be managed via identity provider groups and Atlas roles using group-role mappings.

- **Auditing**: The granular auditing functionality monitors actions in the MongoDB environment to prevent and detect any unauthorized access to data. This includes **create**, **read**, **update**, and **delete (CRUD)** operations, encryption key management, authentication, RBAC, replication, and sharding cluster operations.

- **Data encryption**: The data encryption capabilities offered are robust and comprehensive, ensuring the protection of data at various states:

  - **Encryption at rest**: In MongoDB Atlas, data stored on disks is encrypted by default with AES-256, protecting all volume (disk) data. This process is integrated with the transparent disk encryption service from your chosen cloud provider, which manages all encryption keys. You can also enable the native encryption at rest feature of the MongoDB WiredTiger storage engine. This feature encrypts data files on disk, providing an additional layer of security on top of the cloud provider's storage encryption. It also supports the use of user-managed encryption keys. The encryption algorithm used is **Advanced Encryption Standard – 256 bit – Cipher Block Chaining (AES-256-CBC)**. The encryption keys are rotated every 90 days or according to the user's custom schedule.

  - **Encryption in-transit**: All data traveling between your application and MongoDB Atlas is automatically encrypted using **transport layer security (TLS)**. MongoDB Atlas requires TLS for all incoming connections and has a minimum version requirement of TLS 1.2.

  - **Field-level encryption**: MongoDB Atlas also supports field-level encryption. Specific fields in a document can be encrypted on the client side before the document is sent to the server. This adds an extra layer of security as only those with access to the right encryption key can decrypt and read sensitive data.

  - **Key management**: MongoDB Atlas integrates with the **key management services (KMSs)** of major cloud providers, including AWS KMS, Azure Key Vault, and Google Cloud KMS. These services manage the cryptographic keys for data encryption, allowing for secure key storage, key rotation, and auditing. Additionally, MongoDB Atlas provides the option for users to utilize **customer-managed encryption keys (CMK)** with database-level encryption, offering greater control over data encryption and security.

Figure 11.3 shows various options available for implementing encryption at rest in MongoDB Atlas:

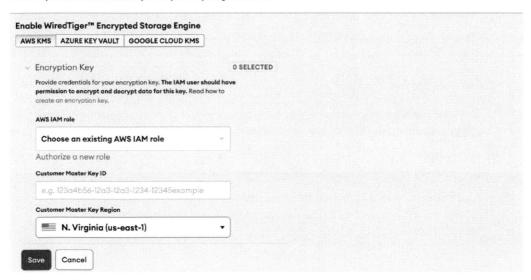

Figure 11.3: Encryption at rest using your Key Management

- **Network security**: MongoDB Atlas offers a variety of secure data access methods for network security. These methods involve the use of dedicated clusters within a unique VPC to isolate and protect data, effectively preventing any inbound network access from the internet. Unidirectional connections from the VPCs or **virtual networks** (**VNets**) of AWS, Azure, or Google Cloud to the clusters via private endpoints are permitted.

- **Encrypted backups**: MongoDB Atlas uses your cloud provider's standard storage encryption method to encrypt all snapshots, securing cluster data when at rest. The management of the encryption keys for this process is handled by your cloud provider.

In projects and clusters where WiredTiger Encryption at rest with Customer Key Management is activated, MongoDB Atlas not only encrypts your snapshots but also adds an additional layer of encryption to your data files.

For any secure environment or system, it is essential to detect the threat at the earliest opportunity and raise alerts that can be responded to with appropriate security measures. The following section explores the monitoring and alerting capabilities available within MongoDB Atlas.

Monitoring and alerting

MongoDB Atlas offers an extensive array of tools and features designed to assist in the monitoring of database deployments with the goal of allowing performance reviews and ensuring reliability. In addition to these monitoring capabilities, built-in alerting functionality is also available, providing an extra layer of oversight and control. This combination of monitoring and alerting offers a detailed and comprehensive approach to managing database performance.

The following is a sample of various monitoring techniques utilized within MongoDB Atlas, along with use cases for how you might utilize each of these features:

- **Use case**: Identifying slow queries

    - **Performance Advisor**: Helps you monitor and improve slow queries, suggesting new indexes and providing insights and recommendations for optimization

    - **Query Profiler**: Monitors query performance, giving a detailed view of how queries are executed and where potential bottlenecks may occur

    - **Real-time performance panel**: Provides real-time insights into the performance of the database, enabling quick identification and addressing of slow queries

- **Use case**: Improving schema design

    - **Frequently used schema design patterns**: Helps in understanding common practices and apply them to specific use cases

    - **Performance Advisor and Atlas UI recommendations**: Offer recommendations to improve schemas tailored to specific database structures and usage patterns

- **Use case**: Diagnosing performance issues via deployment metrics

    - **Disk space utilization**: Includes user data and MongoDB's operational data, essential for assessing storage capacity

    - **Operational data metrics**: Comprises buffer files (temporary storage), journal files (data integrity), and log files (event recording), each playing a role in data management and recovery

    - **Performance metrics**: Indicators such as throughput and latency provide a real-time view of database performance

    - **Scalability and stability metrics**: These metrics help in understanding system scalability under different loads as well as overall stability, including uptime and recovery times

These are only a fraction of the robust set of metrics available to developers, database administrators, and operational administrators offered by MongoDB Atlas.

All the preceding metrics are available for alerting in MongoDB Atlas. Alerts can be set at a variety of levels, intervals, and circumstances, and can be triggered based on specific conditions to maintain optimal database deployment performance. These conditions can be tailored to various aspects, such as specific database metrics, user behavior or actions, account activity, and more.

When an alert is triggered, it can be sent via an SMS or email (including email aliases). All of these are fully configurable in the Atlas UI or via administrative APIs.

Further, MongoDB Atlas has a variety of popular third-party integrations, which allow connection with external monitoring services such as *Datadog, Opsgenie, Prometheus*, or *PagerDuty*.

Another critical aspect of security is creating regular backups and restoring data to avoid any data loss or unfavorable situations.

Back up, restore, and archive

MongoDB Atlas offers many features to back up, restore, and archive data, ensuring data protection and compliance. Backups encapsulate the state of a cluster at a specific time, acting as a safety measure against data loss. MongoDB Atlas utilizes the native snapshot capabilities of cloud providers for full-copy snapshots and localized snapshot storage. For some instances, backups are automatically enabled and can't be disabled; for others, there's much more flexibility. For example:

- **Serverless instance snapshots**: Backups are automatically enabled for serverless instances, supporting full-copy snapshots and localized snapshot storage. Serverless instance snapshots can be restored to other serverless instances and dedicated clusters.

- **Online archive**: MongoDB Atlas moves infrequently accessed data to a MongoDB-managed read-only federated database instance on cloud object storage, providing a unified view of MongoDB Atlas and archived data. This feature is available only on `M10` clusters and above, and is not supported on serverless instances.

> **Note**
>
> Atlas backups are not available for free `M0` clusters, but you can manually back up using `mongodump` and `mongorestore`. Restores must be made to a cluster running the same major release version or the next higher one. Backups made before an upgrade can still be used.

Chapter 12, Monitoring and Backup in MongoDB, discusses backups in more detail.

Automation

MongoDB Atlas integrates advanced automation features for efficient database management. These capabilities minimize manual tasks, optimize resources, and enhance performance. Let's explore how these functions contribute to a streamlined database experience:

- **Cluster creation and user management**: MongoDB Atlas streamlines the process of setting up and managing database clusters by automating key tasks. Cluster creation is simplified with intuitive tools and templates that guide you through the configuration process, enabling quick deployment of customized cluster hardware to meet specific requirements. User management is also enhanced through automation, with features such as RBAC, user provisioning, and security settings that can be easily configured and managed.

- **Auto-scaling**: MongoDB Atlas offers an auto-scaling feature that automatically adjusts the cluster's resources based on demand. It analyzes CPU and memory utilization to scale the cluster tier up or down, ensuring optimal performance. Storage scaling is also provided, automatically increasing storage when disk space usage reaches 90%. The process includes considerations for sharded clusters, storage behavior, and oplog size. Auto-scaling is enabled by default but can be customized or opted out of, and it operates without incurring downtime.

- **Automated upgrades**: Automated minor version updates are applied to upgrade the MongoDB database seamlessly in the background, ensuring that you always have access to the latest bug fixes, security patches, and other critical updates without any manual intervention. Upgrades from one release series to another are also simplified, with no need to modify the underlying operating system or handle package files. By automating these upgrades, the platform enables you to focus on building your applications, thus enhancing efficiency and ensuring that the database is always running the most current and secure version.

- **Automated maintenance**: Maintenance is performed automatically in the background, enabling you to configure a preferred weekly maintenance window for minimal disruption. The process is resilient to replica set elections, and maintenance continues even if there are changes within the replica set. Notifications about upcoming maintenance events are provided, and maintenance is performed on a rolling basis across the nodes, ensuring no downtime. You can monitor the status and access logs for detailed information, though this is not required.

Atlas developer data platform

Having explored MongoDB Atlas as a database service, let's now shift focus to its broader capabilities as a comprehensive data development platform. Over recent years, MongoDB has enriched the Atlas platform with numerous features, enhancing the traditional functionalities of the MongoDB database. These additions establish MongoDB Atlas as a robust data platform, offering vital tools for the development of modern applications, including full-text search, vector search, streams, and data federation. Let's delve deeper into these features.

Atlas Vector Search and its role in AI applications

In 2023, MongoDB introduced a public preview of its new product, *Atlas Vector Search*. Built on the MongoDB Atlas developer data platform, this innovative feature is designed to power intelligent applications with semantic search and generative AI capabilities over any type of data.

What does vector search entail?

Vector search is a technique that enables semantic search, which involves querying data based on its inherent meaning. This method utilizes machine learning models, often referred to as encoders, to convert various forms of data—such as text, audio, and images—into high-dimensional vectors. These vectors encapsulate the semantic essence of the data, which can then be sifted through to identify similar content based on the proximity of vectors in a high-dimensional space. Vectorized search can therefore effectively supplement traditional keyword-based search methods. It's also gaining significant attention due to its potential to enhance the capabilities of **large language models** (**LLMs**) by offering ground truth beyond the LLMs' inherent knowledge. In the context of search use cases, vector search enables the retrieval of pertinent results even in the absence of exact phrasing. This method proves beneficial in various scenarios, including natural language processing and recommendation systems.

To illustrate this, consider that you have a collection of documents in MongoDB made up of articles written for a blog. You'd like to search for documents related to *artificial intelligence*. For a full-text search, you would search for documents that contain the exact phrase of *artificial intelligence* or *AI*, and you would get back a result set. However, this result set is based on matches with that word, rather than any understanding or context of what the words might mean. So, it would include documents that mention artificial intelligence but are not about that topic per se.

Vector search instead takes the query *artificial intelligence* and the documents, and transforms them into numerical vectors using techniques such as word or document embeddings. Documents are then compared to find those that are of similar query vectors using a cosine similarity metric.

The embeddings capture semantic meaning and relationships between words so that you are more likely to receive documents only about AI, as opposed to those merely mentioning it. This provides more accurate and contextually relevant results compared to the full-text search approach.

What is Atlas Vector Search?

MongoDB's implementation of vector search on the Atlas platform is a unified, fully managed feature that integrates the operational database and a vector store. It supports quick integrations into LLMs, making it a fast and user-friendly way to build semantic search and AI-powered applications that utilize data stored in MongoDB.

The platform enables you to search through any unstructured data. You can create vector embeddings using the machine learning model of your choice, such as OpenAI or Hugging Face, and store them in MongoDB Atlas. It powers use cases such as similarity search, recommendation engines, Q&A systems, dynamic personalization, and long-term memory for LLMs.

Figure 11.4 highlights the features of Atlas Vector Search. It illustrates a process where data is placed into Atlas Vector Search from various internal data sources, such as databases, CRMs, and white papers, and stored as embeddings.

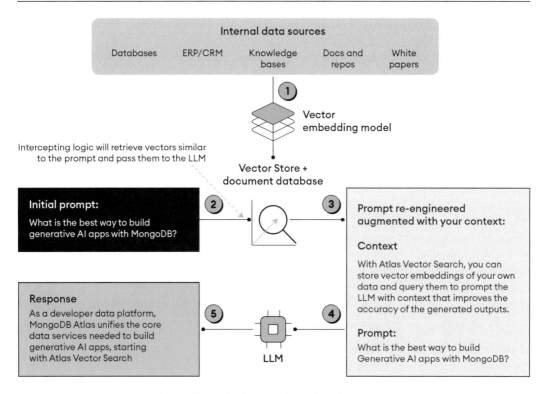

Figure 11.4: Atlas Vector Search in MongoDB

This vector database then serves as the long-term memory for LLMs, expanding its knowledge base by storing private or domain-specific information outside the LLM in the form of embeddings. When you pose a question, the vector database searches for the top results most pertinent to your query. These results are then amalgamated with the original question to formulate a prompt that offers a comprehensive context for the LLM, enabling it to generate more precise answers. This integrated solution is commonly referred to as a CVP stack, comprising ChatGPT/LLMs, a vector database, and prompt-as-code.

Atlas Vector Search simplifies the process of working with databases and vector search by using the unified MongoDB Query API. This allows you to build AI-powered experiences on MongoDB Atlas as part of a single, consistent developer experience. With this, you can access all the data you need; however, you need to query it.

One of the key features of Atlas Vector Search is the ability to store your vector embeddings right next to source data and metadata, thanks to the power of the document model. Vector data is integrated with application data and seamlessly indexed for semantic queries, enabling you to build simpler and faster applications.

Semantic search and vectors

Semantic search is the concept of searching based on the meaning of data rather than the data itself. In this context, a vector is a numeric representation of your data that can be searched using advanced machine learning algorithms.

Atlas Vector Search and Atlas Search have distinct functionalities. Atlas Vector Search enables searching through data using semantic meaning captured in vectors. In contrast, Atlas Search facilitates keyword search based on the actual text and any predefined synonym mappings.

KNN, ANN, and vector embeddings

k-nearest neighbors (kNNs) algorithms are frequently used to find vectors near one another. **Approximate nearest neighbors (ANNs)**, is a technique for finding similar vectors that trade a degree of accuracy for performance. This is one of the core algorithms used to power Atlas Vector Search. The algorithm for ANN search uses **hierarchical navigable small world (HNSW)** graphs.

Atlas Vector Search supports embeddings from any provider that are under the 2,048-dimension width limit on the service. It is supported as a vector store in both LangChain and LlamaIndex, two popular frameworks for building services that utilize LLMs.

Atlas Vector Search can query any kind of data that can be turned into an embedding. This includes images, media files, and other types of data. One of the benefits of the document model is that you can store your embeddings right alongside your rich data in your documents.

How to use Atlas Vector Search

To use Atlas Vector Search, take a look at the following steps:

1. Create your Atlas cluster to lay the foundation for vector search.

2. Set up the embedding creation function. To create embeddings, you must use a specific model, such as `all-MiniLM-L6-v2`. Various methods are available for this, including calling a managed API such as Hugging Face or the OpenAI API, hosting the model yourself, or running it locally.

3. Define and integrate your embedding function into your code, enabling you to generate embeddings for specific texts.

4. Store these embeddings in your database, either in the original collection or a separate one.

5. Go to Atlas Search to create an index, essential for vector search operations.

With everything in place, you can now query your data using the `$vectorSearch` stage in the MongoDB Query Language workflow to retrieve results that align with your search intent.

> **Note**
> Always refer to the official documentation for detailed steps and best practices.

Atlas Search

Not to be confused with Vector Search, Atlas Search is an integrated full-text search feature providing a scalable solution for creating relevance-based application features. It's built on top of Apache Lucene, with the intention of removing the necessity for a separate search system alongside your database. *Chapter 13, Introduction to Atlas Search* will explore the functionalities and uses of Atlas Search in greater detail.

Atlas Application Services

Beyond the robust search capabilities of Atlas Vector Search and Atlas Search, there's Atlas Application Services, enhancing the overall application development experience. This suite provides a range of tools to streamline and optimize your MongoDB applications.

What is Atlas Application Services?

MongoDB Atlas Application Services is a serverless application backend designed to streamline the development of cloud-based applications. It provides a suite of tools and services that allow developers to focus on building unique features rather than managing database and server infrastructure.

Atlas Application Services is designed to address common challenges faced by backend, web, and mobile app developers. It offers configurable functions, integrated data access, and security rules, allowing you to focus on crafting unique features instead of boilerplate backend code.

- For backend developers, Atlas Application Services provides a platform to develop applications that can react to changes in MongoDB Atlas data, connect that data to other systems, and scale to meet demand, all without the need to manage database and server infrastructure.

- Web developers often encounter overhead when sending data from a server to the browser, including tasks such as authentication and data validation. Atlas Application Services provides solutions for these challenges, allowing you to focus on the unique features of their applications.

- For mobile app developers, syncing data across devices can be a significant challenge. Atlas Application Services, in combination with Atlas Device Sync, offers an offline-first, cross-platform solution for syncing data between a backend and mobile devices.

Figure 11.5 illustrates the key features of Atlas Application Services, including Atlas Functions, Atlas Triggers, the Data API, the GraphQL API, and Device Sync.

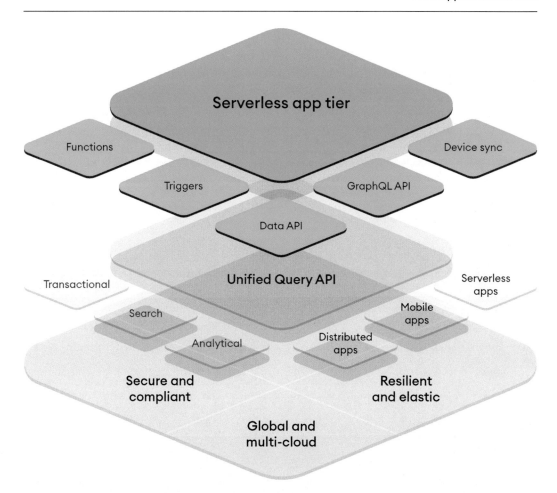

Figure 11.5: Unified key features of Atlas Application Services

Key features

Here are some of the key features of Atlas Application Services:

- **Serverless architecture**: This feature allows you to deploy server-side applications without the need to set up and manage server infrastructure. It covers provisioning, deployment, operating systems, web servers, logging, backups, and redundancy. Furthermore, it enables authenticated clients to interact with specific parts of the database based on their permissions.

- **Dynamic and responsive**: This aspect enables the service to react to data changes in MongoDB Atlas, process data from HTTPS endpoints, and run Functions on a schedule with Triggers. It also offers usage-based pricing, allowing you to pay only for the exact amount of compute you use at any given time.

- **Security**: Security is a paramount feature in Atlas Application Services. It provides built-in user management and authentication methods, making the integration of third-party authentication providers simpler. It also gives you control over which users may read and write data on a per-field basis with role-based permissions.

- **Data synchronization**: Data synchronization across devices is made seamless with Device Sync. This feature eliminates the need for complex synchronization logic with the Realm database SDKs.

Atlas Application Services is anchored by several core components, each essential to its functionality. These foundational elements shape the versatility and efficiency of the platform. Let's delve into these integral parts of Atlas Application Services:

- **Atlas Functions**: Serverless JavaScript functions for backend tasks
- **Atlas Triggers**: Automates actions in response to database changes or schedules
- **Authentication and user management**: Built-in user management and authentication methods
- **Schema validation and data access rules**: Validates and secures data with predefined rules
- **GraphQL API**: Generates a GraphQL API based on the application's data model
- **MongoDB data access**: Provides client-side access to MongoDB Atlas with enforced rules
- **Atlas Device Sync**: Offers offline-first, cross-platform data synchronization for mobile apps
- **Pre-built applications**: Customizable template applications to experiment with App Services

How to use Atlas Application Services

To fully tap into the capabilities of Atlas Application Services, you can interface with it using *Realm*. Realm is an embedded, object-oriented database that lets you build real-time, always-on applications. Its SDKs also provide access to Atlas App Services. Open-source SDKs are available for most popular languages, frameworks, and platforms. You can directly query MongoDB Atlas through the Realm SDKs, or alternatively, you can employ the Atlas Data API to facilitate queries via an HTTP client. The platform also boasts built-in user management capabilities with Application Services Users Authentication, allowing easy integration with JWT authentication and third-party providers such as Facebook, Google, and Apple. To ensure data security and integrity, Application Services rules are in place to dictate data access permissions.

After familiarizing yourself with Atlas Application Services, you'll now explore one of its important components—*Atlas Data API*.

Atlas Data API

The Atlas Data API is a managed service that allows users to interact securely with data stored in Atlas via standard HTTPS requests. This API simplifies interactions with the Atlas cluster, eliminating the need for a driver. It's important to note that the Data API is not a direct connection to your database. Instead, it functions as a fully managed middleware layer that mediates between your cluster and the clients sending requests.

It can be utilized in any platform that supports HTTPS, including web browsers, web servers, CI/CD pipelines, serverless and edge compute environments, mobile applications, and **internet of things (IoT)** devices. It eliminates the need to install any database drivers or libraries, allowing you to send standard HTTPS requests.

Here's an example of a standard HTTPS request using the Data API:

```
curl -s "https://data.mongodb-api.com/app/app-book/endpoint/data/v1/action/
  -X POST \
  -H "Content-Type: application/ejson" \
  -H "Accept: application/json" \
  -H "apiKey: <your API key>" \
  -d '{
    "dataSource": "mongodb-atlas",
    "database": "learn-data-api",
    "collection": "hello",
    "document": {
      "text": "Hello, Packt!"
    }
  }'
```

The Data API supports two types of endpoints:

- **Data API endpoints**: These are automatically generated endpoints that represent a MongoDB operation. They can be used to create, read, update, delete, and aggregate documents in a MongoDB data source.

- **Custom endpoints**: These are app-specific API routes handled by Atlas Functions that you write. They allow you to define operations that fit your use case specifically. For instance, you can create an endpoint that runs a predefined aggregation or integrates with an external webhook service.

Security and authorization

While the Data API requests may resemble traditional database operations, such as `find` or `insertOne`, the Data API adds additional layers of authentication, authorization, and correctness checks. This ensures that your data is accessed or modified only in the ways you allow, making it safe to access data in MongoDB Atlas from potentially vulnerable clients such as web apps.

For each incoming request, the Data API does the following:

- Authenticates the calling user
- Authorizes the request
- Runs the requested operation
- Enforces the access control rules and document schemas defined in your app
- Returns an HTTPS response to the caller

Use cases

While MongoDB drivers are recommended for all types of applications, particularly for high-load and latency-sensitive use cases, the Data API is particularly useful in certain specific scenarios, such as:

- Running MongoDB operations from a web application or other clients that cannot be trusted (i.e., you would rather not give them a direct database connection string).

- Managing a MongoDB driver in a server-side environment is not feasible or desirable.

- Developing a new feature with a preference for a flexible solution on the client side first, before creating and refining the API layer.

- Integrating Atlas data access into a federated API gateway.

- Using MongoDB with applications that are built in a programming language that MongoDB does not yet support. While MongoDB supports the most popular programming languages and has idiomatic drivers for them (Python, PHP, Ruby, C#, Java, Node.js, etc.), more obscure programming languages require using either a community driver or building your own. Since community drivers can be erratically maintained, if you are using a rare, new, or otherwise unsupported programming language, the Data API provides a viable option.

How to use the Atlas Data API

Set up the Data API for your app using either the Application Services interface or Realm. If you're using the Atlas UI, navigate to **HTTPS Endpoints** on the left and then select **Data API**. Once there, activate the Data API, which will create endpoints for any MongoDB source linked to your app. Choose an authentication method, enable the relevant providers, and save your configuration. Next, establish access permissions by setting rules for the linked collections, ensuring data is accessed securely. Finally, save all changes and deploy your app.

Having delved into the capabilities of the Atlas Data API for direct interactions with the MongoDB cluster, it's essential to also consider where this vast amount of data can be efficiently stored and queried. This leads you to Atlas Data Lake, a versatile solution for large-scale data storage and analysis.

Atlas Data Lake

MongoDB Atlas Data Lake is an analytics-optimized object storage service designed for extracted data. It provides an analytic storage service optimized for both flat and nested data, ensuring low-latency query performance.

Essentially, the data lake capability enables you to run a single query that will route to either object storage or a database. This allows for more advantageous data storage use cases, including the ability to handle data stored in various formats outside of JSON and BSON, such as CSV, TSV, Parquet files, and the like.

Atlas Data Lake requires a paid tier cluster usage with backup enabled. It supports collection snapshots from Atlas clusters as a data source for extracted data. The service automatically ingests data from the snapshots, partitions it, and stores it in an analytics-optimized format.

Data storage and optimization

Atlas Data Lake stores data in Parquet files, an analytic-oriented format based on open source standards, with support for polymorphic data. The storage format of Atlas Data Lake is designed to best fit its structure, allowing for fast point queries and aggregate queries. For point queries, the storage format improves performance by finding partitions faster. Aggregate-type queries only scan the column required to provide results.

The data is fully managed, partition-level indexed, and balanced as it grows. The service optimizes data extraction for analytic-type queries, ensures consistent performance, and minimizes data scans by re-balancing existing files when new data is extracted. Moreover, Atlas Data Lake partition indexes improve performance for aggregate queries by returning results directly from the partition index without needing to scan the underlying files.

The following use cases highlight the practical applications and value Atlas Data Lake offers:

- Isolate analytical workloads from your operational cluster
- Provide a consistent view of cluster data from a snapshot for long-running aggregations using `$out`
- Query and compare across versions of your cluster data at different points in time

How to use Atlas Data Lake

To get started with the Atlas Data Lake, perform the following steps:

1. Begin by creating an Atlas Data Lake pipeline. For this, you can use various tools including the Atlas UI, the Data Lake Pipelines API, or the Atlas CLI.
2. Once your pipeline is in place, move on to setting up a federated database instance tailored to your dataset.
3. Connect to your federated database instance, ensuring seamless access to your data.
4. Run queries against your Data Lake dataset, tapping into the vast information reservoir.

As always, referring to the official Atlas Data Federation documentation will provide detailed steps and best practices to enhance your experience.

The stored data in Atlas Data Lake can be integrated with data from other sources for combined analysis. For such integrations, *Atlas Data Federation* is the tool of choice.

Atlas Data Federation

MongoDB Atlas Data Federation is a comprehensive data integration tool that manages operations on data from diverse sources. It is a distributed query engine that enables you to query, transform, and move data across various sources inside and outside of MongoDB Atlas. This feature provides a seamless way to work with data from different locations, reducing the complexity of data management.

Atlas Data Federation can now be deployed in Microsoft Azure as well as querying Microsoft Azure Blob Storage. Previously, Data Federation could be deployed only to infrastructure hosted in AWS. However, with the addition of Azure Blob Storage, Azure users can now query and analyze their data across multiple sources into a single, federated view.

Atlas Data Federation combines data from MongoDB Atlas clusters, Atlas Data Lake, and cloud storage into virtual databases and collections. The data remains in place and in its native format. You can get data insights quickly with federated, parallelized queries across various data stores. Query results can then be sent directly to an Atlas cluster, Atlas Data Lake, an AWS S3 bucket, or an Azure Blob Storage instance in the specified file format.

Data Federation simplifies working with rich data. It allows you to spend more time uncovering insights instead of managing infrastructure. It is fully integrated with MongoDB Atlas, providing a unified data platform with powerful aggregations, native tools and drivers, multiple data formats, and a pay-as-you-go model.

Atlas Data Federation can access data in a variety of storage services, including AWS S3 buckets across AWS Regions, Atlas clusters, HTTP and HTTPS URLs, and Atlas Data Lake datasets. You can set up RBAC for your federated database instances and control how your client connects to your federated database instance.

Data processing

Atlas Data Federation preserves data locality and maximizes local computation to minimize data transfer and optimize performance. It provides an elastic pool of agents in the region nearest to your data where it can process the data for your queries.

It does not persist data inside the system. Once your query is processed, it only stores the metadata in your federated database instance. This ensures compliance with data sovereignty regulations and legal requirements. This feature reduces the time and effort spent on building aggregations that transform and enrich data. It simplifies the complexity of pipelines and ETL tools when working with data in different formats, making it easier to generate insights for real-time applications or downstream analytics.

Data Federation executes certain parts of a query directly on the underlying storage service, reducing the amount of data to move around, making the process faster and cheaper. It uses data partitioning for cloud object storage and tries to push as much of the query to the Atlas cluster as possible. For Atlas Data Lake datasets, it uses partition indexes to speed up queries.

Key features

Here are some of the key features of Atlas Data Federation:

- **Easy conversion of Atlas data to columnar file format**: Data Federation allows the transformation of Atlas data from one or more clusters into a columnar file format. The converted data can be sent to AWS S3, facilitating faster insights and streamlined data movement with analytics tools.

- **Direct querying of Atlas databases and cloud object storage**: You can query Atlas databases and cloud object storage simultaneously using a single API. This enables powerful aggregations to refine datasets, which can be stored in an Atlas database for real-time applications.

- **Support for various data formats in Federation**: Atlas Data Federation accommodates multiple data formats, including JSON, BSON, CSV, TSV, Avro, ORC, and Parquet. This allows you to perform robust, modular aggregations on data in place and save the results to the preferred storage tier.

- **Serverless nature for effortless management**: The serverless nature of Data Federation eliminates the need for infrastructure setup and management. You can create a cloud federated database with a few clicks and begin querying immediately. Similar to an on-demand service, you pay only for the queries you run and only when actively engaging with your data.

How to use Atlas Data Federation

To get started with Atlas Data Federation, you can create a federated database alongside your operational Atlas database with just a few clicks in the Atlas UI. After setting up the federated database, it's essential to configure multiple data sources. For those new to the process, utilizing a sample dataset can be a beneficial starting point. Additionally, for a more streamlined and automated approach, you can also use the Atlas CLI to manage and interact with the federation. This flexibility allows you to choose the method that best fits your workflow and expertise.

While Atlas Data Federation offers a seamless way to integrate and analyze data from various sources, there's another feature that enhances real-time data processing—*Atlas Stream Processing*.

Atlas Stream Processing (preview)

In the realm of data processing and management, the ability to handle streaming data efficiently has become paramount. MongoDB Atlas Stream Processing is a transformative feature that allows you to build event-driven applications by continuously processing streams of data. This feature offers a unified developer experience for all data, whether in motion or at rest.

With the introduction of Atlas Stream Processing, MongoDB has taken a significant step forward in addressing the challenges associated with event-driven applications.

Operational mechanism

Atlas Stream Processing provides a seamless connection to critical data, whether it resides in MongoDB via change streams or in an event streaming platform such as Apache Kafka. It allows you to effortlessly connect to various platforms including Confluent Cloud, Amazon MSK, Redpanda, Azure Event Hubs, or a self-managed Kafka instance utilizing the Kafka wire protocol. By integrating with the native Kafka driver, it ensures low-latency performance. *Figure 11.6* illustrates this in detail:

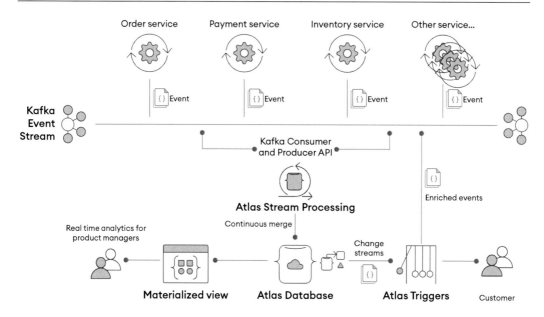

Figure 11.6: Atlas Stream Processing interfacing with various data sources

Figure 11.6 depicts how Atlas Stream Processing allows for the filtering, routing, and aggregation of the data as required before it is stored in a data store by interfacing with various data sources such as Apache Kafka.

Key features

Here are the key features of Atlas Stream Processing:

- **Continuous processing**: By utilizing MongoDB's aggregation framework, Atlas Stream Processing can process data streams from platforms such as Apache Kafka continuously. This real-time processing capability enables immediate querying, analysis, and response to data streams, eliminating the delays associated with batch processing.

- **Continuous validation**: Atlas Stream Processing ensures the integrity of incoming data through continuous validation. It checks the formation of events, detects any message corruption, and identifies late-arriving data that might have missed its processing window.

- **Continuous merge**: The processed data can subsequently be continuously materialized into views that are maintained within Atlas database collections, a process that can be likened to a push query. Applications can access results from the view using either the MongoDB Query API or Atlas SQL Interface through pull queries. The continuous merging of updates to collections is an extremely efficient method for maintaining up-to-date analytical views of data, which can support both automated and manual decision-making and actions. Besides materialized views, you also have the option to publish processed events back into streaming systems such as Apache Kafka.

Setting up a stream processor

Creating a stream processor in MongoDB Atlas with Atlas Stream Processing involves using the familiar aggregation pipeline syntax. Let's consider the following example:

1. You'll first need to define an aggregation pipeline for the data source, validate to exclude data from `localhost\127.0.0.1`, create a tumbling window to group message data every minute, and merge the processed data into a collection in MongoDB Atlas.

2. Next, create a stream processor named `netattacks` using your pipeline p and `dlq` as arguments. This process will handle the desired processing and utilize a **dead letter queue** (**DLQ**) to safely store any invalid data for later inspection, debugging, or re-processing:

```
let p = [
  {
    $source: {
      name: 'kafkaProd',
      topic: 'Nettraffic'
    }
  },
  {
    $validate: {
      validator: {
        $expr: {
          $ne: ["$ip_source", "127.0.0.1"]
        }
      }
    }
  },
  {
    $tumblingWindow: {
      interval: {
        size: Number(60),
        unit: "second"
      },
      pipeline: [
        {
          $group: {
            _id: "$ip_source",
            count_reset: {
              $sum: 1
            }
          }
        }
      ]
    }
  },
```

```
        {
          $merge: {
            name: 'AtlasCluster',
            db: 'ID',
            coll: "DDSattacks"
          }
        }
      ];

      db.createStreamProcessor('netattacks', p, dlq);
      sp.netattacks.start();
```

Let's have a closer look at the syntax of the preceding code:

- The $source stage specifies the source of the data, which is a Kafka topic named Nettraffic.

- The $validate stage filters out any events where ip_source is 127.0.0.1.

- The $tumblingWindow stage groups the events into 60-second windows, and for each window, it groups the events by ip_source and counts the number of events.

- The $merge stage outputs the results to the DDSattacks collection in the ID database in AtlasCluster.

Finally, the createStreamProcessor function is used to create the stream processor, and the start method is called to start it.

After exploring the real-time data synchronization capabilities of Atlas Stream Processing, you might be curious about more traditional querying methods. Let's look at the *Atlas SQL Interface*, which offers a powerful way to interact with your data using the familiar SQL syntax.

Atlas SQL Interface

The Atlas SQL Interface allows communication with MongoDB using SQL. While SQL databases, with their structured schema, have been the traditional choice for applications requiring strict data consistency, NoSQL databases (of which MongoDB is one) have emerged as favorites in scenarios demanding flexibility and horizontal scalability. MongoDB has made a substantial move to close this divide between the two databases with the launch of the Atlas SQL Interface. NoSQL databases, such as MongoDB, provide flexibility and scalability that traditional SQL databases often can't compete with.

SQL continues to be the preferred language for data analysis because of its simplicity and widespread use. This has created a demand for tools that can convert between SQL and NoSQL data models, enabling analysts to apply their existing SQL expertise and tools with NoSQL databases. The Atlas SQL Interface addresses this need by providing a way to query and analyze Atlas data using SQL. It leverages the MongoSQL dialect, which is compatible with SQL-92 and designed for the document model, the data model used by MongoDB. This allows users to apply their existing SQL knowledge to MongoDB data.

The Atlas SQL Interface also uses the Atlas Data Federation functionality, which enables querying across multiple Atlas clusters and cloud storage systems such as Amazon S3. This makes it possible to analyze data from different sources in a unified manner. To see how this interface operates and connects, refer to *Figure 11.7*:

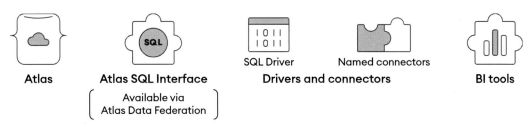

Figure 11.7: The Atlas SQL Interface for SQL queries

Figure 11.7 demonstrates the Atlas SQL Interface in action, allowing SQL queries to be used with MongoDB. It showcases the connection process using a MongoDB SQL driver or a custom connector from a BI tool, highlighting the seamless integration.

The Atlas SQL Interface is comprised of the following elements:

- **Federated database instance**: This refers to an instance of Atlas Data Federation. Each of these instances includes virtual databases and collections that correspond to data in your data storage. It also offers a SQL schema and translates Atlas SQL queries between your BI tool and your Atlas data.

- **Custom connector or SQL driver**: A custom connector or SQL driver offers a conventional way to link to a BI tool. If you're utilizing a BI tool, it's important to verify the connections it supports.

- **BI tool**: A tool for visualization and reporting, such as Power BI or Tableau.

One of the key benefits of these connectors and drivers is that they provide a first-class querying experience of Atlas data through your preferred SQL-based tool. This means that you can use the same SQL queries and tools you're used to, but with the added benefits of MongoDB's flexible document model and scalable architecture.

How to use the Atlas SQL Interface

Activate the Atlas SQL Interface either through the Atlas SQL Quick Start procedure or by setting up your own federated database instance, which in turn activates Atlas SQL by default. Once the Atlas SQL Interface is active, obtain the suitable JDBC/ODBC driver or the custom Power BI/Tableau connector to manipulate and query your document data using your preferred SQL tool. Furthermore, the Atlas SQL Interface employs Atlas Data Federation for its query engine, allowing for efficient querying across various Atlas databases and other resources, including cloud storage buckets and HTTPS endpoints.

While the Atlas SQL Interface provides a robust method for querying your data, you might want a more visual representation of the information in your Atlas cluster. To best visualize the data stored in your Atlas cluster, you can utilize MongoDB Atlas Charts.

MongoDB Atlas Charts

MongoDB Atlas Charts is a contemporary data visualization tool that enables the effortless creation, sharing, and embedding of visualizations from MongoDB Atlas. It stands out as the only native data visualization tool specifically designed for MongoDB Atlas, offering a quick, simple, and powerful way to visualize data.

Whether operating a dedicated cluster or serverless instance or using Atlas Data Federation for robust insights from blended Atlas and S3 data, or archived data in the online archive, Atlas Charts caters to a wide range of data visualization use cases, such as the following:

- **Real-time BI**: Atlas Charts facilitates the creation of dynamic visualizations in just a few clicks. All deployments from an Atlas project are available by default, dashboards can be configured to refresh automatically, and dashboards can be easily shared across a team. This allows for quick, easy, real-time business insights.

- **Direct interaction with JSON data**: Atlas Charts works directly with JSON data, simplifying the analytics workflow. By natively supporting the document model, less time is spent searching for insights and more time is spent making decisions. This eliminates the need for flattening data into tabular structures as is the case with traditional BI tools.

- **Embedded analytics**: With analytics embedded in Atlas Charts, charts and dashboards can be embedded into any application. An `iframe` can be used for quick chart embedding, or the embedding SDK can be used for greater control and customization. This delivers powerful insights and relevant data to users where it is needed.

- **Enhanced collaboration and integration**: Atlas Charts is designed for collaboration, making it easy to create and share secure dashboards. It is also integrated with MongoDB Atlas, requiring zero setup or ETL, enabling quick visualization for all data in Atlas.

To see how this looks in practice, look at *Figure 11.8*. You'll see visualized data from the MongoDB collection, including aspects such as the number of movies, movie ratings, average Metacritic scores, distribution of movies by language, and various comparisons of critic and viewer review scores by decade. This high-level overview provides a powerful and intuitive way to understand and analyze the data within the MongoDB movies collection.

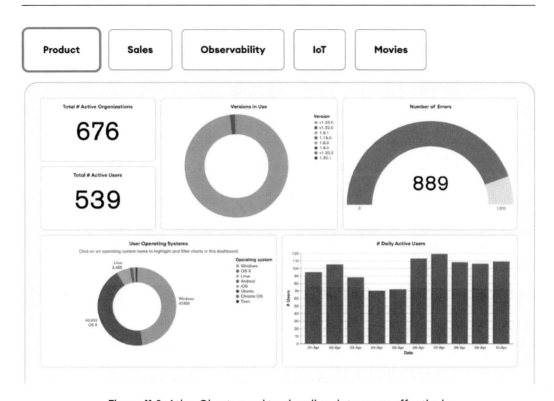

Figure 11.8: Atlas Charts used to visualize data more effectively

Atlas Charts offers several methods for embedding data visualizations into applications. These include the following:

- **Embedding via iframe**: An `iframe` is quick and simple to use. Customization options include sizing, refresh interval, and display theme selection.

- **Embedding through the SDK**: Using the SDK to embed a chart provides further customization options, including dynamic filters, sizing and style, and on-demand refresh.

- **Handling click events with the SDK**: The click event handler can be used to build interactive experiences into embedded charts. Clicking on an element in a chart can open up more details on the clicked element, highlight the element, or create a filter for another chart.

With Atlas Charts, you can also effortlessly manage your Atlas spending using newly launched out-of-the-box billing dashboard. You can design your own unique dashboards with charts aligned to your optimization strategies for streamlined insights and sharing.

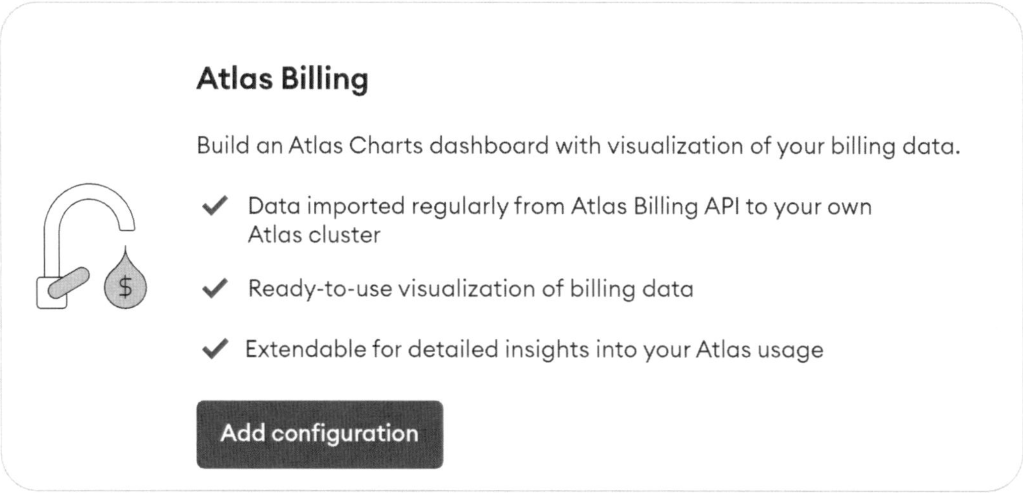

Atlas Billing

Build an Atlas Charts dashboard with visualization of your billing data.

✓ Data imported regularly from Atlas Billing API to your own Atlas cluster

✓ Ready-to-use visualization of billing data

✓ Extendable for detailed insights into your Atlas usage

Add configuration

Figure 11.9: Atlas Billing

MongoDB Atlas Charts is the optimal way to create, share, and embed data visualizations from MongoDB Atlas. It offers a rich JSON format, seamless integration with Atlas, embedded analytics, and sharing and collaboration.

How to use Atlas Charts

Follow the steps outlined below to use Atlas Charts:

1. In MongoDB Atlas, navigate to the Charts option on the navigation bar.

2. On the Charts page, click on the Add Dashboard button in the upper right and insert the basic details including a title and perhaps a brief description.

3. After your dashboard is set up, it's time to introduce your initial chart using chart builder, a user-friendly drag-and-drop mechanism that facilitates swift chart creation.

4. Choose your data source.

5. Incorporate the fields you want in the chart and end with customization.

Notably, the chart builder also empowers you to compose, store, and distribute queries and aggregation pipelines.

With Atlas Charts, you can quickly visualize the representation of information in Atlas clusters. In the next section, let's dive into the *Atlas Kubernetes Operator*.

Operational integrations: The Atlas Kubernetes Operator

When discussing operational integrations, a standout feature is the Atlas Kubernetes Operator. The Atlas Kubernetes Operator, built using CNCF's Operator Framework, is open source. It integrates with Operator Lifecycle Manager and Service Catalog, and supports certified Kubernetes distributions.

What is the Atlas Kubernetes Operator?

In MongoDB, the Atlas Kubernetes Operator is a service that integrates Atlas resources with Kubernetes clusters. This allows you to deploy and manage the lifecycle of cloud-native applications that require data services in a single control plane with secure enterprise platform integration.

The MongoDB Atlas Kubernetes Operator uses **custom resource definitions** (**CRDs**) to manage the Atlas configuration. CRDs are extensions of the Kubernetes API that allow the creation and configuration of custom resources as instances of the CRD.

These custom resources represent various MongoDB Atlas entities and their configurations. The operator watches for changes to these custom resources and applies the corresponding changes to MongoDB Atlas resources. Here are the key CRDs provided by the Atlas Kubernetes Operator:

- `AtlasBackupPolicy`: Represents a MongoDB Atlas backup policy and facilitates the management of backup policies for MongoDB Atlas clusters

- `AtlasBackupSchedule`: Pertains to a MongoDB Atlas backup schedule and allows for the control of backup schedules for MongoDB Atlas clusters

- `AtlasDatabaseUser`: Denotes a MongoDB Atlas database user and enables the handling of database users, their roles, and their access to databases and collections

- `AtlasDeployment`: Signifies a MongoDB Atlas deployment within a project. The configuration of an Atlas deployment, including the MongoDB version, instance size, and region, can be defined using this resource

- `AtlasProject`: Represents a MongoDB Atlas project and allows for the creation, configuration, and management of Atlas projects directly from a Kubernetes environment

- `AtlasTeam`: Refers to a MongoDB Atlas team and facilitates the management of teams, including team members and their roles, within a MongoDB Atlas organization

- `AtlasDataFederation`: Refers the configuration of a federated database instance and its private endpoints in MongoDB Atlas

- `AtlasFederatedAuth`: Enables users to configure federated authentication in Atlas

The Atlas Kubernetes Operator ensures that the state of the projects, database deployments, and database users in Atlas matches the configurations in each `AtlasProject`, `AtlasCluster` and `AtlasDatabaseUser` custom resource that is created in a Kubernetes cluster.

It's important to note that CRDs take priority over settings specified in other ways, such as in the Atlas UI. If a custom resource is deleted, the Atlas Kubernetes Operator deletes the corresponding object from Atlas unless annotations are used to skip deletion. This allows for a Kubernetes-native experience when managing MongoDB Atlas resources.

How to use the Atlas Kubernetes Operator

Creating an Atlas cluster directly from a Kubernetes environment is a simple process. This involves the installation of MongoDB Helm charts and the Atlas Kubernetes Operator.

To add the MongoDB Helm charts repository, execute the following command:

```
helm repo add mongodb https://mongodb.github.io/helm-charts
```

Subsequently, you can install Atlas Kubernetes Operator with the following command:

```
helm install atlas-operator --namespace=atlas-operator --create-namespace
mongodb/mongodb-atlas-operator
```

To ensure the successful installation and availability of the Atlas Kubernetes custom resources within the Kubernetes cluster, a validation step is performed. This step is crucial to confirm that the resources are correctly set up and ready for use:

```
atlasbackuppolicies.atlas.mongodb.com                2023-11-10T22:14:30Z
atlasbackupschedules.atlas.mongodb.com               2023-11-10T22:14:30Z
atlasdatabaseusers.atlas.mongodb.com                 2023-11-10T22:14:31Z
atlasdatafederations.atlas.mongodb.com               2023-11-10T22:14:31Z
atlasdeployments.atlas.mongodb.com                   2023-11-10T22:14:31Z
atlasfederatedauths.atlas.mongodb.com                2023-11-10T22:14:31Z
atlasprojects.atlas.mongodb.com                      2023-11-10T22:14:31Z
atlasteams.atlas.mongodb.com                         2023-11-10T22:14:31Z
```

Following the validation, an Atlas cluster can be created via a Helm chart. The Helm chart installation can be initiated with the following command:

```
helm install atlas-deployment \
mongodb/atlas-deployment \
--namespace=my-book \
--create-namespace \
--set project.atlasProjectName='My Project' \
--set atlas.orgId='<orgid>' \
--set atlas.publicApiKey='<publicKey>' \
--set atlas.privateApiKey='<privateApiKey>'
```

The preceding command will install the `atlas-deployment` from the MongoDB repository into the `my-book` namespace (which will be created if it doesn't exist), and set the necessary parameters for the Atlas project.

> **Note**
>
> There is also a Terraform provider for MongoDB Atlas, which is not covered here. You can refer the following resource for Terraform-specific guidance: `https://www.mongodb.com/atlas/hashicorp-terraform`

While the Atlas Kubernetes Operator offers seamless integration with Kubernetes, there's another tool in the MongoDB Atlas suite, which is a unified CLI for managing MongoDB Atlas, including Atlas Search and Atlas Vector Search, named the Atlas CLI.

Atlas CLI

The MongoDB Atlas CLI is a powerful tool designed to interact with MongoDB Atlas database deployments and Atlas Search from the terminal. It allows you to perform complex database management tasks in seconds using short, intuitive commands.

How to use the Atlas CLI

Check the MongoDB documentation to select the installation method appropriate for your operating system: `https://www.mongodb.com/docs/atlas/cli/stable`.

Capabilities of the Atlas CLI

The Atlas CLI is designed to manage MongoDB Atlas from the command line. With just one command, a quick start is possible:

The `atlas setup` command should be run to configure the CLI for use with a MongoDB Atlas account. This command guides you through registration, login, setting up a default profile, creating your initial free tier cluster, and connecting to it using the MongoDB Shell.

The Atlas CLI also provides a wide range of commands for managing MongoDB Atlas deployments, including creating and deleting clusters, managing database users, configuring network access, and more. For example:

- `atlas cluster list`: Lists all MongoDB Atlas clusters
- `atlas cluster get`: Retrieves detailed information about a specific MongoDB Atlas cluster
- `atlas cluster search`: Manages Atlas Search for a cluster
- `atlas dbusers create`: Creates a database user for a project
- `atlas accessList create`: Creates an IP access list entry for a project

Beyond the basic commands, the Atlas CLI offers a range of advanced features to optimize workflows. By learning the various Atlas CLI commands, complex tasks such as scaling clusters, managing backups, and configuring alerts can all be performed from the command line.

Use `atlas --help` to display all the capabilities of the Atlas CLI.

In 2023, MongoDB announced that with the use of Atlas CLI, it's possible to launch an Atlas cluster locally for testing or development purposes. The Atlas CLI utilizes a ready-made Podman image for this. This image also includes features such as Atlas Search and Atlas Vector Search. To create a local Atlas deployment with the default settings in interactive mode, execute the following command:

```
atlas deployments setup -type local
```

If you want to list your Atlas deployments, run the following command:

```
atlas deployments list
```

If you're logged in to Atlas, both your local and cloud Atlas deployments will be visible. Without Atlas authentication, only your local deployments will be displayed.

In conclusion, the MongoDB Atlas CLI is a powerful tool for managing MongoDB Atlas deployments. It enables the execution of complex database management tasks quickly and efficiently. Whether you are a seasoned MongoDB developer or just getting started with MongoDB Atlas, the Atlas CLI is a valuable tool to have in the toolkit.

Summary

MongoDB Atlas is a fully managed developer data platform offering performance, security, and flexibility, suitable for any organization looking to use MongoDB in a cloud environment.

It's a comprehensive data management platform designed for modern applications. It handles various data types and is multi-cloud compatible. In this chapter, you looked at how this platform integrates data and application services, enabling rapid application development. You were also introduced to new features including Atlas Vector Search and Atlas Stream Processing that help in enhancing information retrieval and data stream handling.

The next chapter will focus on the essential aspects of monitoring the health and performance of your system, along with strategies and tools for effective data backup and recovery.

12

Monitoring and Backup in MongoDB

Effective monitoring and backup are essential when deploying MongoDB in a production environment. They play a crucial role during the development phase, aiding in performance optimization and troubleshooting. Hence, these processes should be established from the outset, not added as an afterthought.

In this chapter, you will explore the operational aspects of MongoDB. You will learn the importance of having a reliable backup strategy, steps to ensure your backups are consistent and accurate, and whether they can be successfully restored when required.

This chapter will cover the following topics:

- Importance of monitoring
- Key metrics to monitor in MongoDB
- MongoDB reporting and monitoring tools
- Understanding cluster backups
- MongoDB backup methods

Monitoring in MongoDB

Monitoring in MongoDB extends beyond the simple task of keeping an eye on your system's health. It provides a comprehensive lens into the database's intricate behaviors, such as how it processes and responds to various requests, manages memory, or deals with concurrent operations. This deep understanding is crucial for spotting inefficiencies, such as slow-performing queries or suboptimal indexing patterns. Monitoring plays a pivotal role in identifying bottlenecks that can hinder performance, allowing for timely interventions.

Another critical aspect of monitoring is ensuring data integrity. Consistent monitoring can detect anomalies or potential data loss scenarios. By using appropriate monitoring tools and best practices, you can ensure that the database not only functions seamlessly, but also aligns perfectly with the specific needs of your applications and end users.

Monitoring clusters

When designing a software system, you make a lot of assumptions—from clear technical expectations to subtle user-experience nuances. Despite of making informed decisions based on what you know, it's possible that you might miss or underestimate certain factors.

This is where monitoring comes in. It helps you check whether your assumptions were correct, or if your software is working as you had planned. If your software needs to serve more users or handle more data, monitoring enables you to handle that growth. A strong monitoring system spots problems in your software, and gives you early warnings about potential security issues.

Figure 12.1 illustrates various monitoring metrics you can measure to monitor your MongoDB Atlas clusters.

Figure 12.1: MongoDB Atlas monitoring metrics

Why monitor in MongoDB?

Before diving into the details of monitoring in MongoDB, let's understand why monitoring is crucial in the first place:

- **Early issue detection**: Monitoring is your early warning system. By keeping tabs on various metrics, you can detect potential issues before they become problems. This proactive approach saves time and effort down the road.

- **Scaling**: As your application gains more users and traction, the load on your database naturally increases. Monitoring helps you understand when it's time to scale up (or down) to meet these demands, ensuring a smooth user experience.

- **Cost reduction**: By keeping an eye on resource usage, you can optimize costs. Overprovisioning can be as problematic as under-provisioning, and monitoring helps strike the perfect balance.

- **Performance optimization**: Monitoring can help identify bottlenecks or inefficiencies in your system, allowing you to optimize for best performance.

- **Backup and restoration**: Regular monitoring ensures backup processes are working as expected. In case of unforeseen issues, having a reliable backup and restoration process can be a lifesaver.

- **Data integrity**: At the end of the day, it's all about data. Monitoring ensures that data remains consistent, accurate, and available—safeguarding the most valuable asset of your application.

What should you monitor?

The most crucial metric in MongoDB is memory usage. Like all database systems, MongoDB heavily relies on system memory to boost its performance. Whether you're utilizing the default WiredTiger storage engine configuration or not, it's essential to prioritize memory usage monitoring. Grasping the basics of how computer memory operates can give you an edge when interpreting metrics from your monitoring tools. Let's look at some fundamental concepts associated with computer memory.

Page fault

RAM provides speed but at a premium cost. In contrast, while **hard disk drives (HDDs)** and **solid-state drives (SSDs)** are slower, they are affordable and ensure your data remains intact during system or power hiccups. Typically, your data resides on these drives. When executing a query, MongoDB seeks the required data from memory. If it's not there, MongoDB retrieves it from the disk and transfers it to memory. This action is called a *page fault* since memory data is structured in pages.

As these page faults accumulate, memory space dwindles. Eventually, to make room for new data, some pages must be discarded, leading to what's called a *page eviction* event. While it's impossible to wholly eliminate page faults, especially with dynamic datasets, it's beneficial to reduce their occurrence. A practical way to achieve this is to ensure that your frequently accessed data, or the working set, remains in memory.

Resident memory

Resident memory is the portion of RAM that MongoDB actively uses. Monitoring this metric is vital. Quick memory access boosts database operations, especially reads. However, excessive RAM consumption by MongoDB can strain other system processes. Persistent high usage may signal the need for more RAM or database adjustments. More importantly, MongoDB's resident memory should ideally stay below 80% of the total available memory. Exceeding this can lead to performance-diminishing swapping, where data moves from RAM to disk. Monitoring this metric ensures optimal performance for both MongoDB and your system.

Virtual and mapped memory

When MongoDB needs a memory spot, the operating system provides a virtual address. Whether this address correlates to a physical spot in the RAM depends on the data's location. MongoDB employs this virtual address to access the underlying data. Now, when journaling is activated (which is recommended unless there's clarity and acceptance of the risks of disabling it), MongoDB maintains a separate address for this journaled data. Post-checkpoint data—typically updated every 60 seconds—gets added to the journal. The term *virtual memory* encompasses the entire data volume that MongoDB requests, journal included.

On the other hand, mapped memory omits journal references. As time progresses, this mapped memory aligns closely with your actively used data or working set. Simultaneously, the virtual memory becomes a sum of this mapped memory and the dataset size since the last checkpoint.

Working set

A *working set* represents the dataset MongoDB actively utilizes. While it sometimes aligns with the dataset MongoDB holds, there are instances when some collections remain untouched, and don't contribute to the working set. You can directly monitor memory in MongoDB Atlas at the MongoDB level, using the **Memory** option shown in *Figure 12.1*. You can indirectly monitor memory usage by using the hardware metrics **System Memory** and **Max System Memory**, found on the same page.

Track free disk space

It's common for databases to run low on free disk space. Just like keeping an eye on memory, you should watch how much disk space you're using. You can set up alerts for when you're using 40%, 60%, or 80% of the total space, especially if you're adding a lot of data quickly.

Having ample space greatly helps with system maintenance, mainly because moving data around can take time. To check on this, you can monitor the **Disk IPOS** metric, and free space to see how much space is left in the **Hardware Metrics** section of the MongoDB Atlas dashboard.

> **Note**
> The **directoryPerDB** option can help with data sizing as you can split your storage into different physically mounted disks.

Monitoring replication

Replica sets use the **operations log** (**oplog**) to hold the synced state. Every operation is replicated to the primary node, and then to the primary node's oplog, which is a capped collection. Secondaries stream this oplog asynchronously, copying the same operations in order.

If the primary node is overwhelmed with copying (i.e. replicating) an increased number of write operations, the secondaries may struggle to read and apply the operations fast enough, resulting in *replication lag*. Replication lag refers to the amount of time it takes to replicate a write operation on the primary to a secondary.

Note

If the time is 4:30 P.M., and the secondary node just applied an operation that was applied on your primary node at 4:25 P.M., this means that the secondary is lagging five minutes behind your primary node. In your production cluster, the replication lag should be close to (or equal to) 0. You can track replication lag by monitoring the **Replication Oplog Window** and **Oplog GB/Hour** metrics on MongoDB Atlas.

Oplog size

Every member in a replica set stores a copy of the oplog in `db.oplog.rs()`. The reason being that if the primary node steps down, one of the secondaries will get elected, and require an up-to-date version of the oplog for the new secondaries to track. The oplog size is configurable, and you should set aside sufficient space. The oplog size doesn't affect memory usage, and can make or break the database in cases of operational issues.

If replication lag persists and continues to grow, you'll eventually get to a point where the secondaries will fall so far behind the primary that the secondary node won't be able to read from the primary's oplog. This issue arises when the earliest record in the primary's oplog is newer than the most recent record the secondary node has processed.

Essentially, in this case, a gap emerges between the secondary and primary oplogs. This gap results in a loss of track of operations that may have occurred, causing the secondary to halt replication. In general, the oplog should hold at least two days' worth of operations. The oplog should be longer than the time it takes for the initial sync with your current I/O and network bandwidth, for the same reason that was detailed earlier.

Network monitoring

Network activity plays a pivotal role in system performance. High or irregular network usage may indicate performance constraints or other issues. Hence, it's crucial to consistently monitor and analyze unusual network patterns. In MongoDB Atlas, under the MongoDB Metrics section, the **Network** metric allows you to track incoming data (bytes in), outgoing data (bytes out), and the total request count, ensuring you're always informed about your database's network behavior.

Cursors and connections

Under the MongoDB Metrics section in MongoDB Atlas, keeping tabs on the number of connections and cursors (both open and timed out) can give you a snapshot of the cluster's health. An excess of connections might burden the database, hinting at potential issues in your application's structure. Conversely, very few connections may suggest that the database isn't being used to its full potential.

Furthermore, a high count of open cursors can strain the database, while an increase in timed-out cursors indicates the database is already grappling with a substantial workload. It's essential to strike a balance to ensure smooth operations.

Document metrics

The MongoDB Metrics section enables you to keep tabs on the number of CRUD operations executed per second on each server within the cluster.

Not all CRUD operations are created equal in terms of adding load to the database, but on average, it's a useful metric for identifying nodes behaving out of sync with the rest of the cluster. For instance, if two identical secondaries in a replica set display a significant disparity in operation counts, it could indicate network bandwidth or configuration issues between that node and the primary.

Monitoring memory usage in WiredTiger

WiredTiger is MongoDB's default storage engine, known for its efficiency and scalability. When you initiate MongoDB with WiredTiger, it establishes an internal memory cache. How sizable is this cache? By default, it's roughly half of the RAM you have, minus 1 GB. Therefore, if you have 16 GB RAM the internal cache is set to about 7.5 GB. But that's not all the memory MongoDB uses. It also sets aside some memory for tasks such as handling connections and sorting data. MongoDB also takes advantage of any extra memory your system has to further improve its performance.

If you want to check or change the WiredTiger cache settings, you can use the MongoDB Shell. Using the parameter `storage.wiredTiger.engineConfig.cacheSizeGB`, lets you adjust the cache size.

> **Note**
> It's usually best to stick with the default cache size. But if your data is highly compressed, you may consider reducing the cache, say by 10-20% to free up some memory for other uses.

Tracking page faults

Page faults might seem harmless when their numbers are low. But if they start to pile up and cross a certain point, they can slow down your system significantly. This slowdown is more noticeable when you're using traditional HDDs, but it remains a concern even with faster SSDs.

To stay ahead of potential issues with page faults, it's advisable to maintain a test environment that mirrors your live setup. This staging environment lets you push your system to its limits, allowing you to see how many page faults it can handle before performance drops. By comparing the stress test data with the actual page faults in your live system, you can gauge the available margin for optimal performance.

If you're curious about the current page fault status, you can look at the `extra_info` section:

```
db.adminCommand({ "serverStatus" : 1 })['extra_info']
```

`serverStatus` outputs the following result in `mongosh`:

```
{ "note":"fields vary by platform", "page_faults":Long("3465") }
```

Tracking B-tree misses

Maintaining proper indexing is crucial to ensure MongoDB operates efficiently and responsively. B-tree misses refer to situations where the system encounters page faults while trying to access a B-tree index. Given that indexes are frequently accessed and are usually much smaller than your main dataset, they should ideally always be available in memory.

An increasing number of B-tree misses or a fluctuating ratio of B-tree hits to misses may indicate that your indexes have grown, or aren't optimally designed. It's essential to monitor these misses for efficient system performance. While MongoDB Atlas provides an integrated dashboard for such metrics, you can also utilize tools such as MongoDB Cloud Manager for a more detailed view or access this information directly through `mongosh`.

I/O wait

I/O wait refers to the time an operating system waits for an I/O operation to complete. It has a strong positive correlation with page faults. If you see I/O wait increasing over time, it's a strong indication that page faults will follow as well. You should aim to keep the I/O wait at less than 60% for a healthy operational cluster. This can buy you some time to upgrade in case the workload increases suddenly.

Read and write queues

I/O waits and page faults can lead to an accumulation of read and write requests. When you notice growing queues for these requests, it's usually a symptom of underlying issues such as page faults or waits. If queues begin to pile up, it's a clear indication that something is wrong and needs to be fixed.

Having discussed the diverse aspects of monitoring, from memory usage to read and write queues, let's take a closer look at the intricacies of memory management in MongoDB. Let's explore the concept of working set calculations, and its significance in ensuring optimal database performance.

Working set calculations

The working set in MongoDB is a vital concept that pertains to the amount of data and indexes that a database accesses over a specific period. This data should ideally be held in the system's RAM to guarantee optimal performance. When it comes to database performance, understanding your working set is pivotal. While MongoDB is capable of managing vast datasets, the speed of data retrieval is significantly affected by whether the data is accessed directly from the RAM or fetched from a disk. Accessing data from the RAM is exponentially faster, which is why the working set—data that is frequently accessed—should ideally reside in memory.

Why is the working set crucial?

As your MongoDB instance serves requests, it tends to pull the required data into RAM. Over time, the most frequently accessed data—your working set—naturally find its place in memory. If this working set fits comfortably in RAM, your database performance remains high. However, if it exceeds the available RAM, you'll find the system frequently evicting data from memory, only to pull it back in shortly after. This constant data movement impacts performance.

Estimate the working set size

There's a direct command to ascertain the working set size, but there are indirect ways to gauge it as well. One method is to examine the data that your application accesses regularly. If you can determine the data needed to satisfy a substantial majority of user requests—say, 95%—you'll have a good estimate. Factoring in the logs, user queries, and datasets, and adding an additional 30 to 50% buffer for indexes can further refine this estimate.

Another indicative method is monitoring page faults. The low frequency of page faults suggests that the majority of the working set is in memory. However, a sudden or steady increase in page faults can indicate that the working set has outgrown the available RAM, implying that it might be time to expand the RAM or optimize the data.

Importance of indexes in the working set

Indexes play a crucial role in speeding up data access. Even if you can't have your entire working set in memory, prioritizing your indexes to reside in RAM can make a notable difference. By ensuring the indexes are in memory, MongoDB can quickly locate the data on disk, even if the actual data isn't in RAM, thus optimizing access speeds.

MongoDB reporting tools overview

MongoDB offers several integrated reporting methods. This section gives a brief overview of these methods and outlines the specific questions they can address.

Utilities

In MongoDB, utilities are specialized tools designed to offer insights, facilitate diagnostics, and aid in the routine evaluation of database operations. They play a pivotal role in ensuring smooth performance, and assisting administrators in understanding and rectifying any discrepancies or issues. Whether you're looking to get a snapshot of the current activity or dive deep into specific operations, MongoDB's utilities are your go-to resource:

- `mongostat`: This tool provides counts of database operations by type (`insert`, `query`, `update`, `delete`, etc.), helping you understand the overall server load distribution.

- `mongotop`: This tool tracks and reports current read and write activities on a collection basis. It is particularly useful for identifying which collections or databases are experiencing the most activity, helping you to precisely discern potential performance bottlenecks.

Commands

MongoDB has various commands that give a detailed status report of the database. These commands can be more granular than the utilities mentioned previously. They can be used in scripts or programs for custom alerts or to adjust application behavior based on database activity. One such method is `db.currentOp()`, which identifies ongoing operations in the database instance. Here are some example commands:

- `serverStatus`: Provides a comprehensive overview of the database status, including disk usage, memory usage, connection details, journaling, and index access

- `dbStats`: Gives a report on storage usage and data volumes, helping monitor a specific database's state and storage capacity

- `collStats`: Provides collection-level statistics, such as object count, size, disk space used, and index information

- `replSetGetStatus`: Returns an overview of the replica set status, providing details on the replica set's state, configuration, and member metrics

Hosted monitoring tools overview

Table 12.1 lists various hosted monitoring tools, available typically via a subscription:

Tool name	Description
MongoDB Cloud Manager	A cloud suite for managing MongoDB deployments, providing monitoring, backup, and automation. For on-premises solutions, MongoDB Enterprise Advanced includes Ops Manager.
VividCortex	Provides deep insights into MongoDB's production database workload and query performance with one-second resolution.
Scout	Provides several plugins, including MongoDB Monitoring, MongoDB Slow Queries, and MongoDB Replica Set Monitoring.
Server Density	Provides a MongoDB-specific dashboard, alerts, replication failover timeline, and mobile apps.
Application Performance Management	IBM's **software as a service (SaaS)** offering for application performance, which includes a monitor for MongoDB and other applications.
New Relic	Supports full application performance management and lets you view monitoring metrics from Cloud Manager.
Datadog	Infrastructure monitoring tool for visualizing the performance of MongoDB deployments.
SPM Performance Monitoring	Monitors all crucial MongoDB metrics and provides a correlation of metrics and logs.
Pandora FMS	Provides the `PandoraFMS-mongodb-monitoring` plugin for MongoDB monitoring.

Table 12.1: Monitoring tools in MongoDB

Having delved deep into the realm of monitoring in MongoDB, you now recognize its pivotal role in optimizing performance and preempting potential issues. Yet, while monitoring is essential for maintaining a healthy system, it's equally important to ensure the safety and integrity of your data. This brings the next vital aspect of MongoDB operations: backups.

The next section will explore the strategies and tools provided by MongoDB for dependable backups that ensure your data always remains safe and restorable.

Cluster backups

"Hope for the best, plan for the worst." – John Jay (1813)

This principle is pivotal when shaping your MongoDB backup strategy. Various unforeseen events can threaten your data's integrity.

Backups are essential in disaster recovery systems. While some might lean on replication—believing that having three data copies is a protective shield—it's crucial to understand the potential risks. If one copy is compromised, the other two can assist in rebuilding the cluster, especially during concerns such as disk failures. These failures become more likely as disks approach their **mean time between failures (MTBF)**.

However, along with disk malfunctions, you must also look into security breaches, human errors, or even large-scale calamities such as fires, floods, and earthquakes. Such events can endanger all data replicas simultaneously. Thus, a solid backup strategy is indispensable to prevent complete data loss during such situations.

MongoDB backup methods

Ensuring data safety and availability is paramount when running MongoDB in a production setting. Several methods can be used to capture and restore backups, providing security against data loss events.

Cloud-based backup solutions

Utilizing cloud **database as a service (DBaaS)** offerings often simplifies the backup process. For instance, with MongoDB Atlas, backups can be easily managed either through its graphical user interface or its API.

MongoDB Atlas provides the Cloud Backups feature. This service leverages the snapshot capabilities of the respective cloud providers—whether AWS, Azure, or Google Cloud Platform. Notably, it allows the following:

- Users can initiate on-demand backups or set up continuous cloud backups. The frequency and retention period of these backups are determined by the specific MongoDB Atlas service tier chosen.

- The Cloud Backups feature is exclusive to the platform's paid plans.

- The continuous cloud backup method uses the oplog to capture data changes. Therefore, it's crucial to ensure that the oplog size can accommodate the volume of writes between consecutive backup sessions. If the oplog is inadequately sized, the backup process might be disrupted.

On-premises backup solutions

For those managing MongoDB on their own infrastructure, two robust backup solutions are tailored to on-premises deployments:

- **MongoDB Cloud Manager**: This SaaS solution can be configured to monitor and back up data from your self-hosted servers. Cloud Manager capitalizes on the oplog, similar to the replication process, making it adept at backing up both replica sets and sharded clusters.

- **MongoDB Ops Manager**: For organizations that have reservations about connecting their servers to an external SaaS due to security or other concerns, Ops Manager is the go-to solution. It essentially brings the functionality of MongoDB Cloud Manager on-premises. To access Ops Manager, you must subscribe to the Enterprise Advanced edition of MongoDB for your clusters.

Using filesystem snapshots for MongoDB backups

For those who wish to back up their MongoDB deployments themselves, creating a copy of the underlying MongoDB data files is a viable approach. Let's see how it works:

- If the storage volume containing MongoDB data files supports point-in-time snapshots, it enables you to obtain backups representing a precise moment in time.

- These filesystem snapshots are a feature facilitated by the operating system's volume manager and aren't exclusive to MongoDB.

- During this process, the operating system captures a snapshot of the storage volume, which then serves as a foundational reference for the data backup storage systems and snapshots.

- Different storage systems have their own snapshot mechanics:

  - On Linux platforms, **Logical Volume Manager** (**LVM**) facilitates snapshot creation.

  - Amazon's EC2 **Elastic Block Store** (**EBS**) system also supports the snapshot feature.

Consistency requirements

For a valid snapshot of an operational mongod instance, certain prerequisites are essential. Firstly, journaling must be active. Additionally, the journal should reside on the same logical volume as MongoDB's other data files. Without meeting these conditions, there's no assurance of the snapshot's consistency or validity.

When dealing with *sharded clusters* in MongoDB, obtaining a consistent snapshot requires several steps. Firstly, the balancer must be disabled to prevent chunk migrations during the snapshot process. To ensure data consistency across the cluster, the fsync command should be executed on mongos, which performs the fsync operation on each shard in the cluster. This command can also optionally lock the cluster to block additional write operations, ensuring that the data remains stable during the snapshot process. By adhering to these conditions, you can ensure reliable and consistent backups, using filesystem snapshots.

Backups using mongodump

The `mongodump` tool is a command-line utility designed to create a backup of the data in your MongoDB cluster. When using `mongodump`, you can continue taking writes in your cluster, and if you have a replica set, you can use the `--oplog` option to include the entries that occur during the `mongodump` operation in its output oplog. Opting for this choice requires using `--oplogReplay` when using the `mongorestore` tool to restore your data to the MongoDB cluster.

`mongorestore` is a great tool for single-server deployments, but once you get to larger deployments, you should consider using different (and better-planned) approaches to back up your data.

One downside is that all the indexes need to be recreated on restore, which may be a time-consuming operation. Another major downside that the `mongodump` tool has is that in order to write data to the disk, it needs to bring data from the internal MongoDB storage to the memory first. This means that in the case of production clusters running under strain, `mongodump` will invalidate the data residing in the memory from the working set; the data would not be residing in the memory under regular operations. This degrades the performance of your cluster.

Backing up with cp or rsync

If your storage system does not support snapshots, you can copy the files directly using `cp`, `rsync`, or a similar tool. Since copying multiple files is not an atomic operation, you must stop all writes to `mongod` before copying the files. Otherwise, you will copy the files in an invalid state.

Backups produced by copying the underlying data do not support point-in-time recovery for replica sets and are difficult to manage for large sharded clusters. Additionally, these backups are large because they include indexes, and duplicate underlying storage padding and fragmentation. By contrast, `mongodump` creates small backups.

Backup and restore on EC2

With MongoDB Cloud Manager, it's simple to automate backups directly from EC2 volumes. Naturally, given your data's residence in the cloud, Cloud Manager stands as the primary choice. However, in scenarios where Cloud Manager might not be accessible or suitable, you can resort to scripting your backup process. Here's a simplified approach:

1. **Prerequisites**: Ensure that journaling is active; this is a crucial aspect for data integrity. Ensure that the MongoDB **database path** (`dbPath`), which houses data and journal files, is linked to a singular EBS volume.

2. **Identifying EBS blocks**: Utilize `ec2-describe-instances` to locate EBS block instances tied to the active EC2 instance.

3. **Locate logical volumes**: Deploy `lvdisplay` to identify logical volumes to which your MongoDB `dbPath` is linked.

4. **Snapshot creation**: With the logical devices in hand from the previous step, employ `ec2-create-snapshot` to generate snapshots. Remember to capture each logical device linked to your `dbPath`.

5. **Backup verification**: To validate the efficacy of your backups, generate new volumes from the created snapshots and mount them. Subsequently, initiate the `mongod` process using the new data. To further ensure the backup's integrity, establish a connection via MongoDB and inspect the datasets.

Backup with queues

Using queues, such as ActiveMQ, is a smart way to back up data. These queues sit between your database and the frontend software. When you add, update, or remove data, it first goes through this queue. This way, data can be sent easily to different places, be it other MongoDB servers or separate log files.

While this method is similar to the delayed replica set approach and solves many backup issues, it's not perfect for every situation.

Incremental backups

As your MongoDB deployments grow, there comes a point where executing full backups constantly becomes impractical due to the size and time required. Instead of daily extensive backups, imagine only doing it once a month and employing incremental backups, such as nightly snapshots, for the days in between. This approach is efficient and minimizes storage requirements.

Tools such as Ops Manager and Cloud Manager come to the rescue, offering support for incremental backups. While it's tempting to craft your own solution when the data size escalates, these tools can be a lifesaver, streamlining the process. However, for those who might be reluctant or unable to use these tools, there's an alternative: leveraging the oplog.

Here are some quick instructions to get you started:

1. Start by making a full backup using any of the methods previously discussed.

2. Temporarily lock writes on the secondary server of your replica set.

3. Identify the most recent entry in the oplog.

4. Export the subsequent oplog entries.

5. Subsequently, unlock writes on the secondary server.

6. In the event of a restore, use the `mongorestore` command with the `--oplogReplay` option, utilizing the `oplog.rs` file you exported.

This approach demands locking writes, which isn't typically recommended. A more efficient strategy might be utilizing the LVM filesystem in tandem with incremental backups. However, this hinges on the specific LVM implementation and the degree to which you can modify it.

Common mistakes and pitfalls in MongoDB monitoring and backup

When managing MongoDB, monitoring and backup are essential. Recognizing potential issues and implementing preventive measures is crucial. Let's explore some common challenges, and tips to sidestep them effectively:

- **Neglecting replica set status**: MongoDB's replica sets offer redundancy and high availability. However, not keeping an eye on the status of your replica sets can lead to potential data loss or availability issues.

  - **How to avoid it**: Regularly check the health and status of each member in your replica set. Set up alerts for any changes in the replica set's status.

- **Back up without oplog data**: The oplog in MongoDB keeps a record of all operations that modify the data. Neglecting to include oplog data in backups can prevent point-in-time restores.

  - **How to avoid it**: Ensure your backup strategy includes oplog data. This allows for point-in-time recovery, which can be crucial for recovering from specific issues.

- **Using default configuration:** MongoDB comes with default configurations that might not be optimized for all use cases. Relying solely on these can lead to performance and storage issues.

  - **How to avoid it**: Regularly review and tailor your MongoDB configurations based on the specific needs and growth patterns of your application.

- **Not monitoring slow queries**: Slow queries can degrade the performance of your MongoDB instance, affecting the overall user experience.

  - **How to avoid it**: Use tools such as `mongotop` and `mongostat` to keep an eye on query performance. Optimize or index collections as needed.

- **Ignoring storage warnings**: Running out of storage can bring your MongoDB server to a halt. Disregarding or not being aware of storage warnings can lead to this situation.

  - **How to avoid it**: Set up alerts for storage metrics. Plan for storage scaling or data archiving based on growth trends.

- **Overlooking connection limits**: Each MongoDB instance has a limit on the number of simultaneous client connections. Overlooking this can lead to refused connections and degraded performance.

  - **How to avoid it**: Monitor the number of active connections and adjust the connection pool settings, or scale your MongoDB deployment as needed.

- **Overlooking backup verification**: Assuming that backups are successful without verifying them can lead to unpleasant surprises during recovery.

  - **How to avoid it**: Regularly test and verify your backups. Restore them to a test environment to ensure data integrity and completeness.

- **Ignoring hardware and OS metrics**: While MongoDB-specific metrics are crucial, ignoring underlying hardware and OS metrics can result in missing early signs of potential issues.

  - **How to avoid it**: Monitor system metrics such as CPU, memory usage, disk I/O, and network bandwidth. These metrics often provide context for database-specific metrics and highlight potential bottlenecks or issues.

Summary

Monitoring and backup are paramount for MongoDB deployments. Monitoring ensures optimal performance, while backups safeguard against data loss. Various tools and methods, ranging from MongoDB Atlas to filesystem snapshots, provide tailored solutions. Whether in the cloud or on-premises, consistent monitoring and robust backup strategies are essential for maintaining MongoDB's reliability and resilience. In today's rapidly digitalizing world, the ability to efficiently search and analyze data is crucial.

This brings us to the next chapter, *Chapter 13, Introduction to Atlas Search*. In this chapter, you will explore the powerful search capabilities integrated into MongoDB Atlas, and discover how to harness the full potential of your data through sophisticated search functionalities.

13

Introduction to Atlas Search

In today's digital age, full-text search capabilities are a necessity for modern applications. The efficiency of search mechanisms plays a pivotal role in enhancing user experience and ensuring easy availability of relevant information. Building relevance-based application features is a complex endeavor. You don't just need to sift through vast amounts of data, but also ensure that the results are tailored to the user's intent and context. The significance of these features is profound because they streamline user interactions, fostering engagement and retention.

Atlas Search is an embedded full-text search feature in MongoDB Atlas, providing a seamless and scalable experience for building relevance-based applications, among other advanced search features. Built on Apache Lucene, Atlas Search eliminates the need to operate a separate search system alongside your database.

This chapter will cover the following topics:

- The features of Atlas Search
- The architecture of Atlas Search
- Atlas Search indexes and operations
- Integration of Atlas Search with Apache Lucene

MongoDB Atlas Search

Before MongoDB Atlas Search, developers had to rely on various other solutions to implement search functionality in their applications. Some of these solutions included:

- **Algolia**: This is a powerful and flexible search and discovery solution. Even though it's used in many applications, it can be quite costly. This cost is driven by the quantity of records stored and the volume of API actions performed. If you have a large dataset, Algolia might not be the best fit for you.

- **Elasticsearch**: This is a distributed, RESTful search and analytics engine suitable for a growing number of use cases. Just like Atlas Search, it is based on Apache Lucene.

- **Solr**: This is another powerful search platform built on Apache Lucene. It's highly reliable, scalable, and fault-tolerant, providing distributed indexing, replication, and load-balanced querying.

- **The built-in $text index of MongoDB**: This is the easiest solution to implement but was not suitable for scenarios involving multiple nested fields.

Traditional solutions for implementing search capabilities often required significant effort and synchronization between multiple services. Atlas Search provides a more integrated and efficient solution, eliminating the need for separate search systems and synchronization efforts, and handling large amounts of data and complex queries efficiently.

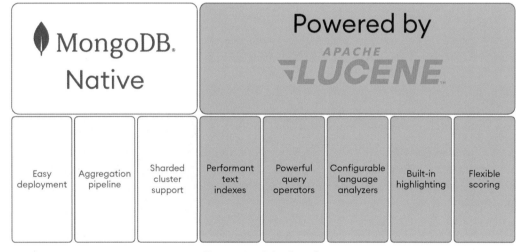

Figure 13.1: Atlas Search

By integrating the database, search engine, and synchronization mechanism into a single fully-managed platform, you can simplify the development of relevance-based search capabilities. A unified API for all operations reduces development time. Both automatic synchronization with the MongoDB database and adjustment to schema changes eliminate the need for manual index remapping, resulting in a streamlined and efficient solution for implementing full-text search functionality.

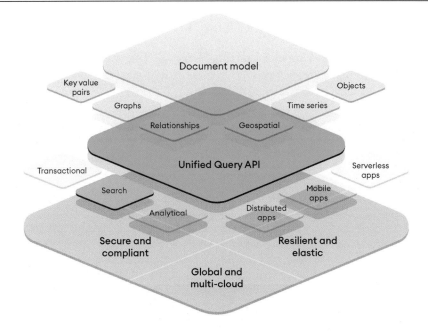

Figure 13.2: Atlas Search in relation with the Unified Query API

The fully managed Atlas platform automates provisioning, patching, upgrading, scaling, security, and disaster recovery. Additionally, it offers deep visibility into performance metrics for both database and search.

Feature overview

Atlas Search is a powerful search platform designed to enhance user experience by providing fast, accurate, and intuitive search capabilities. It's built to handle complex search requirements with ease, ensuring that you always find what you're looking for. Here's a quick overview of what Atlas Search brings to the table:

- **Rich query DSL**: Combines dozens of operators and options to build sophisticated search logic
- **Fuzzy search**: Returns relevant search results regardless of typos or spelling errors
- **Synonyms**: Defines similar search terms to help you find the content you're looking for
- **Custom scoring**: Controls how search results are scored and ranked, and boosts promoted content
- **Visual Editor**: Builds and edits search indexes and queries in a guided and easy-to-use interface
- **Autocomplete**: Suggests matching queries and updates results as you type
- **Fast faceting**: Analyzes and dissects data quickly to surface the most relevant information
- **Highlighting**: Helps you contextualize data by displaying search results in their original context

Version requirements for Atlas Search features

Atlas Search is available on Atlas instances running MongoDB 4.4 or higher versions only. Certain features of Atlas Search may necessitate a specific version of MongoDB. *Table 13.1* outlines Atlas Search features that demand specific MongoDB versions:

Atlas Search feature	MongoDB version
Facets	4.4.11+, 5.0.4+, 6.0+
Facets on Sharded Clusters	6.0+
Stored Source Fields	4.4.12+, 5.0.6+, 6.0+
Query Analytics	5.0+
$lookup with $search	6.0+
$unionWith with $search	6.0+

Table 13.1: Compatibility of Atlas features with MongoDB versions

Atlas Search architecture

Atlas Search is designed to integrate seamlessly with MongoDB, removing the need for separate search solutions and complex data synchronization. Data synchronization is a crucial aspect in systems where the database and search engine are separate entities. In such a setup, the primary data is stored in the database, while the search engine maintains a separate dataset in the form of search indexes. These indexes are optimized for search operations and you can use them to quickly find relevant data based on search queries.

The challenge in such a setup is to maintain *consistency* between the data in the database and the search indexes. Any changes that you make to the data in the database—such as additions, updates, or deletions—needs to reflect in the search indexes in a timely manner. This process is known as data synchronization.

In traditional setups, these synchronization mechanisms operate by continuously polling the database for changes, or by subscribing to a **change data capture** (**CDC**) stream if the database supports it. Once a change is detected, the corresponding update is made to the search indexes.

While this setup can work, it introduces several challenges:

- Adds *complexity* to the system architecture, as there is an additional component to manage.
- Introduces *latency* between the time a change is made in the database and the time it is reflected in the search indexes, leading to inconsistencies.
- Increases the resource overhead, as the synchronization process can be resource intensive, especially for large datasets or high rates of data change.

In contrast, the Atlas Search architecture eliminates these challenges by integrating the search functionality directly within the MongoDB database. Eventually, this ensures data synchronization without the need for a separate synchronization mechanism, simplifying the system architecture and ensuring consistent, up-to-date search results.

Technical overview of Atlas Search indexes

Atlas Search indexes are data structures that categorize data in an easily searchable format. They establish mapping between the terms themselves and the documents that contain those terms, enabling you to retrieve documents faster by using certain identifiers.

An Atlas Search index can be established on a single field or multiple fields. It is advisable to index fields that are frequently used to sort or filter your data, as this allows for the rapid retrieval of documents containing pertinent data during a query.

Index creation and management

When you set up one or more Atlas Search indexes, the `mongot` process is activated on the nodes in the cluster. Each `mongot` process communicates with the `mongod` process on the same node. The `mongot` process interacts with the backend database and opens change streams for each index to create and update search indexes.

When you create an Atlas Search index, you can specify the fields using the following methods:

- *Dynamic mappings* enable automatic indexing of all supported field types in each document by Atlas Search. It's particularly useful when the schema is frequently changing or unknown, or during experimentation with Atlas Search. To use dynamic mappings, set `mappings.dynamic` to `true`. While this approach provides flexibility, it's worth noting that dynamically mapped indexes may occupy more disk space and could be less performant compared to statically mapped indexes.

- *Static mappings* provide the flexibility to selectively identify and index specific fields. By setting `mappings.dynamic` to `false` and specifying the fields to index using `mappings.fields`, Atlas Search indexes only the specified fields with specific options. This approach is beneficial when you have a well-defined schema and want to maintain control over which fields are indexed. It's particularly useful for fields that you don't want indexed dynamically or when you want to configure a single field independently from others in an index. Unlike dynamic mappings, static mappings can help conserve disk space and potentially improve performance, as only selected fields are indexed.

Atlas Search carries out inverted indexing and stores the indexed fields on disk. An inverted index is a connection between terms, and the documents that include these terms. Atlas Search indexes contain the term, the `_id`, and other relevant metadata about the term, such as the term's position in the document.

Even though the data stored in Atlas Search is not a full copy of data from the collection on your Atlas cluster, Atlas Search indexes still consume some disk space and memory. If you enable the store option for fields that contain string values or if you configure the stored source fields in your index, Atlas Search stores an exact copy of the specified fields on disk, which will consume disk space.

Atlas Search offers built-in analyzers for creating indexable terms that account for differences in punctuation, capitalization, stop words, and more. Analyzers apply parsing and language rules to the query. You can also create a custom analyzer using available built-in character filters, tokenizers, and token filters.

For text fields, the `mongot` process performs the following tasks to create indexable tokens:

- Text analysis
- Tokenization, which involves breaking up words in a string into indexable tokens
- Normalization, such as transforming the text to lowercase, folding diacritics, and removing stop words
- Stemming, which involves ignoring plural and other word forms to index the word in the most reduced form

When an existing index is modified, Atlas Search initiates an index rebuild without any downtime. This process allows you to continue using the old index for both existing and new queries until the completion of the index rebuild.

If there are changes to the collection that defines Atlas Search indexes, the most recent data may not be immediately available for queries. However, the `mongot` process monitors the change streams, enabling updates to stored data copies, and ensuring that Atlas Search indexes maintain eventual consistency.

Once an Atlas Search index is established for a collection, you can run text search queries against the indexed fields.

Atlas Search queries

Queries are designed as aggregation pipeline stages, incorporating the $search and $searchMeta stages provided by Atlas Search. When you use them, they must appear as the initial stage in the aggregation pipeline. You can also use them in conjunction with other aggregation pipeline stages within the same aggregation pipeline.

Aggregation pipeline stage	Purpose
$search	Returns the search results of a full-text search
$searchMeta	Returns metadata about your search results

Table 13.2: Aggregation stages and their purpose

The $search pipeline stage

The $search pipeline stage is the core of Atlas Search. It is the first stage in any pipeline that it appears in, and cannot be used in a $facet pipeline stage. The $search stage takes a document with various fields that define the search parameters. The prototype form of a $search pipeline stage is as follows:

```
$search : {
   index : <index-name>,
   <collector-name> : <options>,
   count : <options>,
   highlight : <options>,
   <operator-name> : <options>,
   returnStoredSource : <boolean>,
   scoreDetails : <boolean>,
   sort : <options>,
   tracking : <options>
}
```

Let's break down these fields:

- index: This string specifies the name of the Atlas Search index to use. If omitted, it defaults to default. If you name your index default, you don't need to specify an index parameter when using the $search pipeline stage. Otherwise, you must specify the index name using the index parameter.

- <collector-name>: This field specifies the name of the collector to use with the query. You can provide a document that contains the collector-specific options as the value for this field. Either this or <operator-name> is required.

- count: This is a document that specifies the count options for retrieving a count of the results.

- highlight: This is a document that specifies the highlighting options for displaying search terms in their original context.

- <operator-name>: This field specifies the name of the operator to search with. You can provide a document that contains the operator-specific options as the value for this field. Either this or <operator-name> is required. Use the compound operator to run a compound query with multiple operators.

- returnStoredSource: This flag specifies whether to perform a full document lookup on the backend database or return only stored source fields directly from Atlas Search. If omitted, it defaults to false.

- scoreDetails: This flag specifies whether to retrieve a detailed breakdown of the score for the documents in the results. If omitted, it defaults to false. To view the details, you must use the $meta expression in the $project stage.

- sort: This is a document that specifies the fields to sort the Atlas Search results in ascending or descending order. You can sort by date, number (integer, float, and double values), and string values.

- `tracking`: This is a document that specifies the tracking option to retrieve analytics information on the search terms.

The $$SEARCH_META aggregation variable

The `$search` stage exclusively yields the outcome of the executed query. Any metadata resulting from the `$search` query is stored within the `$$SEARCH_META` aggregation variable. This variable helps you access the metadata outcomes of the `$search` query.

The `$$SEARCH_META` aggregation variable is applicable in any pipeline following a `$search` stage. However, it can't be used after the `$lookup` or `$unionWith` stages in any pipeline.

Let's look at an Atlas Search aggregation pipeline example with `$search`. Suppose you have the following index in the `sample_store.products` collection:

```
{
    "mappings": {
        "dynamic": false,
        "fields": {
            "price": {
                "type": "double"
            }
        }
    }
}
```

The following query searches for products with a price near 100 dollars using `$search`:

```
db.products.aggregate([
    {
        "$search": {
            "near": {
                "path": "price",
                "origin": 100,
                "pivot": 10
            }
        }
    },
    {
        $project: {
            "_id": 0,
            "name": 1,
            "price": 1
        }
    },
    { "$limit": 5 },
```

```
{
    "$facet": {
        "docs": [],
        "meta": [
            {"$replaceWith": "$$SEARCH_META"},
            {"$limit": 1}
        ]
    }
}
])
```

This MongoDB Atlas Search query performs the following operations:

- **Near search**: This searches for products that have a price near 100 dollars in the field of the documents in the specified collection. The `pivot` value is set to `10`, meaning it will consider products within a price range of 90 to 110 dollars.

- **Projection**: This shapes the data that is returned in the result. It excludes the `_id` field and includes the `name` and `price` fields. This means that the output documents will only contain the name and the price of the products.

- **Limiting**: This limits the results to the top 5 matches. This is useful for avoiding too many results, and making efficient use of bandwidth.

- **Faceting**: This organizes the results into two categories:

  - `docs`: This field will contain an array of the top 5 search results

  - `meta`: This field will contain the value of the `$$SEARCH_META` variable, which includes metadata about the search results, such as the search score

Remember to ensure that `name` and `price` are fields in your collection, and make sure to have set the appropriate numeric indexes for the `price` field.

The $searchMeta pipeline stage

The `$searchMeta` stage is a component of the Atlas Search pipeline that is responsible for returning different types of metadata result documents. To run `$searchMeta` queries on sharded collections, your cluster must run MongoDB v6.0 or later. The `$searchMeta` stage has the following prototype form:

```
$searchMeta: {
    "index": "<index-name>",
    "<collector-name>"|"<operator-name>": {
        <collector-specification>|<operator-specification>
    },
    "count": {
        <count-options>
    }
}
```

The $searchMeta stage accepts a document with the following fields:

- index: This is the name of the Atlas Search index to use. If this is not specified, it defaults to default.

- <collector-name>: This represents the collector to be used with the query. A document containing options that are specific to the collector can be provided as the value for this field. The value must be facet to retrieve a mapping of the defined facet names to an array of buckets for that facet.

- <operator-name>: This represents the name of the operator to search with. A document containing options that are specific to the operator can be provided as the value for this field.

- count: This is a document that outlines the options for retrieving a count of the results.

The $searchMeta stage can be only used as the initial stage in any pipeline. The structure of the metadata results document returned by the $searchMeta stage is contingent on the type of results. Atlas Search supports the following result types:

- **count**: The count value included in the results specifies whether the count returned in the results is the total count of the search results or the lower bound.

- **facet**: The result of a facet query is a mapping of the defined facet names to an array of buckets for that facet.

Let's look at an Atlas Search aggregation pipeline example with $searchMeta.

The following query searches for the number of products priced between 50 and 100 dollars using the $searchMeta stage:

```
db.products.aggregate([
  {
    "$searchMeta": {
      "range": {
        "path": "price",
        "gte": 50,
        "lt": 100
      },
      "count": {
        "type": "total"
      }
    }
  }
])
```

This MongoDB Atlas Search query performs a range search with count operation, which searches for products that have a price between 50 and 100 dollars in the `price` field of the documents in the specified collection. The `range` operator is used to specify the range of prices you have interested in, with `gte` (greater than or equal to) set to `50` and `lt` (less than) set to `100`. The `count` operator with its type set to `total` is used to specify that you want the total count of products that match this criterion. This means that the output will be the total number of products that were priced between 50 (inclusive) and 100 (exclusive) dollars.

Here's a concise summary of the differences between the two queries:

- `$search` with the `near` operator: This query returns the top 5 products with prices closest to 100 dollars. It provides actual documents (or parts of them) from the collection that match the search criteria.

- `$searchMeta` with the `range` operator: This query doesn't return the matching documents themselves. Instead, it counts and returns the total number of products priced between 50 and 100 dollars.

> **Note**
>
> When constructing a search interface, it's common to combine these two distinct operators for a comprehensive search experience.

Atlas Search query operators and collectors

In addition to these stages, Atlas Search also provides *query operators* and *collectors* that can be utilized inside the aggregation pipeline stage. These operators enable the location and retrieval of matching data from the collection on the Atlas cluster. Meanwhile, the collector returns a document that represents the search metadata results.

Search operators can be used to search a variety of data types and structures, including terms, phrases, geographic shapes and points, numerical values, similar documents, synonymous terms, and more. They also support search using regex and wildcard expressions. The aggregation pipeline stage incorporates the following operators:

- `autocomplete`: Executes a search-as-you-type query from a partially completed input string

- `compound`: Merges multiple operators into a singular query

- `embeddedDocument`: Searches fields within embedded documents, which are documents that exist as elements within an array

- `equals`: Operates in conjunction with the boolean and `objectId` data types

- `exists`: Checks for the existence of a specified field

- `geoShape`: Searches for values with specified geographic shapes

- `geoWithin`: Searches for points located within specified geographic shapes

- `in`: Searches both individual values and arrays of values
- `knnBeta`: Executes semantic search using the Hierarchical Navigable Small Worlds algorithm
- `moreLikeThis`: Searches for documents with similar characteristics
- `near`: Searches for values in proximity to a specified number, date, or geographic point
- `phrase`: Searches for documents that contain the same sequence of terms specified in the query
- `queryString`: Supports querying a combination of indexed fields and values
- `range`: Searches for values within a specific numerical or date range
- `regex`: Treats the `query` field as a regular expression
- `span`: Specifies relative positional requirements for query predicates within specified regions of a text field
- `text`: Executes a text-based analyzed search
- `wildcard`: Supports special characters in the query string that can match any character

The Atlas Search *compound operator* is a particularly powerful tool, allowing you to combine multiple operators inside the `$search` stage. This enables you to perform complex searches and filters of data based on what *must*, *must not*, or *should* be present in the documents returned by Atlas Search. The compound operator can also be employed to match or filter documents directly in the `$search` stage. Executing `$match` following `$search` is less efficient than running `$search` in conjunction with the compound operator.

Collectors yield a document that signifies the metadata results, typically an aggregation of the corresponding search results. The `$search` aggregation pipeline stage incorporates the `facet` collector. This operator categorizes query results based on values or ranges in specified, faceted fields and returns the count for each of these groups.

The facet collector is a tool that categorizes or groups search results based on the values or ranges present in specified faceted fields. Then, it gives a count for each of these groups, providing a clear view of the data distribution within the search results. The facet collector is applicable to both the `$search` and `$searchMeta` stages. However, you should only use facet with the `$searchMeta` stage when you want to get only the metadata results for the query. Faceted search allows users to filter and quickly navigate search results by category and see the total number of results per category for at-a-glance statistics.

Query execution in Atlas Search

When executing a query, Atlas Search uses the configured read preference to identify the node on which to run the query. The query first goes to the MongoDB process, which is either mongod for a replica set cluster or mongos for a sharded cluster. For sharded clusters, the cluster data is partitioned across mongod instances, and each mongot process is aware of the data on the mongod process on the same node. mongos directs the queries to all shards, resulting in scatter-gather queries.

The MongoDB process then routes the query to the mongot process on the same node. Atlas Search performs the search, calculates the score, and returns the document IDs and other search metadata for the matching results to mongod. Then, mongod implicitly performs a full document lookup for the matching results and returns them to the client.

Relevance scoring in Atlas Search

A key feature of Atlas Search is its association of a relevance-based score with every document in the result set. This scoring system allows Atlas Search to return documents in order—from the highest to the lowest score. Documents are scored higher if the query term appears frequently in a document and lower if the query term appears across many documents in the collection. Atlas Search also supports the customization of the relevance-based default score through boosting, decaying, or other modifying options.

Atlas Search Nodes

MongoDB Atlas Search Nodes are a recent addition to Atlas and are in public preview. This means that while they are fully functional, MongoDB is still actively gathering feedback and making improvements based on user experiences. It's important to note that features in public preview are typically not recommended for production environments until they reach **General Availability (GA)** status.

What are Atlas Search Nodes?

Traditionally, the Atlas Search process, mongot, has been placed side by side with mongod on the same database deployment. This setup necessitates sizing the workload based on both search and database requirements, which could potentially introduce resource contention between the database and search deployment.

In response to this, MongoDB introduced Atlas Search Nodes. These are dedicated nodes within a MongoDB Atlas cluster that exclusively handle search operations. They are separate from the primary and secondary nodes that manage regular database operations. This separation facilitates workload isolation, where search operations do not impact the performance of other database operations.

However, the traditional setup of having mongot and mongod on the same nodes will continue to be available. Users will have the flexibility to choose between the traditional setup and the new dedicated Atlas Search Nodes, depending on their specific requirements. This ensures that MongoDB Atlas can cater to a wide range of use cases and performance needs, providing users with the ability to choose the setup that best fits their application's needs.

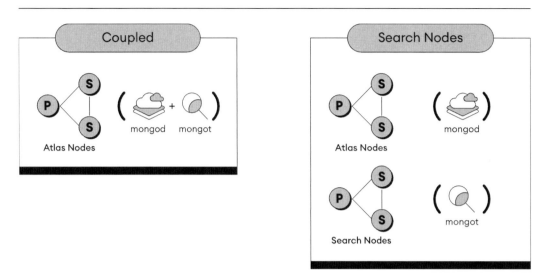

Figure 13.3: Atlas Search Node configurations

Following are the benefits of Atlas Search Nodes:

- **Workload isolation**: By separating search operations from other database operations, Atlas Search Nodes ensure that resource-intensive search tasks do not interfere with the performance of the primary and secondary nodes that manage regular database operations. This isolation allows each type of node to focus on its core tasks, leading to more efficient resource utilization and improved overall performance.

- **Enhanced performance at scale**: Dedicated Atlas Search Nodes are designed to scale horizontally, allowing them to handle increasing search workloads efficiently. As the volume of data or the complexity of search queries grows, additional Atlas Search Nodes can be added to the cluster. This scalability ensures that search operations continue to perform optimally, even under heavy loads. It also means that the performance of search operations does not degrade as the dataset grows, providing consistent search performance at scale.

- **Faster search index build**: Atlas Search Nodes speed up the construction of search indexes. These nodes are specifically optimized for search operations, including indexing. As new data enters the MongoDB Atlas cluster, it is immediately indexed on the Atlas Search Nodes. This real-time indexing ensures that the search index always reflects the most recent data, leading to precise and relevant search results.

Atlas Search index management

Atlas Search Index Management has been enhanced with the introduction of new methods and commands. These improvements provide more flexibility and control over creating, updating, and deleting Atlas Search indexes. Let's take a look at it:

- **Methods for index management**: In addition to the traditional methods (Atlas UI, Atlas admin API, and Atlas CLI), you can now manage Atlas Search Indexes using `mongosh`, the `Node.js` driver, and Compass. These additional methods can be chosen based on preference or the specific requirements of a project.

- **Commands for index management**: Following are the commands to facilitate index management in `mongosh`:

  - `db.collection.createSearchIndex()`: This command creates a new Atlas Search Index. The first argument is the name of the index, and the second argument is a document that specifies the index configuration.

  - `db.collection.createSearchIndex("mySearchIndex", {"mappings":{"dynamic": true}})`: This command creates an index named `mySearchIndex` with dynamic mappings.

  - `db.collection.updateSearchIndex()`: This command updates an existing Atlas Search index. The first argument is the name of the index, and the second argument is a document with the new index configuration.

  - `db.collection.updateSearchIndex("mySearchIndex", {"mappings":{"dynamic": false, "fields": {"description":{"type":"string"}} }})`: This command updates the `mySearchIndex` index to have static mappings and a string field named `description`

  - `db.collection.dropSearchIndex()`: This command deletes an existing Atlas Search index. The argument is the name of the index. For example, `db.collection.dropSearchIndex("mySearchIndex")` deletes the `mySearchIndex` index.

  - `db.collection.getSearchIndex()`: This command retrieves the configuration of an existing Atlas Search index. The argument is the name of the index. If no argument is provided, it retrieves the configurations of all indexes in the collection.

  - `$listSearchIndexes`: This command returns information about existing Atlas Search indexes on a specified collection. It takes either the `id` or the `name` field. You cannot specify both id and name. If you omit both the `id` and `name` fields, `$listSearchIndexes` returns information about all Atlas Search indexes on the collection.

Atlas Search Index Management provides flexibility and control over the management of Atlas Search indexes, making it easier for you to optimize search queries.

Search query analysis

MongoDB Atlas Search's query analytics is a powerful feature that's currently in preview. This feature allows you to view metrics for the Atlas Search query terms tracked using the tracking option on the Atlas UI Query Analytics page.

To use this feature, you must have an `M10` or higher cluster running MongoDB 6.3 or above. Atlas Search does not track search terms or display analytics for queries on free and shared-tier clusters.

The Query Analytics feature provides insights into two key areas:

- **Top search queries**: This feature shows the most frequently used search queries. It's a valuable tool for understanding user behavior and identifying the most popular search terms. This data can guide content creation, improve search engine optimization, and enhance the overall user experience. This information can be used in several ways:

  - **Content strategy**: Content creation and curation is guided by understanding what users are searching for. If a particular topic is frequently searched, it might be beneficial to create more content around that topic to meet user demand.

  - **Search engine optimization (SEO)**: You can use popular search terms to optimize your content for search engines, making it easier for users to find your content when they search for those terms.

  - **User experience**: By understanding what users are searching for, you can tailor the user interface and experience to make those searches easier and more intuitive.

- **Top No Results Queries**: This feature displays the search queries that returned no results. It's an invaluable tool to help you identify gaps in your data or issues with your search configuration. By addressing these *no results* queries, you can improve the comprehensiveness of your data and the effectiveness of your search functionality. You can use this information for the following:

  - **Identifying missing content**: If users are frequently searching for content that doesn't exist in your database, this could indicate a need for that content. You can use this information to guide your content creation strategy.

  - **Improving search functionality**: If certain queries consistently return no results, it may indicate that your search functionality isn't properly configured to handle those queries. You can use this information to refine your search algorithms and improve search effectiveness.

  - **Enhancing user satisfaction**: By addressing the issues that cause no results queries, you can improve user satisfaction. Users are more likely to continue using a service if they can find what they're looking for.

To access the Query Analytics page, navigate to the Atlas Search page for your project, click on the name of the index, and then click on *Query Analytics*. The page displays an overview of the selected index, including index configurations and field mappings in the index definition.

Troubleshooting Atlas Search errors

Atlas Search, like any complex system, may occasionally encounter issues that require troubleshooting.

Understanding and overcoming initial sync challenges

During an initial synchronization process, Atlas Search is unable to execute $search queries on an Atlas cluster. The initiation of this initial sync process can be triggered under the following circumstances:

- When a new cluster is established or specific upgrades are implemented on an existing cluster, an initial synchronization process is initiated.

- When shards are added to a collection that already has an Atlas Search index, an initial synchronization is triggered on the newly incorporated shards for that index.

- If a collection that already contains an Atlas Search index is sharded, an initial synchronization is initiated on the shards where the collection begins to exist.

The initial synchronization process has the following actions:

- The mongod carries out an initial synchronization

- The mongot also conducts an initial synchronization, during which the search indexes are rebuilt

Consequently, you might encounter an error while executing a $search query against a node that has been recently created or upgraded. The query should be attempted again after the completion of the initial synchronizations and the rebuilding of the indexes by mongot. You can verify the status of the initial synchronization of mongot through the following procedure:

1. Navigate to the **Search** tab for the database deployment.

2. In the **Status** column of the index, select **View Status Details**.

3. Observe the state of the index for the node. During the mongot initial synchronization, the status will be INITIAL SYNC. Upon completion of the index rebuilding by mongot, the status will change to ACTIVE.

Understanding the mongot Process Not Installed or Running error

This error is produced when $search queries are executed while the Atlas Search mongot process is either not installed or not operational:

```
MongoError: Remote error from mongot :: caused by :: Error connecting to
localhost:28000.
```

The mongot process is installed only when the first Atlas Search index is defined. If you don't have any Atlas Search indexes in your Atlas cluster, create at least one Atlas Search index to resolve this error.

Understanding and troubleshooting the Empty Result Set error

An empty result set is returned by the mongot process in Atlas Search under the following circumstances:

- **Non-existent index reference**: If a $search query references an index that does not exist, Atlas Search will return an empty result set without any error. By default, Atlas Search uses an index named default if no index name is specified in the query. If there is no default index or if the specified index does not exist, Atlas Search will return an empty result set. To avoid this, a valid index can be specified by its name using the index option.

- **Non-indexed field specification**: If a query is run against a field that is not indexed, Atlas Search will return an empty result set without any error. Only indexed fields should be specified as values for the path parameter. To ensure that all dynamically indexable fields in the collection are automatically indexed, dynamic mapping can be enabled in the index definition for the collection.

- **Text operator used on non-string indexed field path**: If the text operator is used on a field path that is not indexed as a string type, Atlas Search will return an empty result set without any error. Fields with string BSON data type values must be indexed as strings to query the fields using the text operator.

Understanding and troubleshooting the PlanExecutor error

The PlanExecutor error is returned by the mongot process in Atlas Search when a $search query specifies a field that is indexed as an incorrect data type. In such a case, Atlas Search returns an error message identifying the field that was indexed incorrectly and its correct data type:

```
PlanExecutor error during aggregation :: caused by :: Cannot facet on field
"genres" because it was not indexed as a "stringFacet" field.
```

To address the PlanExecutor error, verify that the fields identified in the $search query are indexed using the appropriate Atlas Search field type. For instance, when executing facet queries on string, number, or date fields, these fields should be indexed using their corresponding Atlas Search field types, namely stringFacet, numberFacet, and dateFacet.

Apache Lucene

Atlas Search is a full-text search engine built on top of Apache Lucene, showcasing the versatility of Lucene in a range of search-based applications. Apache Lucene itself is an open-source project focused on the development of search software, and offers a core search library known as Lucene Core.

Apache Lucene Core is a high-performance, full-featured search engine library written entirely in Java. It is a technology that's suitable for nearly any application that requires structured search, full-text search, faceting, nearest-neighbor search across high-dimensionality vectors, spell correction, or query suggestions. The key features of Lucene include the following:

- **Scalable, high-performance indexing**:

  - Small RAM requirements

  - Incremental indexing as fast as batch indexing

  - Index size roughly 20-30% the size of the indexed text

- **Powerful, accurate, and efficient search algorithms**:

  - Ranked searching (best results returned first)

  - Numerous powerful query types (phrase queries, wildcard queries, proximity queries, range queries, and more)

  - Fielded searching (title, author, contents)

  - Nearest-neighbor search for high-dimensionality vectors

  - Sorting by any field

  - Multiple-index searching with merged results

- Allows simultaneous updates and searching

- Flexible faceting, highlighting, joins, and result grouping

- Fast, memory-efficient, and typo-tolerant suggesters

- Pluggable ranking models, including the Vector Space Model and Okapi BM25

- **Cross-platform solution**:

  - Available as an open source software under the Apache License, permitting the use of Lucene in both commercial and open source programs

  - Written entirely in Java

  - Implementations in other programming languages available that are index compatible

Apache Software Foundation

Apache Lucene is a project of the Apache Software Foundation, a community of open source software projects. The Apache projects are characterized by collaborative consensus-based processes, an open, pragmatic software license, and a commitment to creating high-quality software that leads the way in its field. Apache Lucene, along with other Apache projects, exemplifies the power of open source software development and the innovation it can drive.

Atlas Search and integration with Apache Lucene

Atlas Search integrates with Apache Lucene by embedding a Lucene node within each Atlas cluster. This node is responsible for handling search indexing and querying. The data from the MongoDB database is automatically synchronized with the Lucene search index, ensuring that the search functionality is always up to date with the latest data.

The integration of Atlas Search with Apache Lucene is achieved through a dedicated `mongot` Java web process that runs alongside `mongod` on each node in the Atlas cluster.

This `mongot` process is responsible for several key tasks:

- **Atlas Search index creation**: Based on the rules defined in the index definition for the collection, the `mongot` process creates the necessary indexes. This allows efficient and fine-grained text indexing and querying.

- **Change stream monitoring**: The `mongot` process monitors change streams to keep track of the current state of the documents and index changes for the collections defined for Atlas Search indexes. This ensures that the indexes are always up to date with the latest changes in the data.

- **Query processing**: When a query is issued, the `mongot` process interprets the Atlas Search queries and returns the matching documents. This is the step where the actual search operation happens, and the results are returned based on the query parameters.

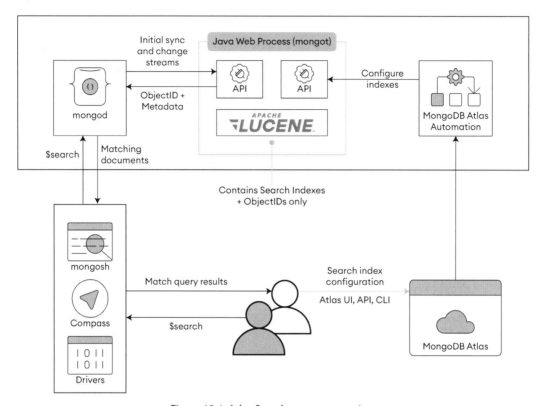

Figure 13.4: Atlas Search query processing

In Atlas Search index definition, there's an option called storedSource that designates the fields from the original document that should be stored by Atlas Search. When stored source fields are defined within an index definition, the mongot process in Atlas Search stores these specified fields.

The storedSource option has the following syntax:

```
{
  ...,
  "storedSource": true | false | {
  "include" | "exclude": [
    "<field-name>",
    ...
  ]
  }
}
```

Upon executing queries that yield matching documents, these stored fields are directly returned by the mongot process, bypassing a full document lookup on the database. This operation hinges on the specification of the returnStoredSource option in the query. Such a configuration can optimize query performance by eliminating the need for an implicit query time lookup on the backend database.

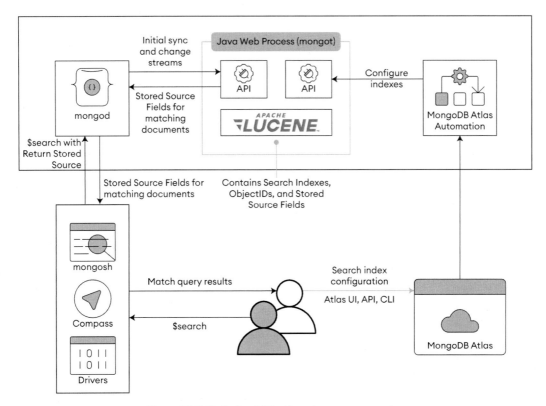

Figure 13.5: Optimized Atlas Search query processing

Summary

MongoDB Atlas Search is a powerful, integrated full-text search solution that simplifies the development of relevance-based application features, and ensures real-time data synchronization. Its seamless integration with MongoDB Atlas and Apache Lucene provides a streamlined and efficient solution for implementing full-text search functionality.

Atlas Search features, such as rich query DSL, fuzzy search, synonyms, custom scoring, a visual editor, autocomplete, fast faceting, and highlighting, allow you to build sophisticated search logic, return relevant search results despite typos or spelling errors, define similar search terms, control how search results are scored and ranked, and more.

Atlas Search integrates with Apache Lucene by embedding a Lucene node within each Atlas cluster, which is responsible for handling search indexing and querying. The integration is achieved through a dedicated `mongot` Java web process that runs alongside `mongod` on each node in the Atlas cluster which process is responsible for creating the necessary indexes, monitoring change streams, and processing Atlas Search queries.

In the next chapter, you will explore another vital facet in detail—integrating applications with MongoDB.

14

Integrating Applications with MongoDB

MongoDB integrates with a wide range of applications and tools, compared to traditional relational databases or even modern NoSQL database systems. This compatibility and ease of use with other third-party applications simplifies application development. Integrating applications with MongoDB opens a world of opportunities for modern businesses seeking agility, scalability, and real-time data capabilities.

As a versatile and developer-friendly NoSQL database, MongoDB enables applications to handle diverse and evolving data requirements, making it a compelling choice for today's data-centric applications.

This chapter will cover the following topics:

- How MongoDB seamlessly integrates with various tools and technologies

- Functions of various tools including the MongoDB Kubernetes Operator, Terraform, Vercel, Datadog, Prometheus, webhooks, and PagerDuty

- How to create a robust ecosystem where MongoDB-powered applications thrive and adapt to dynamic business needs

Technical requirements

Visit `cloud.mongodb.com`, and sign up for a trial account. A free account is enough for most of the examples demonstrated in this chapter. However, a paid account is needed for advanced examples.

Integrating applications in MongoDB

MongoDB offers an array of integrations that span across a variety of use cases. This includes application development and deployment, access and security management, data modeling, project monitoring, application-driven analytics, and receiving alerts.

These integrations provide a seamless interface for third-party tools with which they integrate. Applications that use MongoDB integrations allow you to operate on the database cluster from within those applications. While doing this, you don't need to switch to MongoDB-native applications/tools, such as Atlas or Compass, for managing the cluster architecture setup or performing CRUD operations on the database.

These integrations can help you produce deeper insights from your data through log analysis and send alerts and events. You can deploy and manage the life cycles of cloud-native applications that need data services in a single control plane with secure enterprise platform integrations.

Following are categories of integrated applications based on their primary focus and purpose:

- **Deployment and orchestration integrations**

    - **Kubernetes Operator**: MongoDB offers an official *Kubernetes Operator* that simplifies the deployment, scaling, and management of MongoDB clusters in Kubernetes environments.

    - **Terraform**: Integration with *Terraform* enables automated infrastructure provisioning, making it easier to set up and maintain MongoDB clusters on various cloud platforms.

- **Monitoring and analytics integrations**

    - **Datadog**: Integration with *Datadog* enables real-time monitoring of MongoDB performance metrics and resource utilization, providing insights for optimizing database performance.

    - **Prometheus**: MongoDB integration with *Prometheus* allows custom metrics and alerts to monitor the health and performance of MongoDB clusters.

- **Real-time and event-driven integrations**

    - **Webhooks**: MongoDB's integration with *webhooks* enables real-time event-driven architectures, where applications can respond instantly to database changes and trigger actions or notifications.

- **Cloud and deployment integrations**

    - **AWS / GCP / Azure**: MongoDB Atlas offers seamless integration with cloud providers such as *AWS*, *GCP*, and *Azure*, simplifying database management and maintenance.

    - **Vercel**: Integration with *Vercel* allows for hosting and deploying MongoDB-backed applications on a cloud platform optimized for static and serverless deployments.

- **Development and language integrations**

    - **MongoDB drivers**: MongoDB provides official *drivers* for various programming languages such as Python, Node.js, and Java. This makes it easy to interact with MongoDB databases in your language of choice.

- **Security integrations**

  - **Authentication and authorization**: MongoDB supports various authentication mechanisms and **role-based access control (RBAC)** to secure access to databases and collections.

- **CI/CD integrations**:

  - **Continuous integration and continuous deployment (CI/CD) tools**: Integrating MongoDB into *CI/CD* pipelines allows for automated database migrations and validations during the software development process.

Figure 14.1 shows an extensive list of applications that currently offer integration with MongoDB:

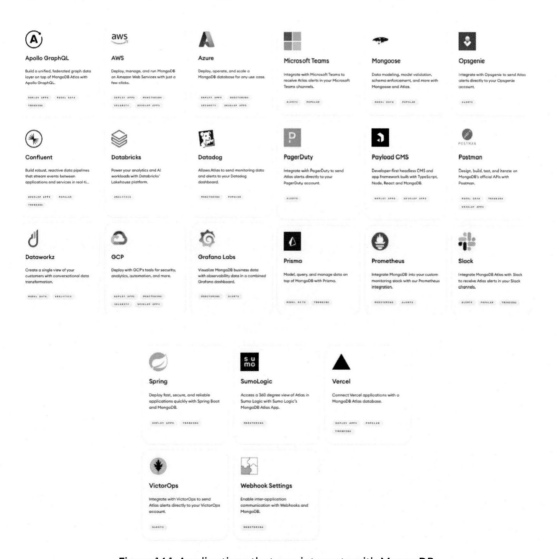

Figure 14.1: Applications that can integrate with MongoDB

The MongoDB Kubernetes Operator

The *MongoDB Kubernetes Operator* is part of the Kubernetes ecosystem, which is an open-source container orchestration system for automating application deployment, scaling, and management. The MongoDB Kubernetes Operator is a tool that helps you manage MongoDB clusters in Kubernetes. It supports features such as authentication, TLS, replication, sharding, and backup.

As Kubernetes grows in popularity, the need to manage stateful applications, such as databases, from within the Kubernetes environment becomes evident. The MongoDB Kubernetes Operator is specifically designed to manage MongoDB clusters using custom resources tailored for MongoDB deployment.

The MongoDB Kubernetes Operator creates, configures, and manages MongoDB deployments from a single Kubernetes control plane. This means, you can manage MongoDB instances on Kubernetes just by creating native objects, such as a Deployment, a `ReplicaSet`, or a StatefulSet.

Installation

The MongoDB Kubernetes Operator is a custom resource definition and a controller, available in three flavors:

- **MongoDB Community Kubernetes Operator**: This is a free operator, mainly used for testing applications, development activities, and small production setups.

- **MongoDB Enterprise Kubernetes Operator**: Available under the Enterprise Advanced license, this operator is used for medium to large-size production environments with all the capabilities of an enterprise setup.

- **Atlas Kubernetes Operator**: This is a new service for integrating Atlas resources with a Kubernetes cluster.

For the Community Edition of the MongoDB Kubernetes Operator, you'll need a Kubernetes cluster with nodes running x86_64/AMD64 processors. ARM64 support was added in `https://github.com/mongodb/mongodb-kubernetes-operator/releases/tag/v0.8.3`.

To begin, install helm by following the installation guide `https://helm.sh/docs/intro/install/`. For testing, MongoDB recommends Kind (`https://kind.sigs.k8s.io/`).

Add the MongoDB Helm Charts for Kubernetes repository to Helm by running the following command:

```
helm repo add mongodb https://mongodb.github.io/helm-charts
```

Install the Custom Resource Definitions and the Community Operator in the `default` namespace using Helm. Execute the install command from the terminal:

```
helm install community-operator mongodb/community-operator
```

Deploy and configure MongoDB using the Kubernetes Operator

Once you have installed the Kubernetes Operator, you can use it for multiple MongoDB operations that you would normally have to perform separately from the database domain—all while staying within the Kubernetes environment.

The configurations that you can handle by using the Kubernetes Operator include the following:

- Deploying a `ReplicaSet`
- Scaling a `ReplicaSet`
- Adding arbiters to a `ReplicaSet`
- Upgrading your MongoDB Community resource version and feature compatibility version
- Deploying `ReplicaSets` on OpenShift
- Defining a custom database role
- Specifying non-default values for readiness probes

The Community edition supports SCRAM and TLS authentication. SCRAM is the default authentication method. To deploy a database using SCRAM, you need to create a user and give it credentials for authentication.

A Kubernetes Secret can be created to store the user's password:

```
kubectl create secret generic dev-mongodb-user-password -n mongodb --from-lite
ral="password=mytopsecretpassword"
```

To deploy MongoDB, a YAML file can be used as input to the `kubectl apply` command. Currently, the Community Operator only supports the `ReplicaSet` type. The Enterprise Operator supports both `ReplicaSet` and Shards.

Following is an example YAML file named `mongoKubernetesOp.yaml`:

```
apiVersion: mongodbcommunity.mongodb.com/v1
kind: MongoDBCommunity
metadata:
  name: dev-mongodb
namespace: mongodb
spec:
# number of desired replicas
  members: 3
  type: ReplicaSet
# the desired version
  version: "5.0.5"
  security:
```

```
# the authentication methods
   authentication:
     modes: ["SCRAM"]
  users:
# the username to be created
  - name: dev-mongodb-user
    db: admin
    passwordSecretRef:
      name: dev-mongodb-user-password
    roles:
      - name: readWrite
        db: dev-db
    scramCredentials SecretName: dev-mongodb-user
```

To apply the YAML file, simply use the following command:

```
kubectl apply -f mongoKubernetesOp.yaml
```

You can check the status while the databases are being created, as follows:

```
kubectl get po -n mongodb -w
```

Once the pods are ready and running, connect to the database using the following command:

```
kubectl exec -it dev-mongodb-0 -c mongod -n mongodb -- mongo ${MONGO_URI}--
username "${USR}" --password "${PASSWD}"
```

This will connect you to the MongoDB Shell directly:

```
MongoDB shell version v 5.0.5
connecting to:
mongodb://127.0.0.1:27017/?compressors=disabled&gssapiServiceName=mongodb
Implicit session: session { "id" : UUID("6268dd8d-bd6b-4463-8036-
4444027a35ae") }
MongoDB server version: 5.0.5
```

The Operator deploys the database with a container called mongodb-agent. This container monitors configuration changes on the cluster, and syncs and applies them to the database. For example, you can just update the manifest if you want to change any configuration for your database and it will be applied. This helps improve database maintainability and helps reform the database to its stable form in case of any database crash for a faster disaster recovery model.

The Atlas Kubernetes Operator

By using the *Atlas Kubernetes Operator*, you can deploy and manage the life cycle of cloud-native applications that need data services in a single control plane with secure enterprise platform integration.

This allows you to manage resources in Atlas without leaving Kubernetes. It ensures that the state of the projects, database deployments, and database users in Atlas match the configurations that you create in your Kubernetes cluster.

The Atlas Kubernetes Operator supports many advanced features within the custom resources, such as X.509 certificate authentication, private endpoints in Azure and AWS, and advanced multi-cloud and multi-region clusters.

The Enterprise Kubernetes Operator

In contrast to its Community counterpart, the Enterprise Operator for Kubernetes is a specialized tool designed to cater to the needs of enterprise-level MongoDB deployments. It distinguishes itself primarily through its ability to deploy sharded clusters, provision Ops Manager, and offer comprehensive backup functionality akin to what Ops Manager provides. These capabilities are essential for organizations operating at scale, where data volumes and complexity demand a more sophisticated approach to database management. The Enterprise Operator's support for sharded clusters allows enterprises to handle vast datasets and high transaction loads efficiently.

The Enterprise Operator's ability to deploy Ops Manager means that you can centralize the management of MongoDB clusters, resulting in enhanced visibility and control over their database infrastructure.

Moreover, the Enterprise Operator's comprehensive backup functionality—using Ops Manager's capabilities—is crucial for safeguarding critical data. It ensures that enterprises can reliably and securely back up their MongoDB databases, minimizing the risk of data loss and simplifying disaster recovery procedures.

While the MongoDB Kubernetes Operator excels at streamlining database deployments within a Kubernetes ecosystem, the need for a tool to manage the evolving landscape of infrastructure management is predominant. Your infrastructure doesn't end with just the MongoDB database. You are likely to have other components, such as virtual machines, load balancers, networking configurations, and cloud resources, that complement your MongoDB deployment. Managing all these resources individually can be cumbersome, prone to errors, and time-consuming. This is where Terraform comes into play.

Integrating Terraform with MongoDB

Terraform is an open-source **infrastructure as code** (**IaC**) tool developed by HashiCorp. It allows you to define and manage infrastructure resources in a declarative manner. This means that you describe the desired state of your infrastructure and Terraform takes care of bringing your actual infrastructure to that state. It's designed to work with various cloud providers, on-premises environments, and third-party services, which makes it a versatile choice for infrastructure automation. The key benefit of Terraform lies in its ability to create, modify, and delete infrastructure resources efficiently and in a version-controlled manner.

Integrating Terraform with MongoDB offers a powerful solution for managing, deploying, and scaling MongoDB databases and infrastructure. With IaC practices, you can ensure consistency, reduce manual errors, and automate repetitive tasks. The collaboration between Terraform's flexibility and MongoDB's NoSQL capabilities provides a solid foundation for building robust and scalable applications that can quickly adapt to changing business needs.

The advantages of having IaC for MongoDB in the form of Terraform include infrastructure automation, scalability of the MongoDB cluster, version control, and collaboration with version control tools such as Git to review, test, and roll back changes as needed. On top of these advantages, using Terraform gives you the flexibility to deploy MongoDB clusters across your preferred cloud platforms such as AWS, GCP, and Azure without having to rewrite the infrastructure code. Since Terraform maintains a state file that keeps track of the current infrastructure state, this file helps Terraform understand the resources it has provisioned, making it easier to manage, update, and destroy infrastructure without causing conflicts or unintended changes.

Installation

To use the Terraform integration, you can install it from the official HashiCorp Terraform downloads page: `https://developer.hashicorp.com/terraform/tutorials/aws-get-started/install-cli`

You can do a manual installation using a pre-compiled binary.

- For macOS, the installation can be done through Homebrew:

    ```
    brew tap hashicorp/tap
    brew install hashicorp/tap/terraform
    ```

- For Windows, Chocolatey can be used in a similar manner:

    ```
    choco install terraform
    ```

- For Linux, HashiCorp officially maintains and signs packages for Ubuntu/Debian, CentOS/RHEL, Fedora, and Amazon Linux.

You can follow the installation steps in the official documentation: `https://developer.hashicorp.com/terraform/install#Linux`

Configuring a MongoDB cluster on Atlas using Terraform

Before you start using Terraform, you need to set up MongoDB Atlas API access and obtain an API key. To begin, follow these steps:

- Log in to your MongoDB Atlas account
- Navigate to the *Project Access* section
- Create an API key with the necessary privileges (e.g., Project Owner or Project Data Access).
- Take note of the API key and the project ID, as you will need them in the Terraform configuration

To start the development of MongoDB Atlas IaC through Terraform, you must create a new directory for the Terraform project and create a file named `main.tf` in it. This file will contain the Terraform configurations. You'll declare the MongoDB Atlas provider in the `main.tf` file.

You must register with the MongoDB Atlas provider first. You can do that with following entries:

```
terraform {
  required_providers {
    mongodbatlas = {
      source = "mongodb/mongodbatlas"
    }
  }
  required_version = ">= 0.13"
}
```

The MongoDB Atlas API key and project ID will be required as part of the configuration:

```
provider "mongodbatlas" {
  public_key = var.mongodbatlas_public_key
  private_key  = var.mongodbatlas_private_key
}
```

The public and private key for `mongodbatlas` can be defined as variables inside a `variable.tf` file as follows:

```
# variables.tf
variable "mongodbatlas_public_key" {
  description = "Mongodbatlas Public Key"
  type = string
}
variable "mongodbatlas_private_key" {
  description = "Mongodbatlas Private Key"
  type = string
}
```

Now, you can define a MongoDB Atlas cluster resource. Create a basic `M10` cluster on AWS in the US East region and enter the following code in `main.tf` file:

```
resource "mongodbatlas_cluster" "cluster-test" {
  project_id   = "<YOUR-PROJECT-ID>"
  name         = "cluster-test"
  cluster_type = "REPLICASET"
  replication_specs {
  num_shards = 1
    regions_config {
      region_name      = "US_EAST_1"
      electable_nodes = 3
```

```
    priority        = 7
    read_only_nodes = 0
  }
}
cloud_backup = true
auto_scaling_disk_gb_enabled = true
mongo_db_major_version       = "6.0"
# Provider Settings "block"
provider_name                = "AWS"
provider_instance_size_name = "M10"
}
```

Now, simply initialize, plan (to preview the changes), and apply the code by running the following commands in the terminal from the folder where main.tf was created:

```
terraform init
terraform plan
terraform apply
```

Terraform will initialize the project, download the MongoDB Atlas provider plugin, and display a plan showing the changes to be applied. Review the plan, type yes to apply the changes, and create the MongoDB Atlas cluster.

To modify the cluster, update the configuration in the main.tf file with the desired changes. For example, if you'd like to increase the cluster size or modify the disk size—after making the changes, run terraform apply again to apply the updates to your MongoDB Atlas cluster.

If the operations on the cluster are completed, you can use the terraform destroy command to delete the cluster and clean up any associated resources.

Using Terraform to create and modify MongoDB Atlas clusters simplifies the management of your database infrastructure. By defining MongoDB Atlas resources as code, you can version-control infrastructure, collaborate with team members, and easily scale clusters to meet changing demands. Whether you are starting a new project or managing an existing MongoDB environment, Terraform empowers you to efficiently manage your database infrastructure with ease and confidence.

Using Vercel with MongoDB

Vercel is a cloud platform that specializes in frontend deployment and serverless functions. Formerly known as *Zeit*, Vercel enables you to deploy front-end applications with ease, handling the complexities of hosting, scaling, and global content delivery. With Vercel, you can build and deploy modern web applications, static sites, and serverless APIs quickly and efficiently. You can start using Vercel by creating an account on its portal: https://vercel.com/.

Vercel and MongoDB are a powerful combination for building and deploying scalable web applications that require both serverless functions and a robust database.

Building a web application with Vercel and MongoDB

To build a web application with Vercel and MongoDB, follow these steps:

1. **Set up a MongoDB database**

   I.   Sign up for a MongoDB Atlas account, create a new MongoDB cluster, and configure the necessary settings, such as region and `ReplicaSet` options.

   II.   Obtain the MongoDB connection string, which you will use to connect your application to the database.

2. **Develop your frontend application**

   I.   Develop your front-end application using your preferred frontend framework (e.g., React, Vue.js, or Angular) or vanilla HTML, CSS, and JavaScript.

   II.   Ensure that the front-end application is designed to interact with a backend API for data retrieval and updates.

3. **Create serverless functions**

   I.   Identify the backend functionality the application requires, such as handling user authentication or fetching data from the MongoDB database.

   II.   Create serverless functions using Vercel's built-in support for serverless functions. These functions will act as your backend API endpoint.

4. **Integrate MongoDB with serverless functions**

   I.   Use the MongoDB Node.js driver or any MongoDB library compatible with Node.js to connect to your MongoDB database from within your serverless functions.

   II.   Implement the necessary logic to interact with the database, such as querying data, inserting or updating documents, and handling database errors.

5. **Deploy your application**

   I.   Push the frontend code, serverless functions, and any necessary configurations to a Git repository.

   II.   Connect your Git repository to Vercel and set up automatic deployments. Vercel will automatically build and deploy your application whenever you push changes to the repository.

6. **Monitor and scale**

   I.   Monitor your application's performance and user behavior using Vercel's built-in analytics or integrate external monitoring tools.

   II.   Use MongoDB's monitoring and logging features to keep track of database performance and identify any potential issues.

Configuring MongoDB Atlas with Vercel

There is already an available pre-built solution as a template that can be used to set up MongoDB Atlas within a Vercel deployment. It's a developer directory app called *MongoDB Starter* and is based on the Next.js framework: `https://vercel.com/templates/next.js/mongodb-starter`

If you're starting a new project, you can add the repo to Vercel and then add the Atlas integration to your project as shown in *Figure 14.2*.

Figure 14.2: Adding MongoDB Atlas integration to an Atlas project

This will redirect you to the MongoDB Atlas login page, where you can log in to your Atlas account. Then, you can select the organization in Atlas that you want to authorize Vercel to have access to and select the project to integrate.

After completing the integration setup and successfully linking an Atlas database to your Vercel project(s), head over to the project's settings page to look at the `MONGODB_URI` environment variable, which is the connection string for the Atlas cluster.

To connect to an Atlas cluster, the IP access list of your Atlas cluster must allow dedicated IP addresses which are generated from Vercel Secure Compute. When enabled, Vercel Secure Compute places your deployments in a private network with dedicated IP addresses.

When you set up the integration, Atlas performs the following actions to secure your Vercel connections to the cluster:

1. Creates a `MONGODB_URI` environment variable that serves as the Atlas cluster's connection string for all Vercel projects that you link this cluster to. When your application doesn't specify a database, the `MONGODB_URI` variable uses `/myFirstDatabase` as the default database name. Replace this name with your database name, or if you use a library to interface with MongoDB, ensure that your application's code specifies your database name.

2. Creates a database user, `vercel-admin-user`, in the admin database and grant the built-in MongoDB database role `readWriteAnyDatabase` to all other non-system databases in the cluster.

Once the integration is completed, you'll start seeing data being populated in your Atlas cluster, as shown in *Figure 14.3*:

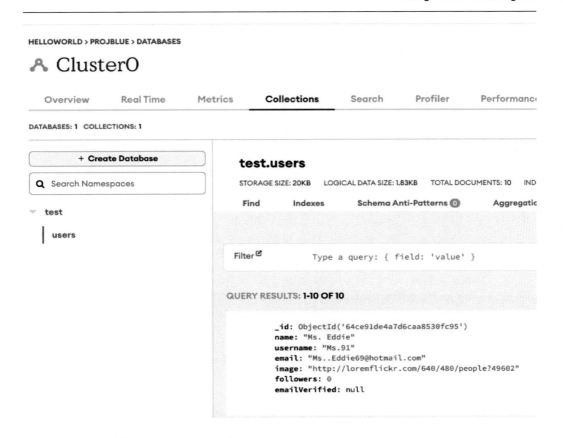

Figure 14.3: Atlas data populating from the Vercel integration

Disconnecting the Vercel integration

You can disconnect the Vercel integration through Atlas UI. However, before disconnecting it, make sure that the cluster's users and network access rules aren't shared with other projects and applications connected to this Atlas cluster.

Here's how to disconnect Vercel:

1. Sign-in to the Atlas UI.

2. Click **Integrations** in the sidebar.

3. Select **Vercel**.

4. Click **Disconnect Vercel**.

5. Choose one of the following options:

    I.   **Delete the database users created as part of this integration**

    II.   **Delete the network access rules created as part of this integration**

6. Confirm that you want to disconnect this Vercel integration:

     I.   Atlas asks you to confirm that you want to disconnect your Atlas organization from Vercel. Disconnecting the integration may result in downtime for your Vercel applications and any other applications connected to the Atlas clusters that you linked to Vercel.

     II.   To confirm, enter the words *DISCONNECT VERCEL* in uppercase, and then click **Disconnect Vercel**.

     III. Atlas removes the integration by removing the environment variables for Vercel projects that it created when you linked the projects to an Atlas cluster.

     IV.   Vercel also removes the integration and no longer displays it in the Vercel UI.

Integrating Datadog with MongoDB

Datadog is a popular monitoring and analytics platform that helps you collect, visualize, and analyze data from various sources, including databases such as MongoDB. It is a leading cloud-scale monitoring and analytics platform that helps you gain valuable insights into your entire infrastructure, applications, and services. It offers a comprehensive set of tools and features to monitor, troubleshoot, and optimize complex environments, including cloud infrastructure, microservices, containers, and more. With Datadog, you can collect, visualize, and analyze metrics, traces, and logs from a wide range of sources, allowing them to proactively identify issues, track performance, and improve overall system reliability. Apart from MongoDB, it provides built-in integration with many popular technologies such as cloud providers (AWS, GCP, and Azure), web servers, containers (Docker and Kubernetes), and other database technologies.

By integrating Datadog with MongoDB, you gain better visibility of a database's metrics, identify performance bottlenecks, and proactively address potential issues. Integrating Datadog with MongoDB can greatly enhance the ability to monitor and manage a database effectively.

By connecting MongoDB with Datadog, you will be able to do the following:

- Visualize key MongoDB metrics

- Correlate MongoDB performance with the rest of your applications

- Create your own metrics using custom `find`, `count`, and `aggregate` queries

> **Note**
> You need MongoDB 3.0 and above for this integration. Integration of MongoDB Atlas with Datadog is only available on `M10+` clusters.

Most low-level metrics (uptime, storage size, etc.) need to be collected on every `mongod` mode. Other higher-level metrics (collection/index statistics, etc.) should be collected only once. For these reasons, the way you configure the Datadog Agent depends on how your MongoDB cluster is deployed, whether it is standalone, a `ReplicaSet`, or a sharded cluster. The interface looks as shown in *Figure 14.4*.

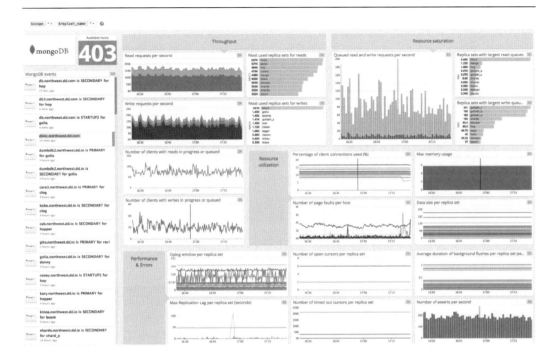

Figure 14.4: Datadog integration

Configuring Datadog

Here are the steps to integrate an on-premises MongoDB deployment with Datadog:

1. **Sign up for a Datadog account**: You can sign up for a Datadog account on the www.datadoghq.com website. There is a trial version to test monitoring as well as a paid version for production setup.

2. **Install the Datadog Agent**: The Datadog Agent is a lightweight piece of software that runs on your servers to collect and send data to Datadog. To integrate Datadog with MongoDB, you need to install Datadog on the server where MongoDB is running. The MongoDB check is included in the Datadog Agent package. No additional installation is necessary.

3. **Configure the MongoDB integration**: Once the Datadog Agent is installed, configure the MongoDB integration. The Datadog Agent supports many integrations out of the box, including MongoDB. To configure the MongoDB integration, edit the Datadog Agent's configuration file and provide the necessary information to connect to the MongoDB instance. Also, specify the hostname, port, and any authentication credentials if required.

4. **Enable MongoDB monitoring**: After configuring the MongoDB integration, restart the Datadog Agent to apply the changes.

5. **Explore the Datadog and MongoDB dashboards**: With the MongoDB integration enabled, Datadog will automatically create pre-built dashboards specifically tailored to MongoDB monitoring. These dashboards display key performance indicators such as connection statistics, memory usage, disk utilization, query performance, and more. Use these dashboards to gain insights into your database's health and performance.

6. **Set up alerts**: Datadog allows you to set up custom alerts based on specific conditions. For example, you can create an alert that triggers when the number of connections to a MongoDB instance exceeds a certain threshold or when the response time for queries increases unexpectedly. Alerts help you identify and respond to potential issues in real time.

7. **Analyze and optimize data**: Continuously monitor the metrics and logs provided by Datadog to identify trends and potential performance bottlenecks. Analyze the data to optimize the MongoDB instance's configuration and improve its overall performance and efficiency.

Table 14.1 shows a few example metrics that can be tracked by using the Datadog and MongoDB integration:

Name	Units	Description
`mongodb.asserts.msgps`	assertions/second	Number of message assertions raised per second
`mongodb.asserts.regularps`	assertions/second	Number of regular assertions raised per second
`mongodb.asserts.rolloversps`	assertions/second	Number of times that the rollover counters roll over per second. The counters rollover to zero every 2^30 assertions
`mongodb.asserts.userps`	assertions/second	Number of user assertions raised per second
`mongodb.asserts.warningps`	assertions/second	Number of warnings raised per second
`mongodb.backgroundflushing.average_ms`	milliseconds	Average time for each flush to disk
`mongodb.backgroundflushing.flushesps`	flushes/second	Number of times the database has flushed all writes to disk
`mongodb.backgroundflushing.last_ms`	milliseconds	Amount of time that the last flush operation took to complete
`mongodb.backgroundflushing.total_ms`	milliseconds	Total number of time that the `mongod` processes have spent writing (i.e. flushing) data to disk
`mongodb.chunks.jumbo`		Total number of 'jumbo' chunks in the mongo cluster

Table 14.1: Tracking with Datadog MongoDB

As part of the paid version, the following log attributes will be automatically tracked and parsed into searchable facets:

Name	Path	Facet type	Group
Database	`db.instance`	list	Database
Operation Type	`db.operation`	list	Database
Duration	`duration`	range	Measure
Client IP	`network.client.ip`	list	Web Access
[Mongo] collection	`mongo.collection`	list	Mongo
[Mongo] PlanSummary Type	`mongo.planSummary.type`	list	Mongo
[Mongo] Query Type	`mongo.query.type`	list	Mongo
[Mongo] Context	`mongo.context`	list	Mongo

Table 14.2: Log attributes

Assets that are part of the Datadog integration include the following:

- **MongoDB overview dashboard**: This dashboard provides a high-level overview of the MongoDB deployment so you can quickly identify potential slowdowns and resource limitations.

- **Recommended monitors**: You can choose a detection method, define metrics to monitor, set alert conditions, and notify the team if needed based on the alerts.

Integrating MongoDB Atlas with Datadog

MongoDB Atlas can also be integrated with Datadog to visualize key metrics. It can even be integrated to correlate MongoDB Atlas performance with the applications running on top.

To install the Datadog integration, first retrieve or create a Datadog API key from your Datadog account. Then, simply log into the Atlas UI portal, and enter a Datadog API key under **Integrations| Datadog Settings**. Click on **Install Integration**.

You can monitor anomalies in MongoDB Atlas in metrics such as CPU usage, memory usage, efficiency of queries, read latency, write latency, and so on.

Figure 14.5 shows the **MongoDB Atlas Overview** in the Datadog portal.

Figure 14.5: MongoDB Atlas overview in the Datadog portal

Integrating Prometheus with MongoDB

Prometheus is yet another monitoring tool that can be easily integrated with MongoDB. It is an open-source monitoring and alerting toolkit designed for monitoring highly dynamic and distributed systems. Prometheus provides a flexible query language called **Prometheus Query Language** (**PromQL**) that allows you to extract and analyze metrics data. This enables you to create custom dashboards, graphs, and alerts based on their specific monitoring needs. By integrating Prometheus with MongoDB, you can gain valuable insights into your database's behavior, identify potential issues, and ensure optimal performance.

Prometheus integration for MongoDB Atlas is available only on M10+ clusters. Just like any other integration with MongoDB Atlas, you'll need to add the IP of the device hosting the Prometheus instance to the IP access list of Atlas.

Configuring Prometheus

Download the Prometheus server binaries from its official website according to the operating system and architecture you're using: https://prometheus.io/download/.

Here are the steps to configure Prometheus and start using it with an on-premises MongoDB deployment:

1. Create a configuration file (prometheus.yml) and define the MongoDB endpoint as a target for data scraping. Specify the MongoDB exporter's URL (http://localhost:9001/metrics) as a target in the Prometheus configuration. This exporter serves MongoDB metrics in a format that Prometheus can understand.

2. Install the *MongoDB exporter*, which acts as a bridge between MongoDB and Prometheus. The MongoDB exporter fetches metrics from MongoDB and exposes them in a format suitable for Prometheus. Download the MongoDB exporter from the GitHub repository: `https://github.com/percona/mongodb_exporter`.

3. Edit the MongoDB exporter configuration file (`mongo.yml`) to provide the necessary MongoDB connection details, such as the *host name*, *port*, and *authentication credentials* (if applicable). Ensure that the exporter has the required read permissions to fetch metrics from MongoDB, as shown in *Figure 14.6*.

```
---
version: '1'
metrics_path: /metrics
listen_address: 0.0.0.0:9001
metrics_relabel_configs:
  - source_labels: [_id]
    target_label: instance
    replacement: ${1}
scrape_timeout: 10s
mongodb_uri: "mongodb://localhost:27017"
```

Figure 14.6: The mongo.yml file

4. Start the Prometheus server using the configuration file created in *Step 1*. Also, launch the MongoDB exporter with the specified configuration file (`mongo.yml`) using `./mongodb_exporter --config.file=mongo.yml`.

5. Once Prometheus and the MongoDB exporter are running, navigate to the Prometheus web interface (default: `http://localhost:9090`), and enter the PromQL queries to validate whether MongoDB metrics are being successfully scraped. For example, you can use a query such as `mongodb_up` to check the MongoDB exporter's health status.

6. Optionally, to visualize MongoDB metrics effectively, integrate Prometheus with Grafana—a popular data visualization tool. Create custom dashboards in Grafana using PromQL queries to display key MongoDB performance indicators such as connection count, memory usage, query response times, and more.

You can use various PromQL queries on the Prometheus portal to run on your MongoDB database. Following are a few examples:

- `mongodb_connections_total`: Monitors the total number of connections to MongoDB

- `mongodb_connections_current`: Monitors the number of active connections

- `rate(mongodb_oplog_operation_total[1m])`: Monitors the operation count per second

- `mongodb_oplog_insert_total`: Monitors the total document inserts

- `mongodb_oplog_update_total`: Monitors the total document updates

- `mongodb_oplog_delete_total`: Monitors the total document deletes

- `rate(mongodb_exporter_mongod_cmd_total{cmd="query"}[5m]) / rate(mongodb_exporter_mongod_cmd_total{cmd="query", status="ok"} [5m])`: Calculates the average response time for queries

These are just a few examples of PromQL queries you can use to monitor and analyze MongoDB metrics collected by Prometheus. You can customize these queries and create more complex ones to suit your specific monitoring requirements.

Figure 14.7 shows what Prometheus integration with MongoDB and Grafana looks like:

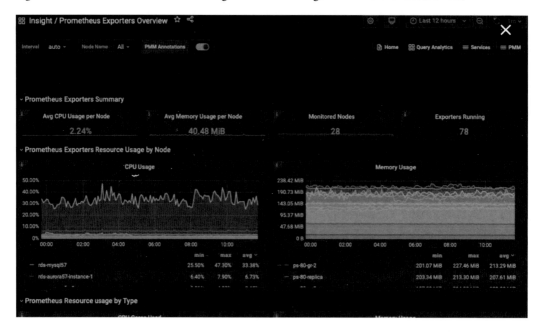

Figure 14.7: Prometheus integration

Integrating MongoDB Atlas with Prometheus

Integrating MongoDB Atlas with Prometheus helps with metric collection that makes it easy for you to send metrics and other data about your Atlas deployments to a Prometheus instance that you manage. Perform the following steps to integrate MongoDB Atlas with Prometheus:

1. Sign-in to the Atlas UI.

2. If it is not already displayed, select the organization that contains the desired project from the **Organizations** menu in the navigation bar.

3. If it is not already displayed, select the desired project from the **Projects** menu in the navigation bar.

4. Next to the **Projects** menu on the top, expand the **Options** (three vertical dots) menu, then click **Integrations**.

5. Click **Configure** under the Prometheus integration card.

6. Enter your preferred username and password. Copy the username and password to a secure location. You can't access the password again once you leave this screen.

7. Select the preferred service delivery method (HTTP SD or file service discovery):

    I.   **HTTP SD**: This method requires Prometheus v2.28 and later. It automatically generates the `scrape_config` part of your configuration file to discover targets over an HTTP endpoint.

    II. **File Service Discovery**: This method allows Prometheus to read YAML or JSON documents to configure the targets to scrape from. You are responsible for providing the targets by making a request to the Discovery API and storing its results in a `targets.json` file.

8. Click **Save**.

9. View **Cluster Metrics** on Prometheus:

    I.   Copy the generated snippet into the `scrape_configs` section of your configuration file and substitute the placeholder text.

    II. Restart your Prometheus instance.

    III. In your Prometheus instance, click **Status** in the top navigation bar, and click **Targets** to see the metrics of deployment.

This integration also allows you to set up custom dashboards in Grafana to visualize the data, providing a comprehensive view of your MongoDB clusters' performance and trends.

Integrating webhooks with MongoDB

Webhooks have emerged as a powerful mechanism for enabling real-time communication between different applications and services. A webhook is an HTTP callback—a simple mechanism through which one application can send data to another in real time. Instead of traditional polling, where an application continuously checks for updates from a server, webhooks allow the server to send data automatically to a predefined URL whenever a particular event occurs. This event-driven approach makes webhooks highly efficient and ideal for real-time data synchronization. When integrated with MongoDB, webhooks can significantly enhance data management capabilities. They enable seamless data synchronization, automation, and event-driven workflows for you and businesses alike.

Here are the advantages of using webhooks integrated with MongoDB:

- **Real-time data synchronization**: Integrating webhooks with MongoDB ensures that data changes within the database are instantly propagated to other systems or services.

- **Automated workflows**: Webhook integration enables the creation of automated workflows triggered by specific database events. For example, when a new document is inserted into a MongoDB collection, a webhook can automatically notify other services or trigger additional actions, such as sending notifications or updating external databases.

- **Efficient data replication**: Webhooks offer an efficient way to replicate data between MongoDB databases or between MongoDB and other databases. This enables you to maintain data redundancy and disaster recovery capabilities seamlessly.

- **Streamlined data updates for external applications**: Integrating webhooks with MongoDB allows external applications or third-party services to receive real-time updates from the database without the need for manual polling. This enhances the responsiveness and efficiency of external applications.

Configuring webhooks with MongoDB

To implement a configuration containing webhooks with a MongoDB cluster, follow these steps:

1. **Configure a webhook endpoint**: Set up an endpoint URL to receive webhook notifications. This endpoint should be secure and capable of handling incoming HTTP requests.

2. **Define webhook event triggers**: Determine the MongoDB events that will trigger webhook notifications, such as document insertion, update, or deletion.

3. **Implement webhook logic**: Develop the logic to process incoming webhook data, validating the authenticity and integrity of the payload. Then, process the data according to the specific use case or application requirements.

4. **Register webhooks with MongoDB**: Use MongoDB's change streams or triggers to register the webhook URLs for specific events. MongoDB will automatically send notifications to these URLs whenever the registered events occur.

5. **Monitor and test**: Regularly monitor the webhook integration for errors or failures. Perform thorough testing to ensure the webhook workflow functions correctly in various scenarios.

To understand webhook implementation, following is an example of a Node.js application with an endpoint as a webhook integrated with MongoDB:

1. Create a Node.js project with MongoDB driver packages installed to interact with the MongoDB database and `Express.js` for the web server.

2. Let there be an `index.js` file to set up an Express web server. Create a POST method to insert a document with JSON passed to the method as seen in *Figure 14.8*. This endpoint will be used as a webhook:

```
app.post('/webhook', (req, res) => {
  // Assuming your data is sent in the request body as JSON
  const newData = req.body;

  // Save the data to MongoDB
  collection.insertOne(newData, (err, result) => {
    if (err) {
      console.error('Error inserting data into MongoDB:', err);
      res.status(500).json({ error: 'Internal Server Error' });
    } else {
      // Send a notification to the webhook URL
      sendWebhookNotification(newData);
      res.status(200).json({ message: 'Data inserted successfully' });
    }
  });
});
```

Figure 14.8: Node.js webhook implementation

3. Create a function with the help of the Axios library to send the webhook notification to the predefined URL and start the integration as seen in *Figure 14.9*:

```
const axios = require('axios');

// Function to send the webhook notification
function sendWebhookNotification(data) {
  axios.post(webhookURL, data)
    .then((response) => {
      console.log('Webhook notification sent successfully');
    })
    .catch((error) => {
      console.error('Error sending webhook notification:', error.message);
    });
}
```

Figure 14.9: Axios library

4. Now, whenever you send a POST request to the /webhook endpoint with JSON data, the server will insert the data into your MongoDB collection and send a notification to the webhook URL.

You can also use Postman to test this:

```
curl -X POST http://localhost:3000/webhook -H "Content-Type:
application/json" -d '{"name": "John", "email": "john@example.com"}'
```

Any data you send to the /webhook endpoint will be saved in the MongoDB collection, and a notification will be sent to the predefined webhook URL in real time.

Integrating MongoDB with alerting applications

Alerting applications can be integrated with MongoDB and used to send alerts or messages to teams or concerned owners of databases or projects. It ensures optimal performance and pre-empts potential issues for the database. Alerting tools such as Microsoft Teams, PagerDuty, and Slack provide real-time notifications and incident management capabilities, enabling teams to respond swiftly to database-related events.

Atlas integrations for webhooks

When configuring an Alert in Atlas, you can send a payload that describes the alert condition using webhooks. To create or update a webhook integration using the Atlas CLI, run the following command:

```
atlas integrations create WEBHOOK [options]
```

The requesting API key must have the organization owner or project owner role to configure a webhook integration. To use this command, you must authenticate with a user account or an API key that has the project owner role.

Microsoft Teams integration

Microsoft Teams is a collaborative platform that offers chat, video conferencing, and real-time communication for teams. To integrate MongoDB with Microsoft Teams for alerting at organization level, follow these steps:

1. Create the Microsoft Teams incoming webhook.

    I.   Navigate to the Microsoft Teams channel where you want to add the webhook.

    II.   Click the ellipses (...) icon from the top navigation bar. A dropdown menu of available options will be displayed.

    III.   Select **Connectors** from the dropdown menu. A modal with available connectors will be displayed.

    IV.   Search for **Incoming Webhook** and select **Add**. A modal with information about the **Incoming Webhook** connector will be displayed.

    V.   Click **Add**. The modal closes.

    VI.   Click the ellipses (...) icon from the top navigation bar, and select **Configure** from the dropdown menu. A modal will be displayed.

    VII.   In the modal, enter a name for your webhook. Alternatively, you can upload a unique image to help you identify your webhook.

    VIII. Click **Create**

    IX.   Copy the incoming webhook URL.

    X.   Click **Done**.

2. If it's not already displayed, select your desired organization from the **Organizations** menu in the navigation bar, and click **Alerts** in the sidebar.

3. Choose whether to create a new alert setting, clone an existing alert setting, or update an existing alert setting.

4. To create a new alert, click **Add Alert**.

5. To clone an existing alert setting:

    I.   Click the **Alert Settings** tab.

    II.   Locate the alert setting you want to clone.

    III.   Select the ellipsis (...) icon, and then click **Clone** in that alert setting's row.

6. To update an existing alert setting:

    I.   Click the **Alert Settings** tab.

    II.   Locate the alert setting you want to update.

III.   Click **Edit** in that alert setting's row.

IV.   Click **User** or **Billing** under **Select a Target**.

V.   Choose the condition as per target selected. For example, organization users do not have MFA enabled/credit card is about to expire.

7.   Configure the Microsoft Teams integration:

I.   Under the **Add Notification Method** heading, click the button for Microsoft Teams.

II.   Enter the incoming webhook URL in the provided text box.

III.   To test the integration, click **Post Test Alert**.

IV.   Under **Recurrence**, set the recurrence conditions in the provided text boxes.

V.   Click **Add**.

You can receive alerts and metrics directly to Microsoft Teams channels with the MongoDB Atlas and Microsoft Teams integration. You can configure the integration to receive alerts including billing alerts, backup alerts, memory alerts, and more. In just a few clicks, you can enable Microsoft Teams integration and keep important stakeholders notified of critical Atlas alerts. Look in the MongoDB documentation for further instructions on integrating with Microsoft Teams: https://www.mongodb.com/docs/atlas/tutorial/integrate-msft-teams/.

PagerDuty integration

PagerDuty is a popular incident management platform that helps teams respond to critical issues promptly. With PagerDuty integration, you can send Atlas cluster event data to PagerDuty when Atlas alerts that you specify are triggered. PagerDuty can create a new incident for the corresponding service, filter additional alerts from the same source into that incident, and alert on-call PagerDuty users.

To integrate MongoDB Atlas with PagerDuty, you must have a PagerDuty account. If you do not have an existing PagerDuty account, you can sign up at https://www.pagerduty.com/sign-up/.

To create or update a PagerDuty integration using the Atlas CLI, run the following command:

```
Atlas integrations create PAGER_DUTY [options]
```

With MongoDB Atlas and PagerDuty integration, you can receive prompt notifications about potential issues through PagerDuty notifications. PagerDuty integration can be configured with a PagerDuty integration key, and once configured, you can determine alert criteria through MongoDB Atlas to start receiving alert notifications to PagerDuty. You can also define escalation rules and alert assignments directly in PagerDuty. If an alert is triggered, PagerDuty tracks incident activity and automatically resolves incidents when the alert has been remedied.

The following link can be followed to integrate MongoDB Atlas with PagerDuty: https://www.mongodb.com/docs/atlas/tutorial/pagerduty-integration/.

Slack integration

Slack is a widely used collaboration platform that enables teams to communicate and share information seamlessly. To integrate MongoDB with Slack for alerting, follow these steps:

1. Set up an incoming webhook in Slack:

    I.   In Slack, create a new Slack app or use an existing one to set up an incoming webhook.

    II.   Configure the webhook to post messages to the desired channel.

2. Install the required packages in your MongoDB environment:

    I.   For Node.js, use the `@slack/webhook` package to send messages to Slack.

    II.   For Python, use the `requests` library to make `HTTP POST` requests to the webhook URL.

3. Implement the alerting logic:

    I.   In your MongoDB monitoring script, identify events that warrant notifications (e.g., high memory usage, slow queries).

    II.   When an event occurs, send a message to the Slack webhook URL with relevant details.

Atlas users will receive alerts and metrics directly to Slack channels with MongoDB Atlas and Slack integration. You can configure the integration to receive alerts including billing alerts, backup alerts, memory alerts, and more. In just a few clicks, you can enable Slack integration and keep important stakeholders notified of critical Atlas alerts. Follow this link to integrate MongoDB Atlas with Slack: `https://www.mongodb.com/blog/post/how-to-alert-your-devops-team-about-your-mongodb-database`.

Splunk On-Call integration

With MongoDB Atlas and Splunk On-Call (previously known as VictorOps) integration, you can receive alert notifications about potential issues through Splunk On-Call dashboards. The Splunk On-Call integration can be configured with a Splunk On-Call API key (and an optional routing key). Once configured, you can determine alert criteria through MongoDB Atlas as well as defining escalation rules and routing rules directly in Splunk On-Call. Only alerts that must be acknowledged can be sent to a Splunk On-Call account. Informational alerts cannot use Splunk On-Call as a notification method.

Further details on Splunk On-Call integration can be found at `https://www.splunk.com/en_us/products/on-call.html`.

Opsgenie integration

With MongoDB Atlas and Opsgenie integration, you can receive alerts and notifications about potential issues through Opsgenie dashboards. Opsgenie integration can be configured with an Opsgenie API key. Once configured, you can determine alert criteria through MongoDB Atlas as well as defining escalation rules and alert assignments directly in Opsgenie. Only alerts that must be acknowledged can be sent to an Opsgenie account; informational alerts cannot use Opsgenie as a notification method.

The following link provides more details on how to create an API integration on Opsgenie: `https://support.atlassian.com/opsgenie/docs/create-a-default-api-integration/`.

Integrating MongoDB with Confluent

Confluent, a leading event streaming platform powered by Apache Kafka, is an open-source distributed event streaming platform. It enables you to build scalable, real-time data pipelines. By integrating Confluent with MongoDB, you can unlock the potential of real-time data synchronization, stream processing, and event-driven architectures. Kafka serves as a central nervous system for an organization, enabling the ingestion, storage, and processing of large volumes of data in real time. It ensures data reliability and scalability by distributing data across multiple nodes, making it ideal for handling high-throughput and low-latency data streams.

You can integrate MongoDB as a source or sink in your Apache Kafka data pipelines with the official *MongoDB Connector* for Apache Kafka. The Connector enables MongoDB to be configured as both a sink and a source for Apache Kafka, which helps you easily build robust applications, reactive data pipelines that stream events between applications and services in real time.

A simple use case for using this integration is replicating data from one MongoDB Atlas data center to another by streaming the data from one region to another using Confluent Cloud Kafka, as shown in *Figure 14.10*.

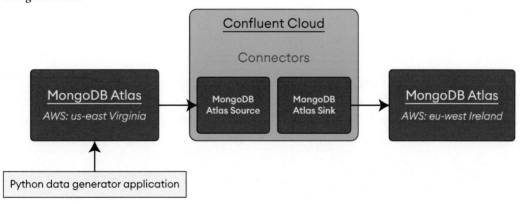

Figure 14.10: Confluent Kafka between Atlas clusters

More details on how to integrate Confluent Kafka with MongoDB Atlas can be found on the official website of MongoDB: `https://www.mongodb.com/blog/post/how-to-get-started-with-mongodb-atlas-and-confluent-cloud`.

Confluent, MongoDB Cloud, and MongoDB Atlas provide fully managed solutions that enable you to focus on the main problems at hand instead of spending too much time on infrastructure configuration and maintenance.

Integrating MongoDB with Postman

Postman, a popular API development and testing tool, allows you to create, test, and monitor APIs efficiently. By integrating MongoDB Atlas with Postman, you can streamline the process of building and testing APIs that interact with MongoDB databases.

Integrating MongoDB with Postman provides benefits such as automation, real-time testing, and a simplified development environment. On MongoDB's official workspace, you can easily work with the Atlas Data API to make development and testing with MongoDB APIs much more simple: `https://www.postman.com/mongodb-devrel/workspace/mongodb-public/overview`.

Summary

This chapter delved into the various methods of integrating applications with MongoDB – both the native and cloud versions of MongoDB Atlas.

The integration of MongoDB with different tools and platforms opens up new possibilities for efficient application development, deployment, and management. You learned how integrating applications with MongoDB using the MongoDB Kubernetes Operator, Terraform, and Vercel enhances the development and deployment process, offering scalability, automation, and flexibility.

This chapter also listed the categories of various applications that can be integrated with MongoDB with ease, using a step-by-step guide with examples. The integration categories included monitoring tools such as Datadog and Vercel, and alerting tools that could be integrated for notifications, such as Microsoft Teams and Slack.

These integrations empower you to build modern, data-driven applications that use the power of MongoDB's NoSQL capabilities. By understanding and implementing these integration methods, you can streamline workflows, accelerate application development, and deliver exceptional user experiences.

The next chapter will explore the security features in MongoDB in detail, including authentication and authorization, and how these features aid in complete data security.

15

Security

When using MongoDB, database security is of utmost importance. Fortunately, it offers easy installation and other benefits such as encryption to protect your data in-transit (SSL/TLS) and at rest, auditing to track executed operations, and so on. This chapter will cover the key aspects of choosing and correctly implementing the types of authentications and authorizations that exist in MongoDB. You'll also look at how **role-based access control (RBAC)** works, and how you can effectively manage users in your database environment.

MongoDB offers mechanisms for controlling access and functions that a user can perform. You can imagine these mechanisms as a tripod composed of different authentication methods, types of authorization, and user management. Authentication identifies the user accessing the database (*who*), while authorization determines the user's allowed actions in the database (*what*). These actions include data operations (read, insert, update, delete), instance configuration, replica set/shard management, backups, and maintenance.

Security in MongoDB is a continuous process of monitoring and evaluation. Even with this well-built tripod, as MongoDB administrators, you must remain aware of these changes. An effective security strategy can be both reactive—responding to incidents as they occur—and proactive, trying to identify and correct potential failures before they become a problem.

This chapter will cover the following topics:

- Authentication methods available in MongoDB
- Enabling authentication in a MongoDB environment
- Creating and changing users
- Creating data access roles

Authentication methods

The first pillar of security in MongoDB is authentication. Authentication is responsible for identifying *who* is accessing the database. For this part, you have four methods.

For the Community version, you have the following methods:

- SCRAM (default)
- x.509

For the Enterprise Advanced version, you also have the following methods:

- LDAP
- Kerberos

Each of these mechanisms has its pros and cons, and to choose the most appropriate one, you must consider your business needs, and the objectives you want to achieve with this step. Let's examine each of these methods in detail.

SCRAM

When you enable authentication in MongoDB, the default method is **Salted Challenge Response Authentication Mechanism (SCRAM)**. Created by the **Internet Engineering Task Force (IETF)**, SCRAM is a robust and secure authentication protocol that enables user authentication without sending the user's password in plain text over the network.

Instead, SCRAM uses a different approach: challenge-response. The client first sends a challenge to the server—in your case, to MongoDB—including its username and a unique random value, known as *nonce*. The server then responds by including its own data concatenated with the client's nonce, and a *proof* based on a hash function applied to the user's password and the nonce.

The client then responds with its own proof, which is computed with the same hash function as the server's data. Finally, the server checks the client's proof, and if it matches its own proof, the server sends a confirmation that the authentication was successful.

The idea behind SCRAM is that at no point in time is the user's password transmitted over the network. Thus, even if a malicious attacker were to intercept this communication, they would not be able to discover the user's password because they don't know the hash function used nor the *salt* (a random value that is used to guarantee that two identical entries for a hash function do not result in the same hash value).

In MongoDB, *drivers* (in this context, drivers refer to any type of access—from MongoDB Shell, application access through programming languages, APIs, or visual interfaces) are responsible for sending the username, handling password information, and the most important pieces of data, along with selecting which database will authenticate a particular user.

Earlier, you could create users in any database in your MongoDB environment. However, it is now recommended that these users are concentrated in a single database. From there, you can provide the necessary privileges and access to functions and other databases. You can do this in any database, but you can take advantage of the `admin` database and centralize all users in that database. Thus, you have the authentication process taking place only in one database, which is very important to facilitate the management of your users and other access requests.

The authentication process is deliberately slow and CPU-intensive to help prevent brute-force attacks. Therefore, it's advisable to perform authentication only when you really need it, creating a single `MongoClient` object in the application and not for each database or service call.

Fundamentals

The fundamentals of SCRAM authentication in MongoDB are as follows:

- **Salted password**: SCRAM authentication in MongoDB begins with the creation of a salted password. A *salt* is a random sequence generated for each user and combined with the user's password. This process makes passwords more secure by preventing brute-force attacks and making hashed passwords unique.

- **Secure password storage**: Salted passwords and authentication data are securely stored in the MongoDB database. This typically involves encrypting passwords and adopting stringent security measures to protect the data.

- **Challenge-response**: When a user attempts to authenticate, MongoDB sends a random challenge (nonce) to the client. The client, in turn, combines this challenge with the user's password (along with the salt), and performs a hash operation to generate a response. This response is sent back to MongoDB.

- **Response verification**: MongoDB verifies the client's response by comparing it with the response it calculates using the authentication information stored in the database. If the responses match, authentication is successful.

- **Number of iterations**: SCRAM authentication in MongoDB supports a configurable number of iterations to enhance security. More iterations require more time to compute the response, making brute-force attacks more challenging.

- **Secure communication channel**: To increase the security of SCRAM authentication, it is important that communication between the client and the MongoDB server is encrypted, typically using TLS/SSL.

- **Roles and privileges**: After successful authentication, MongoDB checks the user's permissions and grants access based on the roles associated with the user's account. This allows fine-grained control over access to database resources.

In the next section, you will learn how to enable authentication on a MongoDB replica set.

Enabling authentication

All examples target the replica set as it is the recommended minimum for a production environment. If you want to enable authentication but have a standalone instance, convert it to a replica set first.

Start with a *keyfile*. This is a file that can be generated from the host where MongoDB is installed. It must be up to 1,024 bytes, contain characters in the base64 set, and have the correct permissions—neither too open nor too restricted. This file must be the same on all the machines that make up your replica set. It is important to consider using x.509 certificates for production environments. Starting in MongoDB 4.2, you can use a keyfile in YAML format for internal membership authentication. This makes it easy to rotate keys to a replica set or a sharded cluster without any downtime.

Here's an example showing the implementation of a keyfile:

```
openssl rand -base64 768 > <path-to-keyfile>
chmod 400 <path-to-keyfile>
```

The following documentation will help you learn more about keyfiles: https://www.mongodb.com/docs/v7.0/core/security-internal-authentication/.

The preceding command uses `openssl` to create a file with `768` random bytes in base64, and the output is sent to a file of your choice. You can then change the permission of the generated file so that MongoDB reads it correctly during initialization.

This file is necessary to identify the hosts that make up the replica set, meaning that a host without this file cannot be added to the replica set. This is called *intra-cluster authentication*. Therefore, you must copy the file to each of the members of your replica set.

Ensure that the user running `mongod` owns and can access the keyfile. Finally, make sure that this file is not on a disk that can be easily removed from the machine or a remote network driver that is mapped to the machine.

With the files in place, and the permissions set correctly, you can now begin working on the MongoDB configuration file. You may have looked at this file before and know that it is a YAML file that contains several sections—security, replication, and net.

In addition to indicating the keyfile path, the `security.keyfile` property also enables both internal/membership authentication and RBAC.

The `replication.replSetName` property contains the name of the replica set. Finally, the `net.bindIp` property defines hostnames and/or IP addresses that define which interfaces the `mongod` process listens on for client connections. You can use `net.bindIpAll` to listen on all available interfaces. However, this may allow incoming connections from interfaces that are public on the internet. This property defines the interface but does not define the IPs or hostnames of servers that can access MongoDB, which can be a point of confusion when configuring it. To learn about this property, refer to this documentation: https://www.mongodb.com/docs/v7.0/reference/configuration-options/#mongodb-setting-net.bindIp.

Here's an example of implementing the `net.bindIP` property:

```
security:
  keyFile: <path-to-keyfile>
replication:
  replSetName: <replicaSetName>
net:
  bindIp: localhost,<hostname(s)|ip address(es)>
```

With these parameters set, you should now start `mongod` using the configuration file:

```
mongod --config <path-to-config-file>
```

It is also necessary to start the replica set. For this, you can refer to *Chapter 2, The MongoDB Architecture,* where you're presented two methods:

- From `mongosh`:

  ```
  rs.initiate()
  ```

- From the terminal:

  ```
  mongosh --eval "rs.initiate()"
  ```

This process triggers an election, and elects one of the members as primary. In this specific case, the process will choose the machine where the command was executed.

You may have noticed that, so far, you've only told MongoDB that it should switch to using authentication, but you haven't created any users or roles to access the data yet. This is because a procedure called *localhost exception* allows you to create a user or role while connected directly via SSH on the member that is the primary of the replica set. This procedure is applicable only when authentication is enabled, and no users or roles exist. Otherwise, you'll have to use existing credentials to authenticate normally.

The possibility of creating a role makes sense when you look at the environment and think about authentication using **Lightweight Directory Access Protocol (LDAP)**, which is covered later in the chapter. Thus, if you're going to use Active Directory, you can create an initial role and link it with the necessary privileges for managing other users or roles.

MongoDB allows users to be created in any database; however, it is strongly recommended that you use the `admin` database to centralize the authentication process. As shown in the following example, you can create a user by assigning a built-in role with privileges to administer users:

```
use admin
db.createUser(
    {
        user: "myUserAdmin",
        pwd: promptPassword(),
        roles: [
            { role: "userAdmin", db: "admin" }
        ]
    }
)
```

Here are the parameters used in this method:

- `user`: This contains the username.

- pwd: This contains the password that will be used. In the case of this example, the `promptPassword` function is being used, and when executing the method in the prompt, you will be asked to insert the password. This prevents the password from being exposed on the screen.

- `roles`: This is an array that can receive one or more roles that will be associated with the user. Note that you have two parameters: `role` and `db`. The `role` parameter takes the name of a built-in role or user-defined role. The `db` parameter receives the name of the database where this user will have that privilege. If you notice, you can use the `admin` database which determines where the user will be created, regardless of its permissions in other banks, that is, where the user will be authenticated.

  When you're executing this procedure, the `localhost` exception will automatically be closed, and any operation on the database will require authentication.

> **Note**
>
> If a malicious user has enough access to perform this procedure, your problem is much bigger than simply accessing the database. So, if you don't have access to credentials, you can simply disable authentication momentarily, restart MongoDB, create a new user, and then re-enable authentication.

Benefits and considerations

SCRAM is secure, simple, and easy to understand. It has been used widely for a long time by various databases and other platforms.

However, it requires some work to manage, especially when users and permissions are not in a single point, such as in a single database. Since authorization is local, it adds additional responsibilities to the environment. You must also know what to do if a credential becomes known, as well as how to secure the credentials of services or applications.

The next section will focus on client authentication, that is, using an x.509 certificate to know who is requesting access to your database.

x.509

User authentication is a fundamental aspect of security in any database management system. MongoDB supports x.509 certificates for client authentication as well as for internal authentication of members of a replica set. For authorization purposes (*what* a user can do), you must combine the use of x.509 certificates with built-in/user-defined roles or LDAP.

In addition to traditional authentication options, such as passwords, it is possible to use authentication based on x.509 certificates in MongoDB. This approach offers greater security and ease of management in corporate and high-security environments. In the following sections, you will explore the process of authenticating users with x.509 certificates in MongoDB, certificate configurations, and best practices to ensure a robust and reliable implementation.

Fundamentals

Before diving into configuration and implementation, it's important to review and understand the key concepts of authenticating users with x.509 certificates in MongoDB:

- **x.509 certificates**: Digital certificates that follow the x.509 standard are used to authenticate clients and servers over secure connections. They contain information such as the user's or server's identity, public key, and the digital signature of a trusted certificate authority.

- **Certificate Authority (CA)**: This is a trusted entity responsible for issuing and signing digital certificates. The CA guarantees the authenticity of the certificates, and therefore, the identity of the users and servers involved in the communication.

- **Client certificate**: This is the digital certificate used by the client (application or user) to authenticate with MongoDB. This certificate is CA-signed and contains customer-specific information.

- **Server certificate**: This is the digital certificate used by the MongoDB server to authenticate with clients, which is signed by the CA as well.

Having acquired an understanding of these concepts, let's look at some essential steps for implementing x.509 certificate authentication in MongoDB:

1. **Choosing a CA**: Selecting or creating a trusted CA is the first step. In corporate environments, there is usually an internal CA, but you can also use recognized public CAs.

2. **Certificate generation**: The CA is responsible for generating server and client certificates. For this, you must create a pair of keys (public and private) for each entity, sign the keys with the CA, and store them correctly.

3. **Certificate distribution**: You must install client certificates on all machines that will access MongoDB. Additionally, ensure that you configure the server certificate in MongoDB and in all applications that connect to it.

Specifically for MongoDB settings, you must define some parameters for the configuration file, in the net section of the mongod.conf file:

```
net:
    tls:
        mode: requireTLS
        certificateKeyFile: <path to TLS certificate and key PEM file>
        CAFile: <path to root CA PEM file>
```

With this done, create a user that will use the certificate for authentication:

```
db.getSiblingDB("$external").runCommand(
  {
    createUser:
"CN=myName,OU=myOrgUnit,O=myOrg,L=myLocality,ST=myState,C=myCountry",
    roles: [
        { role: "readWrite", db: "test" },
        { role: "userAdminAnyDatabase", db: "admin" }
    ],
    writeConcern: { w: "majority" , wtimeout: 5000 }
  }
)
```

For this example, create a user with the certificate, and grant the readWrite role in the test database, along with the userAdminAnyDatabase role in the admin database.

To authenticate yourself in the database, run the following command in the terminal:

```
mongosh --tls --tlsCertificateKeyFile <path to client PEM file> \
    --tlsCAFile <path to root CA PEM file> \
    --authenticationDatabase '$external' \
    --authenticationMechanism MONGODB-X509
```

There are ways to make the transition to requireTLS in environments that are already in production with MongoDB. For that, see the steps outlined in this documentation: https://www.mongodb.com/docs/v7.0/tutorial/upgrade-cluster-to-ssl/.

Best practices

In addition to the basic configuration steps, the following best practices can help further enhance the security and efficiency of authenticating with x.509 certificates:

- **Regular certificate renewal**: Renew certificates periodically to avoid expiration issues and ensure the continued security of the environment.

- **Proper private key management**: Restrict access to private keys for server and client certificates to minimize the risk of unauthorized access.

- **Auditing and monitoring**: Implement an auditing and monitoring system to track authenticated connections, detect suspicious activity, and respond to security incidents if necessary.

Authenticating users with x.509 certificates in MongoDB is a powerful option to strengthen security and ensure the identity of users and servers in sensitive environments. By following the guidelines and best practices presented in this chapter, you can implement a strong and reliable authentication strategy, strengthening data protection and system integrity.

LDAP

MongoDB provides support for both authentication and authorization using Active Directory or OpenLDAP. This is an exclusive feature of the Enterprise Advanced version. On MongoDB Atlas, LDAP is available on dedicated clusters only (`M10` and larger).

When deploying on Atlas, it's crucial to note that there is increased network traffic. You must ensure the continuous availability of the servers because if these servers go offline, authentication and authorization processes won't be successful.

A very important factor when using LDAP authentication or authorization is connecting to servers using TLS/SSL, precisely because user credentials travel in plain text. The use of TLS/SSL encrypts the authentication message, and even if this communication is intercepted, the attacker is not able to access the password.

As you may already know, LDAP employs a hierarchical database that is normally used to store information about devices, users, group permissions, and so on. Probably the best-known LDAP server is Microsoft Active Directory.

LDAP servers allow you to retrieve records by path and search any record or the entire tree for a specific value. Additionally, you can validate a password by hashing it and comparing it to the stored hash value.

But coming back to MongoDB, the biggest benefit is that individual access can be controlled with the join, leave, or switch user policy within the corporation. So, you don't have to keep track of these changes individually. Instead, you can manage the policies in a single place. Once you create the policies/groups in LDAP, link them to a user-defined or built-in role. Thus, all users who use LDAP to authenticate can have their authorizations verified by it.

To start your journey to enable authentication, and later, authorization with LDAP in MongoDB, you can use some tools to help you along the way. One of these is `ldapsearch` for Linux. This is an important tool because, with it, you can diagnose possible connection problems with the servers, validating accesses and other points. To begin, install the `openldap-clients` package on your Linux distribution.

Start with the bind process to authenticate yourself to the LDAP server. Then, use the `-h` parameter to specify the host of your server, `-D` to specify the user (bind distinguished name), and `-w` to specify the password:

```
ldapsearch -h <your_ldap> -D '<your_domain>\<your_user>' -w '<your_password>'
```

You must have a user with bind privileges in your LDAP. The idea is to grant this user read-only privileges, preventing them from performing advanced operations, as their credentials will be exposed in the configuration file. Users with more elevated permissions should not be used as the bind user because, as already mentioned, authentication data must be in plain text.

LDAP queries

After successfully authenticating, you can send queries to your server. Queries should preferably be refined, because searching the entire tree can be a costly operation, especially in large corporations with thousands of users, groups, and roles.

Suppose you want information about the `adminMongoDB` user. You can search all sublevels as follows:

```
ldapsearch -h <your_ldap.net> -D '<your_domain>\<your_user>' -w '<your_
password>' -b 'DC=<your_ldap>,DC=net' -s sub "sAMAccountName=adminMongoDB"
```

As a result, you can see the record for `adminMongoDB` and also see that it is in `CN=Users`. You can restrict your search to this part of the tree and also work on the projection with only the necessary fields:

```
ldapsearch -h <your_ldap.net> -D '<your_domain>\<your_user>' -w '<your_
password>' -b 'DC=<your_ldap>,DC=net' "sAMAccountName=adminMongoDB" -s one cn
name distinguishedName memberOf
```

Protecting your credentials

You must protect your credentials , especially in-transit. Some LDAP servers don't allow sending requests without some type of encryption, causing an error. To avoid this, you must use a certificate to protect this communication. By adding the `-ZZ` parameter, you can encrypt the communication.

In addition to the `-ZZ` parameter, you need a certificate. For example in Linux, this certificate can be found in the `/etc/openldap/certs` directory. Also, execute the following command to add this information to the configuration file found in the following directory: `/etc/openldap/ldap.conf`.

```
grep "TLS_CACERT " /etc/openldap/ldap.conf || echo "TLS_CACERT        /etc/
openldap/certs/ldapCertificate.cert" | sudo tee --append /etc/openldap/ldap.
conf
```

Finally, you can run the query again:

```
ldapsearch -h <your_ldap_server> -D '<your_domain>\<your_user>' -w
'<your_password>' -b 'CN=Users,DC=<your_ldap_server>,DC=net' -ZZ -s sub
"sAMAccountName=adminMongoDB" cn name distinguishedName memberOf
```

LDAP authentication

Now, let's shift focus to the `security` section of the `mongod.conf` file:

```
security:
  authorization: enabled
  clusterAuthMode: x509
  ldap:
     servers: <your_ldap_server>
     bind:
        method: simple
        queryUser: '<YOUR_DOMAIN\your_bind_user>'
        queryPassword:  '<your_bind_user_password>'
     transportSecurity: tls
     userToDNMapping: '[{ match: "(.*)",substitution:
"cn={0},cn=Users,dc=<your_ldap>,dc=net"}]'

setParameter:
  authenticationMechanisms: PLAIN, SCRAM-SHA-256, SCRAM-SHA-1
```

As you can see, the `ldap` subsection contains some known parameters that you saw when executing the queries in LDAP. In the `setParameter.authenticationMechanisms` entry, you added the `PLAIN` option. This refers to the type of authentication used by LDAP (plain text).

You can validate this configuration using a tool called `mongoldap`. This is a bundled component of MongoDB Database Tools Extra package that can be installed with MongoDB Enterprise Advanced. Once this component is installed, it's very simple to use:

```
mongoldap -f /etc/mongod.conf --user <your_user> --password <your_password>
```

This command will tell you whether everything is okay with the authentication part. Next, you will see how to configure authorization.

LDAP authorization

Go back to your MongoDB configuration file, in the same `security.ldap` subsection, add `queryTemplate`:

```
security:
  authorization: enabled
  clusterAuthMode: x509
  ldap:
     servers: <your_ldap_server>
     bind:
        method: simple
        queryUser: '<YOUR_DOMAIN\your_bind_user>'
        queryPassword:  '<your_bind_user_password>'
     transportSecurity: tls
     userToDNMapping: '[{ match: "(.*)",
substitution: "cn={0},cn=Users,dc=<your_ldap>,dc=net"}]'
     authz:
       queryTemplate: "{USER}?memberOf?base"
```

You can revalidate the configuration using `mongoldap` with the same parameters as before. If everything is correct, remember to restart the MongoDB service to apply the changes to the instance.

Binding a group to a role

As the final step, link an existing group in LDAP with a MongoDB role. For this example, you will use the `Admins MongoDB` group from your LDAP, with the built-in `root` role.

Inside the `mongosh` connected instance, add the following code:

```
use admin
db.createRole(
    {
        role: "CN=Admins MongoDB,CN=Users,DC=your_domain,DC=net",
        privileges: [],
        roles: [
            { role: "root", db: "admin" }
        ]
    }
)
```

Now, you can connect using the following parameters:

```
mongosh -u <your_user> -p <your_password> --authenticationDatabase '$external'
--authenticationMechanism=PLAIN  --tls --tlsCAFile=/etc/pki/tls/certs/ca.cert
--host <your_mongodb_server>
```

> **Note**
>
> The `authenticationDatabase` parameter is set to `$external` and `authenticationMechanism` to `PLAIN`, and you also pass the path to your `CAFile` to protect your credentials during transit.

Benefits and considerations

Let's analyze the pros and cons of using LDAP for authentication and authorization in MongoDB.

Pros:

- Unique mechanisms for authentication and authorization
- Allows users to log in to MongoDB with the same credentials they use on their workstation, unifying these credentials
- Easy to add, remove, or change policies and users across all databases
- Quite common in many organizations
- Supports alternative servers. This means that you can add more than one LDAP server in the configuration file to increase service resiliency

Cons:

- Setup requires understanding the LDAP tree and how it works
- Requires the Active Directory (or other LDAP) server to always be online
- Requires a TLS/SSL connection to protect credentials sent to the LDAP server

Kerberos

Kerberos, a standard ticket-based authentication protocol, has become an essential tool for securely managing identities in distributed environments. Originating from MIT's Project Athena, it was designed to provide strong authentication for client-server applications through a cryptographic-based approach to issuing access tickets.

The integration of Kerberos into MongoDB authentication provides the opportunity to use a consolidated and widely accepted solution to ensure that only authenticated users can access and interact with the stored data. This is important to note as Kerberos does not authorize access, which is why another mechanism is needed for this step.

Against this background, you'll further explore how Kerberos authentication works, how it integrates with MongoDB, and its advantages for enterprise and large-scale environments.

Components

To use Kerberos to authenticate against MongoDB, you need to understand and configure a few components, both on Kerberos and MongoDB. Following are descriptions of the main components involved.

Kerberos components

- **Key Distribution Center (KDC)**: It is the heart of the Kerberos system, responsible for managing keys and distributing tickets. The KDC has two main parts:

  - **Authentication server (AS)**: It authenticates users and issues a **ticket-granting ticket** (**TGT**).

  - **Ticket-granting service (TGS)**: Once a customer has a TGT, they can request service tickets for different services—in your case, MongoDB.

- **Principal**: In the context of Kerberos, a principal is a single entity (it can be a user, service, or host) that can be authenticated. In the case of MongoDB, there would be a principal for the MongoDB service.

- **Ticket**: A set of data that proves the client's identity to a server, containing client information, a session key, and other information, all encrypted with the server's secret key.

- **Realm**: This is an administrative domain in Kerberos that groups and manages principals. One can think of it as a namespace for principals.

MongoDB components

- **Configuration file**: As you saw in the LDAP section, you use MongoDB's configuration file to specify security options, including those related to Kerberos authentication.

How the setup and user flow works

The integration of MongoDB with Kerberos follows a structured process to ensure robust security and seamless authentication:

1. Configures the KDC and defines the principals for users and services. The KDC manages keys and distributes tickets.

2. Configures MongoDB to use Kerberos authentication by specifying the option in the configuration file and restarting the server with the appropriate options.

3. Creates users in MongoDB.

4. Clients use their principals to get a TGT from the Authentication Server to the KDC.

5. Using TGT, customers request a service ticket for MongoDB from TGS.

6. The MongoDB driver uses this ticket to authenticate with MongoDB.

7. MongoDB validates the ticket with the service's secret key and establishes an authenticated session.

Thus, MongoDB's integration with Kerberos provides strong authentication, leveraging the established Kerberos security architecture.

Instead of going deeper into Kerberos configuration, you will explore MongoDB-specific configuration. For more information about configuring Kerberos, check `https://web.mit.edu/kerberos/krb5-latest/doc/`.

MongoDB configuration for authentication with Kerberos

Authentication via Kerberos is a robust and widely accepted option in corporate environments. Following are detailed steps and examples on how to configure MongoDB for authentication with Kerberos. Authentication using Kerberos is only available for the Enterprise Advanced version of MongoDB:

1. **Prerequisites**

   Run the following command to check whether you're running MongoDB Enterprise Advanced:

   ```
   mongod --version
   ```

   The output will display a string such as: `modules: subscription` or `modules: enterprise`. This will confirm that your binaries are Enterprise Advanced. The MongoDB documentation (`https://www.mongodb.com/docs/manual/tutorial/control-access-to-mongodb-with-kerberos-authentication/`) contains the steps to be performed, but here are some with a little more detail.

For each instance of `mongod` or `mongos`, you must have a Kerberos service principal. You can add one using the following command:

```
kadmin.local addprinc <username>/<instance>@<KERBEROS REALM>
```

For each host running `mongod` or `mongos`, create a `keytab` file:

```
kadmin.local ktadd <username>/<instance>@<KERBEROS REALM>
```

2. **Creating a user**

As a second step, create a user that has read-only permissions on the `finance` database. Note that this user will be authenticated by Kerberos and authorized by MongoDB (review authentication and authorization concepts):

```
use $external
db.createUser(
    {
        user: "<username>/<instance>@<KERBEROS_REALM>",
        roles: [ { role: "read", db: "finance" } ]
    }
)
```

3. **MongoDB configuration**

Kerberos configuration in MongoDB is done through the configuration file, usually `mongod.conf`. The following example shows how to configure the file:

```
security:
  authorization: enabled
setParameter:
  authenticationMechanism: GSSAPI, SCRAM-SHA-1, SCRAM-SHA-256
```

In this section of the configuration file, specify the `setParameter.authenticationMechanisms` parameter with the `GSSAPI` value, which corresponds to Kerberos, in addition to allowing SCRAM-SHA.

4. **Authenticating using Kerberos**

With everything set up, you can now authenticate to MongoDB using the MongoDB Shell and your Kerberos principal:

```
kinit <username>/<instance>@<KERBEROS_REALM>
mongosh --host <mongodb_hostname> -u " <username>/<instance>@<KERBEROS_
REALM> " --authenticationMechanism=GSSAPI
--authenticationDatabase='$external'
```

> **Note**
>
> It is important to ensure that the MongoDB server can resolve and access the Kerberos KDC. In some cases, it may be necessary to configure the `/etc/krb5.conf` file on the MongoDB server so that it knows your KDC and realm details.

Integration of MongoDB with Kerberos provides a strong and secure authentication method for environments that already use Kerberos. While the setup process is detailed, the benefits of centralized and secure authentication are clear, especially in larger organizations where data security is a high priority.

Having delved into various authentication methods, let's shift focus to access control—specifically, authorization.

Role-based access control (RBAC)

In MongoDB, you can efficiently manage user permissions with RBAC. RBAC allows granularity and flexibility for database resources. You can build functions that define the actions that users can perform, for example, only allowing a user to read data, but not to change or delete it. These can be built-in roles or user-defined roles and can be assigned to any user.

Built-in roles are already defined with MongoDB and you have a variety of them. User-defined roles, as the name implies, are roles that you can create as needed.

Assigning roles to users rather than granting individual permissions simplifies the access management process, especially in large and complex environments.

Using RBAC has several advantages:

- It provides granular control over permissions. Organizations can define a wide range of roles to reflect the different responsibilities and access needs of users.

- It helps enforce the principle of least privilege, a security practice that involves granting users only the permissions they absolutely need to perform their tasks.

- It can help simplify the audit process by making it easier to verify who has access to what.

Whenever you create a role or grant access to a user, you must consider the principle of least privilege, that is, plan what the role or the user must minimally execute in the database. Granting very generic permissions, or with a very high degree of privilege, can cause security problems in accessing data. Further, this can also impact the configuration of the environment.

Knowing about resources, actions, and roles

It's important to understand each aspect of database access creation. These aspects are categorized into three groups:

Resources	Database actions	Database built-in roles
Databases	CRUD	dbAdmin
Collections	Database management	clusterAdmin
Clusters	Deployment management actions	userAdminAnyDatabase
Users	Replication actions	readAnyDatabase
	Sharding actions	readWriteAnyDatabase
	Server administration actions	clusterMonitor
	Diagnostic retrieval actions	read
		readWrite
		backup
		root

Table 15.1: Different aspects of database access creation

If you define roles at the level of resources and database actions, you can create user-defined roles that are granular and flexible, for example, insert permissions in only a certain database and read permissions in another.

It is also important that you separate roles/users that perform administrative operations, such as backup or cluster reconfiguration, from roles/users that have access to data. But that doesn't mean you can't combine those privileges.

Following is a practical example, where you create a user who can read any collection in the database called reports:

```
use admin
db.createUser(
    {
        user: "myUserReadReports",
        pwd: promptPassword(),
        roles: [
            { role: "read", db: "reports" }
        ]
    }
)
```

Note that you use the `use` command so that the user is created in the `admin` database, and within the command in the `roles` array, you determine what this user can do (read-only in this case) and in which database—in this case, reports.

When you authenticate using this user, the command will resemble the following:

```
mongosh --user myUserReadReports
```

Remember that `mongosh` will try to authenticate against the default database, which is `admin`. Further, the expectation is that `mongod` is listening on port `27017`. The password will be requested and then you will be able to access the database.

Combining built-in roles

As mentioned earlier, you can combine roles according to your needs. Imagine that you want a user with read and write permissions in the `finance` database, and with only read permissions in the `reports` database:

```
use admin
db.createUser(
    {
        user: "myUserFinance",
        pwd: promptPassword(),
        roles: [
            { role: "read", db: "reports" },
            { role: "readWrite", db: "finance" }
        ]
    }
)
```

Adding/revoking built-in roles and users

You can also add or revoke the roles of existing users. This procedure may be necessary to use several times throughout the life of your database:

```
use admin
db.grantRolesToUser(
    "myUserFinance",
    [
        { role: "read", db: "log" }
    ]
)
```

Use the `db.grantRolesToUser()` method. As the first parameter, you have the name of the user who will receive the new role. As the second parameter, you have an array that receives one or more roles. In the preceding example, you are passing the `read` role to the `log` database.

The revocation process is quite similar, changing only the name of the method:

```
use admin
db.revokeRolesFromUser(
    "myUserFinance",
    [
        { role: "read", db: "reports" }
    ]
)
```

It is worth mentioning that none of the previous processes require downtime and both start to take effect immediately after their execution. It's also not necessary for the user to authenticate again.

Changing a user's password

Changing the password is an operation that you'll need to do several times during the user management life cycle. As the authentication process using SCRAM-SHA is local, changing the password is a procedure performed by a user with sufficient privileges and connected to the replica set:

```
use admin
db.changeUserPassword(
    "myUser",
    passwordPrompt()
)
```

Remember that even using `passwordPrompt()`, MongoDB sends cleartext data to the server by default. To protect this data with encryption, use TLS/SSL during client and server communication. But it is also important to remember that MongoDB does not store passwords in cleartext, as you saw in the definition about SCRAM. However, there is this point of vulnerability during data transport if you do not use TLS/SSL.

> **Note**
>
> Special characters in passwords are allowed. However, during connection, you must convert them to the URI pattern.

Updating a user

One method that you can use to change user properties is the `db.updateUser()` method. With this method, you can, for example, revoke all permissions of a user. This is useful if you want to keep a certain user but want their access blocked:

```
db.updateUser(
    "myUser",
    {
        roles: []
    }
)
```

Dropping a user

On the other hand, if you want to completely remove a user, use the following method:

```
db.dropUser(
    "myUser"
)
```

> **Note**
>
> If you are removing a user that has privileges such as userAdminAnyDatabase or even root, make sure that there is another user with that same permission level, otherwise, you may have problems with user management in the future.

Listing users

You can use two methods that can return information about a specific user or even all users in the database:

```
db.getUser("myUser")
```

In the preceding method, you are requesting the information of myUser. As the second parameter of the same method, you can specify what you want to return from the user, such as showPrivileges. This parameter returns all privileges the user has:

```
db.getUser(
    "myUser",
    {
        showPrivileges: true
    }
)
```

What sets this parameter apart is that you can drill down into all the features and actions the user has, at the most granular level possible.

When using db.getUsers(), you get back all database users, including their roles and authentication mechanisms.

Role hierarchy

You can classify the role hierarchy into three levels:

- **Level 0 – basic level**: This level concentrates on the most basic operations, with read, readWrite, dbAdmin, and userAdmin, among others. These roles provide essential database privileges.

- **Level 1 – user-defined roles**: You can create custom roles on a specific database. These roles can inherit permissions from level-0 roles or from other level-1 roles in the same database.

- **Level 2 – cluster administration roles**: At the cluster level, you can create custom roles that span all databases in the cluster. These roles can inherit permissions from level-0 roles or from other level-2 roles in the same cluster.

The hierarchy works such that a higher-level role can inherit permissions from a lower-level role. This simplifies permission management because you can set broader permissions on higher-level roles and then grant those roles to specific users.

For example, suppose you have a custom role called `myRole` in the `mydb` database that has read and write permissions on all collections in that database. You can grant this role to `myUser`, allowing them to access all collections in `mydb` without having to specify individual permissions for each collection.

To create custom roles and manage the role hierarchy in MongoDB, you can use the `db.createRole()` command (which you'll see next) to create new roles and `db.grantRolesToUser()` (as you saw earlier) to grant roles to specific users. You can also view existing roles in a database or cluster using the `db.getRoles()` command:

```
db.getRoles()
```

Here's the return example:

```
{
  roles: [
    {
      role: 'dbOwner',
      db: 'products',
      isBuiltin: true,
      roles: [],
      inheritedRoles: [],
      privileges: [
        {
          resource: { db: 'products', collection: '' },
          actions: [
            'analyze',
            'bypassDocumentValidation',
            'changeCustomData',
            ...
          ]
        },
        {
          resource: { db: 'products', collection: 'system.profile' },
          actions: [
            'changeStream',
            'collStats',
            'convertToCapped',
            ...
          ]
        }
      }
```

```
    ],
    inheritedPrivileges: [
      {
        resource: { db: 'products', collection: '' },
        actions: [
          'analyze',
          'bypassDocumentValidation',
          'changeCustomData',
          ...
        ]
      }
    ]
  },
  ...
  ]
}
```

In the output of the command, you can identify all the roles – `inheritedRoles`, `privileges` (and inside it, each privilege in each resource), and finally `inheritedPrivileges`.

Keep in mind that proper management of the role hierarchy is critical to ensuring the security of your database, which includes granting only necessary permissions to users and avoiding excessive privileges that could compromise the integrity of your data.

Managing roles

Along with user management, you also have a lot of flexibility with role management. You can specify privileges for each database resource or even inherit from existing roles.

A practical example widely applicable for creating a user-defined role involves specifying actions that are not covered by the built-in roles, such as having the privilege to find and insert data, but not having the privilege to delete or change data:

```
use admin
db.createRole(
    {
        role: "readAndInsert",
        privileges: [
            { resource: { db: "myDB", collection: ""},
                actions: ["find", "insert"]}
        ],
        roles: []
    }
)
```

In the preceding example, you've created a user-defined role with privileges to read and insert data in any collection of the myDb database. For this, you declare the role parameter, which receives the name of the user-defined role, and a privileges array, which contains the resources and actions (in the case of find and insert).

After creating the user-defined role, add it to a user:

```
use admin
db.grantRolesToUser(
    "myUser",
    [
        "readAndInsert"
    ]
)
```

As mentioned earlier, you can add roles or privileges to an existing role:

```
use admin
db.grantRolesToRole(
    "readAndInsert",
    [
        { role: "readWrite", db: "financeDB" }
    ]
)
```

In the preceding example, you added the built-in readWrite role for the financeDB database to your previously created user-defined readAndInsert role.

Access restrictions

With user-defined roles, you can define access restrictions through a list of IPs that will be allowed. This feature is quite useful because it combines access restrictions with the level of access to data. For this, you have two parameters that can be added when creating a user-defined role: clientSource and serverAddress. Both are inside the authenticationRestrictions array.

The clientSource parameter is the IP address of the client trying to connect to the MongoDB server. The serverAddress parameter is the IP address of the MongoDB server being connected.

Both parameters are used to restrict unauthorized users from accessing the MongoDB server. If the clientSource or serverAddress parameter is set, the user will only be able to connect to the MongoDB server if its IP address is within the restrictions.

For example, if you set the clientSource parameter to 192.168.1.1, only users with the IP address 192.168.1.1 will be able to connect to the MongoDB server. If you set the serverAddress parameter to 192.168.1.100, only users who are connecting to the MongoDB server with the IP address 192.168.1.100 will be able to connect.

The two parameters can be used together to further restrict access to the MongoDB server. For example, you can set the `clientSource` parameter to 192.168.1.1 and the `serverAddress` parameter to 192.168.1.100. This would mean that only users with the IP address 192.168.1.1 could connect to the MongoDB server using the IP address 192.168.1.100.

Thus, the `clientSource` and `serverAddress` parameters are a good way to protect your MongoDB server against brute force and other security attacks.

For these two parameters, you can specify one or more IPs, or a range through an array:

```
use admin
db.createRole(
    {
        role: "readAndInsert",
        privileges: [
            { resource: { db: "myDB", collection: ""},
              actions: ["find", "insert"]}
        ],
        roles: [],
        authenticationRestrictions: [
            {
                clientSource: ["192.168.1.1", "192.168.1.2"],
                serverAddress: ["192.168.1.100"]
            }
        ]
    }
)
```

Summary

This chapter discussed the critical role of security in MongoDB, delving into robust authentication methods such as SCRAM, x.509, LDAP, and Kerberos. However, security doesn't stop at authentication; it extends to proper user privilege management through RBAC. By implementing these best practices, MongoDB not only delivers performance and scalability but also remains a secure and dependable data platform.

In the next chapter, you'll see how auditing works in MongoDB. You'll also get to learn how to enable it in various use cases and tackle possible problems.

16

Auditing

MongoDB auditing is a feature that allows administrators and developers like yourself to track and record operations for a database. This is critical in ensuring data integrity, information security, and regulatory compliance. It also provides a detailed view of operations that are important to the business or that may affect data security. These operations include, but are not limited to, data modifications, management, and authentication operations.

There are several benefits to implementing an auditing strategy in MongoDB. The first is *security*. By tracking activities, you can identify anomalous or suspicious behavior patterns. This can help you detect unauthorized access attempts or an internal compromise. The second is *conformity*, which ensures that data protection and access requirements are being met in organizations that are subject to strict regulations such as GDPR or HIPAA.

The third is *diagnosis* and *troubleshooting*. By logging operations, auditing helps administrators quickly identify and correct issues related to performance or data integrity. The fourth is *accountability*, which ensures that all actions performed on the database can be attributed to a specific user, enforcing individual accountability.

Despite its importance, implementing auditing in MongoDB requires a thoughtful approach. You must consider performance, storage capacity, and a log retention strategy. Furthermore, to avoid information overload, it is essential that you clearly define which activities need to be audited and which do not.

This chapter will cover the following topics:

- Overview of auditing and logging in MongoDB

- How to configure and enable auditing in MongoDB Enterprise Advanced

- How to configure and enable auditing in MongoDB Atlas

- Strategies for troubleshooting auditing issues in MongoDB

> **Note**
>
> Auditing is a feature only available in MongoDB Enterprise Advanced and MongoDB Atlas for `M10` clusters or above.

Auditing and logging in MongoDB

Auditing and logging are essential for effective monitoring and administration of a system. Both provide records of activities that occur in the database, but they serve different purposes and have different characteristics. In certain contexts, the concepts may overlap. Let's explore the differences between auditing and logging in MongoDB:

- **Goal**:

  - **Audit**: The main purpose of auditing is to provide a detailed record of specific actions that occur in the database related to data access and modification. These records are generally created for compliance, security, and investigation purposes.

  - **Log**: MongoDB logs, on the other hand, capture a variety of information about server operations and state. This includes error messages, system alerts, boot information, and other system events. Logs are intended for monitoring, diagnosing, and optimizing system performance.

- **Granularity**:

  - **Audit**: Auditing offers fine granularity, allowing administrators to configure exactly which actions or events they want to monitor. For example, you can set up auditing to track all deletions of a specific document or all accesses by a specific user.

  - **Log**: System logs tend to be more generic, recording a wide variety of activities and system states.

- **Nature of data**:

  - **Audit**: Audit logs are more structured in terms of the data they capture. This includes details such as what actions were taken, who took them and when, and from which IP.

  - **Log**: Starting with MongoDB 4.4, logs are structured as JSON composed of key-value pairs, making it easy to analyze records since they now have a more defined and familiar structure as documents. In previous versions, the logs were in plain text.

- **Retention**:

  - **Audit**: Given their critical nature for compliance and security purposes, audit logs may need to be retained for long periods of time and may be subject to specific regulations.

  - **Log**: System logs, while they may be retained for a while, are usually rotated and discarded after a set period of time to save storage space.

- **Destiny**:

  - **Audit**: Audit logs can be routed to **security information and event management** (SIEM) systems or other specialized analysis tools for analysis and long-term storage.

  - **Log**: Logs are typically stored locally but can also be forwarded to log management solutions for analysis and monitoring.

> **Note**
>
> It is important to remember that MongoDB does not have any type of log truncation, and this must be configured externally. For example, to manually rotate the audit log from the `mongosh` shell, use the following command: `db.adminCommand({ logRotate: "audit" }`

Let's see an example of logging. When you start the MongoDB server, you'll see entries in the log similar to the following:

```
{"t":{"$date":"2023-10-03T10:00:00.000+00:00"},"s":"I",
"c":"CONTROL", "id":23285, "ctx":"initandlisten","msg":"MongoDB
starting","attr":{"pid":12345,"port":27017,"dbPath":"/data/
db","architecture":"64-bit","host":"server_hostname"}}
{"t":{"$date":"2023-10-03T10:00:00.000+00:00"},"s":"I",
"c":"CONTROL", "id":23341, "ctx":"initandlisten","msg":"Build
Info","attr":{"version":"7.0.2","gitVersion":"<git_
version>","OpenSSLVersion":"<openssl_version>","allocator":"tcmalloc"}}
```

This log entry tells you that the MongoDB server started with some parameters; you can see this in the `attr` attribute. In this case, this attribute contains parameters from the configuration file (`mongod.conf`).

As for the audit records, the format will appear as follows:

```
{
    "atype": "createCollection",
    "ts": {
        "$date": "2023-08-14T12:28:30.705-03:00"
    },
    "uuid": {
        "$binary": "BXRyo6adSGSx7WM/ZslYng==",
        "$type": "04"
    },
```

```
    "local": {
        "ip": "127.0.0.1",
        "port": 27017
    },
    "remote": {
        "ip": "127.0.0.1",
        "port": 56292
    },
    "users": [
        {
            "user": "admin",
            "db": "admin"
        }
    ],
    "roles": [
        {
            "role": "root",
            "db": "admin"
        }
    ],
    "param": {
        "ns": "auditTest.coll1"
    },
    "result": 0
}
```

Here, you have information such as the type of operation performed, the date and time, as well as the user who created the collection called `coll1` in the `auditTest` database. This detailed information helps increase traceability.

To sum up, auditing and logging are important for recording activity in MongoDB, where both serve a different purpose and have different characteristics.

Auditing is focused on tracking specific actions for security and compliance purposes. It can be used to track who performed what actions on which database or collection, when the action was performed, and from where they performed it.

Logging is a more comprehensive tool for monitoring and diagnosing system state and performance. It can be used to track a variety of events, including database operations, system errors, and network traffic.

In MongoDB, auditing allows administrators to track and record a series of specific events for compliance, security, and monitoring purposes. The auditing system in MongoDB is quite extensive and can record activities from the system level down to specific document operations.

Types of auditable events

Here are some examples of events that can be audited in MongoDB:

- **Authentication and authorization events**:

    - `authenticate`: Events related to user authentication

    - `createUser`, `dropUser`, `createRole`, `dropRole`, `grantRoles`, `revokeRoles`, and `updateUser`: Events associated with creating, modifying, and managing users and roles

    - `logout`: User logout events

- **Administrative operation events (DDL schema/replica set and sharding)**:

    - `enableSharding`, `addShard`, `removeShard`, and `shardCollection`: Events related to sharding operations

    - `replSetInitiate`, `replSetReconfig`, `replSetElect`, `replSetFreeze`, `replSetStepDown`, and `replSetSyncFrom`: Events associated with the configuration and operation of replica sets

    - `compact` and `repairDatabase`: Maintenance operations on databases and collections

- **Startup and shutdown events**:

    - `startup`: When the `mongod` process starts

    - `shutdown`: When the `mongod` process exits

These are just a few of the many events that can be audited in MongoDB. By configuring auditing, administrators can filter events that are relevant to their needs, ensuring they have a detailed view of critical activities while minimizing information clutter.

Enable auditing in MongoDB

While auditing can be enabled in an environment without authentication, it is most beneficial when used in conjunction with authentication. This allows you to track who performed certain operations on your database in addition to what operations were performed. In this section, you will learn about various configuration file parameters that are required to enable auditing.

First, you'll need to specify where the audit logs will be stored. Depending on the needs of the organization and environment, MongoDB offers different output formats for audit logs. For this example, use the `storage.auditLog` section.

- **Console**:

  - MongoDB can send audit logs directly to standard output (stdout).

  - This is useful for testing, or in scenarios where you have an external tool capturing standard output for further processing.

    ```
    storage:
      dbPath: data/db
      auditLog:
        destination: console
    ```

- **JSON**:

  - Audit records can be formatted as JSON documents.

  - This is useful when you have tools or systems that can process or parse data in JSON format.

  - It is also relevant if you plan to import audit records into a MongoDB collection, or another document-oriented database system.

    ```
    storage:
      dbPath: data/db
      auditLog:
        destination: file
        format: JSON
        path: data/db/auditLog.json
    ```

  The parameters can be specified as follows:

  - destination: In this case, with the value file

  - format: With the JSON value

  - path: With the path where you want to store this file

- **BSON**:

  - BSON is a binary representation of JSON-like data structures.

  - Storing audit logs in BSON can be useful for tighter integrations with MongoDB, especially if you plan to store or process these logs within a MongoDB cluster.

    ```
    storage:
      dbPath: data/db
      auditLog:
        destination: file
        format: BSON
        path: data/db/auditLog.bson
    ```

- **Syslog**:

  - MongoDB can be configured to send audit logs directly to syslog, a standard logging tool for UNIX and Linux systems.

  - This facilitates integration with centralized log management systems, as well as monitoring tools that can capture and alert based on syslog events.

```
storage:
  dbPath: data/db
  auditLog:
    destination: syslog
```

When setting up auditing in MongoDB, it is essential to consider not only what events you want to audit, but also where and how those logs will be stored and processed. Choosing an audit output type can vary based on compliance requirements, available monitoring and analysis tools, and overall system infrastructure.

Audit filters

Audit filters allow administrators to specify and filter the events that should be audited. Rather than recording every event, which could lead to an overwhelming amount of data, audit filters allow you to define specific criteria so that only relevant events are captured. This is critical for both optimizing performance (reducing audit overhead) and focusing on activities of particular interest, such as those related to security or compliance.

Audit filters work by defining criteria for specific fields in audit documents. For example, you can create filters to audit a specific user's activities, operations on a specific collection, or actions of a specific type (such as insertions or deletions).

Here are some basic operations you can perform to set audit filters:

- **Audit activation**: Before setting filters, you must enable auditing in MongoDB. To do this, refer to the *Enable auditing in MongoDB* section above.

- **Filter definition**: The filter is defined using the `auditFilter` option at MongoDB startup or in the configuration file:

```
storage:
  dbPath: data/db
  auditLog:
    destination: file
    format: BSON
    path: data/db/auditLog.bson
    filter: '{ atype: { $in: [ "createCollection", "dropCollection" ] }
}'
```

In the preceding example, a filter was defined just for the `createCollection` and `dropCollection` events.

- **Filter structure**: Filters are structured as JSON documents. For example, to audit all actions of a user named alice using admin as the authentication database, use the following filter:

```
{ "users": [ { "user": "alice", "db": "admin"} ] }
```

- **Audit read and write operations for any user in a specific collection:** For auditing purposes, track all read and write operations for any user in a specific collection.

```
{
    "atype": "authCheck",
    "params.ns": "myDatabase.myCollection",
    "params.command": {
        "$in": [
            "find",
            "insert",
            "delete",
            "update",
            "findAndModify"
        ]
    }
}
```

- **Audit only delete operations**:

```
{ "atype": "delete" }
```

- **Combine criteria**: You can combine multiple criteria into one filter. For example, use the following command to audit insertions made by alice into a specific collection:

```
{
    "users": [
        {
            "user": "alice",
            "db": "admin"
        }
    ],
    "atype": "insert",
    "params.ns": "myDatabase.myCollection"
}
```

You can also change these parameters at runtime by using the following command:

```
db.adminCommand(
    {
        setAuditConfig: 1,
        filter: {
            "atype": "authCheck",
            "param.command": {
                "$in": [
                    "find",
                    "insert",
                    "delete",
                    "update",
                    "findAndModify"
                ]
            }
        }
    }
)
```

In the preceding example, you reconfigured the audit filters for **create**, **read**, **update**, **delete** (**CRUD**) operations on any database.

If you want to check the current audit parameters, you can use the following command:

```
db.adminCommand({ getAuditConfig: 1 })
```

> **Note**
>
> When you change the settings at runtime and restart the server, these settings revert to the default settings defined in the configuration file. Therefore, if you want these settings to be permanent, always persist them in the mongod.conf file.

It is important to remember that auditing can introduce some performance overhead. Therefore, audit filters should be used strategically to capture only the events you need. It is also useful to test any filter in a development or test environment before applying it in production to ensure it captures the desired events without unwanted side effects.

Enable auditing in MongoDB Atlas

MongoDB Atlas supports auditing for all `M10` and larger clusters, and it's worth visiting the documentation to learn about the additional rates and charges (`https://www.mongodb.com/docs/atlas/billing/additional-services/#database-auditing`).

Follow these steps to enable auditing in MongoDB Atlas:

1. Log in to your Atlas project, and select **Advanced** from the **SECURITY** section of the left menu:

Figure 16.1: The Advanced option

2. Toggle the button next to **Database Auditing** to on:

Database Auditing

Database auditing allows you to customize log downloads with the users, groups, and actions you want to audit.

Turning on this feature will increase your daily cluster pricing. Read more.

Figure 16.2: Enabling database auditing

3. When you do this procedure, you will see a few options appear below. These options refer to the audit settings, including the audit filters that you saw earlier.

    The first option allows you to import JSON with the filters you want. Upon clicking the **USE CUSTOM JSON FILTER** button, you will see the following:

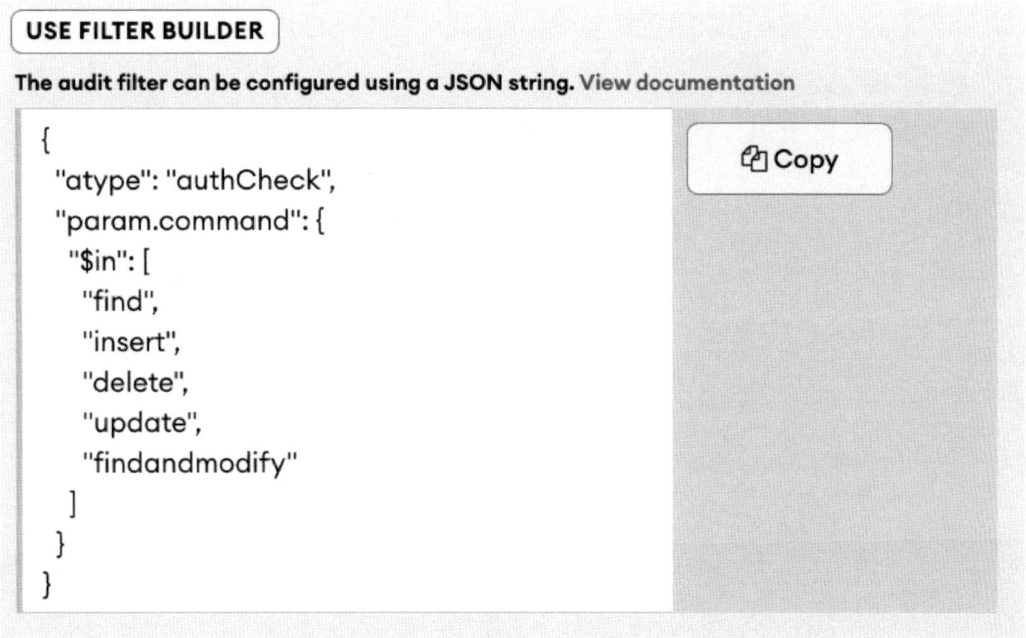

```
USE FILTER BUILDER
```

The audit filter can be configured using a JSON string. View documentation

```
{
  "atype": "authCheck",
  "param.command": {
   "$in": [
    "find",
    "insert",
    "delete",
    "update",
    "findandmodify"
   ]
  }
}
```

Copy

Figure 16.3: Applying audit filters

But if you prefer, you can use **FILTER BUILDER**, where you can easily select the users and/or roles to target for auditing, as shown in *Figure 16.4*:

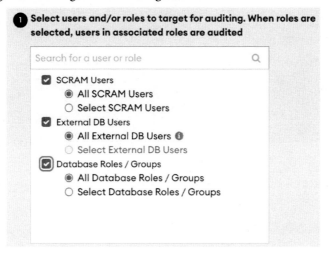

Figure 16.4: Selecting users and roles to audit

Next, you can select event actions you want to audit, as shown in *Figure 16.5*:

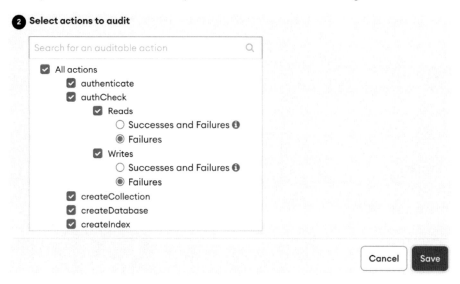

Figure 16.5: Selecting event actions to audit

4. To apply the changes, click the **Save** button.

View and download MongoDB logs

There are multiple ways to get audit logs in MongoDB Atlas. You can navigate directly to the project dashboard in the GUI, click the ellipsis icon (**...**), and select **Download Logs** from the dropdown menu, as shown in *Figure 16.6*:

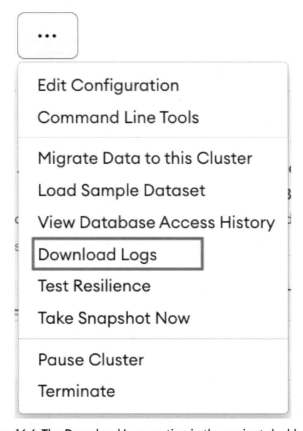

Figure 16.6: The Download Logs option in the project dashboard

However, if you prefer, you can make a call through the REST API. To do this, you will require four parameters:

- The public API key and private API key:

    - Go to the **Organization | Access Manager** page, then click on the **Create API Key** button. On this page, you can generate both the public and private keys, as shown in *Figure 16.7*:

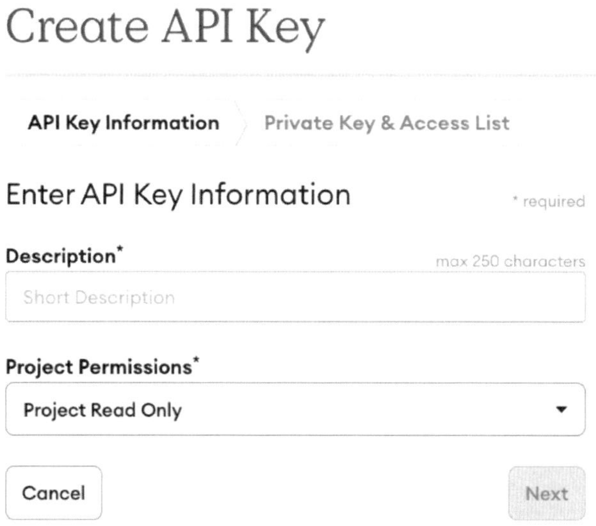

Create API Key

API Key Information 〉 Private Key & Access List

Enter API Key Information   * required

Description*   max 250 characters

Short Description

Project Permissions*

Project Read Only   ▼

Cancel   Next

Figure 16.7: Creating an API key

- The project ID:

  - On the **Organization | Projects** page, you can copy the project ID, as shown in *Figure 16.8*:

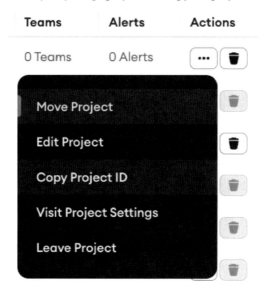

Figure 16.8: Retrieving the project ID

This information is a hexadecimal value that looks like this: `5e65697e0d4ddf42c4ba8d80`.

- The MongoDB cluster hostname, which is available on the **Database overview** page.

Once you have all the four parameters, make the following REST API call:

```
curl --user "{public_key:private_key}" \
  --digest \
  --header "Accept: application/gzip" \
  GET  "https://cloud.mongodb.com/api/atlas/v2/groups/{groupId}/clusters/
{hostname}/logs/{logName}.gz"
```

The `groupId` parameter is a unique 24-hexadecimal-digit string that identifies your project. You can use the `/groups` endpoint to obtain these values. The `hostname` parameter is a human-readable label that identifies the host that stores the log files.

The `logName` parameter can contain `mongodb-audit-log`, referring to the host of a replica set, or `mongos-audit-log` referring to the query router of a sharded cluster.

Case study: The role of auditing in compliance

Let's analyze a use case where auditing is necessary in a healthcare information management system. Suppose you're working for a company that develops a healthcare platform, offering services such as scheduling appointments, managing patient records, and requesting medical prescriptions, among other things. Given the sensitive nature of healthcare information, it is crucial to ensure data security, integrity, and privacy. To comply with regulations such as the **Health Insurance Portability and Accountability Act (HIPPA)** in the US or similar standards in other countries, it is important to implement robust auditing measures:

- **Audit objectives**:

    - Track access and modifications to patient records

    - Monitor the actions of all users with administrative privileges

    - Ensure compliance with data privacy regulations and standards

    - Quickly investigate and respond to any suspicious activity or data breaches

- **Implement auditing in MongoDB**:

    - **Configuration and filtering**:

        - Enable auditing in MongoDB and configure it to capture relevant events such as CRUD on specific collections such as `medicalRecords`, `prescriptions`, and `schedules`.

        - Define audit filters to monitor access and actions by administrative users and those with access to sensitive data.

- **Attribution and identification**:

  - Ensure all users have unique IDs and authenticate using secure methods.

  - Configure MongoDB to log detailed information about the user, such as the user ID, IP address, and action taken.

- **Periodic review and analysis**:

  - Establish a routine for regularly reviewing audit logs, looking for anomalous patterns or suspicious activity.

  - Use tools and solutions that facilitate log analysis, highlighting critical events or worrying patterns.

- **Retention and backup**:

  - Due to the regulated nature of the healthcare industry, audit logs must be retained for a specified period (for example, six years under HIPAA).

  - Implement regular backup routines of audit logs to ensure their long-term availability and integrity.

- **Incident response**:

  - Develop an incident response plan that uses audit logs as a primary source of investigation.

  - In case of a suspected or confirmed data breach, use the logs to determine the scope of the incident, the affected data, and exploited vulnerabilities.

In this scenario, MongoDB auditing is not just a technical tool but a vital component in ensuring patient confidence, regulatory compliance, and the overall health of the eHealth system. By proactively tracking and monitoring data access and changes, the company can ensure that sensitive information is protected while maintaining accountability and transparency with regulators and users.

Troubleshoot auditing issues in MongoDB

MongoDB audits play a critical role in ensuring the integrity, security, and compliance of stored data. By enabling detailed tracking of all activities and operations within the database, auditing facilitates detection of suspicious or anomalous events, making it possible to take immediate measures to protect data and infrastructure.

Furthermore, analyzing audit logs helps identify the root cause of issues, speeding up incident resolution and optimizing MongoDB performance. This is especially crucial in enterprise and regulated environments where legal compliance is essential and data responsibility is an ongoing concern.

Ultimately, audit troubleshooting is an indispensable tool for database administrators seeking to maintain the reliability and integrity of their MongoDB systems.

Let's look at some strategies and practices to help you determine whether there are any audit problems in your MongoDB environment and how you can address them effectively.

How to identify and address issues in auditing using MongoDB

To ensure the integrity of your data and maintain compliance with security regulations, it's essential to identify and resolve auditing-related issues in MongoDB.

- **Check audit logs**: Allow generation of detailed records, and review logs for unauthorized events, suspicious activities, or configuration errors.

- **Analyze audit records**: Utilize log analysis tools to identify abnormal trends or patterns in audit records, and be vigilant about unsuccessful authentication events, unauthorized access, or unusual operations.

- **Set up alerts**: Configure alerts to notify you when critical or anomalous events are recorded. This enables a real-time response to audit issues.

- **Conduct internal audits**: Conduct internal security and compliance audits periodically to assess the current state of auditing in MongoDB.

- **Monitor performance**: Be aware that auditing can impact MongoDB performance, so monitor system resources carefully to identify potential bottlenecks.

- **Stay informed**: Stay updated on best practices and updates related to auditing in MongoDB to avoid known issues.

Tools for MongoDB audit record analysis

Choosing a tool for analyzing MongoDB audit records can depend on your specific needs, the scale of the environment, and personal preferences. Make sure to select a tool that meets your needs for analyzing and viewing audit logs effectively. The following are some examples of tools that can be used:

- **MongoDB Compass**: MongoDB Compass is a graphical tool provided by MongoDB for intuitively viewing and querying audit logs, once the logs are imported into a MongoDB cluster.

- **Custom scripts and command-line tools**: Create custom scripts in languages such as Python or use command-line tools such as `grep` to search and filter audit records.

- **Splunk**: Splunk is a widely used data analysis platform for indexing and analyzing audit logs.

Summary

In this chapter, you explored the key aspects of auditing in MongoDB—audit configuration, auditing in MongoDB Enterprise, advanced auditing in MongoDB Atlas, and use cases for troubleshooting potential problems in relation to an audit. You learned about the various features, advantages, and challenges of auditing in MongoDB, and gained a comprehensive and practical understanding for effective implementation.

Auditing in MongoDB allows you to monitor specific activities in the database, providing a detailed view of operations relevant to business and data security. These operations include data modifications, management operations, and authentication.

However, implementing auditing in MongoDB requires a thoughtful approach, considering factors such as performance, storage capacity, and log retention strategy. It's essential to define which activities need auditing to avoid information overload.

In the next chapter, as the final part of MongoDB security features, you will learn about different types of encryption and how to implement them in your database.

17

Encryption

As the need to protect sensitive information grows, organizations globally are placing increased emphasis on data security. In the realm of database management, encryption plays a vital role in ensuring the integrity and confidentiality of stored and in-transit data. This chapter delves into the details of data encryption in MongoDB and discusses how it's become an essential component in pursuit of compliance with various regulations and security standards.

With data privacy regulations becoming more stringent, organizations are mandated to adhere to strict security standards, including data encryption. Prominent among the regulations that necessitate the implementation of encryption include **General Data Protection Regulation (GDPR)** by the European Union, which aims to protect the privacy of European citizens; the **Health Insurance Portability and Accountability Act (HIPAA)** in the United States, governing data security in the healthcare sector; and the **Payment Card Industry Data Security Standard (PCI DSS)**, a compliance framework for credit cardholder data and security. Additionally, many countries have their own data protection laws that require encryption of sensitive data.

In this chapter, you'll explore how MongoDB provides security features such as encryption at rest and in-transit, to meet these compliance requirements and protect the data stored within its systems. You'll grasp the technical details of these implementations, and discover best practices to ensure your data remains secure and your organization complies with applicable regulations.

This chapter will cover the following topics:

- Types of encryption methods in MongoDB
- Implementing encryption in-transit
- Implementing Client-Side Field Level Encryption
- Implementing encryption at rest

Encryption types

MongoDB offers robust data encryption features to safeguard your data. Here's a summary of three encryption methods, that'll be explored in more detail later in this chapter:

- **Encryption in-transit**: Encryption in-transit protects data during transmission between MongoDB clients and servers. This is achieved using the **Transport Layer Security/Secure Sockets Layer/ (TLS/SSL)** protocol, which encrypts data before it's sent over the network.

- **Client-Side Field Level Encryption**: This method allows the encryption of individual data fields within a MongoDB document. It protects highly sensitive data at a granular level, where only specific parts of documents are encrypted while the rest remain accessible.

- **Encryption at rest**: This method of encryption protects data when it's stored on a disk. Data is automatically encrypted at the file level, ensuring that even if someone gains physical access to the disk, the data remains secure.

Certificates

Certificates, which generally refer to TLS/SSL, play a crucial role in securing information during data storage and transmission. TLS/SSL certificates safeguard communications between clients and MongoDB servers by encrypting transmitted data and authenticating the servers, and in some cases, the clients.

The following key aspects outline the use of certificates in securing data:

- **Server authentication**: Certificates are used to authenticate the MongoDB server to clients. When the server presents its certificate, it proves its identity to clients, ensuring that data stored in the database is only accessed by trusted entities.

- **Encrypted connections**: Certificates are essential for establishing a secure connection between clients and servers. Certificates enable encryption of data at rest and in-transit, ensuring stored and transmitted information remains confidential and protected against unauthorized access.

- **Data integrity**: Certificates contribute to data integrity by encrypting data in-transit. Any unauthorized changes made to the data during transmission are detected during certificate verification, ensuring the data remains uncompromised.

- **Compliance with regulations**: TLS/SSL certificates can be used to encrypt data in-transit between the server and client to meet security and privacy regulations such as GDPR, HIPAA, and PCI DSS, which require database encryption.

The use of TLS/SSL certificates is essential for complete data security. In the next section, you'll take a look at the importance of certificates for encryption in-transit.

Encryption in-transit

Ensuring secure data communication over networks is paramount, particularly when it comes to databases such as MongoDB. In the following sections, you will learn about the fundamentals of encryption in-transit and explore the intricacies of configuring MongoDB for enhanced database communication security.

How it works

Transport encryption protects MongoDB by encrypting all network traffic, meaning that a packet transmitted using TLS/SSL can only be read by the end client. As you saw in the *LDAP* section of *Chapter 15, Security*, this type of encryption ensures that no malicious attackers can read a message in-transit.

Network encryption should be used whenever possible. In MongoDB Atlas, network encryption is enabled by default and cannot be disabled. For on-premises clusters, you may choose to implement TLS/SSL, or it can be optional for clients to connect to the cluster:

- `requireTLS`: The client must use TLS
- `preferTLS`: The client can use TLS, and replication will be used whenever possible
- `allowTLS`: The client can use TLS
- `disable`: The server does not support TLS

The TLS protocol provides the following features:

- **Authentication**: Servers (and optionally, clients) authenticate each other using certificates
- **Confidentiality**: Ensures that data in-transit cannot be read or decoded by malicious actors who may be monitoring the network
- **Integrity**: Makes sure that data is not altered (intentionally or accidentally) during transmission

You should use certificates in the form of `PEM` files for configuring TLS. They can be issued by a **certificate authority** (**CA**), or they can be self-signed. As a good practice, in production, you should use certificates generated and signed by the same certification authority, which can be maintained by you or a third party.

Configure TLS for MongoDB

This section contains quick steps to help you set up your MongoDB environment.

Enable TLS

Let's examine the necessary parameters for enabling the MongoDB environment:

- You can use two options (`net.tls.mode` and `net.tls.certificateKeyFile`) to change the configuration file:

```
net:
tls:
mode: requireTLS
certificateKeyFile: /path/to/certAndKey.pem
```

As you saw earlier, when the parameter mode is set with the value `requireTLS`, this means that all connections to the MongoDB server must be secured. If a client tries to connect without the certificate, it will fail. The `certificateKeyFile` parameter contains the path to the `PEM` file. It is worth noting that the permissions of the `.pem` file must be properly configured. As a recommendation, this file must be readable only by the user executing the `mongod` process.

- The secure permission for this file is `600`:

```
chmod 600 /path/to/certAndKey.pem
```

- Additionally, this file must also belong to the user who runs the `mongod` process. For example:

```
chown mongodb:mongodb /path/to/certAndKey.pem
```

Also, pay attention to the location of the file. Keep the `.pem` file in a secure directory, considering the permissions of the directory containing the file. It is a good practice to ensure that the directory is only accessible by the MongoDB user and that other users do not have read, write, or execute permissions. In short, proper file protection of the `.pem` file is essential for the security of your MongoDB server. Be sure to follow the best practices for protecting your private keys and certificates.

Authenticate clients via TLS

You can configure MongoDB to authenticate and verify client certificates during the handshake with the server. Enabling client authentication via TLS takes security one step further by requiring clients to also prove their identity to the server.

To do this, you can add one more parameter in the configuration file:

```
net:
  tls:
    mode: requireTLS
    certificateKeyFile: /path/to/certAndKey.pem
    CAFile: /path/to/ca.pem
```

The `tls.CAFile` parameter corresponds to the CA file path, which in turn contains the CA's public certificate (or the full certificate chain) that was used to sign the client's certificate. If the certificate presented by the client is signed by the CA, the authentication proceeds successfully, otherwise, it is rejected.

Upgrade a cluster to use TLS

In production environments where TLS in not enabled, you can execute the following procedure to prevent downtime:

> **Note**
>
> It is important to ensure that all clients have TLS connections enabled; otherwise, they will no longer be able to connect once this procedure is complete.

1. Start with secondary servers (and for sharded clusters, all `mongos`). Change the setting to allow TLS:

    ```
    net:
      tls:
        mode: allowTLS
        certificateKeyFile: <path to TLS/SSL certificate and key PEM file>
        CAFile: <path to root CA PEM file>
    ```

2. Do this for each cluster node, remembering that when you arrive at the primary server, you should run `rs.stepDown()`.

3. Move the servers to `preferTLS`. You can do this dynamically via `mongosh`:

    ```
    db.adminCommand(
      {
          setParameter: 1,
          tlsMode: "preferTLS"
      }
    )
    ```

4. At this point, all connections should be using TLS, as it is the preferred option across all nodes.

5. Finally, require connections to use TLS:

    ```
    db.adminCommand(
      {
          setParameter: 1,
          tlsMode: "requireTLS"
      }
    )
    ```

    This procedure must also be persisted in the configuration file:

    ```
    net:
      tls:
        mode: requireTLS
        certificateKeyFile: <path to TLS/SSL certificate and key PEM file>
        CAFile: <path to root CA PEM file>
    ```

Therefore, while avoiding downtime, you can move from a cluster that didn't require TLS, to an environment protecting all network traffic between servers and clients (and between nodes in a cluster).

Importance of CAFile

The proper use of CAFile is critical in securely authenticating clients via TLS for the following reasons:

- **Trust**: Allows MongoDB to trust certificates presented by clients, knowing they were signed by a trusted CA.

- **Protection against man-in-the-middle attacks**: Without CAFile, anyone could present any certificate to the server, and the server would have no way of verifying the validity of that certificate.

In many cases, especially in internal or test environments, you can use a self-signed CA (where the CA and the certificate are generated by a user rather than a large, external CA). However, in production environments, especially those exposed to the internet, it is generally advisable to use certificates from a well-known and respected CA. A CAFile can contain a single CA or a chain of certificates, depending on the certificate hierarchy you are using.

In summary, the CAFile parameter is an important part of the process for authenticating clients via TLS, as it gives MongoDB the ability to verify and trust certificates presented by clients.

Restrictions and considerations

Following are some restrictions and considerations for enabling encryption in-transit:

- **System requirements**: To enable encryption in-transit, you must configure a TLS/SSL certificate on the MongoDB server. This may require obtaining a valid certificate from a trusted CA.

- **Resource consumption**: Encryption in-transit consumes server resources, which can impact performance on systems with heavy read/write loads. It's essential to properly size the system to handle the additional overhead.

- **Driver compatibility**: Ensure that MongoDB drivers used in your application support encryption in-transit. Some drivers may require a specific configuration to use it.

- **Latency**: Encryption introduces some latency due to the encryption and decryption of data. This may be negligible in most cases but is something to consider in latency-sensitive applications.

- **Proper configuration**: Make sure to configure MongoDB correctly to use TLS/SSL connections, and ensure all connections between clients and the server are secure. Neglecting this can result in the leakage of sensitive data.

Encryption at rest

This feature is only available on MongoDB Enterprise Advanced or MongoDB Atlas (M10 and above). Encryption at rest allows you to encrypt data on storage devices, such as disks, arrays, etc. In contrast to encryption in-transit, which protects data while it is being transmitted between the client and the server, encryption at rest protects data directly on physical storage. This means that if your hardware is stolen or disks are compromised, the data remains protected.

MongoDB uses the `AES-256` encryption algorithm to encrypt data. `AES-256` is a strong encryption algorithm which is difficult to crack and is used in a wide variety of compliance standards. This algorithm uses a symmetric key, that is, the same key to encrypt and decrypt data.

Encryption at rest in MongoDB

MongoDB offers various options for implementing encryption at rest:

- **Transparent data encryption** (**TDE**): MongoDB Enterprise provides transparent encryption of data at rest, meaning encryption is completely transparent to applications accessing the database. This eliminates the need for any coding work required by the application to make the encryption work.

- **WiredTiger storage engine**: MongoDB uses the WiredTiger storage engine to support encryption at rest. WiredTiger supports data block encryption at the storage level.

- **Encryption keys**: Encryption requires the use of keys to encrypt and decrypt data. MongoDB allows you to use the **Key Management Interoperability Protocol** (**KMIP**) to manage keys, or you can manage your keys locally. In the case of MongoDB Atlas, you can use AWS, GCP, and Azure Vault services.

Configure encryption at rest for MongoDB

The following sections give a detailed walkthrough of encryption at rest in an on-premises environment followed by MongoDB Atlas.

On-premises

Encryption at rest usually involves multiple levels of keys to provide a combination of security and performance. Some steps must be executed before configuring MongoDB for encryption at rest. Let's look at these steps in detail:

1. **Generate the master key**

   The master key is a highly secret and protected encryption key that is used to encrypt other keys, known as data keys. It is usually stored securely, preferably using an external **key management service** (**KMS**). This is an important point because if the master key is compromised, then all of the data keys that it encrypts will also be compromised. This could lead to unauthorized access to all the encrypted data.

   I.   Use a **cryptographically secure random number generator** (**CSRNG**) to create a strong, typically 256-bit key for the AES algorithm.

   II.   Store the master key securely. This might involve using a **hardware security module** (**HSM**) or a KMS from a cloud provider such as AWS, Google Cloud, or Azure, and as you'll see later, these providers can be easily integrated with MongoDB Atlas.

2. **Generate keys for each database**

   To improve security and performance, it is common to use different keys for each database or even for different sets of data (optional).

   I.   Similar to master key generation, use a CSRNG to generate unique keys for each database.

   II.   These keys are used directly to encrypt the data, so they must be accessible by the database system for read and write operations.

3. **Encrypt data with the database keys**

   With the generated database keys, you can now encrypt the data.

   I.   When data is written to the database, the system uses the key corresponding to the database (or set of data) to encrypt the data before writing it to disk.

   II.   When the data is read, the process is reversed: the encrypted data is read from the disk and then decrypted using the database key.

4. **Encrypt the database keys with the master key**

   To increase security, database keys are encrypted with the master key. So, even if someone gets the database keys, they are useless without the master key.

   I.   Use the master key to encrypt all database keys.

   II.   Store the encrypted database keys in a secure location, but accessible by the database system.

   III. When the database system starts or needs to decrypt data, it first uses the master key to decrypt the database key, which is then used to decrypt the data.

The advantage of this multi-level system is that the most critical master key can be securely stored and rarely accessed. Database keys, which are accessed more frequently, are less critical in terms of exposure because they are always encrypted when stored. Together, these practices provide a high level of security for data at rest. Once the keys are generated, you can configure MongoDB.

Configure MongoDB

- **Pre-requisites**

  - Make sure you're using the MongoDB Enterprise Advanced version, as encryption at rest is only available in this version.

  - Decide whether you want to use MongoDB's internal KMS (local key) or an external KMS. Each option has its own configuration considerations.

- **Local key encryption (WiredTiger)**

  - You can use the openSSL command to generate your master key. It is important to store the key in a safe place outside the MongoDB server. Here's an example of generating a master key using openSSL:

```
openssl rand -base64 32 > /path/to/your/mongodb-keyfile chmod 600 /path/
to/your/mongodb-keyfile
```

- Now, in the configuration file, add the following parameters:

```
security:
enableEncryption: true
encryptionKeyFile: /path/to/your/mongodb-keyfile
```

- Restart the MongoDB service and your data will already be encrypted at rest.

Let's see the specific function of each of these parameters:

- `enableEncryption`: Indicates that encryption at rest is enabled. Possible values are `true` or `false`.

- `encryptionKeyFile`: The path to the file containing the encryption key for the WiredTiger storage engine. The file must have read-only permissions for the owner and should be stored in a secure location.

If you decide to use an external KMS, some additional parameters are required.

- **Configure the KMS**

  - **For AWS KMS**: Create a **customer master key** (**CMK**) and record your AWS access key and secret key.

  - **For Azure Key Vault**: Create a key and configure the service principal ID and secret key.

  - **For Google Cloud KMS**: Create a key and configure the project ID, location, key ring, and key name.

- **Configure MongoDB to use KMS**

  - In the `mongod.conf` configuration file, add the following:

```
security:
  enableEncryption: true
  kmip:
    keyIdentifier: <keyID>
    serverName: <kmipServer>
    serverCAFile: <pathToCAFile>
    clientCertificateFile: <pathToClientCert>
    clientPrivateKeyFile: <pathToClientKey>
```

Let's examine each of these parameters:

- `kmip.keyIdentifier`: Identifies the symmetric key that KMIP/KMS use to encrypt and decrypt data.

- `kmip.serverName`: The hostname of the KMIP server. It can contain the hostname or IP.

- `kmip.serverCAFile`: The path to the `PEM` file that contains the CA certificate that signed `clientCertificateFile`. Used to verify the identity of the KMIP server.

- `kmip.clientCertificateFile`: The path to the `PEM` file that contains the KMIP client certificate for `mongod` or `mongos`. The KMIP server uses this certificate to verify the client's identity.

- `kmip.clientPrivateKeyFile`: The path to the `PEM` file that contains the private key of the KMIP client's certificate for `mongod` or `mongos`.

- `kmip.port (optional)`: The port of the KMIP server.

As with the configuration for the local key, the MongoDB process must be restarted for the changes to take effect.

Use encryption at rest

Encryption at rest protects against direct access to data storage. Therefore, as a best practice, you should ensure that access to the MongoDB server and its backups is secure via a combination of user authentication and user authorization.

When you're first setting up encryption at rest, it is important to back up your complete data, as there is always a risk associated with significant system configuration changes. For instance, inadvertent changes or mistakes when enabling encryption can make your data inaccessible and unreadable.

With these steps, you should now have a MongoDB environment configured to use encryption at rest. You should also consult the official MongoDB documentation, as it may provide specific details and updates for specific versions of MongoDB.

Restrictions and considerations

It is always good to keep in mind the following considerations or even restrictions that may prevent implementation. The following are examples:

- **Secure storage**: Encryption at rest protects data stored in MongoDB's data files. Using a secure filesystem or storage device that supports encryption is crucial.

- **Performance**: Encryption at rest can impact performance, especially during intensive read/ write operations. Carefully choose the encryption algorithm and configuration options to minimize performance impact.

- **Key management**: Key management is a critical part of encryption at rest. Ensure that encryption keys are securely stored, and only authorized personnel have access to them.

- **Backup and recovery**: When creating backups of encrypted data, it's important to ensure that the backups are also encrypted, and encryption keys are stored securely.

- **Version compatibility**: Check the MongoDB version compatibility with encryption at rest since this feature may vary between versions.

- **Lost key recovery**: Ensure robust key recovery procedures are in place. If encryption keys are lost, recovering data may become impossible.

Client-side encryption

While most modern database management systems offer robust security mechanisms to protect data at rest and in-transit, few have managed to address the need to protect data at the granular level of the field within a record. This is the gap that MongoDB seeks to fill with **Client-Side Field Level Encryption (CSFLE)**.

CSFLE represents a sophisticated approach to security, allowing applications to encrypt specific document fields in a collection before sending that data to MongoDB. With this technique, the encryption and decryption processes take place exclusively on the client side, ensuring that the database server never has access to clear text data. Sensitive data is not only stored securely, but also handled and processed with the highest degree of protection. Thus, even in a hypothetical scenario of a total database compromise, even though an attacker could obtain encrypted data from sensitive fields, they would not have the keys or the necessary context to decrypt them. This is an excellent option for organizations that want to encrypt one field, but not every field in their database.

MongoDB 7.0 introduced a very interesting feature when working with CSFLE, called *Queryable Encryption*. Queryable Encryption is based on a fast, encrypted search algorithm that allows the server to process queries on encrypted data without knowing the data, i.e., it allows you to run expressive queries on encrypted data. The data and the query itself always remain encrypted on the MongoDB server, which returns encrypted query results to the driver, providing a secure way for users to run expressive queries on data.

When is CSFLE used

CSFLE protects data at the field or document level. This is particularly useful for scenarios where certain data, such as **personally identifiable information (PII)**, requires extra protection due to regulations or privacy requirements.

MongoDB strengthens its security posture and offers developers flexibility by adopting CSFLE. For example, different fields can be encrypted using deterministic or random encryption, depending on the needs of the application. Deterministic encryption ensures that a specific input value will always result in the same encrypted value, allowing for efficient queries. Random encryption, on the other hand, ensures that the same input value produces different encrypted results each time, providing an additional level of security.

Additionally, MongoDB abstracts away much of the complexity associated with key management, making the process more accessible. However, this does not lessen the responsibility of the developer or administrator to properly manage and protect the encryption keys, especially the master key, which is critical to data integrity and accessibility.

Before exploring how this works, let's look at two important concepts in the CSFLE context:

- **Automatic encryption keys**: When you set up CSFLE, you must define encryption policies that specify which fields in your collections should be encrypted and with which algorithm. MongoDB automatically generates data encryption keys for each encrypted field as defined in the encryption policies. These data encryption keys are automatically generated by the client itself and are never stored on the MongoDB server, ensuring a high level of security. Each client has its own data encryption keys.

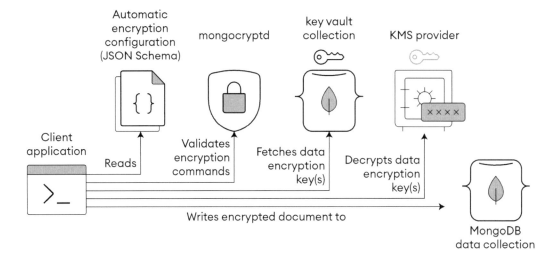

Figure 17.1: Steps to perform a write of field-level encrypted data

- **Transparent decryption**: After encrypting the data on the client, this encrypted data is stored on the MongoDB server, where it is protected against unauthorized access. When a client wants to access this encrypted data, MongoDB automatically provides the appropriate decryption keys (generated by the client) for decrypting the protected fields. The decryption process is transparent to the client application, meaning the client does not need to directly manage decryption keys or perform manual decryption operations. MongoDB takes care of this automatically, allowing the client to access the data in its original format seamlessly.

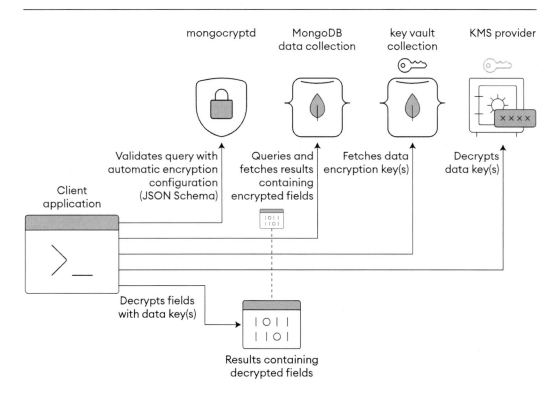

Figure 17.2: Steps taken to query and decrypt field-level encrypted data

How it works

Let's have a closer look at CSFLE works:

- **Client-side encryption**: Unlike encryption at rest, which takes place on the server side, CSFLE is exclusively performed on the client side (at the application level).

- **Automatic encryption keys**: MongoDB can automatically manage encryption keys for each field or document, which simplifies key management. Although the CSFLE feature is also available in the Community version, it is exclusive to the Enterprise Advanced version.

- **Transparent decryption**: When documents are retrieved, they are automatically decrypted with the help of the driver without requiring any additional steps on the application side.

Configure MongoDB

Execute the following steps to enable client-side encryption for MongoDB:

> **Note**
>
> Encryption with CSFLE is only available with MongoDB Enterprise Edition, version 4.2 or later.

1. **Configure the environment**: Install the package corresponding to your programming language. For example, for Python, install `pymongocrypt`.

2. **Generate a master encryption key**: The master key can be randomly generated and must be stored securely, similar to what was discussed in the *Encryption at rest* section.

3. **Create a Key Vault**: A Key Vault is a special collection named `keyVault` on your MongoDB cluster that stores data encryption keys. Don't use the `admin` database to store your keys as the MongoDB client may not be able to access or decrypt your data due to lack of permissions.

4. **Define an encryption scheme**: By using an encryption scheme, you can define which fields will be encrypted. For each field, you can define whether the encryption should be deterministic (the same input value always produces the same encrypted value) or random (the same input value produces different encrypted values in different encryptions). Take a good look at each of these approaches for your scenario.

5. **Configure the MongoDB client**: When you start the MongoDB client, you must specify that you want to use client-side encryption and provide the master key and encryption scheme.

   • `master_key`: Generated in *Step 2*

   • `KeyVault`: Reference to the collection used to store data encryption keys

   • `schema_map`: Requires the encryption scheme, defined in *Step 4*

   ```python
   from pymongo import MongoClient
   from pymongo.encryption import Algorithm, ClientEncryption
   from pymongo.encryption_options import AutoEncryptionOpts
   master_key = ... # Put your master key here kms_providers = {'local':
   {'key': master_key}}

   schema_map = {...} # Your encryption scheme

   auto_encryption_opts = AutoEncryptionOpts(  kms_providers=kms_providers,
     schema_map=schema_map,
     key_vault_ namespace="admin.datakeys"
   )
   client = MongoClient('mongodb://localhost:27017', auto_encryption_
   opts=auto_encryption_opts)
   ```

6. **KMS providers**: Specifies the KMS provider's key to be used. It can be local (using the generated master key) or external (e.g., AWS KMS, Azure Key Vault, or Google Cloud KMS).

7. **CRUD operations**: When performing CRUD operations, specified fields are automatically encrypted before being sent to the database, and decrypted when retrieved.

Restrictions and considerations

The following considerations and restrictions must be kept in mind before implementing client-side encryption:

- **Version**: CSFLE was introduced in MongoDB 4.2 and enhanced in later versions, so any previous versions will not support this functionality.

- **Performance**: Client-side encryption and decryption operations add some overhead. Depending on the volume and nature of the data, this will affect performance. Therefore, it is critical to be mindful of how much encryption is needed.

- **Encrypted data querying**: Querying for encrypted fields requires a different approach, especially if the field is encrypted using random encryption.

- **Master key**: Losing the master key means losing access to data. It is essential to keep secure backups of this key.

- **Driver compatibility**: Not all programming language drivers can support CSFLE to the same extent, or in the same way.

- **Data regulations**: CSFLE can help organizations comply with data protection regulations such as GDPR, as sensitive data is encrypted at the application level and MongoDB never sees the data in clear text.

- **External KMS**: As of MongoDB 4.4, you can integrate with an external KMS such as AWS KMS, Azure Key Vault, or Google Cloud KMS to manage your master key.

The integration of CSFLE varies from application to application, therefore, to implement CSFLE successfully, it is critical to understand your application's requirements, do a thorough assessment of the fields that need to be encrypted, and plan for key management. It's important to refer to the official documentation for the most up-to-date and specific details.

Queryable Encryption

Queryable Encryption builds on CSFLE and allows advanced queries to be executed in your database. Queries that could previously filter only for equality, may contain expressions to search for partial values in their queries, which is a powerful aspect.

Queryable Encryption strikes a balance between security and functionality, allowing users to query encrypted data without having to decrypt it first. In MongoDB, this is achieved by *deterministic encryption*.

Deterministic encryption is a type of encryption where the same input value always results in the same encrypted value. This contrasts with random encryption, where the same input value can result in different encrypted values each time.

Since deterministically encrypted values are consistent, developers can create indexes and queries based on these values, just as they would on unencrypted data. However, while this provides enormous flexibility and efficiency, it also comes with challenges. The predictable nature of deterministic encryption can, in some cases, make data more vulnerable to pattern analysis. Therefore, it is a tool that must be used with care. In this context, the ability to balance security and accessibility becomes an art.

With Queryable Encryption, MongoDB gives you the tools you need to keep data secure while preserving the ability to access and analyze that data effectively. As the digital world continues to evolve and security challenges multiply, solutions such as Queryable Encryption in MongoDB play an essential role in ensuring that organizations can thrive in a secure and efficient environment.

Summary

MongoDB offers a robust range of encryption features to ensure data security at rest, in-transit, and even on the client side. These features are essential for compliance with regulatory standards and safeguarding sensitive information. By combining these capabilities, you can establish a robust security framework, protecting sensitive data from external threats, and meeting regulatory standards.

The beauty of MongoDB is its ability to adapt and evolve. Learning its fundamentals is not just a technical task, but an experience that transforms the way you view data storage and retrieval.

Index

Other Books You May Enjoy

If you enjoyed this book, you may be interested in these other books by Packt:

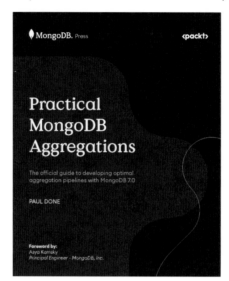

Practical MongoDB Aggregations

Paul Done

ISBN: 978-1-83508-064-1

- Covers the newest features of MongoDB 7.0 and shares insights of the MongoDB aggregation framework

- Provides practical principles and approaches for developing effective aggregation pipelines

- Equips you with examples to address common data processing challenges

- Illustrates complex data manipulation tasks with real-world examples

- Ideal for developers, architects, data analysts, engineers, and scientists familiar with the aggregation framework

Packt is searching for authors like you

If you're interested in becoming an author for Packt, please visit authors.packtpub.com and apply today. We have worked with thousands of developers and tech professionals, just like you, to help them share their insight with the global tech community. You can make a general application, apply for a specific hot topic that we are recruiting an author for, or submit your own idea.

Download a free PDF copy of this book

Thanks for purchasing this book!

Do you like to read on the go but are unable to carry your print books everywhere?

Is your e-book purchase not compatible with the device of your choice?

Don't worry, now with every Packt book you get a DRM-free PDF version of that book at no cost.

Read anywhere, any place, on any device. Search, copy, and paste code from your favorite technical books directly into your application.

The perks don't stop there, you can get exclusive access to discounts, newsletters, and great free content in your inbox daily

Follow these simple steps to get the benefits:

1. Scan the QR code or visit the link below

https://packt.link/free-ebook/9781835883501

2. Submit your proof of purchase
3. That's it! We'll send your free PDF and other benefits to your email directly

Made in the USA
Monee, IL
13 July 2024

bd1cd707-6731-4d69-9103-7b32f6808c3aR01